The 1972 Munich Olympics and the Making of Modern Germany

Gameplan:

Step 1: TAKE ATTENDANCE!

Step 2: Cuba Libre
Step 3: Read book (optional)

Happy 21st Euan,

Hope this book evokes memories of the Kai Times!

Luke

November 2015

WEIMAR AND NOW: GERMAN CULTURAL CRITICISM

Edward Dimendberg, Martin Jay, and Anton Kaes, General Editors

The 1972 Munich Olympics and the Making of Modern Germany

Kay Schiller and
Christopher Young

UNIVERSITY OF CALIFORNIA PRESS
Berkeley Los Angeles London

University of California Press, one of the most distinguished university presses in the United States, enriches lives around the world by advancing scholarship in the humanities, social sciences, and natural sciences. Its activities are supported by the UC Press Foundation and by philanthropic contributions from individuals and institutions. For more information, visit www.ucpress.edu.

University of California Press
Berkeley and Los Angeles, California

University of California Press, Ltd.
London, England

Library of Congress Cataloging-in-Publication Data

Schiller, Kay.
The 1972 Munich Olympics and the making of modern Germany / Kay Schiller and Christopher Young.
p. cm.
Includes bibliographical references and index.
ISBN 978-0-520-26213-3 (cloth : alk. paper)
ISBN 978-0-520-26215-7 (pbk. : alk. paper)
1. Olympic Games (20th : 1972 : Munich, Germany)—History. 2. Terrorism—Germany—Munich. 3. Athletes—Violence against—Germany—Munich. 4. Germany—Politics and government—20th century. I. Young, Christopher, 1967– II. Title.
GV7221972.S35 2010
796.48—dc22 2010004934

Manufactured in the United States of America

19 18 17 16 15 14 13 12 11 10
10 9 8 7 6 5 4 3 2 1

This book is printed on Cascades Enviro 100, a 100% postconsumer waste, recycled, de-inked fiber. FSC recycled certified and processed chlorine free. It is acid free, Ecologo certified, and manufactured by BioGas energy.

This book is dedicated to Hans Schiller, who took me as a young boy to see Klaus Wolfermann win the javelin gold in 1972
(Kay Schiller)

In loving memory to Valerie Young, who first told me about Mark Spitz and spent many years patiently waiting for me to emerge from sports matches
(Christopher Young)

CONTENTS

ILLUSTRATIONS

ACKNOWLEDGMENTS

During the course of conceiving, researching, and writing this book, we have incurred many debts and it is a pleasure to acknowledge them here. It is not possible to record the nature of every assistance offered, but it is true to say that every single person mentioned in the following list combined the giving of their expertise and knowledge with spontaneous acts of generosity and hospitality that added greatly to the enjoyment and fulfillment of completing this project. The brevity with which they are mentioned stands in inverse proportion to the gratitude we owe them and the warmth with which they are all remembered now.

Paul Betts, Erik Eggers, Markus Hesselmann, Manfred Lämmer, Andrei Markovits, Rudolf Spindler, and Alan Tomlinson were there from the beginning, and without their encouragement and support, this work would hardly have stumbled out of the starting blocks. It was funded by the Alexander von Humboldt Foundation, the British Academy, the Arts and Humanities Research Council, the Tiarks Fund in the Department of German and Dutch, and the Fellow's Research Fund, Pembroke College, University of Cambridge, and the Research Funds of the History Department and the Faculty of Arts and Humanities of Durham University.

Colleagues at the Deutsche Sporthochschule and the University of Cologne made every effort to facilitate research: Carl Lennartz, Walter Borgers, Evelyn Mertin, Heike Kuhn, Sandra Esser, Robin Streppelhoff, Susanne Couturier, Wolfgang Steidlinger, Walter Pape, Ursula Peters, Bernd Bastert, Timo Reuvekamp-Felber, Hans-Joachim Ziegeler, Lorenz Deutsch, Douglas Taylor. In an act of unprecedented magnanimity, Lorenz Peiffer included us in his project on GDR sport as well as welcomed us into his family. Many others helped magnificently along the way: Christiane Eisenberg, Klaus von Lindeiner, Gertrude Krombholz, Werner Rabe, Brigitte Maibohm, Manfred Grape, Lorenz Marold, Robert Ide, Heinz Florian Oertel, Winfried Nerdinger, Jürgen Wolf, Jutta Braun, Gunter Gebauer, Wolfram Pyta, Hubertus Knabe, Bob Edelman, Wayne Wilson, Ed Derse, Barbara Keys, John Efron, Kerwin Klein, Liz Leckie Schlüssel, John MacAloon, Richard Holt, Peter Taylor, Saul Kelly, Jo Whaley, Niklaus Largier, Giselher Spitzer, Dan Alon, Richard Bessel, Chris Brooks, Graham Ford, Mary Fulbrook, Michael Geyer, Neil Gregor, Heinrich Jaeger, Norbert Jaeschke, Gerhild Knopf, Howell Harris, Philip Williamson, Carsten Schiller, Tobias Heyl, Lorens Holm, Hans Holzhaider, Manfred Oldenburg, Heinz Koderer, Ferdinand Kramer, Eckard Michels, Winfried Müller, Ingrid and Rolf Muth, Mike Froggatt, Peter Ramsauer, Gavriel Rosenfeld, Mark Roseman, Michael Schaich, Georg Schönfeld, Rudolf Sottung, Kathrin Stadler. Among the many interviews given, we particularly thank Friedhelm Brebeck, Rolf Müller, Dr. Hans-Jochen Vogel, Werner and Anita Ruhnau, Carlo Weber, and the late Markus Wolf.

Archivists in several countries were unstinting in their help: Albert Knoll (KZ-Gedenkstätte Dachau), Peter Franz and Annegret Neupert (Bundesarchiv Koblenz), Anton Löffelmeier and Ulrike Trummer (Stadtarchiv Munich), Gerhard Fürmetz and Caroline Gigl (Bayerisches Hauptstaatsarchiv Munich), Dagmar Rinker (HfG-Archiv Ulm), Claus Brügmann (Archiv für Christlich-Soziale Politik Munich), Gisela Krause (Archiv der Friedrich-Ebert-Stiftung, Bonn), Ruth Beck-Perrenaud (IOC Lausanne), Dr. Freifrau von Boeselager (Politisches Archiv des Auswärtigen Amts, Berlin), Andreas Höfer (Deutsche Olympische Akademie), Wayne Wilson, Shirley Ito, and Michael Salmon (LA84 Foundation), and the helpful staff at the Monacensia library in Munich.

In addition to the extremely helpful readers for the University of California Press, friends, students, colleagues, and, in one case, an inspiring teacher from high school read full drafts of the manuscript with a patient and exacting eye: Lukas Werner, Heike Sahm, Klaus Nippert, Christoph Bertling, Allen Guttmann, John Knox, Barbara Koenczoel, Dieter Schulze-Marmeling, Markus Hesselmann. The usual caveat about residual errors applies. Sarah Bowden provided an outstandingly accurate and efficient first draft of the English translations of German quotations. Sharon Nevill managed the printing of multiple versions with characteristic good humor.

We were fortunate to be able to draw on excellent feedback offered at conferences and after invited lectures at the following universities: Leeds (Stuart Taberner), Birmingham (Association of Modern German Studies), Brighton (Alan Tomlinson), Glasgow (Alana Vincent), Lancaster (Student History Society), London, Institute of Historical Research (German History Seminar), Michigan (Andrei Markovits), Virginia, Charlottesville (Alon Confino), UC Berkeley (Anton Kaes, Niklaus Largier), UC San Diego (Bob Edelman, Wayne Wilson), Johns

Hopkins (Stephen G. Nichols), Illinois, Urbana-Champaign (C.L. Cole), Applied Arts Vienna (Roman Horak), Liverpool (Andrew Plowman), as well as the German Historical Institute Washington (Uta Balbier, Stefan Wiederkehr).

It is an honor to appear in the series Weimar Culture and Now, and we thank the editors Anton Kaes, Martin Jay, and, in particular, Ed Dimendberg who encouraged submission to the Press when this project was barely a twinkle in the eye and saw it through to contract with consummate professionalism. The same goes for Niels Hooper, Nick Arrivo, Suzanne Knott, and Christopher Pitts at the Press, who nursed the book through to completion.

At no stage would this project have been possible without the support of our families, Uta Papen and Fabian Schiller, and Angela, Alex, and Peter Young, whose love and support was too often repaid by a patiently indulged dereliction of duty. To them we owe our greatest debt.

1

Introduction

Telcon: 12:05—9/2/72
Mr. Kissinger
The President
K: Mr. President.
P: Oh, Henry, I was thinking—you know Fischer will be coming in having won that chess thing sometime. And I want you to see if we can get the other fella to come to *[sic]*.
K: Spassky.
P: Yes, you know what I mean.
K: Right.
P: They have had a long match, etc.
K: No, we better not, Mr. President, because Spassky is thinking of defecting and we better stay away.
P: Oh, is he?
K: Yes.
P: OK. Thanks.[1]

As Richard Nixon soon learned in this brief exchange with Henry Kissinger on 2 September 1972—one day after Bobby Fischer's victory over Boris Spassky in the most famous match in chess history, and one week into the Games of the twentieth Olympiad in Munich—the relationship between sport and politics is not always easy. At best—as the president might have deduced had he reflected for a moment on the irony of Fischer's one-man assault on the Soviet system at the height of East-West détente—it can be slippery.[2] At worst, as the world would be forced to conclude just days later, it can prove tragic. By 6 September, the conclusion of the Fischer-Spassky saga had been eclipsed by events in Munich, and Kissinger was pondering the etiquette of changing his plan to combine a meeting with West German government officials in the Bavarian capital with a visit to the Olympic Games.[3] He had good reason to hesitate. In the early hours of 5 September, members of the Palestinian group Black September had broken into the Olympic village, shot dead two members of the Israeli Olympic team, and taken nine of their compatriots hostage in a day-long siege that turned Munich into "the cockpit of world events."[4] When this seismic moment of globally televised terrorism ended in a farrago of police errors that led to the death of all the Israeli captives, the bleakest day in the histories of the Olympic movement and the young Federal Republic was complete. As Chancellor Willy Brandt later recalled: "My disappointment at the time was intense [not least] because the Olympics on which we had expended so much loving care would not go down in history as a happy occasion."[5]

Brandt's prediction has proved all too accurate. Sports retrospectives might remind us of the athletic prowess displayed in 1972: Lasse Virén's double in the men's distance events; gymnast Olga Korbut (whom Nixon did soon manage to attract to the White House) "playing like a kid in the sun";[6] or Mark Spitz's colossal, and until Beijing 2008, unsurpassed seven golds in the pool. But over thirty years later, the Munich Games are still dominated by their moment of nadir. Memorialization of 1972 has tended to caricature the Germans as hapless fall guys with a pantomime baddy's past. Recent cinematic treatments such as Kevin MacDonald's Oscar-winning documentary *One Day in September* (1999) and Steven Spielberg's controversial *Munich* (2006) are but prominent cases in point.[7] The aim of this book is to redress the balance and tell the story of Munich from the beginning rather than the end. Late in the evening of 4 September, the Olympic stadium witnessed the "romantic triumph of a slender German schoolgirl in the high jump," a moment "that united the minds and emotions of spectators from a hundred different nations in a common celebration of unique athleticism."[8] Were it not for events that began just hours later, sixteen-year-old Ulrike Meyfarth's joyous leap to victory might well have stood as a metaphor for West Germany's successful rehabilitation on the world stage through the Olympics. This book seeks to examine the significance of those Games to the Federal Republic and explore, for the first time on the basis of extensive archival research, the "loving care" it invested in them.[9] With the exception of a few brief essays, this topic, which sheds critical light on West German culture, politics, and society in the 1960s and the early 1970s, remains virtually unexplored.[10]

It hardly needs stating that the 1972 Olympics were of vital importance to West Germany. Until that point, its international representation had relied upon membership to NATO and the European Communities, as well as the usual forms of cultural diplomacy such as state visits, participation in world fairs, and specific initiatives such as the German Academic Exchange Service (DAAD) and the Goethe Institute.[11] By comparison, the symbolic capital on offer via the Olympic Games was immeasurable. As calculated by the organizers, it would have taken thirty-four years of filling the eighty-thousand-person-capacity Olympic Stadium on a daily basis to accumulate the number of worldwide television viewing figures for the opening ceremony alone. This same fact had not escaped the Black September terrorists who, during a pause in their negotiations on 5 September, congratulated the Germans on "produc[ing] an excellent Olympic Games," which at the same time "offered the Palestinians a showcase where they could bring their grievance to the millions watching around the world."[12] In bringing the Games to Munich in the first place, the West Germans had an equally urgent message to convey. A letter in 1970 from Brandt's vice-chancellor and foreign minister, Walter Scheel, urging German embassies and consulates around the world to devote the forthcoming Olympics their utmost energies, outlined some of its main components:

> More than ever before, the 1972 Summer Olympics in Munich and Kiel [where the sailing events took place] will attract the attention of the world to the Federal Republic of Germany. We must be aware that other nations will be more interested in and critical of us than they have been of other countries that have hosted the Games hitherto. The memory of the Olympics in Berlin in 1936, of our historical past, and not least the awareness of our peculiar political situation will play no insignificant part in this.
>
> IOC statutes might state that cities rather than countries host the Games, but it is on their success or lack of it that the whole country and its population is judged.
>
> This therefore offers us the unique opportunity to use the worldwide interest in sport to draw attention to the portrayal of our development and state and to project to the rest of the world the image of a modern Germany in all its political, economic, social, and cultural facets.[13]

Bonn's diplomats would doubtless have sensed the Olympics had more to offer still. When the president of the International Olympic Committee (IOC), Avery Brundage, made his valedictory speech a week before the Munich event, his tour d'horizon of recent host cities provided further insights into the allure and potential of Olympic regeneration:

> The Games of the XVth Olympiad in 1956 in remote Melbourne . . . represented the best investment Australia ever made. . . . Four years of positive, world-wide publicity: an enumeration of positive achievements in contrast to the reports of crime, war, political machinations and catastrophes that were disseminated in the news media, led to increased immigration and expanding tourism. The economy and industry were stimulated, and not only Australia, but the lands of the entire South Sea area were increasingly integrated into the modern world of the twentieth century. . . . Tokyo [in 1964] was able to accelerate its urban development by ten years. The city was practically newly built and will thereby always be more attractive and efficient. . . .

> Japan will one day reap a multiple of its investment in material and intellectual benefits. . . . [In Mexico 1968] the self-assurance of these peoples *[sic]* was strengthened, and particularly all Latin American countries were proud that one of them was capable of organizing this huge and expensive event just as well as the other capital cities of this world.[14]

Brundage, like IOC presidents before and since, might have believed his own rhetoric, but the durability and continued desirability of the Olympic brand today speaks clearly of the positive outcomes of investing in and hosting the Games. In 1972, it is clear that the Federal Republic could hope to gain much from its investment: urban regeneration, civic boosterism, increased tourism, economic development, and, of course, the chance to overlay residual images of the recent past with new narratives about the country's political, economic, social, and cultural acumen. All in all, it was an irresistible opportunity.

The historian, however, must be cautious not to recount the West German Olympic project on such a simple storyboard or reduce it to the one-dimensionality of actor Michael Douglas's commentary in *One Day in September*: "The Germans saw the Games as an opportunity to erase the negative memories many still had of the 1936 Berlin Olympics, which had been used for propaganda purposes." To a certain extent, such statements are true, but they conceal the richly textured and complex tableaux of discourses, ideas, and circumstances against which the 1972 event was developed and played out. The question of how "the Germans" saw the Games or rather *which* Germans saw the Games *in which ways* requires considerable teasing out for a start. For one, political power remained far from static in the period, the government changing twice in the six years prior to 1972—from right-liberal (CDU/CSU and FDP) via grand coalition (CDU/CSU and SPD 1966) to left-liberal (SPD and FDP 1969)—in line with the turbulent social climate of the late 1960s ("1968"). For another, the idea for hosting the Games did not originate with the federal government but with an ambitious and opportunistic alliance between two particular individuals: Willi Daume, the head of West German sport, and Hans-Jochen Vogel, the mayor of Munich. Subsequently, Bonn was not solely or even predominantly responsible for their preparation, the Organizing Committee (OC) consisting, rather, of "an unusual and unique grouping" of "the Federal Republic, the Free State of Bavaria, and the State capital Munich" on the one hand and "individual representatives of the world of sport" on the other.[15] Finally, in the IOC German officials had to negotiate the traditions and peculiarities of one of the world's most powerful but idiosyncratic international NGOs. Each of these aspects—the changing social and political climate in 1960s West Germany, the influence exercised on the Olympic project by a determined cluster of individuals, and the nature and agenda of the IOC—must be understood as essential factors in the formation of the Munich Games.

THE FEDERAL REPUBLIC IN THE 1960S: CAUGHT BETWEEN FUTURE AND PAST

As Olympic history has shown, the Games have been used from their inception in 1896 "by host nations both to celebrate an historical legacy and to aspire to the expression of their modernity."[16] In the Federal Republic of the 1960s, this dual focus on the past and the future-orientated present was writ large in debates about policy and national self-understanding. If the past had been repressed in the 1950s, the problematic legacy of Nazism lingering uncomfortably just below the surface, it returned with a vengeance in the 1960s. For whatever reasons the public and politicians let "bygones be bygones" in the first decade of the new Republic, the strategy became unworkable in the long-term. From the late 1950s onward, a complicated interplay between internal and external stimuli led to a change in attitude toward the Nazi past in West Germany. An increased internalization of this history developed because of events at home, such as the Ulm Einsatzgruppen trial in 1958 (when the practice of exterminating Jews on the Eastern Front first came to public attention), the anti-Semitic wave of 1959 and 1960 (which soon encouraged ten Länder [federal states] to make the teaching of German history from 1933 to 1945 compulsory), and the first debate about the statute of limitations for Nazi crimes in 1960. Influences from abroad, such as the media drama of the Eichmann trial in Jerusalem (1961) and the continual waves of the German Democratic Republic's (GDR) destabilization campaigns, also played an important part. Just ten years after its foundation and anxious not to lose the moral high ground to its ideological rival, the Federal Republic had no option but to treat charges against its citizens with the utmost seriousness. With the clock ticking too on the (later extended) 1965 statute of limitations, war-criminals were increasingly brought to justice.

Remembering, therefore, became less "selective" in the years running up to the mid-1960s as the "burden of the past" took on ever more virulent tones in public debate. The student revolt of 1968, which projected itself as the critical interrogator of the older generation's past, only radicalized a theme that had already been the subject of public debate for the best part of a decade. Although the eleven years from 1958 to 1969 marked the highpoint of both the public's demand for reflection on the Nazi past and the juridical activity aimed at punishing its crimes, the 1960s remained a complex prism of perspectives. While the past increasingly featured in public debate about German identity, and its variegated forms of continuity into the present were critically examined, voices stressing German victimhood and the need to bring recent history to a close still retained their vigor. The number of those wishing to draw a line under Nazi crimes rose from 34 percent in 1958 to 67 percent in 1969—a fact exploited not only by the newly formed National Democratic Party (NPD, 1964), whose overall vote potential reached 15 percent in 1968, but also by mainstream politicians such as Franz Josef Strauß, leader of the

Bavarian Christian Social Union (CSU). In 1969, Strauß, who chaired the committee responsible for constructing the Olympic venues (Olympia-Baugesellschaft) for three years, felt secure enough to declare: "[A] people that has achieved such remarkable economic success has the right not to have to hear anymore about 'Auschwitz.'"[17] A year later, Willy Brandt's act of penitence, when he famously fell to his knees in the Warsaw ghetto, did not meet with universal popularity in West Germany. Some 48 percent told a *Spiegel* poll that the chancellor had exceeded his remit, and a few weeks later an assailant protesting the presumption of Brandt's gesture in the Polish capital punched him to the ground outside the offices of the 1972 OC in Munich.[18] Leaving aside Brandt's extraordinary good humor on this occasion and the lax security that would later mar the Games themselves, the incident aptly summarizes the attitude of West German society to the past in the 1960s.[19] This was, in Detlef Siegfried's words, "strangely ambivalent" and full of "disintegrative moments."[20]

By 1965, the year in which the Munich Olympic bid was conceived, a paradoxical mix of heightened sensitivity and moral ambiguity toward the past had clearly been established. The divergence—which was to increase as the decade progressed—between the views and decisions of politicians and public-opinion formers and the attitudes of the general public was also already evident. The Auschwitz trial confronted Germans for the first time with the industrial scale of the Nazis' destruction of human life. By the time of its conclusion in August 1965, those in favor of dropping such court cases in future had risen to 57 percent (from only 15 percent four years earlier during the Eichmann trial). At the same time, however, the Bundestag voted (in March 1965) to prolong the statute of limitations on war crimes (in the first instance to 1969, for thirty years thereafter, and indefinitely in 1979), despite opposition from 60 percent of the general population. In contrast to 1960, when original calls for an extension had emanated solely from the Social Democratic Party (SPD), the decision in 1965 was supported by the Free Democratic Party (FDP) as well as a significant number of Christian Democratic Union/Christian Social Union (CDU/CSU) members of parliament. But even as mainstream politicians moved closer to each other and away from their respective publics, they would nonetheless continue to exploit the past for party-political purposes. As before in 1961, the CDU made capital in the general election of 1965 out of Willy Brandt's wartime "desertion" of the fatherland to fight in the Norwegian resistance. In so doing, as Brandt's advisor Egon Bahr accurately observed, they were appealing to and feeding a significant "nationalistic propensity to prejudice."[21]

Soon, however, successive chancellors were attempting to remove the past from the public agenda. In his declaration of government in 1965, just weeks before learning of a potential bid to host the 1972 Olympics, Ludwig Erhard struck a very different chord from the campaign trail when proclaiming the "end of the post-war era." This topos might have had "the character of an ideology that [was] invoked all the more vigorously the more evident Germany's entanglement in the Hitler legacy [became],"[22] but in the context of a de Gaulle-driven revival of nationalistic rhetoric in Europe,[23] it also represented an attempt to overcome the difficulty of establishing a national identity without recourse to a problematic past. The following year, Kurt Georg Kiesinger continued in similar vein at the head of the Grand Coalition, exhorting the nation on the Day of German Unity to turn away from history whose "teaching leaves us in the lurch."[24] By the time of Kiesinger's own declaration of government in December 1966, the focus had fully shifted toward economic success as the potential bedrock of a new German identity. Rainer Barzel, the leader of the CDU/CSU Fraktion in the Bundestag, invited the country to rejoice in its elevated status in the world ranking-lists for production, trade, and social services.[25] These much vaunted achievements might have provided material comfort, but they could not plaster over the ruptures in the social fabric caused by the past. By the time the SPD won power in 1969, the legacy of Nazism had come to the fore again. Although Brandt interpreted the student rebellion in his declaration of government in October 1969 as a sign of the Republic's maturing democracy, he soon began to worry about the unwillingness of the younger generation to learn from recent history and its subsequent unreflecting flight into radicalism. At the Bundestag's first official commemoration of the end of the Second World War on 8 May 1970, the chancellor famously noted that no German could consider themselves "free from the history they [had] inherited."[26] From the conception of Munich's Olympic bid in 1965, therefore, to the moment of the Games themselves in 1972, the past faded out before reemerging in government discourse.

At the same time, the 1960s witnessed the shoring up of a belief in the present and, more importantly, the future. From the beginning of the decade, the idea of planning or steering society lost political stigma. Increasingly, schemes such as Göring's Four-Year Plan to make Germany fit for war or the economic models of Eastern European socialism were forgotten or ignored, as politicians and publics of every persuasion invested in the optimistic feasibility ("Machbarkeit") of the future. Planning the future of society in general or the urban environment in particular was reinvested with positive connotations and gained support from the majority of the working class, the main political parties, and the younger functional elites: "politics no longer focused solely on the solution of problems at hand but, from the end of the 1950s, was increasingly directed toward the future; indeed the future itself became the subject of politics."[27] In the 1960s, West German democracy at Land and national levels became characterized by a proliferation of plans—from the Bundesfernstraßenplan (1957) and the "Großer Hessen-Plan" (1965) to the Grand Coalition's Economic and Stability Law of June 1967, and, in the world of sport, the Golden Plan for Health, Play, and Recreation (1960).[28]

The Federal Republic was not alone in its desire to turn the future in its hands and shape it with present policy. In fact, as the French government's efforts at *planification* in the immediate postwar era indicate, West Germany was simply catching up with its capitalist neighbors in the 1960s, its planning euphoria merely indicative of the country's increasing "Westernization."[29] The widespread conviction that the development of society could be reliably predicted via social-scientific means was nourished specifically in the Republic by the experience of the "economic miracle" and underpinned by the belief that the domestic and global economies would continue their steady growth without major long-term shocks or crises. Despite fears of inflation in 1964 and the first recession of 1966 through 1967, West German optimism held firm throughout the 1960s and remained intact until the first dramatic hike in oil prices of 1973.

This common optimism went hand in hand with an increasing conviction, particularly among social-democrat and liberal politicians, that ideological struggle had had its day. Not only had the country's two main parties drawn closer after the SPD shed most of its Marxist heritage at the Bad Godesberg conference of 1959, but the "end of ideology" was also perceived in an apparent diminishing of differences between the two Germanys.[30] The fact that East and West had managed to sustain comparatively rapid economic growth while financing expanding welfare states even raised hopes that the two systems were set to converge. Such beliefs began to ease the "German question" into a new dimension and would eventually frame the changing attitudes of the Federal Republic's political elites toward the GDR's unqualified participation in the Munich Games. The motor behind intra-German détente—articulated in Brandt's "Two states—One nation" theory and culminating in the Ostpolitik treaties with the Soviet Union, Poland, Czechoslovakia, and the GDR from 1970 to 1972—presumed a new understanding of the state that severed its link with the concept of nation: "The state was no longer an 'ethical idea' in the Hegelian sense, but a modern organization which had to adapt and transform according to new requirements and demands."[31]

This sense of modern organization—a reaching for the future while addressing the issues of the day head-on—set the climate in which a West German bid for the Olympics could be conceived and, indeed, flourish. Paradoxically, while the past increasingly dominated public discourse in the 1960s, it was the Republic's future-orientation that gave the Olympic project its essential pulse. When planning ahead for 1972, technocratic optimism, economic growth, and the "end of ideology" each played a vital role.

KEY INDIVIDUALS: WILLI DAUME AND HANS-JOCHEN VOGEL

Yet crucially, there would have been no West German Olympics at all, were it not for two individuals who met for the first time when one walked into the other's office looking, at the eleventh hour, for a potential city to host the next Olympics but one. When Willi Daume arrived at Munich City Hall on 28 October 1965, he was eager to ride a brief wave of international sympathy that had gathered behind the Federal Republic after a crushing political defeat at the IOC over the controversial status of the GDR (see chapter 6). In Hans-Jochen Vogel, he encountered a politician equally keen to seize the moment of improbable opportunity. Ambitious and opportunistic in equal measure, Daume and Vogel formed a perfect team and went on to exert a formidable influence on the shape of the 1972 Games. Any analysis of West Germany's Olympic project would be inaccurate if it neglected the crucial role of central individuals and their respective worldviews. The form and content of the Games often owe as much to individual visions, passions, and convictions as they do to local and national circumstances, and Munich was no exception. In 1972, a somewhat unlikely pairing came together at an auspiciously productive moment in the nation's history.

Both men were firmly established in their respective spheres and appeared to be riding an upward curve. Daume had served as president of the Deutscher Sport Bund (DSB, German Sports Association) since 1950 and in 1961 had secured an unassailable position as "head of German sport" when he was elected simultaneously to the presidency of the National Olympic Committee for Germany.[32] A recipient of the Großes Bundesverdienstkreuz (Great Cross of Merit) in 1959, he was held in equal esteem internationally. A member of the IOC from 1956, he was elected its vice president on the eve of the Munich Games in August 1972 and later headed its important admission committee (Commission d'Admission).[33] Reputed to have enjoyed great credibility among the athletes themselves,[34] he was later voted "Sports Personality of the Twentieth Century" by the German press.[35]

Vogel was no less dynamic. A talented lawyer, he had become, at the age of thirty-four, the youngest mayor of any European metropolis in the 1960 Munich city elections. Nearly forty years younger than his predecessor and running under the campaign slogan of "Munich of Tomorrow," he secured some 63.4 per cent of the vote for the SPD. Given this clear "breakthrough for the younger generation," there is probably some truth to his claim that the Munich victory encouraged Brandt to stand against the elderly Adenauer in the 1961 general election.[36] After his spell in Munich, Vogel would spend twenty-two years at ministerial level in Land and national governments, most famously as minister for justice during the "German Autumn" of 1977, when he steered debates away from a possible reintroduction of the death penalty for kidnappers, and later as leader and chairman of the SPD (1983–1991 and 1987–1991 respectively).

Despite conspicuous successes, both men were to miss out on the office that would have crowned their careers. Daume—against an increasing "Latinization" of world sports' hierarchies in the 1970s and early 1980s[37]— harbored hopes of becoming the IOC president, until the West German boycott of the

FIGURE 1. Federal President Gustav Heinemann visiting the Olympic venues with Lord-Mayor Hans-Jochen Vogel and OC President Willi Daume in 1971 (photo: Alfred A. Haase, courtesy of Süddeutsche Zeitung Photo)

Moscow Olympics ruined his chances in the election year of 1980.[38] In the same period, Vogel suffered high-profile defeats, losing first as governing mayor of Berlin to the CDU's Richard von Weizsäcker in 1981 and then to Helmut Kohl in the 1983 general election. In the 1960s and early 1970s, however, Daume and Vogel were enjoying both their best times and an aura of those destined for even greater things. One was the "Bundeskanzler des Deutschen Sports" (Chancellor of German sport),[39] the other the "Karajan der Kommunalpolitik" (Karajan of local politics).[40]

These two central figures at the heart of the Munich Games were confident and, indeed, typical representatives of the first two political generations of the Federal Republic—Daume (born 1913) in the vanguard of postwar reconstruction, Vogel (born 1926) in the subsequent wave of ideological skepticism.[41] Vogel, in fact, was a typical "1945er" (a generation which significantly shaped the Games).[42] As such, both were regarded as above suspicion when it came to the Nazi past.

Only thirteen years old at the outbreak of the Second World War, Vogel had benefited from the "Gnade der späten Geburt." The shock of German defeat and his experiences as a young soldier—who firmly believed in the "Endsieg" and was probably saved by an injury received in Italy in March 1945—converted him into a committed democrat, wary of the dangers of ideology.[43] He shared the same attitude to the past as his party leader Brandt. While accepting the illogicality and imprudence of imposing guilt on those born after the fact, he believed nonetheless that "even they [could] not free themselves from the history of the people to whom they actually belong[ed]."[44] On his return from a visit to Leningrad in 1966, he reported widely on the open wound the war still caused in much of Europe.[45] As his later publications would suggest, he acknowledged and was perhaps even driven by the guilt of having simply "swum along in the general current and . . . only asked questions and expressed doubts to those he trusted."[46]

Born thirteen years earlier, Daume's relation to the past was more complex than Vogel's. Having played team handball at the highest level (in the Gauklasse with Eintracht Frankfurt from 1934 and once for the national team in 1938) and attended the Olympics both as a spectator (1928 and 1932) and a participating athlete (1936), his later memories of dealing with the Nazis tended to focus on sport and its self-projection as a realm apart, even under threat, from the regime. Reminiscing on the closing ceremony of the Los Angeles Olympics of 1932, for instance, he would recall an "unforgettable melancholy" born of a feeling that "something [was] coming to an end in Germany that would never return. Economic calamity, the Nazis ante portas."[47] His image of the Berlin Games—during which he was removed from the gold-medal-winning team handball squad to join a makeshift basketball team, a sport massively popular in the United States but virtually unknown in Germany—drew from a similar emotional stock: "Athletes who were as active in sport as I was and were competitive sportsmen were all critical. But we avoided the issue more than anything, and sport was a way of doing that."[48]

Nevertheless, as recent research has shown, Daume's past was less clear-cut than he portrayed. A prosperous, middle-ranking industrialist who took over the family's Dortmund iron foundries on the death of his father in 1938, Daume had joined the party in May 1937.[49] After a brief spell in the army, he was granted a *uk-Stellung* (i.e., classified as indispensable in his civilian job) because of the importance of his factory for the manufacture of tank parts. Much of the war was spent overseeing a company branch in Belgium, where—as he later claimed—under the threat of deportation to the Stalingrad front he wrote spying reports for the SS Security Service of such dubious quality that he was finally left in peace.[50] Be this as it may, like Vogel and countless other Germans, Daume had "looked away." In April 1942, one thousand Jews were held for several days in the sports hall of his local club, TV Eintracht Dortmund, which was under his supervision, before being transported to Zamo near Lublin, a holding point for the death camp at Belzec. In 1944, sixty-five forced laborers kept production at his factory going.[51] In the early 1940s he had also penned articles in TV Eintracht's club magazine and *NS-Sport* that were infused with "a militaristic understanding of sport charged with [nationalistic] pathos."[52] Nonetheless, as the paucity of documentary evidence gathered against him after the war and the fact that the Stasi's collaboration with the KGB to find incriminating material against him proved so unsuccessful clearly shows, in the grand scheme of things, Daume was a negligible figure in Nazi Germany.[53] Like the majority of his generation, he benefited from his marginality before 1945 and the new Republic's willful amnesia in the 1950s.

To varying degrees, therefore, Daume and Vogel had both flirted with Nazism but avoided serious indictment. In 1945 Daume, who had begun rising through the ranks as a sports functionary under the National Socialists, found himself in the right place at the right time. At the age of thirty-two, he had a young and apparently uncompromised face that fitted the needs of the moment. With the politically and confessionally divided landscape of pre-1933 sport providing little traction to postwar German needs, the organizational tabula rasa offered considerable opportunity for self-advancement. Under the watchful eye of the Allies, the emphasis in the second half of the 1940s fell heavily on regional and federal development. Much the same as over the previous decade, Daume used the luxury of time and administrative facilities afforded him by a prospering but not overburdensome business life to maximize his political advantage.[54] Continuing at a local level with almost no interruption, he fostered good contacts with the Allies and became chair of the West German handball association in 1947. Soon, there was scarcely a regional or supraregional committee on which he did not sit, and by the end of the decade he had become both vice president of the new-guard Arbeitsgemeinschaft Deutscher Sportämter (ADS, Consortium of German Sports Offices), a forerunner of the DSB, and treasurer of the old-guard National Olympic Committee (NOC)—two rival factions eager to secure complete control of West German sport. In the event, Daume's interpersonal and negotiating skills saw him elected as the first president of the DSB in 1950—a compromise candidate who was soon to make the post and German sport his own. Aged thirty-seven, he had been placed in charge of an association of some four million members, the largest German "Volksbewegung" since the demise of the Nazi Party.[55]

The ability to straddle rival factions, make the right move, and assert one's will against the grain of competition and expectation was a skill that Daume shared with his Munich partner, Hans-Jochen Vogel. Vogel, who came from an educated middle-class family of professors, civil servants, and judges that stretched back several generations, and who had also worked in the Bavarian state chancellery, would have been a natural candidate for membership of the CDU/CSU, like his younger brother, Bernhard, a future CDU minister-president.[56] On finding no welcome in the party, however, he joined the SPD—a socially counterintuitive move that he nonetheless carried off with considerable aplomb. He "conducted himself in the artistic circles of Schwabing and public meetings with equal aplomb";[57] practiced the folksy beer-barrel tapping (Bieranstich) that officially opened the Oktoberfest with a Braumeister until he had it off to a tee; and later became the first middle-class, Bavarian, and practicing Catholic chairman of the SPD.[58] Daume and Vogel might have been opportunists, but their careers were cemented on a reputation for forthrightness and trustworthiness.[59] It was doubtless this combination that made two men pursuing great things—Daume, the world's greatest sporting event, Vogel, the transformation of his city—into ideal partners.

As Vogel later recalled, there were differences of style and opinion, but these did not prevent the two from developing an excellent working relationship.[60] This close and—as the historical record of many hundreds of letters and meetings over six years shows—largely harmonious cooperation was founded on a productive mix of opposite but complementary skill-sets and similar, if not identical, core beliefs. Daume was renowned for his exuberant generosity, flights of fancy, and visionary qualities;[61] Vogel, by contrast, for technocratic sobriety, studied parsimony, and exactitude to the point of pedantry.[62] If Vogel's "computer-brain stored data, people, meetings, and events more precisely than almost anyone else could have,"[63] Daume—as his partner would remember—regarded the organizational detail of the Games with "bewilderment." While Vogel kept his eyes firmly on the bottom line, Daume produced results "which an administrative expert would have considered completely impossible."[64] Both men were driven by a strong work ethic fuelled by an awareness of the responsibility placed upon them to improve society.[65] A member of the CDU, Daume's worldview was marked by enlightened-liberal, civil-society thinking. Tolerant and international, he held to a basic Christian-humanist orientation and was conscious of the need to develop new structures within the young Republic.[66] As a vital facet of democracy, sport equated to fairness, community, and freedom of choice.[67] Christianity and social justice formed the archimedic point of Vogel's personal convictions too.[68] An admirer of Wilhelm Hoegner—the SPD's Bavarian leader whose speech on the relicensing of the party in November 1945 arguably foreshadowed its seminal Godesberg reforms fourteen years later—he bristled with the "common cause of humanity regardless of religious, national or class differences," notions of "human dignity," "freedom," "justice and . . . solidarity" and believed "passionately" that "every individual, be they the poorest, had the right to expect some modest good fortune in life."[69]

For all their differences, Vogel and Daume—two men from moderately conservative backgrounds motivated by moderately progressive convictions—shared enough common ground to form a cohesive unit with a firm will to succeed. Their respective talents as visionary and ruthless pragmatist made them the ideal composite for the "short summer of concrete utopia" that looked to the future with a belief in progress by technocratic means.[70] And when it came to persuading the federal government to back the bid, steering their Games through innumerable committees and dealing with the IOC, they knew what had to be done and formed their own Grand Coalition.

THE INTERNATIONAL OLYMPIC COMMITTEE

Vogel, Daume, and the Federal Republic would need to be resourceful, since in the IOC they were engaging not only with "one of the world's greatest institutions" but one that believed its own hype, clung to traditions, and behaved on occasion with the random unaccountability of a self-electing gentlemen's club.[71] As a West German Foreign Office official witheringly observed on his return from Lausanne in 1969: "The general impression one gets of this IOC conference is of scant organization teetering constantly on the brink of disaster. The IOC consists for the most part of old and very old men, whose independence borders on the unmanageable."[72] The committee's dysfunctional workings were matched by an increasingly outmoded set of principles. Even in the 1960s it was still largely imbued by the ethos of its founder, Baron Pierre de Coubertin (1863–1937), who had conceived the Games as part of a broad program of educational reform in the wake of the Franco-Prussian War.[73] An enlightened reactionary, who embraced the nascent peace movement, de Coubertin developed a set of ideals that shared core values with analogous idealistic and international movements of the time such as Scouting (1908), Esperanto (1887), and the Red Cross (1863).[74] Each of these was characterized by a rhetoric of universal membership, "an insistence on political neutrality," "a professed interest in peacemaking or pacifism," "a complex and problematic relationship between national and international loyalties," and "the emergence of a (marginalized) 'citizen-of-the-world' style radical supranationalism."[75] Olympism, in particular, sought to transfer the mood and feel of religion, which had lost its function in the modern world, to the domain of sport and aimed to resynthesize body and mind via competitions in music, literature, art, and design. It revered the body as a locus of moral endeavor in the midst of the atrophy and decadence of modern industrial society and maintained the purity of its participants by insisting on their amateur status.[76]

Despite its fin-de-siècle creed, Olympism proved highly durable and thrived in the twentieth century despite the disruption of two world wars. Governed by a code of such "obvious and banal character" that it found "eager subscribers of every political stripe," the IOC preached universalism, practiced maximum inclusiveness and resolutely refused to become ensnared in world events beyond its control.[77] De Coubertin and his successors had been proselytizingly ambitious about the movement's global reach and clearly willing to make concessions.

While the founder's early writings concerned themselves primarily with the ideals of the Games, his later output focused increasingly on how to preserve their existence irrespective of "ideological cleavage."[78] In an interview given after the 1936 Games in Berlin, he asked provocatively: "What's the difference between propaganda for tourism—like in the Los Angeles Olympics of 1932—or for a political regime? The most important thing is that the Olympic movement made a successful step forward."[79] Doubtless de Coubertin would have applauded the irate sentiments of the IOC when several teams withdrew from the 1956 Melbourne Olympics over the Suez crisis and the Soviet invasion of Hungary. As Brundage still maintained in 1972: "The Olympic Games are competitions between individual athletes, and not between nations. . . . In the imperfect world in which we live, precious few international competitions would take place if the participation in sporting events were interrupted every time politicians offend against the laws of humanity."[80] Yet despite such ideals, the movement became increasingly entwined with politics and politicization as the twentieth century progressed: the more political agencies provided the necessary financial and institutional support needed to stage the Games, the harder it became for the IOC to maintain its independence.

In the 1960s, however, politicization was but one of the problems facing the IOC as the world changed and fresh generations of sports functionaries from new nations and ideological alliances began to find their voice. The rise of decolonized nations in Africa led to threats of boycott over the participation of Rhodesia and South Africa; organizers of ambitious regional games flexed their muscles; and the Soviets backed calls for the creation of a transparent IOC parliament to replace the restrictive, self-electing model that had maintained IOC continuities from its inception. The international sports federations had become restless too, demanding fairer representation and annual consultation; athletes and organizers of sports events found it difficult to adhere to the committee's Victorian code of amateurism and anticommercialism; and the metropolises of Rome (1960) and Tokyo (1964) had taken such a shine to their Olympic projects that many feared the Games' recent "gigantism" would, if unchecked, damage their ethic and aesthetic beyond repair.[81] In short, the IOC was under siege on more fronts than perhaps at any other point in its history. The organization might well have benefited from a forward-looking tactician at the helm, such as Willi Daume. Although somewhat swept along by the "economic miracle" and the technocratic optimism of the 1960s—predicting once, for instance, that in the age of space travel scientists would democratize winter sports by inventing year-round ice—Daume was imbued with a deep sense of realism and responsibility for sport's role in a changing world. For Daume (with unmistakable echoes of de Coubertin), sport had a vital part to play in easing the mental and physical woes of society, a task it would fulfill, critically, only by focusing on the future.[82] In Avery Brundage, however, the IOC was run by a president who still believed in the Olympics as a modern religion, "the like of which," he claimed in 1967, had "never happened before."[83] As the modernization and professionalization of sport continued apace after the Second World War, Brundage unrepentantly turned his face to the past, seeking to "arrest the decline and to restore and preserve Olympic ideals" before "promoters and the politicians" caused it to "disintegrate and collapse entirely."[84]

Brundage was powerful. Coming from a poor background, success in the Chicago construction industry had eased his passage into the higher echelons of the Olympic movement. As president of the U.S. Olympic Committee (1923–53), then vice president (1945–52) and president (1952–1972) of the IOC, he was an uncritical, even fanatical follower of de Coubertin's ideas. An isolationist by early political conviction—he chaired the Citizens' Keep America Out of the War Committee—his Olympic heritage also, paradoxically, made him an internationalist. Like de Coubertin, ethics played little part in his outlook. Rather, his behavior was dictated by a rigid cultural code based on an uncompromising understanding of the founder's principles. In word and deed, Brundage "never understood . . . the profound vulgarity of applying the Olympic outlook to every situation he encountered."[85] Most famously, this attitude caused international outrage at the memorial service held in Munich's Olympic Stadium the day after the terrorist attack, when any admiration for his impassioned dictum that "the Games must go on!" quickly evaporated over his claim that the Olympics had been the victim of "two great attacks"—the other coming from the enforced expulsion of Rhodesia after the African nations threatened to boycott. Both sentiments originated from a blind adherence to the notion of the Games' sacred autonomy. To Brundage—and in 1972, as the IOC's hastily issued apology against their departing president's wishes show, to Brundage alone—killing Israelis and being pressured to expel a team of any political hue were one and the same affront.

Such obsession with the letter of Olympic law has been cited as one of the motivations behind Brundage's behavior in 1935 and 1936, when, as president of both the U.S. Amateur Athletics Union and Olympic Committee, he derailed the famous Jewish-led campaign to boycott the 1936 Games. Playing the noninterventionist card and drawing on the widespread belief among U.S. sports functionaries of the interwar years that "sport, American style, could transform other ideologies and social systems,"[86] Brundage returned from Berlin insisting claims about Nazi anti-Semitism were massively exaggerated.[87] In Germany, he had been chaperoned by IOC member Karl Ritter von Halt, with whom he had maintained a close friendship since the two competed in the decathlon at the 1912 Olympics in Stockholm. His role in keeping the United States in the 1936 Games was duly rewarded with a seat on the IOC at the expense of fellow American and pro-boycott member Lee Jahncke.[88] Sports-political convictions, the willingness to show good will, and the desire to progress within elite networks serve only in part, however, to explain Brundage's actions. Of equal importance was a visceral anti-Semitism that surfaced no later than the 1930s and recurred throughout his life.[89] In a speech to the German-American Bund at Madison Square Garden in October 1936, he exhorted his listeners to learn from Germany on how to eradicate the risk of communism.[90] Brundage would become a world-establishment figure in the decades following the war, but his dubious proclivities were known to some West Germans, at least, in the 1960s. In an interview given shortly before his death in 1996, Daume revealed that he had been in little doubt as to the president's political preferences: "He was a Nazi, of course. Some say he would have founded a Nazi party in the U.S.A. I visited him once around that time. At one point, there was a knock on the door, and it opened and there was a real SS-man in a brown uniform with a swastika and armband wanting to collect. He actually supported it all. . . . And—I have to laugh—he showed me all these anti-Jewish newspapers from all over the world, which he loved, it was very odd."[91]

Daume's recollections were doubtless conflated but they reveal that the Munich OC president was aware of the general drift of the American's views. Certainly, as he also remembered, Brundage ensured that no Jew was ever elected to the IOC despite a range of good candidates during his presidency, and that Jewish descent hampered applicants' chances of gaining even relatively minor posts within the organization.[92] His disdain for Jews was matched only by his admiration for Germany. In 1973 he fulfilled his ambition to marry a German princess and lived out his latter days within walking distance of the site of the 1936 Winter Olympics at Garmisch-Partenkirchen.[93] Such Germanophilia would have advantages and disadvantages for the Munich organizers. The fair wind of presidential approval would be cancelled out by his passion to achieve German reunification via sport, an unrealistic but tenaciously pursued ambition that often ran contrary to the mood and policy of the federal government. At the same time, the precarious position in which the president found himself as opposing forces gathered momentum made him vulnerable to self-serving political intrigue. He became a "fellow traveler" with an attraction to strong leaders, especially when they produced, as in the Eastern bloc, magnificent sports displays. As the 1960s wore on, Brundage became a brittle ally and the IOC a tricky forum to read.[94]

GERMANY AND THE IOC

In the six years between the awarding of the Games in April 1966 and their completion in the late summer of 1972, the structure and power of the IOC would by necessity curtail the organizers' attempts to frame their own agenda. Since the values and aspirations of Olympism were articulated almost exclusively through the ceremonial aspect and protocol traditions of the Games themselves, the IOC maintained a vested interest in the form and content of each Olympics and ventured to keep local organizers on a short leash. The Games offered immeasurable symbolic capital, but they came at a fixed-rate currency. Olympic Games were not, in other words, based on a straightforward donor-recipient model whereby the NGO handed over ownership of its flagship event for a given period to individual cities and (by extension) states. Rather, it kept at least one protective hand on its precious commodity, admonishing, cajoling, and even threatening host nations whenever its expectations were disappointed or its regulations remotely contravened. The relationship between the IOC and its hosts, therefore, was symmetrical in outcome but asymmetrical in premise. While both partners would enjoy the party and benefit from its legacy, one was left to foot the bill in its entirety.

Such are the parameters within which host cities, at least since the 1930s (see chapter 3), have agreed to play. The Munich organizers were no exception and, as we shall see throughout this book, were often involved in intricate and irritating negotiations with the IOC over matters of taste, vision, and diplomacy. What is intriguing about the 1972 event, however, is the extent to which West Germany's organizing team staked its claim as an active participant in the Olympic movement, setting itself up as its self-proclaimed savior in its period of greatest turmoil. Time and again, Daume would return to this theme, stressing both the extraordinary trust the IOC placed in Germany and Germany's responsibility to renew the Games for the present day.[95] Admittedly, the archive shows little trace of either the federal government or Munich obsessing over the state of the Olympic movement, but Daume's convictions and all-encompassing energy meant that his perception of the nation's function within a larger Olympic narrative would have a significant impact on the eventual shape of the event. If the "Schicksalsspiele" (threshold Games) of Munich sought to portray a modern Germany, they were equally concerned, in the mind of their chief organizer at least, with giving the Olympics "a new self-understanding."[96]

This bifocal approach to the Games fits neatly with a general practice in cultural diplomacy, in which—as Johannes Paulmann has shown—West Germany differed markedly from other European states. Unlike its counterparts, which after 1945 continued to rely on nineteenth-century techniques of cultural *export* for self-representation abroad, the Federal Republic placed its emphasis intellectually and materially on *exchange* and *dialogue.*[97] Daume's dual commitment to the national and the international was, therefore, very much in keeping with Bonn's cultural program. More importantly, however, he was influenced by a deep-rooted historical relationship—on personal, institutional, and ideological levels—between German Olympians and the IOC. The 1972 event was affected by Daume's close friendship with Avery Brundage and the insipid but pervasive legacy of what we shall term the "German Olympic imagination."

Despite some differences on matters of principle (see chapter 2), Daume stood firmly in the IOC president's corner. By the mid-1960s, they had been acquainted for some thirty years, having met at the 1936 Games and again at close quarters when Brundage lodged with the Daumes in Dortmund shortly after war. While recognizing the president's overt Nazi tendencies in one breath, Daume would admire his grand stature in the next. "He was a great man," he enthused toward the end of his life: "He was the kind of American who made that country great, a pioneer type."[98] Daume, the middle-class, middle-ranking industrialist from the Ruhr was in awe of the Chicago tycoon and reveled in his company and the glamorous world of the IOC.[99] On the invitation of U.S. President Johnson, he flew to Brundage's eightieth birthday celebrations in 1967, Alt-Nymphenburger porcelain under his arm and a telegram of congratulation from President Lübke in the post.[100] When it came to hosting the pampered IOC, nothing was good enough: in 1963, secretary Otto Mayer had to plead with him to curb his spending as he prepared to welcome its session (an annual meeting which dovetailed with the Olympics every four years and took place at other times in different cities around the world) to Baden-Baden.[101] Such munificence would later lead to problems with the Munich city representatives on the 1972 OC, for whom the clash of economic cultures (such as an estimated accommodation bill of three million deutschmarks from the Vier Jahreszeiten and Sheraton hotels) sometimes proved too hard to stomach.[102]

Much of Daume's determination to regenerate and indeed perfect the Olympic event was fuelled by his obvious pleasure in being a member of an exclusive club. But his passion also stemmed from a long-held devotion to its aims and principles among German sports functionaries in general. The Olympics of the modern era might have been invented by a Frenchman, modeled on English sporting ideals, and celebrated for the first time in their ancient home in Greece, but no other country in Europe took to the Games with such philosophical zeal as Germany. This enthusiasm was buoyed by and displayed certain affinities to the country's deep-seated philhellenism, but did not, crucially, depend on it. In the first instance, the Olympics became popular in Germany because they represented the de facto world championships of a form of bodily culture, modern sport, that found itself in ideological struggle with an indigenous counterpart, gymnastics (Turnen). The arrival of sport from Britain in the years between the foundation of the Reich in 1871 and the First World War pitted two different forms of citizenship against each other: the newcomer offering the inherent competition of the industrial age as an alternative to the incumbent's collective mentality and top-down institutional structures. The innate modernity of the import found a natural home in burgeoning urban centers, where it offered alternative loci of sociability and, eventually, mobility for the new service professions such as engineering, sales, and journalism.[103] When sport made the dramatic leap in spectatorship and participation in the interwar years that established it as one of *the* cultural phenomena of the twentieth century, its rise was all the more bitterly contested by the Turner, who frequently condemned the Olympic Games as a pursuit unworthy of German patriots. Within the institutional memory of German sport, therefore, the Olympics became both a cherished ideal and a national preoccupation.

Most of this tradition drew breath from one man, Carl Diem, whose influence spanned the twentieth century until his death in the early 1960s. Born into humble circumstances, Diem latched onto the new phenomenon of sport as a form of social advancement at the end of the nineteenth century.[104] By the age of twenty he had become secretary of the Deutsche Sportbehörde für Athletik (1903, German Sports Authority for Athletics), and as a journalist traveled to the intercalendric Games in Athens in 1906. Appointed general secretary of the aborted Berlin Olympics of 1916, he rose to the rank of general secretary of the Reichsausschuß für Leibesübungen (Reich Committee for Physical Education) in 1917, helped found the first sports university in the world (Hochschule für Leibesübungen, College for Physical Education) in Berlin in 1920 and, finally, organized the Games of 1936. After the war, he founded the Deutsche Sporthochschule in Cologne in 1947, where he became rector a year later and established himself as the *éminence grise* of West German sport. At one remove from the real center of power, now occupied by the young Daume, Diem was nonetheless instrumental in formulating central facets of the Federal Republic's sports landscape (e.g., Deutsches Sportabzeichen, Bundesjugendspiele, Deutsche Olympische Gesellschaft).

Despite hefty debate in recent years, the nature of Diem's relation to National Socialism is still unclear.[105] While this is not the place to rehearse well-worn arguments, it would be fair to conclude that Diem, like many of those who worked with him, entered into serious compromises with the regime. Certainly his will requested the burning of all but family correspondence after his death, and the sentiments of his wife, Liselott, who confided these final wishes to Daume, succinctly articulate a life of moral dilemma: "He had to go along with some things, which, deep down, he really didn't like."[106] In the mid-1960s, though, Diem's reputation had not yet been exposed to the serious revisions that tainted it in later decades. Immediately after the war, Adenauer and his ministers realized his global connections represented the best chance of expedient reintegration into the conservative world of Olympic (and by extension, therefore, international) sport and were happy to bless a continuity at national level that ensured his survival.

But Diem was more than just a functionary who traded on (and quite possibly believed in) the neutrality of sport. Throughout his prolific career he assumed the mantle of Pierre de Coubertin's principal exegete.[107] In the torch relay, which envisaged human hands transporting a flame from ancient Olympia to the modern metropolis, he invented for the occasion of the 1936 Games a perfect piece of

Olympic symbolism. In voluminous writings he championed the thoughts of the founder, inculcating a generation of West German sports teachers on their way through the Sporthochschule with the message of Olympic fundamentalism: sport's affinity with religious experience; a belief in the ability of massed festivals to express deep human impulses; the paradoxical compatibility of patriotism and internationalist ideals; and above all the neophyte responsibility to spread the word. His influence proved as wide as it was enduring. In 1964—just one year before the Munich bid was conceived—the Japanese, who had commissioned him as their first consultant for the Tokyo Games,[108] said prayers for his departed soul at the Holy Temple in Daianji.[109] And when Daume presented the Greek Olympic Committee with the official invitation to Munich seven years later, its president exalted his predecessor simply as "der 'Olympische.'"[110] The title was apt: together with Brundage (who kept the Diems alive with CARE parcels after the war) and de Coubertin, Diem formed "the great triumvirate of modern Olympic history."[111]

Diem's writings and persona meshed into an "Olympic imagination" that characterized the way in which a certain group of West Germans conceived of the Olympic movement and its Games. This particularly German inflection of Olympism consisted of an uncritical appreciation of the 1936 Games (see chapter 3) and a strong emphasis on the country's long-standing archaeological contribution to Olympic legacy. After Ernst Curtius's original expedition to Olympia in the nineteenth century, the site underwent two further excavations, from 1936 to 1943 and in 1961 when the DSB, Deutsche Olympische Gesellschaft (DOG, German Olympic Society), and the West German NOC financed its final clearance. In their enthusiasm for the sacred home of the ancient Games, West German sports functionaries recounted narratives of national philanthropy which glossed over basic historical facts. The fifty thousand reichsmarks appropriated from Hitler's personal disposition fund to finance the second dig were conveniently forgotten, as were the Nazis' counterintuitive idea of using the ancient location to commemorate the Games of 1936 and the endeavors of Walter Wrede, the highest ranking member of the NSDAP in Greece, to unearth "new Reich exemplary warriors, unnamed heroes of state [and] Aryan strongmen masquerading as Olympic athletes."[112] In 1961, under Diem's direction, the West Germans lorded it over the Greeks when "handing Olympia back" after the final dig and moving the casket containing de Coubertin's heart from one part of the site to another. Throughout the 1960s, they embellished their worldview with institutions such as the Internationale Olympische Akademie (IOA, International Olympic Academy) in Olympia, which—in a manner chiming with Germany's archaeological guardianship of Greek culture—was founded and run under German auspices (until the Greek military dictatorship removed Prince George of Hannover from the directorship in 1969).[113]

This form of Olympic imagination did not, of course, sit comfortably with the mood of the 1960s and 1970s, by which time the trope of philhellenism that had dominated German culture for the previous two centuries had run its course. "Demographic, philosophical, and historical trends" and in particular the need to prioritize different school subjects to aid the expansion of higher education meant that the "the singular propaedeutic power of the Greeks," which had been under siege even before the Nazis came to power, was "decisively . . . broken" by the time Munich bid for the Games.[114] But this very particular understanding of Olympism could not go ignored, because its adherents, seeing themselves as the keepers of a pure tradition, remained highly vocal. There were also ties of personal loyalty. Sports representatives on the OC still held Diem in high esteem, and Daume, although never sharing Diem's vision or regarding himself as a protégé, stayed in close contact until his death in 1962. Diem dedicated his *Weltgeschichte des Sports* to Daume,[115] and Daume called for further excavations in Olympia on the grand old man's seventy-fifth birthday,[116] struggled in vain to secure him an honorary doctorate at a German university,[117] and sought his advice on Olympic matters. After his death, he often enlisted Liselott's help as a ghostwriter for his speeches.

. . .

These were the complicated, overlapping discourses *within, around,* and *away from* which the Munich project would unfold over the six years between 1966 and 1972: a political climate that would experience three different governments, social turmoil, and a radical change of policy toward the Eastern bloc; an international NGO buffeted by internal strife, political interference, and institutional intrigue; and an indigenous concept of Olympism that clung to outmoded notions of the classical inheritance and an unfashionable veneration of the 1936 Games. Within and without these coordinates, the Federal Republic, the city of Munich, and the representatives of the West German sports world were faced with the multiple tasks of presenting the world with a new Germany, envisioning and accelerating dramatic urban development, and making the Olympics speak to a new generation. All the while, they would be oscillating between the two conceptual constants that characterize every Olympic Games: historical legacies and visions of modernity.

The problematic nature of the German past, together with the progressive views of the two key organizers, would make for a predominantly future-orientated Games. Munich's own classical heritage would play a surprisingly minor role. Although nineteenth-century Bavarian rulers, with King Ludwig I in the lead, plundered Greece for architectural ideas and even modeled Munich University's colonnade on the dimensions of the ancient stadium, the planners aimed instead for a "vision of the future" that would "match the spirit of the age and serve the needs of modern man and the modern Games."[118] The committee may have decided against launching Carl Diem's torch relay, as initially suggested, into orbit by satellite. But with the help of cutting-edge computer technology and architectural and design experts from the vanguard of the postwar revival of Germany's Bauhaus legacy, they delivered innovation on a grand scale and created a landscape that was already of tomorrow. When James Caan acted in the 1975 cult sports movie *Rollerball,* the futuristic world of the year 2018 was shot in the precincts of Munich's Olympic park. Before Munich, and indeed the Federal Republic, could serve as an imaginative matrix for the modern world, though, six years of extraordinary German endeavor would have to make sense of the past, future, and present.

2

Urban, State, and National Capital

Buying, Paying for, and Selling the Games

Hosting the Olympic Games had been a twinkle in Willi Daume's eye since the early 1960s. The German sports functionary had become a devoted member of the International Olympic Committee (IOC) in 1956, and two events just four years apart must have given him a taste of what it would be like to stage the movement's premier event. In 1959, Munich, the home city of Avery Brundage's longtime friend and fellow committee member Karl Ritter von Halt, hosted the IOC session. When Nairobi refused to admit the South African delegation in 1963, the Federal Republic stepped into the breech, offering the spa town of Baden-Baden as an alternative.[1] The latter proved a sumptuous occasion with "six princes, one marquis, two counts, three barons, five generals, two sheiks [and] a sprinkling of millionaires" settling into a "casino . . . overlooked by turreted castles."[2]

The erection of the Berlin Wall gave political grist to Daume's private ambition. In the winter of 1962 to 1963, he and the then mayor of Berlin, Willy Brandt, plotted to bring the 1968 Olympics to both parts of the divided city.[3] Without troubling to contact the German Democratic Republic (GDR) and ignoring the disapproval of three Western allies[4] and a Christian Democratic Union (CDU) and Free Democratic Party (FDP) cabinet in Bonn reluctant to hand political capital to a rising Social Democratic Party (SPD) star,[5] Brandt submitted a confidential bid to the IOC.[6] Daume worked the committee's networks, conducting private discussions with the influential Russian member Konstantin Andrianow, who, in the spirit of Khrushchev's new politics of coexistence, assured him of Soviet support.[7] But when news of the secret bid leaked, the Western allies brought the matter to a swift conclusion with an unambiguous call to the West German Ministry of the Interior.

By the time it came to bidding for the next Games in the schedule, disputes between East and West Germany at the IOC had become so heated that the committee would have treated a Berlin proposal as a deliberate act of provocation (see chapter 6). By the same token, the West Germans, and Daume in particular, enjoyed some measure of sympathy among committee members, and after Asia (Tokyo 1964) and the forthcoming foray into Latin America (Mexico 1968) there was a widespread view that the Games should return to Europe in 1972. The decision was due to be made in Rome in April 1966, and after consulting Brandt (who in the meantime had lost the 1965 general election but established himself as the undisputed leader of the SPD) from the IOC session in Madrid in October 1965, Daume had to move quickly to find a German city willing to undertake the task.[8]

It is not clear whether Brandt recommended Munich. At any rate, the Bavarian capital would have suggested itself for several reasons. First, Munich had made a very favorable impression on IOC members in 1959.[9] Second, and more importantly, in Brandt's party colleague Hans-Jochen Vogel, the city possessed an energetic young mayor who could be relied upon to rise to the challenge. Vogel's rivals in other potential cities belonged to the prewar generation and, despite their moral standing, risked reminding international voters of the recent past. Arnulf Klett had governed Stuttgart continuously since 1945, and Herbert Weichmann, a former Jewish refugee from Nazi Germany, led Hamburg's senate. Frankfurt, under Willi Bundert, a former member of the Kreisau circle and the war-time resistance who had spent eight years in a GDR prison on charges of espionage, would have engulfed any Olympic enterprise in East-West controversy. Vogel's fresh face and dynamism stood out by comparison and offered the possibility, at least, of assuaging residual suspicion abroad of Munich as the former "capital of the Nazi movement" *(Hauptstadt der Bewegung).*

Third, the fact that Munich was not a capital but only a medium-sized city would offer an antidote to what Olympic insiders had begun to see as the age of "gigantism." From 1960 to 1968, in Rome, Tokyo, and Mexico City, the Games had sprawled over increasing distances (in Mexico up to 589 kilometers) and aroused fears about the event's practical and ethical sustainability. As a city renowned for high culture, Munich would allow an ideological rescoping of the Olympics, selling itself as a return to the founder's belief in the harmony of sport and the arts.[10] Finally, unlike comparable cities in the Federal Republic, Munich had not yet built a major stadium such as Frankfurt's Waldstadion or Hamburg's Volksparkstadion. Conveniently, however, the city possessed a brown-field site of around 280 hectares (about a square mile) just four kilometers from its historic center. Already approved by the city council for future use as a stadium, it simply awaited funding. Munich, therefore, would not only be in a position to mount a swift bid, but its lack of sporting venues would count in its favor: faced with a tabula rasa, the international sports federations, whose opinions weighed heavily when the

IOC made its final decision, would have the opportunity to demand and influence the creation of state-of-the-art modern facilities for their respective disciplines.[11]

While IOC statues stipulate that Games are awarded to cities, these require the backing of national governments. The only Olympics since 1945 to circumnavigate this condition took place in Los Angeles 1984, when a troubled IOC had only one candidate from which to choose. In West Germany, the federal structure of government potentially complicated matters in that the Land of Bavaria would be required to give its consent as well. In the event, however, the three political agencies agreed almost immediately. Daume put his proposal to Vogel on 28 October 1965; Chancellor Erhard, the cabinet, and the budget committee (Haushaltsausschuß) of the Bundestag consented on 29 November, 2 December, and 8 December respectively; the Bavarian government assented on 14 December, the West German National Olympic Committee on 18 December, and Munich City Council on 20 December. When the application was submitted to the IOC in Lausanne before its deadline at the end of the year, the first stage of Munich's bid had taken barely three months. The astonishing rapidity with which each party pledged its support is clear indication of what was at stake.

MUNICH

When Daume visited Munich City Hall in October 1965, Vogel was flabbergasted. Folklore has it that he met his visitor's inquiry with an exclamation of "Sauber!"—a Bavarian term scarcely translatable into High German let alone English, but which revealed his mood to be one of "productive desperation."[12] After consulting widely—with the city's Council of Elders (Ältestenrat), some fifty-four local institutions, associations, and pressure groups,[13] close associates (probably Hubert Abreß, then head of the city development department, and Klaus Bieringer, head of Munich's cultural affairs department), and national party-leader Brandt[14]—Vogel's shock subsided and his initial concern about costs soon developed into excited cooperation.[15] Even in the precommercial days of the 1960s, the Olympics' effect on civic boosterism was fairly evident. One year earlier, the city's deputy mayor, Georg Brauchle (CSU), had wistfully remarked at the 1964 Winter Olympics in Innsbruck that Munich would get its long-cherished "Großstadion" (major stadium) much sooner if it were to host the Games.[16] Munich, moreover, was in the midst of radical planning. In March 1960, an SPD initiative had led the council to commission a strategy that aimed to produce "desirable order for the city's urban and traffic development for the [subsequent] thirty years."[17] In keeping with the technocratic spirit of the age, the ambitious young mayor had won his first election the same month on a pledge of "farsighted and efficient city planning" and duly established one of the first specially dedicated groups of its kind on taking up office.[18]

In 1960s West Germany, however, financial means lagged somewhat behind wishful technocratic optimism. As the population growth of the "economic miracle" years began to outstrip fiscal capacities, communes experienced increasing difficulty. While private consumption and investment continued to rise dramatically, public expenditure on housing and municipal infrastructure remained largely stagnant. Set against dramatic increases in motorization and demands for greater living space, cities struggled to provide an acceptable quality of life. While the communes (excluding the city-states of Hamburg and Bremen) had invested around DM 500 billion in construction between 1948 and 1962, they had done so largely on credit. By 1968, debtor communes owed a total of DM 35 billion, and Munich, whose individual debt had increased ninefold from DM 172 million at the end of 1955 to over DM 1.5 billion in early 1965, topped the table.[19] In 1965, the city's budget had to cover two-thirds of expenditure on roads, housing, schools, and hospitals on credit despite strong advice from the regional government of Upper Bavaria to reduce borrowing.[20] By the eve of the Games, the mayor would be openly lamenting a system that required a city to host the world's largest sports event in order to fund basic public facilities.[21]

The parlous state of Munich's finances resulted from a period of accelerated growth after 1945 which led to housing shortages, rising land and property prices and pressure on basic infrastructure and amenities. Having served largely as a regional administrative center, underindustrialized Munich attracted more returnees and evacuees after the war than any other West German city. Its immediate postwar population of 480,000 increased by an average of 24,200 each year from 1950 to 1971, with the growth rate reaching a net gain of almost 110,000 between 1969 and 1971 alone. As early as 1950, it had matched its prewar population of 830,000, crossed the one-million-barrier in 1957, and hit 1.2 million on the eve of the bid in 1965.[22] During the Olympic year itself, the population peaked at 1.34 million.[23] In twenty years, therefore, both in absolute (462,795) and relative terms (55.7 percent), Munich had grown more than any other West German commune. At the same time, the negative fallout associated with rapid expansion also brought significant economic advantages, as Munich benefited from the relocation of many vital industries. While cities in the Ruhr such as Essen and Dortmund shed more than 40 percent of their industrial employment in the 1960s, and Hamburg, the second-largest city in the Federal Republic, experienced an 11-percent decline, Munich increased its share in the secondary sector by 11 percent.[24] The city profited from the Cold War in general, and the marginalization of (West) Berlin and division of Germany in particular. Taking in seventy thousand expellees from the Sudeten region of Czechoslovakia, the area became home to its export-oriented industries.[25] The influx of highly qualified refugees from the GDR, too, meant that the printing trade of Thuringia and the textile manufacturing and machine-building of Saxony took hold in Southern Bavaria, while important publishing houses relocated from Leipzig, and the film industry abandoned the UFA grounds in East German Babelsberg. Electrical and, later, communication technology giant Siemens moved its headquarters from Berlin to Munich in 1949, creating fifty thousand work places.[26]

There was a certain inner logic to the largest center in the south replacing the former capital in the north as the country's "Olympic city." Between 1950 and 1970, the population of West Berlin had stagnated, with minor fluctuations, around 2.2 million, its age profile tilting firmly toward the elderly.[27] Munich, by comparison, boasted the youngest population in the Federal Republic, a fifth of its residents having been born after 1945 and two-fifths predicted to be under thirty by 1972. When Vogel emphasized this fact in his speech to the IOC in Rome,[28] he was doubtless hoping to banish thoughts of the 1938 Munich Agreement and its aftermath.[29] But the vital truth behind the mayor's statistics was that in the mid-1960s, Munich desperately needed to rebalance the positive and negative consequences of its postwar boom. Influenced by prominent critiques of postwar America—John Kenneth Galbraith's *The Affluent Society* (1958) and Jane Jacobs' *The Death and Life of Great American Cities* (1961, German translation 1963)—Vogel had been concerned for some time about the fabric of modern society. In it he saw a world increasingly defined by a disparity between private wealth and public poverty, spending on trivial consumer needs over vital communal services, and an unnatural functionalist division between work and living spaces.[30]

For the city administration, this meant solving crucial problems of housing and transport and, as Vogel regularly put it, "adapting communal institutions to the growing and ever-changing demands of [the municipality's] citizens."[31] In 1963, his chief city-planner, Herbert Jensen, had been given council approval for ambitious plans to "resist [any further] shapeless accidental development and the very alarming dissolution of the city."[32] In late 1965, therefore, it must have been clear that hosting the Olympics would accelerate the city's cause by many years, and do so largely on someone else's tab. Indeed, some of Jensen's grander projects, such as the development of the S-Bahn and U-Bahn, would be completed within five and seven years rather than the fifteen originally anticipated.[33] With Land and federal support, the city paid only DM 31 million of the total DM 490 million for the former, with Bonn covering the lion's share of the latter.[34] It is hardly surprising, then, that even before the bid was properly formulated, other communes believed Munich had struck gold, and a conglomerate in the Rhine-Ruhr region mounted a short-lived counter-bid of its own.[35]

BAVARIA

Despite the strong majorities that secured the SPD's power in Munich after 1945, Bavaria was a conservative stronghold. Minister-president Alfons Goppel remained virtually unchallenged between 1962 and 1978 and was surrounded by a strong cast of Christian Social Union (CSU) politicians, most notably party chairman Franz Josef Strauß. As a result of the latter's stints in two Adenauer governments (as minister for special tasks, nuclear energy, and defense), Munich and its surrounding region had cornered a large share of the German aircraft, atomic, and armament industries (e.g., Messerschmitt-Bölkow-Blohm and Krauss-Maffei). Superficially, one might have expected a certain tension between the region's left-wing core and its right-wing milieu, but an underlying similarity of outlook compensated for the sometimes heated differences. Vogel, after all, might have become a CSU member, and within the SPD he had attached himself to the informal but powerful right-wing, conservative grouping known as the Seeheim circle and stood firmly behind the modernization decided at Bad Godesberg. Pragmatic rather than ideologically obsessed, Vogel shared the same convictions as the CSU leadership when it came to Munich and Bavaria: the imperative of economic growth. His relationship with Goppel and Strauß was cordial enough for them to channel resources to Upper Bavaria, and Munich in particular, as one of the Land's main areas of expansion.[36]

Although the bid initially met with opposition from high-ranking civil servants in the finance and culture ministries of the Bavarian government, senior party figures gave it their full support. Strauß, a south German cycling champion in his youth, was a keen sportsman and Goppel—along with the two ministers most closely involved, Ludwig Huber (minister for culture and later an influential member of the Organizing Committee) and Konrad Pöhner (finance minister who later played a key role in the Olympia-Baugesellschaft [OBG], the public corporation entrusted with the construction of the Olympic venues)—understood the potential benefits for the region. While there could be little doubt about the financial strain, many came to agree with the Bavarian minister-president, whom the *Spiegel* quoted as sighing patriotically: "One has to grasp the nettle."[37] The CSU grandees presumably calculated they had little to lose. If Munich won, the overall gains for the Land would outweigh their own financial outlay and any kudos given to the "red" mayor of Munich. If it failed, the defeat would be Vogel's alone. When Strauß portrayed the Games in the Bundestag (on 30 November 1965) as a golden opportunity to correct Germany's "distorted self-representation" abroad, his remarks were doubtless sincere but masked considerable Bavarian self-interest.[38]

Just as Munich bargained on the Games enhancing financial support for the city, the Land could count on a flow of investment to its designated growth area at only minor additional cost to taxpayers. While Munich would profit most, significant sums would spill over into surrounding CSU strongholds and help counteract the drift of young people, in particular, from the countryside to the cities.[39] In this sense, Munich and Upper Bavaria shared common interests and incentives.

Unfortunately, no comprehensive economic analysis was conducted at the time, but as a few examples indicate, exposure to international audiences offered Bavarian businesses unprecedented public relations opportunities.

Occasionally, local companies were outbid by international rivals. Coca-Cola, for instance, which had enjoyed a strong association with the Olympics since Amsterdam 1928, out-priced Pepsi and two local firms for exclusive soft-drinks rights on the Olympic sites by guaranteeing the OC at least DM 2 million from its profits.[40] Sometimes national competitors with key personal contacts, such as Daimler-Benz, would work themselves into pole position too.[41] The Stuttgart company had its Mercedes logo and slogan—"Fair in sports. Fair on the road"—printed on the back of every Olympic ticket for an undisclosed sum, in addition to loaning 1,700 cars, buses, and trucks for the Games, offering 275 middle-of-the-range MB 200s at significantly reduced prizes for the Olympic lottery, and providing drivers, luxury MB 600s, and price reductions for the IOC and other VIPs.[42] Without Vogel's intervention, the Munich-based automobile and motorcycle manufacturer BMW would not have even broken into the Olympic car pool.[43]

On the whole, however, local firms, if competitive, were given the rub of the green. Siemens, rather than its American competitor IBM, won the contract to supply the data-processing system Golym (in Mexico 1968, the Italian firm Olivetti had been prone to embarrassing glitches).[44] Although the DM 22.5 million charged to the OC barely covered a third of the cost, the company's investment was easily recouped in exceptional profits, long-term research and development advances, and publicity gains.[45] Golym held much fascination for those reporting on the high-tech nature of the Games, was discussed extensively in the foreign press, and lingered upon lovingly in the official film. Junghans, a Black Forest firm owned by a Nuremberg holding company, almost lost the timing-keeping contract to a free offer from its Swiss competitor Longines, but various interventions led to both firms sharing the responsibility.[46] Local sports-shoe rivals Adidas and Puma were granted contracts to sell and—against strict IOC regulations—give their products away for free in the Olympic village, thus ensuring that athletes' feet (the only part of the body on which a logo could appear) would be clad for all the world to see in Bavarian brands. Adidas built a hotel to host prospective medal-winners, branched into sportswear, and calculated that 80 percent of competitors chose to wear its shoes at the Games.[47] Despite a better offer from foreign manufacturers of tartan tracks, the distinctive Adidas stripes ran and jumped across native *Rekortan,* Hans-Dietrich Genscher having persuaded the OC that "giving this contract to a foreign company would completely undermine the German manufacturer in the eyes of the world and give the international competitor a worldwide monopoly."[48]

The Land would also benefit from the logistical impossibility of hosting every event in Munich itself. Despite disagreements within the IOC, several competitions took place outside the city limits, in some cases even in newly built facilities.[49] The opening rounds of the soccer tournament took place in Passau, Regensburg, Ingolstadt, Augsburg, and Nuremberg, with some team handball games being played across the state border in neighboring Baden-Württemberg (Böblingen, Göppingen, Ulm).[50] A riding stadium was built east of the city in Riem; and, under pressure from the international rowing and canoeing federations, a luxurious water-sports site was constructed north of the city in Feldmoching at the cost of US$23 million (approximately 5 percent of the final Olympic budget).[51] In Augsburg, some eighty kilometers to the north, an "Ice Channel" was commissioned for the Olympic canoe slalom competitions, much to the ire of Avery Brundage who grumbled that this new event had been included in the program for 1972 on the condition that it took place in Munich itself.[52] In light of the infrastructural, economic, and sporting boost that would inevitably accrue to the region, it is hardly surprising, therefore, that the Bavarian parliament's decision to back the bid and bear one-third of the cost was unanimous.[53]

THE FEDERAL GOVERNMENT

Of the three parties responsible for winning and carrying out the Games, the federal government proved the most difficult to convince. There are different accounts of what happened when Daume, Vogel, Brauchle, and Goppel visited the chancellor's bungalow on 29 November 1965.[54] Least credible is Daume's claim that Ludwig Erhard was "immediately all for it," even uttering the phrase synonymous with West Germany's remarkable postwar rise: "*Wir sind wieder wer* [We are back]. We are able to do this and we are not that poor."[55] Vogel's version, in which the chancellor appeared at first to waver, seems more realistic.[56] Clearly warned by Ludger Westrick, the head of the Chancellor's Office, Erhard doubted Vogel's budget of DM 497 million. A handwritten note from the meeting shows the Munich mayor spinning the deal, pointing out that the Bund, which normally contributed 40 percent of the cost of urban road building schemes, had already agreed the funds for traffic infrastructure.[57]

Two hours later, however, Erhard consented, supposedly remarking that "one shouldn't always mope around and give the country unpleasant news."[58] That same day, in fact, he had been forced to announce public-spending cuts in the Bundestag because of slow economic growth in the second half of 1965.[59] But in all likelihood, the chancellor's agreement came from more than a whim or the transient desire to sweeten a bitter pill. As with Vogel a month earlier, the moment of personal opportunity would not have escaped him. Having stepped in as chancellor after Adenauer's resignation in 1963, Erhard had been granted a popular mandate for the first time in the general election of September 1965. A controversial replacement for the great patriarch and disliked by many in his own party, he nonetheless enjoyed wide popular support for his role as economics minister during the "economic miracle."[60] Arguably the Games offered a chance to follow through on his election campaign and consolidate his image as the "people's chancellor" *(Volkskanzler).*[61]

Ideological reasons, of course, would have featured in Erhard's thoughts too, not least the notion of a *formierte Gesellschaft* ("aligned society"), which had been introduced at the CDU's national conference in 1965. In Erhard's view, West German society was increasingly driven by the dictates of consumerism and performance, the competition within the pluralist system neither catering for the individual nor contributing sufficiently to the common good.[62] As a diffuse concept aimed at recalibrating such developments, the *formierte Gesellschaft* would wither quickly on the vine but, having been underscored three weeks earlier in his declaration of government, the idea would have been lodged in the chancellor's mind when the Munich delegation arrived in Bonn. A successful bid would provide the ideal opportunity to stage a grand and dignified occasion that would demonstrate the cohesion of German society, its public spirit and a belief in nonmaterialistic values.[63] Furthermore, Erhard would have been keen to capitalize on the noticeable shift that had occurred in West German identity by the mid-1960s—away from the 1950s' projection of a reunified nation toward an acceptance of the status quo of the Republic's economic and democratic strength. The *formierte Gesellschaft,* which breathed contemporary theory's optimism about technology and social engineering, sought to orientate the Federal Republic firmly toward the future. Hosting the Olympic Games would rearticulate for audiences at home and abroad another major claim of his declaration of government: that the postwar era had now "ended."

Such was the chancellor's mindset as he took the matter to the cabinet on 2 December. Although full cabinet minutes have not yet been released for this period, a short protocol affords some insight into how the discussion unfolded. The meeting was certainly not unanimous, opinions—where recorded—splitting along party-political and regional lines. CSU voices (Richard Stücklen, Richard Jaeger, and Werner Dollinger—the first two from the Munich region) backed the chancellor, while CDU and FDP members (Rolf Dahlgrün, Jürgen Seebohm, Hans Katzer) urged caution. Dahlgrün (the FDP finance minister) estimated the cost at DM 1 billion, more than double Vogel's projection (the final bill would come to twice that again), and Seebohm (the CDU minister for traffic) noted that the Bund faced other pressing infrastructural obligations. Stücklen (minister for mail and communication and MP for Dachau) and Jaeger (minister for justice and MP for Fürstenfeldbruck), by contrast, played the national prestige card, arguing that "cost should not be the main priority" given the "extraordinary political importance" of hosting the Olympics "thirty-six years after the Berlin Games."[64] Just as Strauß had argued two days earlier in the Bundestag, Bavarian politicians in the cabinet pushed the case for Munich, and by extension their region, on grounds of national representation. As the cabinet fell in-line with the chancellor, this particular pattern of influence and loyalties was set for subsequent governments, when strong regional ties would cross party boundaries.

That said, the preparation for the Games would be characterized by a general unanimity of purpose between city, Land, and Bund, despite inevitable and sometimes petty tensions that occasionally arose. Bavaria would seek, largely in vain, to gain advantage over Munich: in early 1966 the names of three CSU MPs—Konstantin von Bayern (a member of the Wittelsbach family), Hans Drachsler, and Franz Josef Strauß (who had just refused a position in Erhard's cabinet)—were floated as the potential "federal and Bavarian Olympic representative" to serve at the helm of the OC before it was established that IOC statutes gave exclusive organizational rights to the host city and National Olympic Committee (i.e., Vogel and Daume).[65] Likewise, Konstantin von Bayern would continue to bait Vogel with independent CSU-driven funding initiatives (the so-called *Flammenpfennig*) until brought to heel by the overwhelming power of the OC.[66] Vogel, for his part, tried to preserve Munich and SPD interests, failing most prominently perhaps to elevate a member of his personal staff in the city hall, Camillo Noel, to head of the Games' press office against a better qualified and well-connected applicant.[67] (The successful candidate, Hans "Johnny" Klein, had worked for a number of newspapers, acted as press attaché at German embassies in the Middle East and Indonesia, and been part of Erhard's 1965 election campaign and chancellery.) On the whole, however, the Munich Olympics stand as a clear example of "cooperative federalism."[68] Despite a highly decentralized administrative and executive system, the SPD-governed city, the conservative-run Land, and three different federal governments conducted their business largely unswayed by political differences. Technically too, the ten-man board of the OC would be set up so that the political partners assumed a distinct common identity: in a system that required a two-thirds majority, the four votes belonging to those bearing financial responsibility for the Games granted the politicians a "veto-minority" against the six representatives from the world of sport.[69] Generally, however, sport under Daume did little to upset the equilibrium between the political camps.[70] The 1972 Olympics was a "mega-event" (M. Roche) that none of the three agencies could shoulder on its own or, for that matter, in partnership with only one of the others. Success, from which all of them would benefit, depended on each of them pulling together.

THE BID

Munich's chances were boosted enormously when Vienna pulled out after the Austrian government refused to underwrite its finances.[71] As the capital city of a neutral European country that had yet to host the Summer Games, it would have been the strong favorite. But Munich still faced stiff competition, not so much from ill-starred Detroit, which was submitting its seventh application, but Madrid and Montreal. The former could bask in the reflected glory of Europe's dominant soccer team (Real Madrid), while the latter enjoyed the prestige and organizational advantages of hosting the upcoming 1967 World Fair. In April 1966, however, the German performance in Rome was a tour de force. Munich's promise—as originally laid out in its bid document and elaborated over the subsequent months by a small group around Vogel—of spatially compact Games that aimed at a Coubertinian synthesis of culture and sport struck a chord.[72] The general desire for a return to "humane Games within reasonable limits," as Vogel reiterated in subsequent years, seemed acute amongst IOC members.[73]

Munich ranked top in the IOC's consultations with the international sports federations and, at a time when technical professionalism had not yet become standard practice, excelled with its presentation.[74] Three years previous, Buenos Aires's bid for the 1968 Games had foundered on basic errors that earned the city a paltry two votes.[75] Munich, by contrast, left nothing to chance, all elements coming out "a class ahead" of the competitors.[76] On the Foro Italico, the Bavarian capital produced a convincing exhibit of its projected venues. Although these bore only a passing resemblance to what was later built, the fact the council had already passed a development plan and held an architectural competition for a stadium (unlike the Spaniards whose model was a simple replica of Barcelona's Nou Camp) proved vital in demonstrating the city's intent.[77] The Germans exploited modern methods of communication, investing around forty thousand deutschmarks in a carefully scripted film *Munich—A City Applies.* For fifteen minutes the inhabitants of Munich, young and old, were depicted as sports enthusiasts with active lifestyles; the city's rich artistic, cultural, and architectural heritage was highlighted; its love of folkloric traditions such as the Oktoberfest flaunted; and its self-proclaimed image as a "metropolis with a heart" (originally dreamed up for its eight hundredth anniversary in 1958) trumpeted again. Playing on IOC members' penchant for luxury and scenic locations, the film emphasized the city's experience in hosting international conferences, blending in the baroque palaces of Nymphenburg and Schleißheim for visual finesse.

After Montreal had overrun, Vogel and Daume ostentatiously shortened their speeches, taking just a few minutes to highlight the main features of the document already sent to committee members in February.[78] It turned out to be a convincing effort. Having topped the first round with a good third of the sixty-one possible votes, Munich eased to the total of thirty-one required for an overall majority after Detroit dropped out and its eight votes were redistributed at the second stage. Madrid (sixteen votes in the first round, fifteen in the second) and Montreal (sixteen, then thirteen) failed to pose the serious threat that many had feared.[79]

FIGURE 2. Special announcement by the local *Süddeutsche Zeitung*: "Munich is an Olympic city," April 1966 (photo: Fritz Neuwirth, courtesy of Süddeutsche Zeitung Photo)

Before the outcome was known, Vogel thanked the rival cities for the fairness with which the competition had been conducted, but the spirit of his remarks was not entirely clear.[80] At its 1964 session in Tokyo the IOC had explicitly forbidden applicant cities from making "special approaches to the IOC either in person or through diplomatic channels"; the giving of presents had also been outlawed, not least in reaction to rumors of bribes involving prostitutes that had helped Tokyo itself win the Games at the 1959 session in Munich.[81] However, Vogel's Montreal counterpart Jean Drapeau had conducted a worldwide tour of IOC members and pledged free board and lodging for participants at the Games (as opposed to the subsidized fee of US$6 per day offered by Munich)—a promise, in Daume's words, that "would have had de Coubertin turning in his grave."[82] And while the Spaniards lacked funds, the shadow of withdrawal having hung over their bid from early 1966, they matched hard currency with political capital. Ironically, given Franco's dictatorship and the only recently lifted ban on citizens from communist states entering Spanish territory (1962), Madrid portrayed itself "grotesquely" (as

Daume later recalled) "as a stronghold of freedom and democracy," playing on the West Germans' recent difficulties over East German transit issues (see chapter 6) and guaranteeing free movement to athletes from the GDR.[83]

Before leaving for Rome, Vogel had stressed that Munich had adhered "absolutely to the letter" of IOC rules.[84] But it is clear that the Germans had not been so naïve.[85] At the first opportunity, Vogel had written to Brundage stressing that Munich "would make special efforts to ensure that IOC members and their families enjoyed the pleasures offered by [the city] and the surrounding area."[86] IOC dignitaries were duly invited, for maximum discretion by the German Olympic Society rather than the organizers, to stop over *before* the session in Rome.[87] He announced his intention to visit Brundage in Chicago (see chapter 3) and massaged the president's prejudices, congratulating him for his (even then outmoded) stance against the abuse of the Olympic Games by business interests.[88] Despite being an outspoken critic of the IOC's strict amateur guidelines, Daume went even further. Shortly before Rome, he persuaded figure skaters Marika Kilius and Hans-Jürgen Bäumler to hand back the silver medals they had won at the 1964 Winter Olympics on national television. Darlings of the German public, the skaters had been disqualified by the IOC for signing professional contracts with *Holiday on Ice* before the Innsbruck Games began.[89] By returning the medals of their own accord, the whole affair, which had caused a storm throughout 1965, came to a convenient end.[90]

Behind the scenes, too, a working party—consisting mainly of city administrators, Walther Tröger (a National Olympic Committee member who later became mayor of the Olympic village) and representatives of the Land and Bund—was set up in January 1966 to "prepare suitable measures for the representation of the Munich bid." One of its main objectives was to create a positive mood in the international sports press.[91] Bruno Schmidt-Hildebrand, a member of the city's public relations department and head of the Munich-based Association of the German Sports Press (Verband deutscher Sportpresse), exploited his connections in the Association Internationale de la Presse Sportive (AIPS), regaling twenty opinion-makers across Europe with the autonomous sporting aspect of the application and the "dynamic personality" of the young mayor. In a spurious twist to the bid's major tenet, he claimed the Games were not intended "to show the world the new Germany [or] . . . to present the new German youth."[92] Journalists were invited on three-day information-gathering visits to the city, where they were received by the mayor and other officials and treated to first-class accommodation, tours, and tickets to the opera. In the months leading up to Rome, so many invitations were accepted that the visits had to be staggered to avoid arousing suspicion.

Western journalists featured in the program and those with potentially hostile IOC members were especially courted. Because of concerns about British member and International Amateur Athletics Federation (IAAF) president David Lord

Burghley, the U.K. press alone received three invitations. Widely tipped to become Brundage's successor, Burghley was regarded as a GDR-sympathizer because of the IAAF's recognition of the East German athletics team in 1964.[93] But for obvious reasons, the working party's main interests lay beyond its natural Western allies. Given that Eastern bloc members were likely to vote against the Federal Republic, great effort was invested in the "Third World." For although IOC members acted as ambassadors from the committee to their respective nations and not—as in normal international nongovernmental organization practice—vice versa, Daume knew that representatives from developing countries would vote in-line with their government's wishes.[94] Accordingly, West German emissaries were sent around the world with the informal authority to make promises of financial aid to enhance such countries' preparation for the Games.[95] The trips alone cost the Foreign Office Cultural Fund around DM 50,000.[96] Nonetheless, the working group was cautious about flaunting its official backing, since exerting influence via diplomats could prove counterproductive. Burghley himself reacted petulantly to an approach on Munich's behalf by Aubrey Halford MacLeod, British Ambassador to Iceland and former general consul in Munich (1960–65), promptly announcing his support instead for little-fancied Detroit, which had missed out on hosting the 1968 Games by a single vote.[97] Naturally, the Foreign Office offered support, embassies and consulates being asked to observe the visits and spy on rivals.[98] But in general, high-ranking sports functionaries with untainted political reputations and good contacts in the relevant countries were preferred for the task. Such considerations were particularly important in Africa because of Germany's colonial past. Surrogate diplomats included Max Danz, the president of the West German athletics federation and a vice president of the West German NOC, and Alfred Ries, a Jew persecuted by the Nazi regime with impeccable credentials for representing the Federal Republic abroad: not only was he president of Werder Bremen soccer club and a board member of the German Soccer Federation, but had served as ambassador to Liberia under Adenauer before becoming general manager of the major German coffee company Kaffee Hag.

Danz concentrated on South America, Ries mainly on Africa. While cultural reasons alone dictated that the eleven members from South America (including Cuba) would probably vote for Madrid, positive responses from the two Brazilian members João Havelange and General Sylvio de Magalhães Padilha gave a glimmer of hope.[99] The German embassy in Buenos Aires also brought Bonn good news, reporting that Argentine member Mario L. Negri had expressed "full sympathy" to the cause.[100] The prognosis for Africa, however, was much more favorable from the outset. Unlike ten member states of the Arab League (including Syria, Saudi Arabia, and Egypt), Morocco and Tunisia had maintained diplomatic relations with the Federal Republic after its formal recognition of Israel in 1965; and—with the exception of the apartheid regime in South Africa—the poverty of the remaining nations (e.g., Kenya, Nigeria, Senegal, West Sahara) would make them amenable to persuasion.

In the age of decolonization, Africa had rapidly become a theater of superpower struggle over ideological allegiances and the new economic world order. In view of its growing fiscal strength, the Federal Republic was called upon to "accept greater responsibilities and an increased share of the burden for securing the future of the Western alliance . . . and the development of the Third World."[101] In this context, the term *cooperation* concealed a myriad of intricate and duplicitous power relations between first- and third-world countries, the latter exploiting the former, as much as vice versa, and "demanding ever more [development aid] as the price" for their loyalty.[102] The realm of sport was no exception. If in the run-up to the 1972 Games the Federal Republic educated athletes from countries sympathetic to the West—almost 10 percent of students at the Sporthochschule in Cologne came from abroad in 1970—the GDR followed suit at the College for Physical Education in Leipzig; if the Ministry of the Interior sent West German coaches to train soccer players in Senegal, Ghana, Cameroon, Mali, Ivory Coast, Togo, and Uganda, the GDR did likewise by dispatching physical education teachers to the Middle East, Asia, and sub-Saharan Africa.[103] If the Soviet Andrianow wanted to expand the power of the socialist bloc by democratizing the IOC and giving representation to all NOCs, Western sport functionaries like Daume did everything in their power to prevent it. Sport, therefore, was a keenly contested subfield of the Cold War "fight for Africa."

When it came to securing the success of the Munich bid, the Federal Republic's surrogate diplomats were bolstered by President Heinrich Lübke (CDU), a hard-line opponent of East German recognition.[104] Set to embark in early 1966 on a tour of Morocco, Kenya, Madagascar, Mali, Togo, and Cameroon (the latter two with former colonial ties to Germany), the president agreed to canvass the relevant local authorities. Only Morocco had an IOC member, but the Munich team hoped for a ripple effect across an African continent famous in the 1960s for its love of sport. In Morocco, Lübke secured King Hassan's support against the ongoing GDR campaign to "reinforce the division [of Germany] in the realm of sport" but left the question of the bid open, since the monarch was keen to cultivate equally good ties with Spain.[105] However, by the time Danz arrived a week later, Moroccan IOC member and high-ranking Muslim cleric Hadj Mohammed Benjelloun assured him not only of his country's vote but of his determination to bring his colleagues from Tunisia, Senegal, and Egypt on board.[106]

While it is impossible to say how individual votes were cast, it is likely that the combination of presidential influence and surrogate diplomacy had a considerable effect on the outcome in Rome. Pressed twice by the Foreign Office in the following months to divulge the secrets of the voting chamber, an initially reluctant Daume "was strongly convinced that all Africans . . . from north to south without any exception whatsoever" had supported Munich. With success, Daume noted, came "responsibilities, the fulfillment of which would be of eminent political value for the Federal Republic."[107] The Foreign Office clearly agreed. In 1969, Daume was able to diffuse Vogel's fears about threats of an African boycott over the participation of Rhodesia and South Africa in 1972, bullishly assuring the mayor that the Africans had just picked up "a fat check from the federal government" and were turning down invitations from the Eastern bloc.[108] Foreign Office figures certainly bear him out. In the run-up to Munich, sport development aid for "third world" countries increased steadily as a part of foreign cultural policy. The total expenditure of DM 685,000 in 1966 rose to nearly DM 1.2 million in 1970 and, including DM 500,000 for the preparation of athletes for the Munich Games alone, DM 1.8 million in 1971. Originally, DM 2.43 million and DM 2.95 million had been earmarked for 1971 and 1972, though these figures were later reduced as part of general cuts in the 1971 federal budget.[109]

Compared to West Germany's official development aid, which was funded by the Economics Ministry and ran into the hundreds of millions per year (e.g., DM 600 million in 1965), these were small sums.[110] But developing countries sympathetic to the Federal Republic's representational claims, as Lübke stressed all the way across the African continent in early 1966, could, of course, hope to receive from the bigger pot as well.[111] Despite complaints from Rabat that development aid and military equipment had been slow in arriving, the Federal Republic paid large sums to keep African nations onside.[112] Even before Lübke's visit, Morocco had been offered almost DM 194 million for the next several years.[113] As Heide-Irene Schmidt has shown, West German development policy in the 1960s operated on a fine balance between favors given and received: although "aid was granted according to recipients' needs" and the Federal Republic "did not expect 'active support' . . . in return for aid," it nonetheless appreciated "mutual respect of national interests as a foundation for co-operation."[114] Thus, when the president assured King Hassan that support for the Munich Games was not a "question of principle," a subtle but very definite ritual of expectation was at play.[115]

It is little wonder, then, that Daume's speech in Rome sold the Munich Games as a bridge not only between sport and the arts, East and West, but also "young" nations and "old" nations.[116] In later years, Daume would portray the wooing of African votes as a kind of "social justice."[117] In early 1966, at a time when regional games threatened to lure African countries away from the Olympic movement altogether, the West German NOC president felt able to confide his plans to Brundage: "We have . . . offered—if it should be in agreement with the IOC's views—to support the young nations in Africa and Asia financially and technically in their preparations for the Games and when they send their athletes."[118] Taken together, the Cold War and decolonization eased the Munich bid toward success. West German money was already flowing into Africa, and with the IOC, the Western allies, and the Federal Republic wanting to hold on to it, the continent was only too open to persuasion.

Such agendas meant that Africa—much more than Asia or South America—remained firmly on the Federal Republic's radar after the Games were won. Although the organizers could not expect many visitors from the continent, they were keenly aware of a "certain political and sports political obligation to keep [its] population[s] well-informed" about the event.[119] By the same token, the Olympics provided the Federal Republic with a much-needed opportunity to enhance its stale and outmoded image in this strategic region of Cold War struggle. In the wake of German colonialism and two world wars, an internal position paper noted, African views of the Federal Republic were still largely shaped by the "masculine . . . soldier, brave both in attack and defense, loyal and adept at using his weapons." "Self-restraint, unconditional obedience and the prioritizing of honor ahead of other criteria" also determined the picture, with Bismarck and Hitler, for the Arab populations of North Africa at least, appearing the very "incarnation of Germandom." Across the whole of Africa, moreover, the "un-rhythmical" Germans played second fiddle to NATO allies such as the "sensitive" French.[120] Thus the Games allowed for a more positive projection of the German character: namely as "peaceful, conciliatory, serene, sensitive, sober and accurate and looking for harmony."[121] One million deutschmarks of additional funds, donated to the OC by the record company Ariola (equaling some 10 percent of the overall PR budget), were invested in specific advertising initiatives. In particular, the urban middle-classes of the twenty-eight nations with NOCs were targeted in English, French, and Swahili; a highly popular Olympic poster competition was organized for African artists; and the customary activities of the federal agencies and ministries involved in cultural diplomacy were intensified. The Federal Press Office organized seminars for African sports journalists in the Republic.[122] Daume hand-delivered invitations to African NOCs, making impassioned speeches about their integral role in the Olympic movement and bearing gifts of material and financial aid.[123] In Lagos he handed over DM 1 million to help West African athletes participate in the 1972 Games and a track made of the same material as the one at Munich's Olympic Stadium.[124] Until African solidarity against Rhodesia's participation strained relations and almost led to a massed boycott in mid August 1972, the Munich Games received hugely positive coverage across the continent and allowed the Federal Republic, via sport and its ever-popular functionaries, to bestow "great honor"—as one Foreign Office report duly observed—on the people of Africa.[125]

PAYING FOR THE GAMES

Once the euphoria of Rome had dissipated, the organizers would be tossed between the Scylla of financial burden and the Charybdis of Cold War politics for some time to come. (The latter is discussed fully in chapter 6.) When informed of the bid's success, Erhard hailed it as a "mark of great distinction" for the Federal Republic.[126] Four years later, in April 1970, Genscher, the interior minister of the new SPD/FDP government, captured the chancellor's original mood at an Olympic exhibit arranged for politicians in Bonn: "This is an historical opportunity to convey a desirable image of this state and the society which sustains it on the occasion of the Olympic Games to hundreds of thousands of international guests as well as hundreds of millions of TV viewers, radio listeners and newspaper readers."[127] From the earliest moment, it was obvious that Munich would be a "national task." Olympic Games "mean a great deal," as Willi Daume stressed when inviting the great and the good to join the OC's advisory council (Beirat), "particularly for the country that gets to invite the youth of the world."[128] But it was not until 1969 that Bonn *officially* recognized the Games as such. There is a simple reason for this. Federal law dictates that matters of national representation must be financed predominantly by the federal government. The essential difference between Erhard's reaction in 1966 and Genscher's speech in 1970 was the vital promise of additional funding: in view of the task's significance to the nation, Genscher went on to note, the Bund would be carrying "the largest financial share of the investment and organizational costs."[129] This discrepancy between emotional and bureaucratic understandings of the Olympics' importance made for years of protracted negotiations between the city of Munich and Bavaria on the one hand and the federal government on the other.

In 1965, the head of Erhard's Kanzleramt and skeptical members of the cabinet had not been alone in their fears about the Games' funding. Before the bid had passed through the various parliaments, the country's leading financial newspaper, the Düsseldorf *Handelsblatt,* published a damning article warning that the three parties were rushing headlong into "an expensive plan."[130] Soon after the success of Rome, five CSU MPs (led by Franz Gleißner) sent an open telegram to Vogel, demanding the Games be stopped to protect essential expenditure on schools and hospitals; they had to be muzzled by the CSU caucus in the city council (under Hans Stützle).[131] As soon became apparent, though, the doubters had called it right. A memo from the Ministry of the Interior shows how Daume and Vogel had arrived at the initial estimate of DM 497 million: 158 million were to be spent on the Olympic venues, 120 million on the Olympic village, 3.5 million on administration and organization, and 185.5 million on traffic infrastructure, leaving 30 million in reserve for unforeseen circumstances.[132] But by the summer of 1966, the costs had already increased by 23 million, and much steeper rises were to follow. All told, the Games cost DM 1,967 million, just shy of the eye-catching DM 1,972 million later enshrined in the official report.[133] Put another way, the checks made out to the Africans had shrunk over six years from 0.6 to a mere 0.15 percent of the total bill.

TABLE 1. 1972 Munich Olympic Games' Expenditure and Income (in millions of DM)

Expenditure		Income	
Building costs Munich	1,350	Olympic coinage	679
Building costs Kiel	94	Olympic lottery	252
Production costs	523	Income from ticket sales, donations, and television rights	359
		Federal subsidy for Zentrale Hochschulsportanlagen	42
		Contribution of the Federal Republic	311.7
		Contribution of Bavaria	154
		Contribution of the city of Munich	154
		Contributions of Schleswig-Holstein and the city of Kiel	14.4
Total	1,967	Total	1,967

SOURCE: Deutscher Bundestag, 7. Wahlperiode, Drucksache VII/3066: Abschlußbericht über die Gesamtfinanzierung der Olympischen Spiele in München, 9 January 1975.

These cost increases were largely caused by local inflation, not least because the event set an absolute deadline for the completion of venues and their supporting infrastructure. In 1965, the Munich Chamber of Trade and Industry warned the Games would lead to an "excessive boom in the construction industry with adverse effects on the makeup of local prices and wages," a prediction that proved all too accurate.[134] Between 1968 and 1973 Munich's price rises outstripped the national average, and the city became the most expensive in the country by 1971.[135]

In his study of Olympic finances, Holger Preuss makes a basic but useful distinction between expensive and inexpensive Games. Olympics tend to be "cheap" if, as in the two most recent North American examples (Los Angeles 1984, Atlanta 1996), "costs are largely limited to organizing and staging the Games" with profits made or deficits avoided by exploiting existing infrastructures. Games work out to be expensive, by contrast, if they require "extensive investments in traffic infrastructure, communication systems, housing and sports facility construction."[136] On the surface, 1972 fits the second category, but the actual costs, when compared to other Games of the period, place it some way back across the spectrum. The figures for Rome 1960 and Mexico 1968—doubtless for good reason—were never published. But Tokyo 1964 cost US$2.8 billion at a time when one dollar bought four deutschmarks and Montreal 1976 made a colossal loss, with Mayor Drapeau spending like "a Roman Emperor" and allowing costs to soar from an estimated US$300 million to 2.8 billion.[137] Famously, the Canadian government declined to contribute from the outset, leaving the taxpayers of the city and the province of Quebec to struggle with debt until 2006.[138] Munich's total of US$500 million—less than the price of two aircraft carriers, as Richard Mandell trenchantly observed—paled by comparison.[139]

In point of fact, the Games represented extraordinary value for money.[140] In the end, only DM 634 million (i.e., 142 million more than anticipated in the original estimate) came from the three public coffers.[141] Munich city's total expenditure of 154 million, around DM 20 million per year from 1966 to 1972, equated to less than 1 percent of the municipality's annual budget in 1970.[142] Apart from shrewd and—as time went on—forensic financial management, the fiscal health of the Games benefited from several crucial factors.

First, between them the organizers already owned a largely undeveloped site approximately twice the size of Munich's historic city center. The Bund immediately declared itself willing to remove its army barracks and virtually no costs were incurred for relocating businesses.

Second, the Games drew on unorthodox and inventive methods of financing, the single most important revenue stream coming from coinage. From 1969 onward, 100 million ten-deutschmark silver coins generated DM 679 million in revenue—some 34.5 percent of the cost of the Games and more than the combined contribution of the city, Land, and Bund. Initial fears about inflation were unfounded as the West German public avidly snapped the coins up, keeping them for posterity rather than spending them as currency. Inspired by a similar venture at the 1968 Games, the scheme enjoyed unprecedented success, not least when the Eastern bloc protested the wording "Games of the Twentieth Olympiad 1972 in Germany (Spiele der XX. Olympiade 1972 in Deutschland)" (rather than "in Munich")—a debacle that turned them into a collector's item.[143] An Olympic lottery, established in 1967, brought in DM 252 million, while its television equivalent, the *Spiral of Fortune,* which played off the Olympic emblem and was supported by high-profile guests such as Franz Beckenbauer and *Avengers* star Patrick Macnee (in Bavarian dress!), produced DM 187.6 million between 1970 and 1972.[144]

Third, the Games pushed commercialization up to and beyond the legal limit. The 1972 Olympics were the first to be regulated by a specific contractual agreement between the IOC and the host city about the distribution of television revenues, which had been rising rapidly since the first substantial screening of the Games in Rome 1960. The Germans not only quadrupled the sum procured by Mexico City (receiving US$13.5 million from ABC) but—much to the ennui of the IOC—also maximized their share by arguing that equipment and technical costs should redound directly to the hosts.[145] More importantly, deals with leading companies and the sale of commercial rights to the Games' emblem generated significant (although largely undisclosed) sums. Falling through the cracks opening up between ambiguous IOC statutes and the burgeoning spirit of free enterprise in sport, such arrangements had been commonplace for several Olympics, and

Munich was well placed to take advantage. In the Society of Sponsors, which had liaised with local industry and commerce since 1955 to help finance the city's future "major stadium," the organizers could exploit an existing fund-raising apparatus. Renamed Olympic Sponsors Association in 1966 and working closely with the OC, the society collected some five hundred promises of consumable donations and loans of equipment. In addition to the companies mentioned earlier, a host of household and local names lent their support. From Kodak to Wella AG, companies donated everything from television sets and hair salons to petrol, toothbrushes, and, in the case of Franz Zimmermann KG Nittenau, five tons of German chicken. The total savings for the organizers—none of which appear in the final table of costs—amounted to a staggering DM 300 million in loans and around DM 48 million DM in cash donations (i.e., the equivalent of almost one-fifth of overall actual expenditure).[146]

After the IOC's lucrative capitulation to television and commerce in the 1980s, this financing of Munich might seem arcane. But for the 1960s and 1970s, Munich was superlatively managed. Unfortunately for the organizers, though, this was not apparent at the time. The first ten-deutschmark coins were not minted until 1969, the scale of their success only filtering through over the following years; and lengthy negotiations meant that the television contract with ABC was not signed until 1969, despite the OC having to pay out annual advances of DM 500,000 to Lausanne from 1967.[147] In other words, as costs began spiraling at an early stage, the OC and its political backers had a difficult battle on their hands.[148] Their struggle was inevitable from the beginning, since Erhard's government had cloaked its original assurances in a straightjacket. When the Bundestag's powerful budget committee (headed by Vogel's SPD colleague, Erwin Schöttle) agreed to bear one-third of the estimated cost, it did so with important provisos: all alternative avenues of funding were to be explored and, crucially, the cost-sharing formula was to be renegotiated should the total sum exceed DM 168 million.[149]

If Bavaria played a relatively minor role in the bid, it was to come to the fore in the fight for funding. In times of increasing tax revenues, it could probably have afforded the expenditure, even if this was not widely acknowledged. But standing, perhaps, to gain the least of the three partners, it guarded its purse strings tightest, and in so doing benefited not only itself but the city of Munich as well. As costs rose in the summer of 1966, Bavarian Minister-President Goppel pressed Erhard in vain to reconsider the ungenerous nature of Bonn's fiscal conditions.[150] His successor Kurt Georg Kiesinger, who led the Grand Coalition government from December 1966 to 1969 with Bavaria's Franz Josef Strauß as finance minister, brought some relief, however. In a consortium agreement of 10 July 1967, Bonn agreed to bear one-third of the real construction costs of the Olympic venues, the contract containing an apparently convenient subclause for the impecunious city and Land, which stated that it should be renegotiated if the actual cost exceeded

DM 520 million.[151] Given the deal did not actually commit the Bund to further expenditure, however, this caveat proved a mixed blessing.

It was not long before the funding issue became acute. In February 1968, little over six months after the agreement was signed, the OBG revealed that the cost of the Olympic venues had risen to DM 820 million.[152] The announcement shocked Bavaria, a Land that had historically required heavy subsidy from the center and been in net receipt of the federal equalization of burdens for a large part of the postwar period. Not surprisingly, opposition grew. On 21 March, CSU deputies in the Bavarian parliament tabled a motion to limit building investment from public funds "to the absolute minimum" and in future reject all "uneconomical proposals."[153] The reasons for cost increases were complex, but not surprisingly Behnisch and Partners' futuristic tent roof served as a lightning rod for public and political discontent. In 1967, the Stuttgart firm's idea of draping a Bedouin-style cover made of Plexiglas over the Olympic stadium and nearby sports halls had impressed the architectural jury with its boldness of vision (see chapter 4). But in practice its construction entered uncharted territory in building technology, and costs rose tenfold from DM 15 to 18 million to 188 million, for only half the stadium.[154] The dramatic nature of the overall price increases and residual doubts about the aesthetic fit of a modernist design in an architecturally conservative city formed a political powder keg.

A former property developer from Bayreuth (Franconia) who had made his money in concrete, Bavarian finance minister Konrad Pöhner was considered an authority on construction. Sensing how things might develop (the full extent of the roof inflation would only become clear the following year when it hit DM 37 million in spring and DM 130 million by the end of the summer),[155] he broke ranks with his colleagues on the OBG, publicly lambasting the modernist roof and suggesting that Munich should withdraw from hosting the Games.[156] His deputy, Staatssekretär Anton Jaumann, attacked the extraordinary expenditure, too, in a widely publicized speech in Parsberg/Oberpfalz in the Bavarian provinces. Whether Pöhner and Jaumann were genuinely scandalized or set out merely to score political points against their SPD rivals in Munich, siding with the region's concrete lobby against the architects from Baden-Württemberg, the city soon responded by accusing Bavaria of mounting an "anti-Munich campaign."[157] Once again, Hans Stützle of the city council's CSU caucus was called upon to calm troubled waters. Daume intervened with Goppel too, reminding him of the long-term benefits and stressing the crucial importance of Behnisch's architecture "as a yard-stick to measure the spiritual integrity and credibility of a new, young and democratic Germany."[158]

This fracas over, the Land and the city closed ranks again, the former in particular impressing on the Bund that it stood to gain most from the Games. In May, Jaumann wrote to Strauß as chair of the CSU, preparing the way for Goppel to approach Strauß, Kiesinger, and Ernst Benda (minister of the interior, and therefore responsible for sport) in July with a request to renegotiate a 50–25–25 split.[159] In the same month, the Munich City Council passed a similar resolution.[160] But the parliamentary budget committee rejected the requests, taking the view—expressed by several CDU representatives, most notably Heinrich Windelen, an MP from Lower Saxony—that it would be "inappropriate for the Federal Republic to stage the most lavish Games of the [twentieth] century."[161] Hoping nonetheless that the Bund would relent at some point and assume 50 percent of the overall burden, the city and Land would repeat their arguments mantra-like over the next few years.

Despite Strauß's innate desire to help his native Land and the emotive pressure of CSU colleagues who appealed to him to respond "with his Bavarian heart," unconducive economic conditions and long-term structural changes to federal funding mechanisms dictated that he could not give in.[162] In light of the first economic downturn in the history of the Federal Republic in 1967, the dramatic announcement about cost increases in 1968 came at an inopportune moment. Although the economy was to rally again soon, returning by the end of 1969 to growth rates reminiscent of the 1950s, additional federal expenditure on what many saw as a one-off spectacle would have been impossible to sell to the West German taxpayer. As late as July 1969, even the Bavarian section of the German taxpayers lobby wrote to express its grave concerns about the consequences of the Olympic cost explosion.[163] Moreover, Strauß felt embarrassingly misled about the roof. As minister of defense, he had normally doubled the estimates presented to him by civil servants and weapons experts and prided himself on the accuracy of his figures. When it came to the Olympic roof, however, this simple algorithm broke down, Strauß agreeing with Vogel that it was the worst case of public price inflation he had ever encountered and pointing out to the OBG board that the press took them all for "philistines, inexperienced lawyers, and bureaucrats who thought in terms of finance and had no idea of the demands of aesthetics."[164]

Strauß's deliberations would have been complicated further by the final negotiations over the federal Finance Reform Law of May 1969, which required a change to the Basic Law (Art. 91a, b) and represented a compromise deal between the municipalities, regions, and the center. Throughout the 1960s in a struggle over the financial muscle of federalism, the three agencies had argued about their respective powers to raise, spend, and distribute public funds.[165] Essentially, the regions, communes, and Bund had traded off over the right to maximize financial autonomy and manage "shared responsibilities" *(Gemeinschaftsaufgaben)* such as health and education. It did not help Munich's case that the greatest intransigence in these negotiations came from the Bavarian government and Munich's Hans-Jochen Vogel, who was regarded as the communes' outstanding expert on financial matters.[166] With his dogged persistence on issues of Olympic and urban finance,

FIGURE 3. Signing of the consortium agreement on the financing of the Games between representatives of the city of Munich (Hans-Jochen Vogel, second from right), the state of Bavaria (finance minister Ludwig Huber, third from right), and the Federal Republic (interior minister Hans-Dietrich Genscher, fourth from right) on 29 June 1972 (photo: Fritz Neuwirth, courtesy of Süddeutsche Zeitung Photo)

Vogel became the object of a joke in government departments, to wit that it was "best to avoid mayors from Munich when they were in Bonn."[167] Even in 1971, two years after the passing of the reform, Vogel was still on the urban warpath, addressing international audiences about the need for increased devolvement of fiscal powers to cities.[168]

Nonetheless, calls for a redistribution of costs were beginning to reverberate around parliament. In June 1968, a question-and-answer session in the Bundestag (instigated by Josef Ertl, an FDP MP from Bavaria) had indicated that the majority of parliamentarians were in favor of a new settlement.[169] Moreover, parliament's special sports committee—set up in the final stages of the Grand Coalition government to discuss a range of questions dealing with sport and society, the 1972 Games, and the 1974 FIFA World Cup—concurred. For the rest of 1969, this committee's meetings were dominated by cross-party lobbying from Munich and Bavarian MPs.[170] Finally, in the last days of the Grand Coalition, Strauß gave way. Informing Bavaria and Munich in advance, he held out until after the SPD's election victory before giving his ultimate consent and left his successor Alex Möller to deal with the consequences.[171] Despite Brandt's reference to the Games as a national responsibility in his declaration of government in October 1969, Möller hardly rushed to pick up the bill. Although Vogel and Pöhner were invited to Bonn for summit talks in December 1969 and given verbal assurances that the Bund would cover 50 percent of expenditure, the budget committee continued to withhold its consent until almost a year and a half later, with the federal parliament itself not able to vote for a redistribution until April 1971. The final consortium agreement was settled on 29 June 1972, just eight weeks before the Games began. Much to the chagrin of Otto Schedl, Pöhner's successor as Bavarian finance minister, and Munich's city treasury, the Bund took an inordinately long time to clear the debts it had accumulated over the previous five years.[172]

PUBLIC RELATIONS OPPORTUNITIES

Aside from finance, the differences between city, Land, and the federal center were mainly academic. As it transpired, the city of Munich enjoyed a glowing reputation with visitors from abroad, and this would be most valuable to the cause of national prestige. The Federal Republic certainly gained as much from Munich's international radiance as Munich profited from Bonn's belated financial munificence. In fact, the choice of Munich as the West German host, rather than rivals with little international profile (Hamburg or Frankfurt) proved extremely serendipitous. When it came to it, the lavish expenditure on architecture and design led the OC, under pressure from the political agencies, to make budgetary cuts, leaving its PR department with only DM 10 million. Astonishingly, a project with a potential worldwide audience of one billion could draw on only 0.5 percent of the overall budget.[173]

Formulated in January 1969, the OC's publicity campaign had three obvious goals: to "win friends for the Federal Republic"; to use the "unique occasion" of the Games to "refine or, where necessary, correct the image" of the nation abroad; and to increase West German tourism revenues by encouraging foreign visitors to spend time in the country as a whole.[174] Quite apart from pragmatic considerations—such as ensuring that every event in the Games (no matter how obscure) played to a capacity stadium, or siphoning visitors away from a host city short of hotel accommodation—this third objective sought to use the Olympics as a magnet for every part of the Federal Republic. However, if the stated aim of the organizers' strategy was to "attract as many visitors as possible from as many countries as possible to Munich and Germany," the reality of budgetary constraint reduced the ambition.[175] In short, the PR department was forced to target specific groups and do so, largely, on the basis of existing information.[176]

Going on statistics from the 1960 Olympics in Rome, the organizers deduced that 50 percent of visitors to the Games were likely to come from four or five countries: the United States and Canada (in the case of Rome, 18 percent), Germany, France (12 percent each), and the United Kingdom (11 percent). North Americans' commitment to Olympic tourism was underlined by statistics from Tokyo and Mexico City, where they had also formed the largest visitor group, and tourist board records for Bavaria and Munich in 1966 and 1967 pointed in the same direction. While the vast majority of overnight guests in the Land originated within the Federal Republic (22 percent from within Bavaria itself, 71 percent from other federal states), one-fifth of the remaining 7 percent came from the United States and Canada. Figures for the city of Munich itself showed a similar breakdown.[177] Boxed in financially, the Munich organizers thus developed an advertising strategy that functioned along Darwinian lines: with the politically determined exception of Africa, only those regions that could guarantee a high yield of tourists were targeted. Latin America and other poorer regions of the world were mostly neglected until relatively late.

The organizers devoted their energies to changing perceptions of Germany in their key target areas of Western Europe and the North Atlantic. The U.S. market was especially attractive because of the high disposable income and spending habits of its Olympic tourists. But while U.S. citizens were believed to respect West Germany's technical and economic achievements after the war, they did not seem to hold the country in any great affection. This "quasi-neutral" stance would need to be corrected by the production of a "more colorful" picture of Germany. Nevertheless, the United States offered reasonably fertile territory, the author of a report on the OC's participation in the New York Steuben parade less than a year before the Olympics claiming that he "could not discover any reservations about the Games taking place in the Federal Republic and in Munich specifically" and reporting the assurances of the editor-in-chief of *Aufbau,* the German-Jewish émigré daily, that his paper would do all it could to make them a success.[178] Western Europe, despite new allegiances and alignments in the Cold War, proved a trickier prospect, however. While the overall concept of the Games—with its serenity, modesty, and humane dimensions—would probably prevent audiences in Western Europe from "suspecting [the country of] relapsing into totalitarian mentalities," there was still much work to be done.[179] France, for instance, perceived its neighbor's post-1945 manifestation as "nouveau-riche, perfectionist and emotionally cold."[180] There, as in Britain, it was considered best to address the younger generations, who displayed "a more flexible and partly more positive attitude to the Federal Republic" than their elders who had direct experience of the war. But while the French and other Western European audiences could be seduced by references to culture and folklore, "umpa music and Lederhosen" were to be downplayed in the United Kingdom to avoid negative stereotypes.[181]

Munich itself had much to contribute to this effort. A 1969 Infratest poll showed that the city was held in such extraordinarily high esteem by U.S. tourists—concerns about unfriendly service in hotels and restaurants notwithstanding—that it clearly offered the best hope of correcting negative or value-neutral aspects of Germany's image as a whole.[182] The transfer of Munich's inherent charms ("metropolis with a heart") and the texture of its Olympics ("the serene Games") to the Federal Republic in general, therefore, became a major feature of the PR strategy.[183] Thomas Clayton Wolfe, whose praise of the city came to be cited as often as that of Thomas Mann, reflected on the Bavarian capital in his 1939 novel *The Web and the Rock:* "How can one speak of Munich but say that it is a kind of German heaven? Some people sleep and dream they are in Paradise, but all over Germany people sometimes dream that they have gone to Munich in Bavaria. . . . The city is a great German dream translated into life."[184] The 1972 PR campaign sought to exploit such images, turning them inside out and mapping the city's charm and allure onto the country as a whole.[185] Although not reflected upon by the organizers, the untroubled nature of Munich's relation to the past certainly made their task easier. Even today, the city lacks an adequate memorial to its complicity in the Third Reich, and in the 1960s and 1970s, its self-image was embedded between the regional and the global. After 1945, Bavarian historiography distanced itself from "Prussian" militarism and focused on the region's European and cultural connections, while from the 1960s, generations of Munich schoolchildren were presented with the tellingly titled book *München. Heimat und Weltstadt* (Munich: Hometown and Metropolis).[186] Similarly, lectures later given to the Olympic hostesses in preparation for dealing with the public at the Games would skirt around the Nazi era and concentrate on local traditions.[187]

The main Olympic brochure, *In the Middle of this City,* published in fifteen languages with a print run of 1.5 million, exemplifies the transfer strategy very clearly.[188] Lavishly illustrated, it led its readers out in concentric circles, from the Olympic stadium to the furthest reaches of the Republic. From the building site on the Oberwiesenfeld where, as a sign of the city's openness, tolerance, and cosmopolitanism, "15,000 workers from twenty-three countries" were reported to be creating "a new piece of Munich," the booklet whisked its audience to the architectural beauties of the historical city center—an opposition that connoted the synthesis of tradition and modernity. From there, via Wolfe's eulogy, the focus moved to positive associations of the city—its *joie de vivre,* youth and beauty (represented by the PR model known as the "schöne Münchnerin"), relaxation (beer, Hofbräuhaus), strolling, shopping, and easy-going social interaction. After the arts and cultural festival, which was as much a part of the "grand celebration of 1972" as the Games themselves, came Bavaria, characterized by its cuisine (dumplings, veal sausage, meatloaf, and local delicacies), folklore (Lederhosen, farms), mountains, castles, lakes, and finally—with Kiel's hosting of the sailing events on the

Baltic coast acting as a linchpin—the rest of the Federal Republic. In keeping with the depiction of Bavaria and its capital, the nation-state was represented by the twin achievements of modern technology (Volkswagen, Autobahn) and cultural legacies (Bach and Beethoven, Marx and Mendelssohn, Goethe and Gutenberg, Dürer and Diesel), supported by stunning landscapes (the Black Forest, Rhineland), historic cities (Heidelberg, Cologne), wine, food, and *Gemütlichkeit*. In short, prospective visitors were being told that Munich's special atmosphere could be found wherever they went in Germany.

The scarcity of funds available to the PR team was counterbalanced by support from governmental agencies involved in cultural diplomacy and local and international companies. Although even the standard form of advertisement in foreign newspapers proved beyond its financial reach, a fair wind of internal and external assistance helped the Munich campaign reach a large international audience.[189] The state-owned carrier Lufthansa earned the right to call itself the official airline of the Games by offering free trips to senior organizers and distributing PR material during flights.[190] Fifty-five foreign airlines and tourist organizations were also persuaded to show Munich's Olympic films, display models of the sports venues, and hand out leaflets free of charge.[191] Coca-Cola, despite being irked by the IOC's prohibition of explicit advertising at the Games, showed the films at service stations and sports events it was sponsoring.[192] And Inter Nationes and the Federal Press Office each bought almost five hundred copies to play at trade missions, consulates, and embassies abroad.[193] Thus, *Munich—A City Prepares* (1969), the third in the organizers' trilogy, reached an estimated audience of 40 million in 110 countries, including those in the Eastern bloc.[194] On the sea, too, the North German Lloyd (which had catered in the Olympic village in 1936) and its Hamburg competitor German Atlantic Line provided two luxury vessels each, at half price, for publicity purposes.[195] The liners not only distributed materials during routine crossings and cruises but, in 1970, served as platforms for high-profile Olympic receptions in major harbors such as New York, Lisbon, Copenhagen, Leningrad, Helsinki, and Stockholm. As the OC concluded, the ships alone had brought "incalculable" goodwill to the Federal Republic.[196]

Making the most of the available funding and assistance from public and private agencies, Olympic advertisement abroad proved a resounding success. Not only were the 1972 Games a near complete sellout, with 4.5 million visitors overall, but an estimated total of 1.1 million tickets went to foreigners alone.[197]

PRESS

If the PR team's major aim was to bring new visitors to Germany, then the organizers knew that they faced the equally, if not more important, task of taking Germany to the world. In fact, since an audience of almost one billion—including over half the households in the United States—would be tuning into the Games, this was at once a simpler and incomparably more daunting undertaking.[198] Via newspapers, radio, and television, West Germany would be transmitted and scrutinized around the globe. The number of media personnel attending the Olympics had risen steadily throughout the 1960s: Rome was covered by 1,442 journalists, Tokyo by 3,984, and Mexico City by 4,377. While the figures for Munich and Kiel (four thousand and 250 respectively) fell just short of the previous Games, the role of the 1,200 radio and television journalists among them had grown immensely. Important advances in broadcast technology, such as the wider availability of color television and the ubiquity of television sets and transistor radios by the end of the 1960s, were certainly one factor.[199] The Games themselves also contributed to the spread of media hardware—sales of colored television sets in the Federal Republic rising in 1972 by over 70 percent against the previous year.[200] But Munich 1972, as the *Spiegel* announced in its cover story immediately prior to the opening, represented the "first total optical exploitation of an international meeting of athletes," with broadcasters able to select from 1,200 hours of footage. These "TV Olympics," as the magazine concluded, "unite[d] Western Europe's Eurovision and Eastern Europe's Intervision, Communists and Capitalists, Hamites and Semites, Mongolia and Monaco, the old, the new and the third world."[201]

Given the immense significance of the coverage, the OC established a department solely for the press. Led by the energetic and experienced "Johnny" Klein, it received DM 11.3 million between 1969 and 1971, a shade more than the sum earmarked for PR. The organizers canvassed opinion broadly, seeking assistance internationally—as they had done during the bid—from the Association Internationale de la Presse Sportive (AIPS).[202] Leading members of the professional organization for sports journalists advised them throughout the preparation of the Games, commenting on their experiences of comparable events. The association's administrative secretary, Edgar Joubert, proved particularly helpful. A well-known sports journalist of German-Jewish descent, Joubert had left Germany in the Nazi period and was a friend of Daume. Daume had proposed him, predictably to no avail, to Avery Brundage for the post of IOC general secretary in 1966.[203] As a member of the 1972 press committee, Joubert, along with a number of influential local and national journalists, compiled regular reports on the treatment of the press at international sports meets. From the 1968 Winter and Summer Games in Grenoble and Mexico City the committee gleaned that their organization would need to "work with clockwork precision," since this "justly or unjustly" was "perceived to be [a] typically German" trait.[204] While the French, "traditional masters of improvisation," had excelled in keeping the mega-event largely on track, the Mexicans had paid scant attention to the requirements of the increasingly disgruntled press. Reacting "over sensitive[ly]," the South Americans read AIPS's advice and suggestions as "lecturing and interference" and felt insulted by the perceived "lack of trust in their organizational capabilities."[205] In addition to poor housing, communication, and transport systems, journalists often found their seats occupied by unauthorized personnel, with the print media, in particular, finding it difficult to work efficiently as they were exposed to frequent downpours.[206]

Aiming to please at all costs, Munich arguably treated the journalists better than the athletes. The organizers spared no expense in building the state-of-the-art Deutsches Olympia-Hörfunk-und Fernsehzentrum (DOZ) for radio and television, which later became Bavaria's Zentrale Hochschulsportanlage, and DM 5.57 million alone were invested in the Olympic Press Center for print media, with a further DM 4 million going to furnish the journalists' living quarters in the "press city" situated just a short walk from the main venues. In contrast to 1968, each journalist had a single room, equipped with television and telephone. More funds were devoted to keeping the price of food, transport, and housing artificially low before, during, and after the Games: at US$10 to 17 per day, excellent food and wine plus the service of thousands of well-trained hostesses and stewards from the German army acting as guides, chauffeurs, and coffee makers all came at a fraction of the real cost.[207] As a matter of course, sports writers were supplied with sufficient workstations, shielded from the elements at all Olympic venues, and could sit at some 1,800 places in the main stadium alone.[208] Even a critical observer such as Richard Mandell, who traveled to Munich with natural suspicion having just published the first academic account of the 1936 Games, could not help but be impressed.[209] Mandell marveled at the press center's facilities, "filled with hundreds of typewriters in all the world's scripts, more hundreds of compliant, many-languaged hostesses, a restaurant seating 1,000, a place to buy the world's newspapers, telex machines, banks of long-distance phones, conversation pits with deep upholstered furniture, acres of carpeting and bars with deliberately enforced low prices."[210]

Such luxurious hospitality was supplemented by an intensive information campaign. Erhard's former press guru Klein believed strongly in the value of providing journalists with regular and accurate information, claiming in a seminal position paper that "correct information possess[ed] imminent advertisement value." While IOC regulations prohibited host nations from producing materials of a political nature, communications could be written in a way that gave international audiences a clear picture "of conditions in the Federal Republic a quarter of a century after the end of the war." Talking openly about critical debates over cost increases and shared expenditure would even serve to highlight "the democratic transparency of the state." And, "report[ing] that journalists [would] have television sets on their desks at each of the individual Olympic venues, where they [could] choose between ten different programs, or that a swarm of satellites [would] beam television programs and telephone calls from Munich's Olympic Park all over the world" was, Klein concluded, "advertisement in itself for the economic power of [the] country."[211]

Klein's fetishization of facts and figures shaped the press-department materials destined for the IOC, NOCs, and international newspapers, radio, and television networks. Seven glossy bulletins were issued from late 1968, with the third *(2,638 Information Items),* more than any other perhaps, boiling Klein's philosophy down to a single publication. Later read out by the announcer as the stadium filled up before the opening ceremony, it contained details such as the athletes' likely consumption of twenty-three thousand pounds of steak, twelve thousand chickens, forty-three thousand sausages, and more than one million eggs in the 2,600-seater cafeteria.[212] From June 1969, monthly and later biweekly newsletters *(Olympia Press)* were also produced in German, English, French, Spanish, and Russian, with free copyright worldwide. Buttressed with human-interest stories (usually about leading personalities in the OC), these fact-filled information booklets emphasized the image the organizers sought to project: the technological modernity of the country aligned with the charm and tradition of Munich and its surrounding region. In the occasional series "Adorable Munich," for instance, the Bavarians, with their thousand-year-old drinking pedigree, were portrayed as odds-on gold medalists in any Beer Olympics and the possessors of a relaxed and idyllic lifestyle in which the individual could achieve simple harmony with his or her environment.[213] The same press releases, however, also luxuriated in descriptions of the technological infrastructure (from NASA rockets and satellite transmission) that underpinned the Games and, by implication, the nation as a whole.[214] Modernity, tradition, Bavarian charm, and a technological prowess perhaps even to rival the superpowers: these were the messages the organizers wished to beam to the world. A somewhat unlikely blend, it seemed nonetheless to work. In an article entitled "The World Looks to Munich," published in the city's final official guide to the Games in the summer of 1972, Klein congratulated himself on an evening organized for sixty leading U.S. journalists:

> Alpine horns, folk dancing, smoked meat, rustic bread, jazz, yodeling, zither music, beer, gentian, the Olympic film, few speeches, a bit of fun and talking shop. After just under two hours, Roone Arledge [the powerful head of ABC who had bought the North American television rights to the Games for a record fee] said: "A sensational party!" The mix had worked. A little white-blue cliché, which is nonetheless the happy truth, and the open admission that we Germans have no improvisational talent and therefore have to organize everything.[215]

Considering Arledge grew up, as he confessed in his memoir, knowing only three things about the capital of Bavaria—Hitler's putsch, Chamberlain's "peace in our time," and the Oktoberfest—the Munich team had done an excellent job.[216]

As the Federal Press Office (which collated international media coverage) recorded in its *Echo Olympia 72,* such positive messages reverberated around the world. Leaving the more nuanced responses from the Eastern bloc aside (see chapter 6), Munich was clearly anticipated with critical optimism or outright enthusiasm:

"An Affluent West Germany Seeks Acceptance" (*Christian Science Monitor,* 24 May 1972); "Les Jeux qui ne ressembleront pas à ceux de Berlin" (*Sud-Ouest,* Bordeaux, 30 July 1972); "Munich la cosmopolite" (*Gazette de Lausanne,* 23 June 1972); "Roof Über Alles" (*Harpers and Queen,* London, July 1972); "German Efficiency Hits its Peak in Olympic Games Installations" (*Los Angeles Times,* 29 February 1972).

• • •

Not surprisingly, the Olympic project had moved on considerably from the moment Daume first approached Vogel in Munich City Hall. It had required municipal, regional, and federal approval, the support of official and semi-official international diplomacy, public funding, and the backing of infrastructural networks and local and worldwide commercial enterprise. Protracted and intense negotiation over cost-sharing and heated debates about price increases played out against the development of innovative and ultimately inexpensive finance initiatives—but not in time to prevent a reduction in publicity funds. The international PR operation, working on limited budgets, appealed to the specific strengths of the widely popular host city, mapping it onto the Federal Republic as a whole. Members of the world press, come to cover the sports event, were treated as VIP guests and received no less than what they had expected all along: "organizational standards . . . that put all previous Games in the shade."[217] They, and ultimately their readers, listeners, and viewers, were presented with a city acting as a bridge between tradition and modernity. In Munich, past and present sat comfortably together. Such cross-temporal harmony was not as simple to achieve, however, when it came to dealing with Germany's specific Olympic legacy. If the public relations and press departments could ignore the Berlin Games of 1936—which they did without discussion—other organizers could not.

3

The Legacy of Berlin 1936 and the German Past

Problems and Possibilities

Munich's hosting of the Olympics fitted the geopolitical pattern of the International Olympic Committee's (IOC) decisions after the Second World War, which had gradually ushered the defeated nations back to the heart of the international family. The first three Games after 1945 went to the victors and (semi)neutrals (London 1948, Helsinki 1952, Melbourne 1956), with three of the following four heading to the losers (Rome 1960, Tokyo 1964, and Munich 1972). In Rome and Tokyo, the Olympics allowed the hosts to puff out their chest and present a new and forward-looking image. For the Federal Republic, the potential was similar but at the same time very different. Not only did Germany occupy a special place in the opprobrium of world opinion but, unlike Italy or Japan, it had hosted the Games before. Whereas the Italians provided a touchstone with antiquity and the technologically innovative Japanese facilitated the event's expansion into Asia, the Germans were welcoming the Games back after an absence of only thirty-six years. Berlin 1936 had been "the most controversial Games ever" and, not surprisingly, Munich's relation to them was complicated.[1]

In the week of the opening ceremony, the opinion-forming magazine *Spiegel* launched a brutal salvo at the Olympic movement and its hosts.[2] In a report entitled "Ein Geschenk der Deutschen an sich selbst" (A Present from the Germans to Themselves), it paraded a litany of contemporary crises, attacking the politicization of sport (the African boycott threat), the sham of amateurism, the privileging of high performance over massed participation, and the spiraling cost of the event and the "Münchhausen economics" of its defenders. Happy to feed the organizers' greed for money but too lazy to protest against "hypocritical Olympic ideals," the *Spiegel* concluded acerbically, the German public was about to be served the Games it deserved. In all of this, Berlin 1936 was relegated to a subclause, but the inference was clear: Munich had much in common with its predecessor. Quotations from Otto Szymiczek—the German Curator of the International Olympic Academy and significant guardian of the German "Olympic imagination"—appeared in sarcastic montage, and the Games' potential to improve the nation's image was undermined by juxtaposing Munich's "frothy advertising" with what the magazine saw as a real need for "credible, stable policies." The magazine might have avoided a direct *verbal* comparison of the two Games—a common platitude of the GDR (see chapter 6)—but was more than comfortable citing the *image* of 1936 to deliver a negative verdict on modern sport and national attitudes. In the center of the article, its insinuations were lent visual weight by a large picture of the opening ceremony in 1936, swastika prominent, and a caption reading "Olympic Games in Berlin 1936: perjury and monumentalism."

This dissonance between image and words in the *Spiegel* was symptomatic of a broader public unease with the memory of 1936. The reissuing in 1972 of a cigarette card album from the 1936 Games by the Frankfurt publisher März caused the most notable stir. Under the title *Die Nazi-Olympiade,* the press printed the original images alongside a scathing epilogue by Gerhard Zwerenz, a regular contributor to the radical left-wing magazine *Konkret.*[3] As one reviewer astutely noted, the publication relied on an unresolved tension between its attractive visual material and flimsy verbal critique. Egon Franke, federal minister of Intra-German Relations, had little doubt about the publisher's cynical commercial intent, lamenting to its head, Jörg Schröder, how it was already apparently possible "to glorify the darkest times of our nation again." Schröder's reply in the *Frankfurter Allgemeine Zeitung*—"Obviously the Minister is only capable of grasping the critical nature of books if he sees the words 'critical analysis' in the title"—might have been a superlative rhetorical parry, but it masked the ambivalent position that 1936 occupied for the majority of the album's readers.[4] In 1972, the relatively recent Berlin Games were still highly valued by sports enthusiasts as an outstanding *athletic spectacle.*[5] Whether, beyond that, they were fascinated by the "schöner Schein" (beautiful semblance) of the Third Reich (Reichel), convinced by the political critique of it, or moved at the same time by both—is impossible to tell.

At any rate, in 1972 there were contesting views of 1936, which could swirl and fall across a broad spectrum of opinion. Much depended on the discourse within which such opinion was expressed—the "German Olympic imagination," the critical left-wing press, the "innocent" pleasure of sports fandom—and Berlin could be viewed simultaneously from different angles. Moreover, the nature of the Olympics, an event that drew its lifeblood from tradition, made it impossible to ignore the legacy of 1936. The Munich Games, therefore, offer a potent example of what Friedrich Kießling recently described as the major dilemma of postwar German representation: "on the one hand, the desire for recognition and acceptance again in the international community and at the same time, on the other, the search for a suitable way of engaging with the National Socialist past."[6] For the Organizing Committee (OC), winning, planning, and executing the Games for the IOC and the young Federal Republic involved a series of problems, contradictions, and opportunities.

THE IOC AND 1936

Today, the IOC's website reflects the widely held (and particularly Anglo-American) view that 1936 represented the nadir of Olympic history.[7] However, such notions airbrush the committee's own changing relation to the Berlin event over time and reduce a complex bundle of influences and perspectives to a moral shorthand. In point of fact, although initially worried about Hitler's designs on the Olympics, the IOC seemed enraptured with Germany's contribution to the movement. Famously, Leni Riefenstahl was awarded the Olympic Diploma in 1937 for her film *Olympia* and the Nazi leisure organization "Strength through Joy" (Kraft durch Freude) won the Pierre de Coubertin Cup in 1938. In 1937, Carl Diem was allowed to establish an International Olympic Institute in Berlin, and General Walter von Reichenau—a convinced National Socialist member of the 1936 organizing committee, later Reichssportführer and eager military leader on the Eastern Front—was readily accepted as an IOC member. When Sapporo withdrew from hosting the 1940 Winter Olympics because of the onset of war, the event was switched back to its 1936 venue, Garmisch-Partenkirchen.

Scholarship has often criticized the IOC, specifically in this period. Certainly the committee's natural right-wing leanings can hardly be denied.[8] Not only did a number of its members come from countries (Italy, Germany, Spain) whose governments and sports organizations had lurched definitively to the right, but, as aristocrats and businessmen, both they and their Anglo-American counterparts viewed communism, and the Soviet Union in particular, as a serious threat. The personal convictions of some members also harmonized, to differing degrees, with Nazi viewpoints. Feeling undervalued by his native France, the aging de Coubertin let himself be wooed and manipulated by the Nazi regime. Focusing on apparent philosophical affinities (e.g., the body as moral regenerator), he publicly endorsed the 1936 Games and, in the last years of his life, was saved from penury by Nazi funds channeled through Carl Diem.[9] Other prominent Olympians showed even clearer signs of ideological weakness. Henri de Baillet-Latour, IOC president during the Berlin Games (1925–42), was not "very fond of Jews," and his vice president and successor (1946–52), Sigfrid Edström, expressed a "hearty hatred" of those in the United States who publicly opposed the 1936 event.[10] An engineer from Gothenburg, Edström was a Germanophile who spoke the language fluently, visited the country frequently on business, and argued strongly for the readmission of the Federal Republic to the IOC after the war. In such company Avery Brundage looked very much at home.

Yet the emphasis these facts are typically given has often skewed the narrative of 1936. As argued more fully elsewhere, the IOC was not, even loosely, a Nazi body, nor did the magnitude and effect of the Berlin Games stand in isolation.[11] If the IOC began in 1894 as a small, self-selecting group of aristocrats with a big idea, its quadrennial festival grew incrementally from 1896 toward a climax forty years later. The Olympic idea had leapt into a new dimension not only in 1936 but four years earlier in Los Angeles as well, and the two Games must be seen together. Both benefited from the growing internationalization and exponential popularity of sport in the interwar period. Moreover, the United States and Germany were two of the foremost sporting nations in the world, with an awareness of athletics' potential to embody nationalistic ideals and enflame common passions. The warmongering vitriol emerging from *both* sides of the Atlantic when Joe Louis fought the former German world heavyweight champion Max Schmeling in 1938 was perhaps the culmination.[12] The impact of both cities on the Games was immense. The total ticket sales doubled in Los Angeles, then more than doubled again in Berlin, with thirty-two years elapsing before the Games would attract more live spectators (at Mexico 1968). Stadium capacity increased by around 60 per cent (and has hardly been exceeded since), and in the Olympic village (Los Angeles) and the torch relay (Berlin) the final elements were added to the Games' symbolic inventory. After Berlin—ignoring the hastily arranged austerity Games in London 1948—record numbers of cities and countries would apply to host the event.

These two Games helped the Olympics achieve some parity with the world fairs that had inspired them in the late nineteenth century. In 1932 and 1936, they assumed a scale of precision, organization, and spectacle that would come close to the expos for awe, keep pace with their socialist sporting rivals (the Workers' Olympics of 1931 in Vienna, not to mention the Soviet spartakiads, had hosted one hundred thousand spectators in a purpose-built stadium), and put the Olympics firmly on the cultural map.[13] Having just witnessed the greatest Games in the "leading sport nation of the world," as the 1936 official report later put it, Germany had much to emulate.[14] Overwhelmed by the experience of 1932, Diem was nonetheless quietly confident, and soon received an unexpected boost.[15] From 1933, National Socialism became a syncretism of all things popular and, after initial reluctance, rode the wave of sporting enthusiasm and gave the Olympics its first full backing from a national government.[16] Having planned an event that would cost four million reichsmarks, Diem ended up with a stadium that alone was worth over six times that figure.[17] With such support, the Berlin organizing committee gained the financial and political infrastructure to add to the organizational momentum of Los Angeles. Communication technology was raised to the highest level, reaching the largest ever international radio audience and, for the first time in Olympic history, television viewers in special centers around Berlin.[18] The worldwide publicity campaign tapped into the psychology of prospective tourists and Berlin, a swinging metropolis of the 1920s and home to the world-famous UFA film studios, put on the Ritz as well as Hollywood, organizing receptions, banquets, balls, and a summer evening festival with great panache.[19] Writing in his diary about a garden party thrown by Goering, U.S. Ambassador William E. Dodd noted "there was hardly anything that modern inventors could have added."[20]

Most importantly, the Games proved a huge success with competitors and sports enthusiasts alike. The athletes were housed in a sumptuous village, and Jesse Owens famously observed that he had experienced no discrimination in Germany.[21] The spectacle elements offered fantastic entertainment. In the most "elaborate show" Dodd had "ever seen," the stadium was "lighted by electric machines . . . [and] curious electric streams of lights meeting some two or three hundred feet above the performances."[22] Ticket pricing was leveled out in comparison with Los Angeles, ensuring full stadia for almost every event. The childhood memories of German-Jewish émigré and cultural historian Peter Gay brim with excitement. The occasional sight of Hitler might have been "a nauseating by-product," but the Games were "breathlessly anticipated and just as breathlessly enjoyed"—"the atmosphere was electric and contagious."[23]

In terms of organization, spectacle, and symbolic capital, subsequent Games have done little more than tinker with Berlin's blueprint. In this important sense, 1936 was the making of the modern Olympics. Brundage, typically, embarrassed the 1972 organizers on public visits to the Federal Republic by comparing the forthcoming event with its "infamous" predecessor, but Nazi sympathies were hardly a prerequisite for holding the 1936 Games in esteem.[24] Some IOC members (such as Britain's vociferous Lord Aberdaere) might have resented the Germans, but the Games themselves did not come under attack. In fact, continuity of personnel after 1945 ensured that the majority of IOC members would remember the Berlin Games with fondness. At the London Olympics of 1948, Diem was delighted to hear the crushing verdict on the English capital's inferior management of the event—"*pas de comparaison.*"[25] Vitally for the Munich organizers, this—now unfashionable—attitude to Berlin still broadly held sway when they were conceiving and executing their plans in the 1960s.

IOC member and former Olympic horseman Vladimir Stoytchev was a prominent case in point. Despite liberating the Balkans at the end of the Second World War as commander in chief of the Bulgarian army, he was a close ally to Daume and Brundage and a great admirer of 1936.[26] When invited to represent the president as the guest of honor at the seventy-fifth-anniversary celebrations of the German Olympic movement in 1971, he gave a speech portraying Germany as the incubator of Olympic ideals. These, he claimed, had emerged not despite, but almost because of, unfavorable political conditions, and the IOC had gladly awarded the Games to a German city again because of the country's proven ability to protect Olympism against all odds. Munich, he had little doubt, would be "a triumph—a triumph of peace and friendship between nations, a triumph of advancement and the progress of humanity."[27] In the absence of a reliable biography, it is difficult to determine the nuances of Stoytchev's political convictions, socialization, and worldview: the grandson of the mayor of Sarajevo and a graduate of the Maria Theresia Military Academy in Vienna, he held prestigious posts as military attaché in Paris and London in the interwar years and headed the Bulgarian diplomatic mission in Washington from 1945 through 1947.[28] Yet it is safe to say that he typified the IOC old guard which, on account of its seniority, past distinction, and membership of an autonomous global elite, retained and exercised a right to individual opinions and decisions regardless of political circumstances that were changing around them. His less than referential attitude to communist apparatchiks in the 1960s and 1970s is clear evidence of this.

The Bulgarian's ideological allegiance to German Olympians might have been more pronounced than others'. Daume certainly kept Federal President Lübke (who became the target of a GDR smear campaign in 1965), footage of the torch relay, and any memory of Leni Riefenstahl out of the application film *Munich—A City Applies.*[29] And Polish IOC member Włodzimierz Reczek slammed the Games' slogan in Rome announcing that "short distances" in Germany could only refer to the proximity of the concentration camp to the gas chamber.[30] But this outburst might well have helped rather than hindered Munich's cause, and a decisive appreciation of Germany's organizational pedigree seems to have been widespread in sporting circles around the world. If the letters received by Munich's mayor before the bid in 1965 and 1966 are anything to go by, the memory of 1936 was central to some decisions to vote for the Bavarian capital. Brazilian IOC member Magalhães Padilha gave Vogel an "expression of his undivided support" as "the German city and German organizational talent [were] all very familiar to [him] since participating in the Olympic Games in Berlin."[31] Once the Games were awarded to the city, the world press was equally convinced the Germans would put on a "perfect" show, a mantle the organizers were happy to cite as an encouragement to their team or to justify the financial and emotional expenditure on the Games.[32]

However, explicit linking of 1972 with 1936 would have been anathema to German public discourse in the 1960s. In fact, one of the first responses in the Munich City Council when Hans-Jochen Vogel presented the proposal addressed the negative image of national prestige and the 1936 Games.[33] Daume might have casually remarked that dictatorships had it easy when putting on large sports festivals, but the OC never publicly used 1936 as a reference point.[34] In its appreciation of Berlin, therefore, the awarding body stood critically at odds with the sensitivities of the recipient nation. If Munich was about the making of modern Germany, it would have to negotiate Berlin's making of the modern Olympics.

DEALING WITH BRUNDAGE

The Munich organizers tended to counter Brundage's entrenched opinions with pragmatism, and when it came to the memory of 1936, they behaved no differently. Arguably, they even played fast and loose with it. Vogel had little knowledge of Brundage before the bid. In fact, his recent assertion that he was unfamiliar with the president's exact involvement with the 1936 event is probably true, since this was not told in detail until the publication of Richard Mandell's book *The Nazi Olympics* in 1971.[35] The mayor and his colleagues in the city council would have relied heavily on Daume's intimate acquaintance with the workings of the IOC and its dominant leader. Brundage had already assured Daume in November 1965 that he would welcome a bid from Munich because the Germans had shown their organizational competence in 1936, and when Vogel and Deputy Mayor Georg Brauchle took a sixty-hour round trip to Chicago for a ninety-minute meeting with him a few months later, they were well primed.[36] Vogel recorded stressing the modest Helsinki Games of 1952 rather than Berlin as a model for Munich,[37] but notes taken in Brundage's hand capture how the president perceived the politicians' pitch as it unfolded.[38] For those who knew Brundage, the "reasons for selection" would have formed a predictable set of bullet points: "1964–68: Europe's turn"; "German archaeology"; "1936 (Dr. Karl von Halt, so well known, lived in Munich)." Under a line on Brundage's notepad, the category "new things" (such as "fine facilities," "cultural aspect," "less expansion," which would indeed become essential objectives over the subsequent six years) also played their part. While it was these "new things" that the German visitors highlighted in a press conference on their return, in the Midwest they had not shied away from elements of the "German Olympic imagination" that appealed to their host: archaeology and Berlin.[39] These were targeted at a particular audience and after the successful outcome of the bid were rarely used again.[40]

Several weeks later, in his speech to the IOC in Rome, Daume was due to use the archaeological argument again, but it was cut from the final draft.[41] Nonetheless, signals of German continuities were clearly embedded in the address. Drawing to a close, Daume simply mentioned Karl Ritter von Halt as a citizen of Munich.[42] The name was certainly not without resonance. Halt had been the only German to serve for significant periods on the IOC during the Third Reich and the Federal Republic. With the exception of five years in Soviet captivity in Buchenwald, he had enjoyed a high-profile career both before and after the war too.[43] With a distinguished record as a decathlete, soldier, banker, and prominent sports administrator, Halt leapfrogged Diem into the class-conscious IOC.[44] He had become a Nazi party member in May 1933, been appointed to the board of Deutsche Bank as personnel director in 1938, and—as revealed in the Nuremberg trials—belonged to the "Freundeskreis Heinrich Himmler."[45] He headed German track and field (1934–45), and in 1944 was appointed the last acting Reichssportführer by Himmler when hope of victory was all but lost. In the difficult period before Berlin 1936, he had been valued highly both by the IOC for "bringing Hitler into line" and by Hitler "for assuaging the IOC's fears." Certainly more inculcated in the regime than Diem, he returned, like many, to a senior position in the new Republic, becoming director of the Süddeutsche Bank in Munich in 1952 and chair of the Bavarian Council of Banks (Bayerischer Landesbeirat der Banken) from 1957 until his death in 1964, also taking over from Adolf Friedrich von Mecklenburg as president of the NOC. He was readmitted to the IOC (with the strong support of Brundage, who had pleaded with the Allied High Commission for his release from Buchenwald) and eventually to its executive board (1958–63), for the second time since 1937.

Daume's reference to Halt at the critical moment in 1965, as later admitted, was strategic: "I wanted to call him to mind because he was, in the eyes of his many friends, the epitome of the German Olympian."[46] An earlier draft of his speech, in fact, even contained the emotive line: "He is standing next to me in spirit, asking you with me to 'entrust the 1972 Olympic Games to the Bavarian capital, Munich.' "[47] But by that point in the bid, the task of reminding the IOC of German continuity had already been completed most successfully by Halt's widow who spent five days in Rome talking to old friends at the expense of Munich City Council.[48]

When it came to the lives of others, however, Daume was by no means hypocritical. The previous year, he had delivered a heart-felt *laudatio* at Halt's funeral, praising his NOC predecessor for "his impeccable intentions" and reputation "in the whole sporting world" as a "respected protector of the great Olympic legacy."[49] Around the same time, he—warmly but somewhat unbelievably—recalled his winning over hostile journalists in occupied Brussels when announcing the death of IOC president Henri de Baillet-Latour.[50] The explanation for such remarks lies both in the amnesiac nature of German public life after the war and Daume's willingness to engage across generations. Socialized in the old world of German sport, Daume had reached maturity on assuming responsibility for the new. At the national and international level, his skill lay in the ability to foster innovation without alienating tradition. And it was precisely this difficult balance that played a major role in winning the Games. While currying favor with Brundage and Halt's old friends, the Munich team simultaneously secured the goodwill of the IOC's progressive new guard.

Throughout the 1960s, younger members of the committee had harnessed various currents of discontent in a bid to topple Brundage. Most prominently, a campaign to democratize the IOC aimed to permit each nation an elected representative on the committee and regularize meaningful exchange with the international sports federations.[51] Giulio Onesti, president of the Italian National Olympic Committee (CONI) and warmly supported by the Eastern bloc and the underrepresented

African nations, played a key role in these debates.[52] First voicing his complaints in 1963, he went on to stand against Brundage in the 1968 presidential election. As Daume noted, however, "there is always something the host [of the session at which the bid is decided] can do," and Onesti and the Italian Olympic establishment proved very useful.[53] Daume presented Onesti with an original wooden sculpture from the Grünewald era, and the Italian responded by providing vital access to the anti-Brundage lobby and invaluable assistance to the German team.[54] Italian journalists accepted invitations to Munich and were treated with great care "to ensure intensive press coverage in Rome before and during the IOC meeting."[55] CONI advised visitors from Munich's tourist office that "important circles in the IOC" were keen to get away from "concrete" Olympics and approved the winning slogan "Spiele im Grünen" (Games in green surroundings).[56] They helped plan the successful exhibit at the Foro Italico, arranged a press conference on Munich's behalf, and, perhaps most importantly, gave council on how to influence IOC members without causing irritation.[57]

Bringing the Games to Munich, therefore, involved dealing with the old and the new in equal measure. Such a balancing act was both necessary and possible in a relatively closed international setting, well away from the eyes of a critical public. When it came to staging the Games under domestic scrutiny, the emphasis inevitably tilted toward the new. De Coubertin, Baillet-Latour, Edström, and Diem—depicted in Daume's funeral oration as waiting to welcome Karl Ritter von Halt to heaven[58]—were never mentioned again in the same breath. Dead and buried, their problematic legacies, however, would resurface over the following six years. In terms of personnel, public personalities, central Olympic events, locations, and the concentration camp at Dachau only thirty-five kilometers from the new Olympic stadium, 1936 was never far away.

PERSONNEL

The number of people required to organize an Olympic Games runs well into the thousands. It is a simple fact of 1960s West German society that a representative sample of its talented and well-positioned citizens would carry some burden from the past. In such cases, Daume tended to give the benefit of the doubt, writing in one of his first major position papers on the Munich Games: "A view of history, in which everything a nation did under a dictator or criminal regime is thought of as bad . . . seems questionable to me."[59] On matters of individual selection, he was, typically, ungrudging. Assessing a proposal to appoint the famous self-confessed SS officer, poet, and American university professor Hans Egon Holthusen to the arts committee, he noted: "Personally, I am inclined to look at all these things magnanimously and leave it at that."[60] And in 1971, he was happy to defend the appointment of August (formerly Baron) von Fink, one of Hitler's great financial supporters, to the new curatorium of the NOC's proselytizing sister society, the German Olympic Society (DOG).[61] Daume's attitude was firmly in keeping with the times: even at the height of the protest movement in 1968, 41 percent of non-student youths (as opposed to 13 percent of students) and 43 percent of the population in general considered an individual's past irrelevant to their suitability for public service. Yet as Daume realized too, it was "also necessary, of course, to safeguard the international image and avoid presenting targets."[62] There were obvious sensitivities in many other parts of the world, and sustained and vigorous attack could be expected from the GDR (see chapter 6).

The past tainted the highest echelons of the OC. The most senior post on the full-time payroll (general secretary) was occupied by Daume's tennis partner, Herbert Kunze, a tax lawyer in the Ruhr, treasurer of the German Sports Association (DSB) and vice president of the NOC. As Kunze's Stasi file reveals, he had become a member of the Nazi party in May 1933 (attending the Referendarlager of the NSDAP/SA in Jüterbog, where young Nazi lawyers received both military and ideological training) and was involved in the SS from its foundation (as a student at the SS-Reichsführerschule in Bad Tölz) and a range of other Nazi organizations. Although the timing of his party membership (as a "Märzgefallener" he was not an "old fighter," but joined the NSDAP opportunistically only after the elections of March 1933) and departure from the SS in 1936 ("honorable discharge for professional reasons") could be interpreted as ideological reluctance, his progression through the legal profession to middle-ranking civil servant *(Regierungsrat)* with responsibility for military expenditure in the Reich Finance Ministry suggests he kept his own interests at heart. The formulaic nature of his denunciation in the East German files might indicate that he was only a minor player in the Nazi state, but it seems that Kunze set aside any reservations he might have had for the sake of his career.[63] Bernhard Baier, a sports representative on the OC board and a *Ministerialdirigent* in the Ministry of the Interior of Lower Saxony, had also been involved with the regime. During the Third Reich, he had belonged to the party (1937) and the SA (1937, *Scharführer* 1942) and served as *Regierungsrat* (1942) in the Nazi administration.[64]

Such appointments were not uncommon, of course, in the Federal Republic. When applying for the post in Munich, Kunze felt no compunction in naming Heinz Maria Oeftering, his former boss from the Reich Finance Ministry who himself had become the first president of the German railways (Deutsche Bundesbahn) in 1957, as his referee.[65] In terms of susceptibility to GDR propaganda, however, those members of the OC who had been involved in the organization of the 1936 Games were more vulnerable. Such cases allowed the East German propagandists to construct a focused narrative of fascist continuity in sport. In the month the Games took place, for instance, the East German journal *Deutsches Sport-Echo* attacked Hans-Joachim Körner, a "disciple of Diem" who had been placed in charge of the 1972 Olympic Youth Camp.[66]

Risky though they were, such individuals were highly valued for the organizational experience on which Daume laid a premium, particularly in the early planning stages. He enlisted the advice of the architect of the Berlin Olympic stadium, Werner March,[67] and argued for the employment of Adam Nothelfer[68] and Gerhard Hübner,[69] two key members of "Diem's staff." Despite Munich City Council's reluctance to countenance an old guard return, as the president would recall, the 1972 team contained "a range of people . . . who were there in '36."[70]

A central figure in this cohort was Guido von Mengden, *Generalreferent* to the Reichssportführer von Tschammer und Osten at the time of the 1936 Games and a supporter of Daume's appointment as general secretary to the DSB and NOC in the 1950s.[71] Mengden had formed part of the entourage that told Brundage what he wanted to hear on his tour to Germany before the 1936 Games. Daume, however, knew the value of Mengden's experience ("ten times better than Kunze"), and made his own participation in the Games contingent on that of his organizational confidant, despite the fact he had retired in 1963. In 1964, he had defended his integrity in the face of the GDR's threat to expose him to the IOC.[72] "An awkward character sometimes," as Daume later noted, Mengden was "really incriminated, a dreadful Nazi," and even had "great clout with Hitler."[73] Probably in anticipation of the sharpening of East German knives[74] and acknowledging his unpopularity in certain circles of West German sport, Mengden accepted a carefully shielded post away from the spotlight,[75] where he worked as an advisor on a paid contract with the role of "making sure that the issues at hand were properly conceptualized and formulated."[76] He acted as Daume's doorkeeper,[77] even advising him on the degree to which applicants to the OC had been involved in the Nazi regime.[78] Most significantly, Mengden was to shape one of the Games' defining moments from behind the scenes. Although he stepped back from the limelight, the iconoclastic opening ceremony (see chapter 4), which made one of the clearest statements about Germany's desired break from the past, bore his stamp.[79]

Not everyone, though, "adapted . . . to their role" as conveniently as Mengden.[80] Although not tainted by the past in the way that others were, his ally Walter Umminger nonetheless inflicted considerable damage on the Games. As editor of the NOC's house journal *Olympisches Feuer* and the standard work *Die Olympischen Spiele der Neuzeit—von Athen bis München* (1969) (The Modern Olympic Games—from Athens to Munich), Umminger was the natural choice to take charge of the *Olympisches Lesebuch* (1971), an Olympic reader designed to help school teachers prepare their pupils for the Games on behalf of the DOG. However, when the four-hundred-page compendium appeared, a domestic and inner-German storm broke out. The book contained a wide range of opinions on modern sport—from de Coubertin and four-minute-miler Roger Bannister to Brecht, Habermas, Mitscherlich, and Camus. But it was defined by and ultimately repudiated for its unadulterated articulation of the "German Olympic imagination." A central article by Umminger himself cited the modern Olympics as one of the few exceptions to the historic paradigm of European cultural influence in which the French had "hit on all the big ideas first" with "the Germans seeing them through to their absolute conclusion."[81] French hegemony could be reversed, Umminger suggested, by a venerable German Olympic genealogy stretching down from Leipzig Academy director, Adam Oeser, and his pupil Johann Joachim Winckelmann, author of the seminal eighteenth-century history of ancient art, via Goethe, Schiller, and the romantic author Bettina Brentano (who wrote to Achim von Arnim about reinventing the Olympic Games in 1813) to archeologists Ernst Curtius and Wilhelm Dörpfeld. Sweeping seamlessly across two centuries, the Olympic line ended with Carl Diem, to whom special merit was given as de Coubertin's successor.[82]

It was not Diem's name per se that caused furor in Germany, but an uncritical and trumpeting appreciation of the 1936 Games, which seemed to cling to every expression of philhellenism in the world of German sport. In this case—as an assessment by the West German Foreign Office put it—it was accompanied by an unreconstructed view of the events of the twentieth century.[83] Quite against the run of German historiography, which was undergoing a paradigm shift in the 1960s,[84] the causes of the First World War and the year 1939 went unmentioned and dubious phrases abounded: "After the Blitz campaign against France, German troops entered Paris. This success meant that peace seemed just around the corner."[85] The GDR had a field day, organizing an international press conference and using the book as a convenient straw-man to rehearse their standard complaints about West German sport.[86] The Soviets duly followed, but their case was already eloquently put by the vitriolic reaction of the domestic press.[87] In West Berlin, the senator for Schools and Youth refused to distribute the book unless the history section was removed, and the general uptake outside Bavaria proved very poor.[88] The Games had taken a significant propaganda hit at home and abroad.

The same potent mixture of Olympic imagination and unqualified admiration of 1936 was evident, perhaps not surprisingly, in the outlook of Carl Diem's wife, Liselott, who occupied a prominent position in West German sports-science in the 1960s and 1970s.[89] A Jew who had been sacked from her position as head of women's education at the Deutsche Hochschule für Leibesübungen in Berlin when the Nazis came to power in 1933, she had taken up an identical position at the newly founded and Sporthochschule in Cologne in 1947, where she eventually received a titular professorship (1965) and became rector (1967–69). Daume's confidante and ghostwriter,[90] she was also feted by her old family friend Brundage.[91] His allegiance along with the worldwide connections she enjoyed from her husband's former network imprinted themselves on the "aristocratic" tone of her correspondence with the "parvenu" Daume. Although like Mengden, her ideas were often progressive, she too was decidedly "old world" in outlook and image.[92] Daume appointed her to the founding group of twenty-one on the OC as well as several committees, but she was excluded from the board where the real power lay. She enjoyed minor triumphs, such as resurrecting an exhibition of the German excavations at Olympia, which had been rejected by the arts committee, and then colluding to stage it in a technically outmoded fashion akin to 1936.[93] But her attempts to push Carl Diem to the fore and establish continuities with the past were constantly frustrated, in particular by chief designer Otl Aicher (whom she once childishly taunted about the Games' mascot Waldi)[94] and press officer "Johnny" Klein (to whom she sent a picture from the 1936 official report of a bare-chested Diem on his morning jog with the organizing team, in the hope that he might use if for publicity).[95]

However, despite hostility from some chief organizers, Liselott Diem succeeded in making a lasting contribution to the way the Games would pass into historical record. Perhaps raising unfair expectations, Daume had approached her at an early stage to write the official report, with logistical support from the Carl Diem Institute at the Sporthochschule.[96] Diem initially imagined she could work her way to the center via the back door, but her hopes were never realized.[97] Correspondence with her assistants over many months catalogued a plethora of complaints about blatant obstruction and exclusion in Munich, particularly from the department of visual design.[98] Quite apart from ideological differences, personal conflicts of interest were also at work. Aicher, who was responsible for the layout of the three-volume report, was also planning a rival tome on the Games' design.[99] By September 1973, with the 1974 World Cup beginning to capture the public's imagination, the report was so behind schedule that the OC forfeited DM 400,000 for late delivery and the board allowed Kunze to end Diem's contract and take control himself.[100] At the publishers proSport Verlag, Walter Umminger, who had met frequently on editorial issues with Diem and her team, argued his ally's corner without success.[101] The missed deadlines influenced the decision, but the board also harbored concerns that the emerging text was both "unusable" and "full of flaws."[102] Doubtless the bias of Diem's historical perspective played a key role in their dissatisfaction, Hans-Jochen Vogel distancing himself, much to the editor's ire, by personally removing all his own quotations from the manuscript.[103] But within months, lawyers had established that Liselott Diem's words could only be changed if factually inaccurate.[104] She was reinstated, Aicher's volume IV was blocked by Umminger at proSport, and the official report of the 1972 Olympics opened with a triumphant articulation of the "German Olympic imagination," complete with German archaeologists trumping the French and the organizational excellence and implied innocence of the 1936 Games. The underlying assumptions of Umminger's publicly decried *Olympisches Lesebuch* were writ large on the first page of the Games' official history.

The Liselott Diem affair shows the tenacity of those who held firm to the "German Olympic imagination" in the early 1970s. Despite fighting a lost cause, they always strived to have the last word.

PERSONALITIES

In contrast to those who worked behind the scenes in Berlin and Munich, the public personalities of 1936 were easier to reject or engage for the cause. Athletes who had competed in Berlin were viewed entirely positively. In March 1969, former German medal winners were invited to Munich along with high-profile Olympians from other countries to launch the 1972 domestic publicity campaign live on Second German Television (ZDF). Quadruple gold medalist Jesse Owens, whose presence on that occasion proved a major coup, and former world heavyweight boxing champion Max Schmeling (although not an Olympian) were both fully involved. By contrast, Leni Riefenstahl, whose *Olympia* had lingered with such fascination on Owens and captured the "Schönheit der faschistischen Feier" ("beauty of the fascist ceremony"), was persona non grata.[105] Each of these prominent figures could be conveniently categorized in the Federal Republic, but their relation both to 1936 and to public beyond Germany was far from straightforward.

Despite protesting otherwise, Riefenstahl, as a holder of the Olympic diploma, was given a Category C card in 1972, which gave her privileged access to all Olympic venues. While the German organizers attempted several times to block this decision, Daume leaving the IOC in no doubt that he was "very much against Frau Riefenstahl," Lausanne proved robust in defending someone it viewed as the maker of an "exceptional film."[106] Other Olympic cities bore her little grudge, Helsinki inviting her to film its Games in 1952 (declined), and Brundage, of course, was an admirer.[107] He supported her during her difficult U.S. tour after Kristallnacht and, responding to a prompt from Carl Diem in 1948, she was presented with the Olympic Diploma originally awarded to her at the IOC session in London in 1939.[108] In 1965, Brundage arranged for a "director's cut" of the film to be purchased for his private use.[109] The situation in Germany offered a sharp contrast: President Heinemann's office removed Riefenstahl's name from the guest list for a reception of Olympic VIPs (to which her diploma would normally have provided automatic entry), and the OC did its best to stop Munich cinemas screening *Olympia* during the 1972 Games.[110]

But as the decision by domestic cinemas to show her work suggests (one to packed audiences throughout the Games), neither Riefenstahl nor her film were as universally deplored as the organizers thought. A few years later, when the audience turned on Riefenstahl during the talk show *Je später der Abend*, 90 percent of letters and calls to the television station defended her.[111] In the 1960s, Riefenstahl had begun to enjoy a less fractious image in the rest of the world, and by the early 1970s she was undergoing a renaissance among young antiestablishment figures keen to flout taboos. In 1966, the New York Museum of Modern Art returned her to the big screen with the first retrospective of her films, and in the 1970s Andy Warhol invited her to his art factory. Steven Spielberg said he longed to meet her. In Britain, the tone-setters of hip culture went a step further, turning her into the "foundress of an anarchic pop-ideal."[112] In 1972, Mick Jagger used imagery from her Nuremberg Nazi rally films in his stage shows and allowed her to photograph him with his wife Bianca for the *Sunday Times.* David Bowie called her a "rock star," noting for good measure that Hitler was more of a media artist than a politician.

In autumn 1972, the *Sunday Times* decided to ride this wave of popularity and commissioned the seventy-year-old director of "one of the great documentaries of all time" to take a series of pictures of the Munich Games for its magazine.[113] On 1 October, its cover duly announced "Leni Riefenstahl's Second Olympics" across a split page with her pole-vaulting images from 1936 (black and white) and 1972 (color). Although the shots prompted little retrospection (sports photography since 1936 had modernized following Riefenstahl's impulse), the identity of the photographer caused consternation among the Jewish communities of Germany (especially Berlin) and Britain.[114] Even before their publication, the British section of the World Jewish Congress denounced them as an affront, not least in the wake of the terrorist attack. The paper remained unmoved, however, vaunting Riefenstahl as "the world's best photographer in [the] field" and arguing "if her former connection with the Nazi Party . . . were a reason for a permanent ban on her work, then the world's television and cinema companies should never show her classic film . . . again [when] in fact they do so continuously."[115]

The *Sunday Times*'s recital of the familiar line about sport's neutrality loses all force when read alongside comments made to Günter Grass a week after the Jewish Society's complaints. Having agreed to be interviewed about the Games as a representative of the 1972 arts committee, Grass was taken aback by the aggressiveness of the opening question. Asked if the Games had "reawoken any national guilt or paranoia" in Germany, the left-wing author, who had helped Brandt to election victory in 1969, retorted: "I find it hypocritical if the representatives of other European countries, who God knows have a record of guilt, a national record of guilt, point the finger at the Germans like Pharisees on every possible and impossible occasion."[116] In 1972 Britain, Hitler's legacy seemed good for sales. "His" Games could be used to conjure up the undifferentiating British obsession with German war guilt, while his filmmaker could be hired for fashion and chic.

The Munich organizers' commissioning of Max Schmeling and Jesse Owens intended the opposite effect. Both were chosen for their "positive image worldwide" as part of a "very small and exclusive" circle that would have included middle-distance star Emil Zatopek but for the political turmoil in Czechoslovakia.[117] Payments were made to Owens's PR agency, and Max Schmeling, who owned the north German franchise for Coca-Cola was assured that money would be no object.[118] Schmeling, who had established himself as the Federal Republic's omnipresent talisman, was a natural choice. For the West German public, he represented "a kind of witness for a better Germany in a time of darkness . . . a sportsman with a conscience who refused to bask in the nationalist rhetoric and racial superiority of the Nazis without ever claiming to have done anything spectacular to oppose it."[119] As one society hostess noted in *Der Spiegel* in the early 1960s: "He [stood] for too much to be expendable: German strength, German heart, Coca Cola."[120] A friend of the newspaper mogul Axel Springer, he visited Khrushchev (in 1958) to plead the case for German reunification, and was hailed on his seventieth birthday by President Scheel as "Germany's number one sportsman for life."

Although little heeded, a small minority of left-wing commentators denounced Schmeling for entering a pact with the Nazis.[121] Leaving arguments about naivety and possible coercion aside, it is certainly the case that the regime enjoyed his support in late 1935 when Brundage asked Reichssportführer von Tschammer und Osten to send the boxer or tennis star Gottfried von Cramm to help derail the American boycott. Knowledge of Schmeling's collusion with Brundage entered the public domain well before 1972. In fact, the boxer's own accounts of what happened in New York always talked up his role in events.[122] Mistaking Brundage's concern about discrimination against the Jews and Negroes on the U.S. (rather than the German) team as genuine, Schmeling claimed to have greatly influenced the Americans' deliberations.[123] Not unlike the *Sunday Times*'s defense of Leni Riefenstahl, this—albeit deluded—admission in his 1956 autobiography *8-9-aus* feeds off the presumed innocence of athletes, even in the face of obvious political intrigue. Tellingly, when Schmeling admitted his "boundless naïveté" in the boycott debacle, he did so only in the context of Hitler's later refusal to receive Jesse Owens after the black athlete's medal-winning performances.[124] In the popular imagination, the infamous "Jesse Owens incident" had become a convenient shorthand for the evil of the 1936 event—one that reduced Hitler to a spoilsport in a stadium while containing the positive ending of a morality tale. It also omitted complicating subplots such as many black athletes' opposition to the boycott due to racial discrimination in the United States, as well as Owens's own initial reluctance to travel to Berlin and sudden volte face in 1935.[125]

In the 1960s, however, the narrative of Owens and Hitler was widely disseminated and made Schmeling and Owens the perfect partnership for the 1972 publicity campaign. Owens would kick it off in West Germany. Schmeling would sail into New York harbor, as he had done in 1935. And amid the opulence of a gala dinner on board the cruise ship *Bremen* in 1971, the two former greats would

FIGURE 4. Former Olympic gold medalists awaiting the arrival of the Olympic flame in Munich, 25 August 1972 (front row from left to right, Gerd Fredriksson, Swedish six-time kayaking gold medalist, Emil Zatopek, Czech distance runner, Bikila Abebe, Ethiopian marathon winner in 1960, and Jesse Owens) (photo: Fritz Neuwirth, courtesy of Süddeutsche Zeitung Photo)

stand together and invite the world to Germany. Only the GDR commented on the tangled web.[126]

As is now well established, Adolf Hitler did not snub Jesse Owens. Having congratulated all the medal winners on the opening day except the high jumpers whose competition had finished after he left the stadium, Hitler was asked the next morning by the IOC either to congratulate *all* medalists or *none at all.* Before Owens even took to the track, Karl Ritter von Halt had announced that the Führer would not be greeting athletes personally for the rest of the Games (possibly because the high-jump final had produced two black American medalists).[127] Nonetheless, the Hitler-Owens story was to become part of an "extensive . . . mythology" of 1936.[128] Despite telling an audience of a thousand blacks in Kansas City immediately after the Games: "Hitler didn't snub me—it was our president who snubbed me. [He] didn't even send me a telegram," it was one that Owens spun primarily himself.[129] It surfaced with particular currency in the run-up to the 1968 Olympics in Mexico City, when a group of black sporting activists under the title of Olympic Project for Human Rights (OPHR) made a list of demands, including the banning of Rhodesia and South Africa from the Olympic Games, the desegregation of the U.S. Olympic Committee's (USOC) administrative and coaching staff, and the removal of Brundage from the IOC.[130] As an Olympic boycott gathered worldwide momentum, the whole of independent Africa joining in at one stage, Brundage found a close ally in the unlikely figure of Jesse Owens. The famous athlete was the only man to match him as a "strident, obsessive, and omnipresent public critic of the boycott."[131] He shared the president's blind and idealistic belief in sport as a meritocracy in which fair rules were applied regardless of race, class, and background, and argued repeatedly that a U.S. boycott in 1936 would have deprived him of the opportunity to destroy Hitler's racial arguments with his athletic performance. Although Brundage was quoted as saying he would rather sell his beloved New York Athletics Club before admitting "niggers and kikes," he promptly proposed Owens for membership of the USOC board.

Owens's unlikely allegiance with Brundage climaxed when two of the OPHR's prominent representatives, John Carlos and Tommie Smith, famously raised black-gloved fists on the medal rostrum at the 1968 Olympics. After failing to temper the mood of the national squad's black athletes in the Olympic village, Owens continued his rebuttal of OPHR in his 1970 *Blackthink: My Life as a Black Man and White Man.*[132] Premised on a belief that equal opportunity really existed for blacks in the post–civil rights era, the book pulled no punches, making inflammatory statements (if the "Negro doesn't succeed in today's America it is because he has chosen to fail"), comparing the Black Power salute to the gestures of Nazi soldiers, and equating "the collectivist, separatist rhetoric of post–civil rights activists" with Hitler's *Mein Kampf.*[133] Finishing with an extensive account of the "snub of 1936," *Blackthink* was positively reviewed in the mainstream American press and received rapturously at the citadel of the "German Olympic imagination"—the Carl Diem inspired Olympic Academy at Olympia—where Owens read from it prepublication in 1969.[134] Understandably, however, it did little to change his detractors' view of him as an "Uncle Tom" figure.

At the 1972 Games, some of the racial tensions of 1968 were replayed, albeit less virulently, within the U.S. team. As a sign of apathy rather than all-out protest, Vincent Matthews, a particularly vociferous opponent of Owens in Mexico, and Wayne Collett shuffled their way through the victory ceremony for the men's 400 meters, refusing to turn toward the American flag, stroking their beards and swirling their medals as they left the stadium to jeers from the crowd. Once again, Owens entered the village in an attempt to persuade the recalcitrant athletes to apologize, alluding to enticing job offers he claimed to have collected from good American companies, while the IOC, in collusion with the U.S. Olympic Committee, was in the process of issuing a life-long ban.[135] Owens's efforts to reconcile Collett and Matthews to his point of view proved as futile as four years earlier. Likewise his attempt to assuage his radical critics earlier that year with a new book, *I Have Changed,* had equally run aground. Intended as a modification of *Blackthink,* the book inadvertently moved Owens closer to Hitler: "I never doubted for a single minute that I *was* totally on 'the other side,' never dreamed there might be some parts of me—and of almost everyone—which resembled parts of *him.* What I think I've learned, you see, is that—perverted as he was—Adolf Hitler wasn't really the villain. Even millions of Germans who fought behind him—many of them who stood in Berlin stadium and applauded me—weren't the villains. *Ideas* were the villains."[136]

One can scarcely imagine a more contorted articulation of the "Hitler snub" than Owens's final twist. In 1972, however, the ruminations of the Munich Games' special ambassador on Hitler's culpability remained unknown in Germany. As in the United States, the Owens myth would probably have proved robust enough to withstand scrutiny and as it happened, world events swayed such issues Owens's way. With the controversial medal ceremony taking place only three days after the deaths of the Israeli athletes, most of the world, including Matthews's own family, was not in the mood for "any more intrusion."[137] For a brief moment at least, Owens's views became de rigueur.

The confusion of the Owens myth is instructive, nonetheless, of the contradictions that surrounded the three key public players from 1936 at Munich. Schmeling, the rehabilitated "ordinary German," fitted the common postwar narrative of selective remembering and new prosperity, with Leni Riefenstahl his mirror-opposite. Conspicuously close to the regime, she was one of a small minority to whom the door of public acceptability in the new Republic remained closed. Yet, in certain Western countries, her star was rising again and, in Britain at least, provided a strangely neutral platform from which to launch uninformed attacks on Germany's relationship to its past. Generational conflict amongst black athletes in the United States led Jesse Owens to align himself with Brundage, the "nigger hater," over an antiboycott movement some thirty years in the past and for which scarcely anyone outside IOC circles, not even Schmeling who had assisted it at the time, could still voice support. These cases show that coping with the past *(Vergangenheitsbewältigung)* could be as complicated outside Germany as it was within it. At the time of the Games, however, such complexity was hardly reflected upon.

THE TORCH RELAY

The same was true of the torch relay, the 1936 Games' most prominent legacy to the Olympic movement. The universal symbolism of the flame had been so readily adopted by every host nation since the war that it hardly registered as a German invention. Yet it is surprising—initially, at least—that those involved in its technical and infrastructural organization in 1936 were so keen, and indeed able, to make cultural capital out of it again in 1972. Having contributed in some material or commercial form to Berlin was, of course, no bar from supporting Munich. Many companies offering their services to the OC (such as the German Atlantic Line that transported Schmeling and others to high-profile PR opportunities around the world) emphasized their link with tradition. The torch relay, however, was of a different magnitude altogether. In 1936, it had been sponsored by Krupp, Hitler's major armorer and one of the high-profile industrial-sector imprisonments at the (second) Nuremberg trials. For Berlin 1936, the steel magnates helped establish the Olympics Fund of German Industry[138] and advertised their wares by donating engraved torches made of V2A polished Nirosta (stainless steel), a multifunctional material they had discovered almost simultaneously with Swedish and British rivals in 1912.[139] In 1936, Nirosta steel stood as much for modernity and the coming of German industrial might as the flame did for the values of the classical age. Of the many nebulous aspects of the Games' dealings with the Nazi regime, the Krupp connection is one of the least clouded.

Several incidents suggest the OC went to great lengths to insure the firm's participation again. For instance, at least one other company offered to supply torches and technical backup free of charge[140] before the board decided to invite tenders and allow Krupp to enter the running.[141] Daume, much to the irritation of his general secretariat, nudged negotiations along via direct and often biased intervention.[142] And an unwieldy compromise had to be struck between the model for the torch and the weight of the material from which it was constructed. Coming in at 2.5 kilos,[143] over and against the committee's optimal range of 670 to 740 grams, Krupp's stainless steel was too heavy for Otl Aicher's design.[144] Discussions about switching to aluminum proved unfruitful,[145] and caught between artistic intransigence and industrial determination the organizers settled on a model which at 1.35 kilos was not only twice their ideal weight but, by some margin, the heaviest torch in Olympic history.[146] The value of the 6,700 torches Krupp supplied (just over DM 125,000) might not remotely have matched the sums given by comparable firms (see chapter 2).[147] But the real point of interest lies in the company's desire to have its stainless steel identified with the event for a second time and the committee's willingness to accommodate it.

A major reason for its inside track was the presence of Berthold Beitz on the OC board. As soon as the water sports were awarded to Kiel in 1967, a town in which Krupp enjoyed considerable influence, it was evident that it would be represented at the highest level of the event.[148] At any rate, as one of the most celebrated businessmen in postwar Germany, Beitz was a real catch. Appointed by Alfried Krupp as his general plenipotentiary in 1953, he enjoyed an extraordinary rise in fortune, helping the company by the 1960s to become "the largest privately owned industrial empire in history" with a stake in virtually every foreign economy and a fortune worth US$1.25 billion more than Rockefeller's.[149] Having prevented the deportation of Jews to concentration camps while working for German Shell in Poland, his war record, moreover, made him a rare commodity: an internationally recognized "good German" with positive press in the Jewish world and the Eastern bloc. One of the few Germans honored in Yad Vashem, he was hailed in Warsaw as "an outstanding emissary" of his country.[150] Suspicious to the oversensitive Adenauer, he later provided invaluable advice to Brandt and his Ostpolitik team. In business, he was no respecter of tradition and represented the "newer model of manager" that emerged in the Federal Republic and marked the death of the mythological " 'factory father' who cared as much for his firm and his family of workers as he did for profit."[151] A modernizer with an untainted past, Beitz was an inspired choice for Krupp and the OC alike. A newcomer to the world of sports management, he quickly proved promotion material and was fast-tracked onto the IOC ahead of the successful mail order magnate, travel agent, and multiple Olympic medalist Josef Neckermann.[152]

Yet Krupp's relation to the past was marked by continuities and repression.[153] Its PR department relegated the Nazi period to a footnote in a narrative about the company's exemplary provision of social care for its workers reaching back to imperial times. In the 1950s and 1960s, this selective account was both underpinned by and used to support the West German state. No other firm played such a significant role in state visits: the federal government, aware of the public's critical gaze, conveniently outsourced the pomp and ceremony of its representative duties to the legendary magnificence of Krupp's receptions, while Krupp exploited the state's backing to oppose the Allies' intention to remove it from coal and steel production. The massive site in Essen promoted positive discourses about postwar Germany and the "Kruppian social cosmos," with its workers' apartments, food stores and hospitals, was often shown to visitors on their way through to the Eastern bloc.[154]

The acceptance of Krupp must be seen, of course, against the broader rehabilitation of the German business world both at home and abroad. In the Federal Republic, leading industrialists, incensed at the stripping of Krupp's assets and the twelve-year prison sentence passed down to Alfried by the Nuremberg judges, rallied round their colleague and bombarded the American authorities with letters demanding his release. The West-Verlag rushed out its defense of German industry *Schwerindustrie und Politik* (Heavy Industry and Politics) and Krupp itself commissioned Tilo Wilmowsky to write *Warum wurde Krupp verurteilt?* (Why was Krupp Convicted?). Both books—based on the mantra about power relations in Nazi Germany, "the state commands the economy"—were well received by politicians and many sections of the West German public.[155] Over forty years later, Daume's assessment of Krupp as an "all-round decent man" and "representative scapegoat" is typical of the mood of the time, particularly among industrialists.[156]

In the United States, too, conservative intellectuals and business leaders closed ranks around their German counterparts in an act of solidarity intended to protect Western interests in the burgeoning Cold War.[157] These self-regarding, internationally connected elites readily picked up their prewar contacts. There is no direct evidence that Brundage encountered Alfried Krupp at the 1936 Olympics, but given the latter's gold medal in the sailing competition and the lively forum for business exchange that the Olympics had provided since Los Angeles 1932, it would be surprising if they had not met.[158] Brundage pleaded Krupp's case with the U.S. authorities, and might well have played a part in the German's early release in 1951.[159] Nationally and internationally, then, German industrialists in the 1950s could successfully portray themselves both as victims of the Nazi regime and defenders of the nation's culture and economy.

As S. Jonathan Wiesen demonstrates, West German industrialists' relation to the past was based on a "paradoxical urge" both to bury it and control it via careful self-projection. More than "anguished confessions of guilt or . . . the achievement of psychic closure," memory for this important segment of German society "was about the very public presentation and manipulation of symbols, lessons, and experiences."[160] There is surely no finer example of this than Krupp's reappropriation of the torch relay in 1972. Having secured the right to supply the vital equipment, the company exploited its symbolic capital. In a full-page advertisement for stainless steel in 1972, Krupp trumpeted the continuity between 1936 and 1972 and its own role in preserving it.[161] Underneath the Olympic rings and framed by large pictures of the two torches, a text projected Krupp's supposed stainless past as a means for creating an aesthetically pleasing and durable future:

> Nirosta—the steel that's eternally young
>
> Munich 1972—where the world's young sporting elite will meet. Sporting games, comradely competition, finding out how good one is. Looking forward to being there. Being there like NIROSTA, Krupp's high-grade steel—forever young. Like these Games, indestructible, and multifaceted in use. Whether as an elegant cup or an aesthetically pleasing symbol such as the Olympic torches for Berlin 1936 and Munich 1972. NIROSTA—Krupp's high-grade steel—a material to master the future with.

It matters little that the reality almost failed disastrously, the Bundeswehr having to prevent major embarrassment by reassembling six thousand torches when one in ten turned out to be faulty.[162] Nor is it of importance that in 1972 Krupp needed the flame more than the flame needed Krupp, the firm at this stage still recovering from its shock collapse as a private concern and forced conversion into a single-stock company in 1967. Rather, the real significance of Krupp's advertising rhetoric is the self-assurance with which it could latch onto the presumed innocence of a sporting symbol and transfer it to itself. Equally telling is the company's complete expectation of and—as a glowing comparison of its two torches in the sports magazine *Kicker* testifies—gaining of public approval.[163] For postwar German industry, this was business as usual.

In other domains, however, the nature of the continuity suggested by the torch was open to debate. Not surprisingly, Liselott Diem, who was a member of the relay committee, read the event in a manner similar to Krupp. Her working notes for the relevant chapter of the official report contain an account by Fritz Schilgen, the final runner of the 1936 relay,[164] and her proposal for the 1972 route—which she envisioned going to former Olympic sites around the globe—breathed an unproblematic, all-enveloping universality.[165] Despite the committee rejecting the grand scheme, her concept and convictions remained unshaken. In a speech at Olympia during the summer of 1972, she talked up the itinerary on which the OC finally settled as the longest stretch the flame had actually been carried by *runners* (as opposed to riders, drivers, and cyclists) and drew parallels with the one her husband had planned for the 1940 Games between the ancient civilizations of Greece and Japan.[166] Once again, however, Diem was forced to conjure up her dead husband from the margins, as much to her regret the OC gave no publicity to the inventor of the event.[167]

Weeks later, at the official flame-lighting ceremony in the same location, Hans-Jochen Vogel delivered a somewhat different speech. Taking as his theme the "timelessness" of the Games and the relay and "their ability to span the whole world and bring nations together," he observed that Olympism both "disappointed and uplifted." Just as the festivals of ancient Greece had excluded all but a small minority of free men, he argued, the Games of the modern era scarcely lived up to the "immaculate nature" of their ideal. Nonetheless, Munich hoped to be enveloped, if briefly, by the assembly of all humanity, a longing most aptly expressed by Albrecht Haushofer, who had set out his poetic vision of the Olympic flame for posterity in 1944 while a political prisoner in Moabit.[168] Haushofer's verses, which Vogel cited at length in his climactic invitation to Munich, had a double edge. For one, they skillfully wove rupture into a narrative of continuity, and opened up the issue of German guilt and the 1936 Olympics without direct or simplifying accusation. For another, they served as a subtle but unmistakable broadside to the military dictatorship that had governed Greece since 1967. (Vogel, ever the political animal, had even sought advice from Brandt's office as to whether he should go to Olympia if the Greek prime minister was in attendance.)[169] Unlike Krupp and Diem, the only thing that Vogel found "forever young" in this setting was a sense of German culpability and the lessons that needed to be learnt from it. Unfortunately, the Greek hosts provided a less than conducive setting for his sentiments. Night and day, the army guarded every step of the torch's way, serenading it in heavily militaristic tones that the Munich organizers had expressly wanted to avoid. To rub salt into the wounds, the populace greeted the German delegation with the predictable "Heil Hitler."[170]

PLACES

The contradictions over the treatment of inherited events continued into the OC's handling of particular places. Where possible, the organizers avoided potent memories of the Nazi regime. A proposal to route the relay via Dachau, for instance, was rejected,[171] the relay committee even instructing the Bavarian Sports Association to distance itself from mini-relays that were scheduled to split off from the main event and carry the flame to smaller communities.[172] Of course, it was not always practical or desirable to eradicate every trace of 1936 or avoid locations sullied by the regime. Generally speaking, despite their relative innocence as symbols of sporting achievement, actual physical or projected places associated with the Berlin event—the Olympic Stadium, or the desire in some quarters to name one of the new streets in Munich's Olympic park after Diem—were treated more critically than sites with unambiguous connections to Nazi power in Munich.

In Berlin itself, the Olympic Stadium—like other sports facilities, buildings, industrial plants, and military installations that had sprouted up under the Nazi regime—found rapid reuse after the war in a city ravaged by heavy infrastructural damage. After the removal of Nazi insignia, such buildings were treated as "the products and proof of a non-political sphere of industrial modernity" and "as if they did not belong in any specific sense to the history of the Nazi state."[173] Renamed Olympiastadion by the Berliner Magistrat, the Reichssportfeld soon played host to a wide range of sporting and cultural events. Max Schmeling fought for the last time in front of twenty thousand spectators at the Waldbühne in 1948, one hundred thousand soccer fans watched Germany lose two to one to Turkey in 1951, and in the 1950s and 1960s, the complex hosted an illustrious mix of Catholic and Protestant Kirchentage, the annual "Große Polizeischau," British army tattoos, and a range of rock concerts, including a riotous Rolling Stones gig in 1965.[174] For West Berliners, the site of the 1936 Games, therefore, provided a pragmatic and stigma-free home for large-scale events in the city. This view was largely shared across the Federal Republic: five out of ten German soccer championships in the 1950s were held in the Olympic stadium, and in 1951 even Jesse Owens returned with the Harlem Globetrotters, stepping out of a helicopter to a rapturous welcome from seventy-five thousand spectators from all parts of the city.[175]

On one level, the Munich organizers went to some lengths to articulate their solidarity with West Berlin. Although they rejected the Berlin Senate's attempts (supported by the federal Ministry of the Interior) to appropriate elements of the cultural program,[176] they held their board meetings in the city on two occasions with the expressed aim of maintaining "close contact with the sports authorities and organizations of Berlin"[177] and "once again embodying the connection between the Olympic cities of Munich and Berlin."[178] In the midst of Cold War tensions, proudly highlighting the link between Germany's two Olympic cities made political sense as an act of civic boosterism for the beleaguered former capital. On another level, however, the idea of transplanting even the smallest symbolic recollection of Berlin to the heart of the Munich project met with a distinct chill. As a site of memory, rather than simply a location of sports and popular festivals, the Berlin Olympiastadion had made no effort to "open up the doubtless difficult context that made the place infamous."[179] A merging of pragmatism and presumed sporting innocence had been evident in the restoration of Nazi features around the site: from the natural stone cladding and the Führerloge to, most patently, the bell tower and the militarily resonant Langemarckhalle (renovation by the original architect Werner March between 1960 and 1963). At the 1968 Oktoberfest, an international PR agency presented Vogel with a stone from the stadium for laying at the new Olympic site. However, as Press Chief "Johnny" Klein later informed the donors, at a time when delegates at the IOC session in Warsaw were taken to see the graves of 1936 participants murdered during the Nazi occupation, Berlin would have to remain off limits.[180] What might have been perfectly acceptable in West Berlin—in 1966, the stadium became one of only two architectural objects to be placed on a 182-strong conservation list—was clearly not in Munich.[181]

The name Carl Diem—commemorated with others at the Berlin stadium after the war—proved equally unpopular in Munich.[182] Although some seventy streets or squares were already named after him in the Federal Republic, the Munich City Council remained resolutely opposed to following suit. Vogel had informed Daume that in Munich, a city with "particularly strict regulations and binding resolutions when it came to the memory of the Third Reich," "desk drawers were full of the appropriate material" in anticipation of a Diem-proposal.[183] To avoid "raking up the political past" at an open session of the city council, it was decided to restrict the naming of the twenty-two streets, bridges, and squares in the Olympic district to renowned former champions from abroad, with the exception of de Coubertin, the archaeologists Curtius and Dörpfeld, and the deceased deputy mayor Georg Brauchle (d. 1968) who had been instrumental in the city's bid. Some of those honored were virtually unknown to the wider public.[184] Few could have identified James Connolly (the triple U.S. medalist in the jumping events at the inaugural Games in Athens) as the name behind the infamous Connollystraße of the terrorist siege. The council's grasp of German Olympic history proved shaky too. Willibald Gebhardt, the first German member of the IOC who tenaciously fought modern sport's corner against the Turner, was mistaken for an athlete. Helene Mayer, the half-Jewish silver-medal-winning fencer on the 1936 German team, was honored too, but her inclusion rested on a myth of resistance similar to that of Jesse Owens. Remembered as one of the few Jews on the German team and viewed by dint of her victory as a triumph over adversity, she had in fact simply flown in from her home in the United States to compete, after which, having given the Nazi salute and won her medal, she returned to safety.[185]

Diem's omission from the "carefully" constructed list nonetheless caused a variety of complaints, not just from his wife.[186] Some sections of the press followed the issue supportively, distinguishing between the deserving Diem on the one hand and party diehards such as Ritter von Halt and von Tschammer und Osten on the other.[187] Max Danz, a sports representative on the board, felt sufficiently moved to raise the issue at two critical meetings of the committee: first at an extraordinary session three days before the opening, at which sponsorship of an exhibition at Dachau to commemorate sport's fight against fascism was being contemplated,[188] and secondly four months later during a discussion about the erection of a monument to the Israeli victims of the terrorist attack (see chapter 7).[189] Danz's interventions at such insensitive junctures demonstrate the almost militant, residual belief in Diem's innocence amongst certain functionaries. Daume, as usual, attempted to mediate, suggesting that the independent fundraising body for the Games (the Olympic Sponsors Association) might quickly organize a Diem exhibition that could evolve into a permanent Olympic museum under the aegis of the Sportpark GmbH.[190] Despite his best efforts, no one in Munich would rescue the architect of Berlin.

Beyond Berlin and its central *acteurs*, decisions about locations followed a more pragmatic line. The choice of Kiel to host the water sports for the second time is a case in point. When various international federations refused to compete on a southern German lake, the landlocked Munich organizers were forced to look to the north coast.[191] Ranked equal with its rival Lübeck on sporting and infrastructural criteria,[192] Kiel eventually won the day for reasons of national security.[193] Amid a plethora of dissenting voices from other government offices, the Ministry of Defense advised that westerly winds around Travemünde could blow the naval support teams into zonal waters and provoke retaliation from the GDR.[194] Strikingly, the lengthy discussions and correspondence over the difficult issue of selection never touched on the city's link with 1936. For this, Kiel doubtless had its annual international regatta to thank—the "Kieler Woche," which dated back to 1882 and, despite misuse for Nazi propaganda, had been reconvened in the summer of 1945 by enthusiastic British occupiers. By the early 1960s, Kiel had become an annual focal point of world-class sailing, Baltic culture, and Scandinavian performing arts—features prominently reflected in its contributions to the 1972 cultural program.

In the former "capital of the movement," too, discussions about locations for central cultural events proceeded with scant attention to a site's status under the Nazi regime. Thus, the Olympic flame, which for practical reasons arrives in the host city on the eve of the Games, was housed overnight on the Königsplatz. This square—framed on three sides by nineteenth-century buildings celebrating Bavaria's Hellenophilic past (Glyptothek, Propyläen, and the Neue Staatsgalerie) and completed on the fourth by Paul Ludwig Troost's "severely neoclassical"

1930s Führerbau and Verwaltungsbau—marked "the political and administrative nerve center" of the party.[195] Its shrubbery and trees had been replaced by twenty-two thousand square meters of flagstones to facilitate military parades and other infamous scenes of Nazi history, such as the book-burnings of 1933. The most significant single project of the arts program—a world-leading exhibition costing DM 5 million and entitled Weltkulturen und moderne Kunst (World Cultures and Modern Art)—was housed in Troost's other Munich commission, the Haus der Kunst.[196] The regime's first major piece of architecture, the lime-faced neoclassical museum "possessed immense ideological significance," not least as the site of the Große Deutsche Kunstausstellung from 1937 to 1944.[197] Neither location was first choice. Originally, the Theresienwiese had been selected as a suitable place to receive the Olympic flame with a "joyful celebration," and the Neue Pinakothek chosen to house the showpiece exhibition.[198] But the former foundered due to the Oktoberfest, which was normally half erected by late August, and the latter came to nothing because the 1967 prize-winning design for Alexander Freiherr von Branca's gallery was still in the planning phase and the Bavarian state government prudently refused to prioritize spending in a rush to have it completed for the Games.[199] In the event, the Königsplatz and the Haus der Kunst were chosen with the same insouciance that had informed their omission in the first place. In selection and nonselection alike, the Nazi past played no role whatsoever.

The reason for this is twofold. First, in postwar Munich—much as in West Berlin—the devastated urban landscape demanded that undamaged buildings and infrastructural hubs be put to use again with little regard to their Nazi legacy. Thus, the Haus der deutschen Kunst soon reopened, with a subtle airbrushing of its title, as an exhibition space in 1946. It hosted a show by Blauer Reiter artists in 1949 (who had previously featured as prominent exemplars in the infamous "Degenerate Art" display) and in the 1950s drew in crowds of up to eighty thousand and one hundred thousand respectively for its annual Große Kunstausstellung München and displays by international artists.[200] At the Königsplatz, the largely unscathed Nazi party buildings provided homes for incongruously civilized institutions, the Führerbau eventually becoming the Hochschule für Musik, and the Verwaltungsbau the Haus der Kulturindustrie, which housed the Zentralinstitut für Kunstgeschichte. The "flagstone sea" ("Plattensee") on the square gradually transformed itself into a city-center parking lot, a natural urban development enshrined officially by city council law in 1961 (but prohibited for aesthetic reasons for the period of the Games).[201]

Beyond such pragmatic amnesia, there was a second reason for the organizers' apparent historical indifference. At the time they were making their decisions, the public discussion addressing the practical use of former Nazi sites in Munich had not yet reached consensus. In the mid 1960s, the normalization of architectural legacies that characterized the 1950s was increasingly problematized, with the

Königsplatz and the Haus der Kunst featuring prominently in the debate. Conservatives angry at the city's modern development highlighted the concreted indignity of the Königsplatz and pleaded for a return to the green idyll of prewar days; opponents argued that the square possessed a beauty and functionality that transcended its Nazi influence.[202] At the same time, traditionalists and modernists clashed when the Bavarian State Architectural Commission proposed demolishing the Haus der Kunst as part of a road-widening scheme for the Altstadtring, the former arguing its neoclassical look enhanced the city better than recent progressive architectural choices, the latter wanting it razed to the ground.[203] In the end, the Haus der Kunst survived virtually unaltered, although the Games' space requirements provided the modernist lobby with an opportunity to wrap two temporary Plexiglas frames around the back of the building and "conceal its strongly monumental character."[204] Both debates show that in the vital preparatory phase of the Games, architectural "memory was anything but stabilized."[205] With matters unresolved in the 1960s, it is not surprising the organizers stayed within the common postwar parameters of pragmatic usage.[206]

Nonetheless, although not primarily chosen for their historical resonance, both the Königsplatz and the Haus der Kunst became sites of rupture and reflection during the Games. In the case of the Königsplatz, there was a gentle remolding of expectations. Although set against a heavily classical backdrop, the arrival of the flame in Munich was celebrated with a mix of local and international folkloric talent rather than military pomp. The Munich Bläserbuben accompanied a short ceremony in which Daume and Vogel delivered brief speeches, and the scene was lightened with airy performances by folk groups from Romania, Mexico, and the famous Medau dance school.[207] The contrast to Berlin's bombastic embrace of the flame and the heavy tone set by subsequent host cities could not have been greater.

The Haus der Kunst issued an even more obvious invitation to reflect. Searching for a theme "that was not restricted to national or sporting motifs," local curator Siegfried Wichmann conceived an exhibition of importance to the world of art in general and to West German self-presentation in particular.[208] In its final manifestation, Weltkulturen und moderne Kunst sought to demonstrate the influence of the Asian, African, and American continents on European art in the late nineteenth and twentieth centuries.[209] This reversal of the donor-recipient model between first and third worlds (which played a key role in the diffusion of the Olympic ideal) intended to suggest that many parts of the world had achieved cultural freedom long before decolonization. Although pilloried by Liselott Diem[210] and Avery Brundage (a collector of Asian art who reported to his advisor: "It was as well that we did not participate"),[211] it was widely regarded as a cutting-edge international event. At the same time, exhibiting supposed "primitive" art forms at a resonant Nazi location in a display of mutual enrichment with European modernity would also, as the official report suggested, "eradicate an inhuman prejudice and demonstrate a new cosmopolitan understanding of art."[212] In its desire to fuse time and space, the report even erroneously located the show at the same site as the "Degenerate Art" display, and gave the year as 1936.[213] The agenda of international art history, therefore, blended with the organizers' second choice of venue to create a statement that read as an atonement for pan-European arrogance and Nazi ideology. The exhibition and the Haus der Kunst had both a "cultural-political value" and an "immanent political significance."[214]

In the official report's account of the exhibition, broad cultural politics certainly softened hard politics per se and smoothed off the edges of overt German reflection. Such hedging about of the German past was evident elsewhere too. For despite laying out the national significance of the exhibition in their rationale, the artistic organizers made no such reference in their catalogue that accompanied the event.[215] President Heinemann was a reluctant patron and declined to write a foreword. Daume expressed diametrically opposed opinions to different groups of listeners. Writing to Heinemann, on the one hand, he stressed the "particular significance" of the location—with the official report's Freudian slip—as a counterpoint to the "site of the [Nazi] exhibition" in 1936.[216] In *Stern* magazine, however, he denied the venue's symbolism and, referring to the Italians' unselfconscious use of the Foro Mussolini for the 1960 Olympics, bemoaned "the inability of the Germans to come to terms with their own history."[217] Daume's contradictions typify the way in which the 1972 organizers dealt with historically resonant locations in Munich and potential transfers from Berlin. As generally the case in both cities after the war, pragmatic usage of the Third Reich's architecture became a part of everyday life. But as the impossibility of transposing a single stone from Berlin to Munich suggests, the problems began when the everyday unfolded onto the symbolic. At Munich 1972, the Haus der Kunst was suspended between its everyday status and a carefully embedded statement about the German past.

• • •

Berlin 1936 and other traces of National Socialism around the city of Munich, therefore, found themselves enmeshed in a variety of discourse-distinct contradictions at the 1972 Olympics. For the IOC, 1936 represented the tipping point from which it would go on to realize its ambition as an institution with truly global reach in the twentieth century. For the Munich OC, Berlin provided welcome sports-political capital during the bid and organizational expertise and select PR opportunities after it. At the same time, it fuelled certain individuals' indulgence in a "German Olympic imagination," which translated clumsily onto the public domain of the late 1960s and posed awkward questions about commemoration and the symbolism of places. Paradoxically, the presumption of sport's inherent innocence and the self-representation of the young Republic's management elites could allow a central player such as Krupp to take up the running where it had left off thirty-six years earlier. All the while, 1936 acted not unlike the psychoanalytical "real": that which could never be fully expressed, it nonetheless structured almost every engagement with the Germans' Olympic past. As this chapter has shown, when speaking in public, few Munich officials dealt with 1936 in anything but circuitous fashion. As a result, the blunt simplicity of Heinemann's remark to the IOC Session a week before the Games stands out for its rarity: "The older generation still remembers the 1936 Games in Berlin well, which were manipulated by Germany's rulers at the time for their own purposes."[218]

But Heinemann was not without contradiction himself. In 1969, he pledged to support a memorial service at the Dachau concentration camp in conjunction with the Games, telling Daume and the OC personally that "it would round off the image the Games would give of Germany."[219] After giving further assurances of his intention to attend, he withdrew unexpectedly in the summer of 1972.[220] Although "diary commitments" were presented in August as the official apology and a wreath sent in lieu,[221] an internal memo from five months earlier tells a different story: "BP [Federal President] does not wish to participate in the memorial."[222] It is not clear why the president changed his mind—leaving the political sphere to be represented by federal minister Egon Franke, Vogel, and opposition leader Rainer Barzel—but his behavior is symptomatic of a strange mixture of well-meaning obligation and distinct unease that characterized the OC's relation to the event as well.

Although the idea for the service originated from and was nurtured by the board—not least to draw the sting from potentially more critical events planned by other nations—the OC held the event publicly at some distance.[223] "A potentially tricky matter of protocol,"[224] as Daume observed, it was organized officially in Munich by the two Christian churches and the Israelitische Kultusgemeinde, and, because it was impossible to circumnavigate, the International Comité Dachau, the representative body of former camp inmates who had established an inalienable right to participate in all such activities on the site.[225] After difficult negotiations with the latter over the program, the event went ahead on the eve of the Games (25 August) with some two thousand participants from around the world.[226] Four actors read texts composed in Dachau and Berlin in 1936; William Pearson, a black soloist (as the press constantly noted) from the Cologne Opera, sang from the Psalms; and the cantor of the Kultusgemeinde gave a rendition of the Hebrew Lament for the Dead. Neither Brundage nor any other IOC official attended, and—rather hypocritically—the OC declined to cover the costs.[227]

In the end, Dachau was to host three significant memorial events during the Games. At each of them, 1936 was treated differently. At a rally convened by the Bund der Antifaschisten Bayern und the Vereinigung der Verfolgten des Naziregimes (3 September), Heinz Laufer, a prominent member of the German Communist Party (DKP) and competitor at the 1956 Olympics in Melbourne, drew parallels between 1936 and 1972.[228] At the OC's quasi-official ceremony, by contrast, the Archbishop of Lusaka in Zambia, Adam Kozłowiecki, who had been deported to the camp shortly after the German invasion of Poland in 1939, recalled both the joyous sporting hopes of all who had attended the Games and their dreadful failure to recognize suffering around them, admonishing his listeners to guard against similar sins of omission.[229] By contrast again, at a special service organized for the Israeli Olympic team, Heinz Galinski, chairman of the Jewish congregation of Berlin, maintained that the Federal Republic was a "fundamentally different state to the German Reich of 1936" with human dignity "at the centre of its constitution."[230]

As this chapter has shown, such differing ways of citing the 1936 complex were fully in keeping with the time. In terms of the 1972 project, however, Galinski's unambiguous endorsement of the Federal Republic carries most significance. For if 1936 shadowed the organizers, it hardly *overshadowed* them. They dealt with it as and when, sometimes with more appetite and conviction than at others. Berlin 1936 might have been unavoidable but, as we shall see in the chapters that follow, the past was not an obsession for those mapping out the new Germany.

4

Germany on the Drawing Board

Architecture, Design, and Ceremony

Although singular in scale, Munich was not without precedent as a public relations exercise of national importance. Well before the bid, the Federal Republic had presented itself with great success at a series of international exhibitions, not least the Brussels Expo of 1958, the first World Fair since the war. Under the title "Progress and Humanity," the Belgians aimed to sweep aside the aggressive nationalism that had culminated in the symbolic saber rattling of Paris 1937, and the West German contributors were only too willing to oblige. Seizing the opportunity to "make good the mistakes of the [previous] occasion," the young Republic devoted itself to a "project of conscious and deliberate modernization . . . that clearly broke with the National Socialist past."[1] Although supervised by the Economics Ministry under Ludwig Erhard and controlled, ultimately, by the cabinet in Bonn, Germany's image in 1958 was largely constructed by representatives of the Deutscher Werkbund (DWB), an association of artists, architects, industrialists, and politicians founded in 1907 and reestablished in 1950 to promote the aesthetic quality of German products, economic recovery, and cultural reform. The involvement of nongovernmental agencies in the Brussels event is hardly surprising given, as Paul Betts has shown, the huge importance of industrial design to the Federal Republic in the 1950s and 1960s. A vital contributor to the country's export revenues after the currency reform of 1948, modernist design occupied a significant position within the cultural economy as well. While the National Socialists had openly embraced modernist design, in the postwar era its representatives successfully reinvented themselves in rejection of Nazi "blood and soil." Modernist design was therefore freer than almost any other form of intellectual expression to transform "the wreckage of the past into a brave new world of post-fascist modernity."[2]

Warmly supported in North America, where its foremost exiles had settled before the war, but at the same time independent of that continent's pervasive influence on the arts in the 1950s, design became a peculiarly potent articulation of West German identity during the Cold War.

The DWB luminaries who took charge of the Brussels project rejected original plans to present "the complete German cultural production" (with Gutenberg, Goethe, et al.)[3] and infused it instead with the guiding principles of postwar German design: transparency in public architecture connoting the openness of the new democracy, and an emphasis on everyday objects in the private sphere to rebalance the intrusion of the National Socialists into domestic relationships.[4] DWB president Hans Schwippert, who had overseen the reconstruction of Düsseldorf and the new parliament in Bonn, devised a concept to be housed in a building commissioned from his modernist contemporaries Egon Eiermann (the Neckermann building in Frankfurt) and Sep Ruf (the American Consulate in the Munich). The "German pavilion" that took shape in the Brussels suburb of Heysel was the very antithesis of Albert Speer's monumental tower in Paris. Constructed of glass façades resting on steel skeletons, a series of quadratic, two-story units appeared to float naturally within the contours of the site's uneven landscape. Inside, the exhibit was sparingly furnished with domestic objects of the highest quality that gave a stunning impression of contemporary German living spaces. Celebrating the postwar era's restored "happiness in life" *(Lebensheiterkeit),* the German Pavilion stressed the "friendliness" and "beauty" of its workplaces and homes as "bulwarks against fascism and communism, A-bomb anxiety, and Cold War militarism."[5] By integrating products from foreign manufacturers, it sent clear signals about the country's internationalist intent too. Somewhat controversial among conservatives at home, the German effort was praised both nationally and internationally. Erhard hailed it as a confirmation of the Federal Republic's honorable membership of the Western alliance; Federal president Theodor Heuss, a DWB president himself before the war, drew parallels to an exhibition planned by the association during the Weimar Republic; and, warmly supported by the press, the Brussel's Expo jury awarded the Germans joint second prize (behind Czechoslovakia) in the competition for best overall exhibit. The strategy of allowing design elites to focus on their own work had proved a winning formula.

Nine years later, Bonn aimed to repeat the performance at the 1967 World Fair in Montreal.[6] Now supervised by a special Generalkommissar (Peter von Siemens, great grandson of the company's founder and president of the BDI, the Federation of German Industries), the Germans' preparations appeared to follow a familiar pattern. Hans Schwippert (along with Mia Seeger of the German Design Council, and Walter Rossow and Gustav von Hartmann of the DWB) took responsibility again for the overall concept, while further high-caliber modernists, Rolf Gutbrod and Frei Otto, held the architectural reins. Otto's roof design for the

German pavilion soon became legendary. Replacing the rigid skeleton and glass façades of Brussels with steel ropes and a transparent plastic skein, he created not so much a building as a "new, unique form," a "floating cloud" that respected the surrounding landscape and "marked the building out as an improvisation that was to be used for only six months." Perched beside a lagoon, eight masts were arranged in a "light-hearted, lilting structure that integrated the island in front of it."[7]

Against such innovation, however, the content of the pavilion seemed to regress. Given more exacting guidelines by the Canadian organizers about the themes of the fair—"man the creator," "man the producer," "man the explorer," "man the provider," "man and his health," "man and the community"—the German team had to look beyond the horizons of its own design excellence, and after initial delays, neither a satisfactory nor a unified concept emerged. Nonetheless, hoping to show "that Germany was a creative and indispensable part of European culture," the Federal Republic went to great lengths to present the riches of its historical legacy.[8] While the famous Ulm College of Design was featured, there was in effect a return to the traditional conception that would have gone to Brussels in 1958 had the DWB not intervened; design per se was crowded out by exhibits on music (a glass wall tracing its development in manuscript form from Bach to Stockhausen), church life (the Kaiser-Wilhelm-Gedächtniskirche in Berlin and ecclesiastical architecture), theater, museums (a cast of the Kugelzahn fish from Solnhofen, a Roman gravestone from 70–100 AD in Cologne, and the Bockhorst Triumphkreuz from 1200 AD), and displays of a historical nature on industry and research. The show was completed by a library and display of the best sculptors of the twentieth century.

In contrast to Brussels, Montreal was far from an unqualified success. While the 1958 jury had mildly criticized the German exhibit for the "abstract nature of some of its topics and presentational aspects that lacked warmth and feeling," these complaints were writ large over the Germans' efforts at Montreal.[9] Briefed by the German organizing team in June 1966, U.S. and Canadian consultants to the exhibition were alarmed at what they had seen. Writing immediately to Bonn, they praised the pavilion as a "highly impressive . . . architectural achievement," but expressed strong reservations about the exhibits it would house:

> The total effect is one of unrelieved heaviness. The average North American will come out of the Pavilion with the feeling that he has been subjected to an extremely intellectualized lecture in a rather dull museum with no opportunity to relax. . . . The teacher, i.e. Germany, will be respected, but he will not be liked because he will be demanding too much . . . There is nothing warm and personal, nothing charming and friendly about anything in the Pavilion. . . . There is an absence of feeling of hospitality, of communion between the visitors and the hosts . . . the story it tells is dull because the light touch is missing.[10]

The German press tended to concur.[11] In the summer of 1966, therefore, just as the Munich Olympic team was beginning to turn the preliminary blueprint of its bid into a viable long-term vision, Bonn seems to have reached a crossroads in its self-presentation at international events. While the excellence of German architecture and design could be relied upon to make an impact abroad, the essence of the country's image remained in some doubt. The archive shows no connection between the incipient planning for Munich and the final preparations for Montreal. This lack of coordination is not surprising, perhaps, given the highly devolved nature of the Games' organization, especially in the early phases when the line of communication ran mainly between Daume and Munich City Hall. It was certainly echoed later when the Munich team was scarcely consulted about the 1971 World Fair in Osaka. The Munich organizers set their own agenda, without explicit reference to Brussels or Montreal. Their main achievements, however, should be seen in the context of, and measured against, West Germany's performance in the Canadian capital. While exploiting the country's recent strength in design, Munich, without realizing it, would go on to turn the North Americans' critique about style and substance on its head.

ARTS

Athletes arriving early at the Olympic village in 1972 might have been forgiven for agreeing with the consultants. Waiting for them on their bedside tables was the Organizing Committee's official present, a four-hundred-page book entitled *Deutsches Mosaik,* translated into English, French, and Russian. Originally intending to condense the monumental and much-acclaimed anthology of German intellectual endeavor *Deutscher Geist* (published as an act of "inner resistance" by Peter Suhrkamp not long before his deportation to a concentration camp in 1940 and reissued to international acclaim in 1966[12]), the committee had settled on a new version targeted at foreigners.[13] Aiming to act as "a calling card for Germany's recent intellectual rehabilitation," the volume concentrated on the twentieth century and made few compromises on intellectual standards.[14] It was originally to be edited by Inge and Walter Jens, before governmental misgivings led to their removal.[15] Featuring Einstein, Benjamin, Heidegger, and Freud, to name but a few, it would, in fact, have made an excellent university primer in modern German studies.

Not surprisingly, Vogel could muster little enthusiasm for the idea when it was first mooted, fearing, with some justification, "that the text would be too demanding for the majority of competitors."[16] But Daume was a bibliophile who delighted in the sumptuous editions of Brecht and Proust that Suhrkamp owner Siegfried Unseld sent to adorn his bookshelves.[17] An educated "Bürger," he scavenged literature for *bon mots* that he scattered extravagantly and eclectically in his public addresses.[18] He could weave a speech to a Chinese audience around Goethe (comparing his ideas on continuity and change to the Olympic movement), or pepper another with Luther, Bernard of Clairvaux, and Nietzsche in quick succession.[19] Later president of the Erich Kästner Society (from 1981) and chair of the e.o.plauen-Gesellschaft (from 1992), Daume mixed business and pleasure from an early stage, inviting the Spanish philosopher Ortega y Gasset, for instance, to give a lecture at the annual conference of the German Sports Association (DSB) in 1954. The *Deutsches Mosaik* was Daume to a tee: after two years of discussion—as one irate government minister was informed—he had pushed the arts committee to approve it "with misgivings and only lukewarm support," and given his word to the publisher before final consultation with the board.[20]

Daume promoted his own interests in similar fashion with the *Edition Olympia*—twenty-eight posters commissioned from world-famous artists to be published, against Vogel's better judgment again,[21] by the OC and Munich's Bruckmann Verlag.[22] An art lover, whose office at the OC's headquarters in the Saarstraße "looked like a studio with all its kinetic objects and contemporary sculptures,"[23] Daume chased major names (Picasso, Chagall, Miró) with substantial honorariums.[24] He reveled in hosting leading figures in his Feldafing villa, for instance, to discuss a possible ballet spin-off with the Bavarian state operas. Ultimately infeasible—because of Miró's excessive demands—the dance project proved an unfavorable omen for the posters.[25] Some artists made only a perfunctory effort to link their work with the sports event, and the early results caused "the shaking of heads" and "barely stifled mockery" in the OC.[26] Oskar Kokoschka, who opened the series with a somewhat lethargic depiction of the Greek Kouros, caused a flood of letters to Munich City Hall[27] and was lambasted in the press for reproducing a figure with "the posture of someone who had spent too long at a desk."[28] Although generally deemed one of the many successes of the Games—more popular participants including Serge Poliakoff and David Hockney—the art project hardy matched initial expectations.

The *Deutsches Mosaik* and the *Edition Olympia* stemmed from the same cultural matrix as the content of the Federal Republic's exhibit in Montreal, and in the same way, they enjoyed no more than a mixed reception. But the connection between sport and the arts that manifested itself in Munich drew its inspiration from Olympic discourse as well. De Coubertin had always perceived sport as part of high culture and persuaded the delegates at the 1906 IOC congress in Paris to conjure up the muses with competitions in literature, music, and the visual arts from 1908 onward. In 1912, under a thinly veiled pseudonym, he won a medal for literature himself. The founder's enthusiasm was not always shared, though, and some hosts embraced the competitions with more zeal than others. Berlin expended great energy on them, the Germans carrying off no fewer than thirteen gold medals, whereas London 1948 (like its counterpart immediately after the First World War,

Antwerp 1920) treated them coolly.[29] In the 1950s, the competitions faded and were replaced by burgeoning cultural programs that could draw in world-class artists no longer affronted by the obligation to submit their work or performance to judgment by jury. Daume's love of the arts might have come from the innate sensibilities of the educated German bourgeoisie, but it was enhanced by the Olympic ethos and the "German Olympic imagination," sustained under Carl Diem's influence either side of the war. For Daume, like Diem and de Coubertin, sport was a cultural entity, and he worked hard to nurture its relations with music, art, and literature in universities, businesses, churches, and the media.[30] Brundage too was both a believer and aficionado. Almost as well known in the 1960s for his art collection as his Olympic office,[31] he bought jades and bronzes from the Asian market with a millionaire's passion and purse, taking his own expertise very seriously in the process.[32]

This confluence of personal, national, and international interests gave the Munich event a particular shape, not least when the bid was being prepared. Before submitting, Vogel and Daume wrote individually to Brundage, assuring him that "the art-loving city of Munich" would stage "Games of extraordinary beauty characterized by the uniting of bodily and spiritual development"[33] and suggesting that "no city in the world" was better suited to "enriching [the Olympics] with cultural values" and "returning [them] to the classical 'contest of carriage and songs.'"[34] In April 1966, Vogel told Italian journalists that "Munich would put on Olympics in the spirit of Baron de Coubertin."[35] And at the decisive session in Rome, the president duly gave delegates a steer by bemoaning the disappointing standard of the fine arts program at recent Games.[36] In their efforts to return to Coubertinian principles, the Munich team even planned to revive two events last conducted—either at all or with any real passion—at the Berlin Games of 1936: a lavish festival play to be performed (à la Diem) on several evenings in the main stadium and the aforementioned arts competitions.[37] Like many of the group's initial ideas, however, both projects were quietly dropped when planning began in earnest, despite Günter Grass's suggestion of a "Lyrikolympiade" (Poetry Olympics) with a final to take place in the Olympic precincts.[38]

Nonetheless, a forty-day arts program *(Olympic Summer)* soon took shape and drew exclusively on artists "who could match the high level of the sports events."[39] Undeniably elitist in tone, it was leavened, more successfully than either the *Deutsches Mosaik* or the *Edition Olympia*, by a sense of progressiveness and cooperative internationality. Led by an arts committee that included leading representatives from different generations—Grass, Hans Egon Holthusen, Erich Kästner, Alexander Kluge, Günther Rennert, Carl Orff, Carl Zuckmayer, Friedrich Luft, and Herbert von Karajan—it was divided into classical, contemporary, and avant-garde sections. Major exhibitions (such as Weltkulturen und moderne Kunst) were accompanied by classic and modern theater, from Schiller and the Royal Shakespeare Company to Broadway's Negro Ensemble Company and Moscow's puppet theater.[40] Twelve countries performed over seven weeks at an International Folklore Festival, which was complemented and contrasted by jazz and the *MUSIK, FILM, DIA, LICHT* Festival, offering countless first performances of electronic, vocal, pop, beat, improvised, and computer-generated music. The Olympic village cinema showed films from twenty-two countries, and a meeting of young European writers, journalists, painters, sculptors, and scientists discussed the Olympic ideal, "often in strong and irreconcilable terms."[41] Kiel produced its own impressive, if more high-end, program, with an exhibition *Man and Sea* that brought together the nations of the Baltic coastline, a Stockhausen premier, and operas and ballets from Stockholm, Sofia, Hamburg, and Copenhagen.[42]

De Coubertin would have been delighted, but Avery Brundage—in the contrary spirit that characterized the final years of his presidency—was not. Recent events had given Lausanne grounds for concern. As the Munich team was going to the drawing board, their counterparts in Mexico had been putting the final touches on an arts program that surpassed all others. Exploiting the unique opportunity to attract nations that would not normally have given the country a second thought, Mexico organized a year-long program that drew in five million visitors. Orchestras, ballets, and jazz artists from thirty-five nations took part, and some forty countries (from Guatemala to Ethiopia and China) contributed to the folk festival.[43] The IOC fretted about the viability of such large-scale events in the future, and the following year clearly instructed the Munich team to restrict its arts program to a national venture. The OC, however, had already approved a full international festival, and Daume, with the scheme so close to his heart, proceeded regardless, giving false assurances that it would comply with the IOC's wishes.[44] Over the following two years, Lausanne reiterated its position on numerous occasions but the Munich organizers remained evasive until it was too late.[45] At the IOC session during the Winter Games in Sapporo in February 1972, Brundage finally capitulated, but not before stressing deep regret and clamping down on the cultural dimension of the next two Games in Montreal and Moscow.[46] Although considerably shorter and attracting fewer visitors than Mexico, the Munich arts program eclipsed it in real terms: fifty nations provided fifty-seven operas, seven operettas, three musicals, ten ballets, thirty plays, forty-two orchestral concerts, eight choral concerts, twenty-four chamber and solo concerts, twenty-two orchestras, fifty-six conductors, seventy soloists, and six exhibitions. It was attended by 14 percent of the 4.5 million who traveled to the Bavarian capital.[47]

The OC's disregard for the IOC's stipulations would have had much to do with an innate sense of German identity premised on high culture. The organizers would not have wished to be outdone by their immediate "Third-World" predecessors either. But their plans for an international arts program also served the vital purpose of cultural diplomacy. In 1972, "the time was not right for a form of self-projection that emphasized the national," as Klaus Bieringer later reflected. "We worked," instead, "on the principles of openness, internationalism, and high standards."[48] Like Mexico before it, the Federal Republic could scarcely afford to squander the opportunity to open itself, in any way it could, to the world.

DESIGN

In the period after 1945, Mexico City and Munich were exceptional in their cultural engagement with the Olympics. In its texture and composition, however, Munich had more in common with Berlin. The reason for this, again, is that both German Games were imbued with a sense of responsibility to the founder's original vision. Inspired by Wagner and the philosopher John Ruskin, who created the English arts and crafts movement, de Coubertin conceived the Olympics as an event that not only contained art and music but formed a complete work of art itself. Few cities recognized the Games' fundamental aspiration to create "a unity of the athlete with the spectator, . . . the surroundings, the decoration, [and] the landscape,"[49] and only Munich and Berlin ever attempted it. In 1930, Diem noted that "the festive character of previous Games had left much to be desired from the viewpoint of harmony" and set himself the goal of producing a "Gesamtkunstwerk" by means of a festival play.[50] *Olympische Jugend* (Olympic Youth) became an impressive undertaking that involved a cast of ten thousand, singing and dancing to music by Carl Orff and Werner Egk under a cathedral of light whose beams met high above the stadium, and culminating in the choral movement of Beethoven's Ninth Symphony. But when the Nazi government took a shine to the Games, the "work of art" expanded to an unprecedented dimension and the whole of Berlin transformed itself into a harmonious Olympic organism. Decorative schemes combining "utility with beauty, simplicity with colorfulness,"[51] massed gymnastic displays, and perfectly flowing traffic arteries "produced a rare density and fullness of signs" across the city.[52] The continued fascination of the Berlin Games lies predominantly in the power of its unified aesthetic. In 1972, no one set out to create a *Gesamtkunstwerk,* the concept forming neither part of the bid nor holding much appeal for the organizers who found it "presumptuous."[53] But—immeasurably more than the cultural program—it was the outcome that most clearly defined their Games. Whether originally intended or not, Munich 1972 became a *Gesamtkunstwerk,* albeit one created by a core group of specialists working to transcend the memory of 1936.

OTL AICHER

When it came to defining the Games' aesthetic, it is hardly surprising the organizers turned to one of the country's international experts. "Modernist design of the rationalist functionalism mode," after all, had been "officially showcased" and successfully combined with politics and public relations "to great effectiveness"—not least in Brussels and Montreal—throughout the late 1950s and 1960s. With industrial design "now virtually synonymous with the best aspects of West German modern culture," the forty-five year-old Otl Aicher (1922–91), winner of the Prix d'Honneur at the 1961 Triennale in Milan, was an obvious choice to lead the design department.[54] By 1966, Aicher had modernized the image of the chemical giant BASF, shipbuilders Blohm & Voss, electrical durables company Braun (with Hans Gugelot), and the national airline Lufthansa (1962–64).[55] But the call to Munich put all previous commissions in the shade, the critical left-wing Catholic later joking that the Vatican was all that was left for him to do.[56] Certainly, the role placed Aicher—along with Daume, Vogel, architect Behnisch, PR guru Klein, and police chief Manfred Schreiber—at the heart of a select group whose input and vision gave the Games their ultimate form.

Aicher's involvement was opposed by some, mainly older, members of Munich's art and design establishment. Graphic designer Richard Roth (b. 1908), backed by Ludwig Huber, an OC vice president and the Bavarian minister of culture,[57] accused his younger colleague of profiteering, complaining he neither came from Bavaria nor had studied there for any length of time.[58] But Aicher enjoyed warm support from many in the local scene. The head of the Bavarian section of the DWB, Werner Wirsing—who had cooperated with Roth on an exhibit in Brussels, was later to chair the OC's design committee (until 1969), and would build the women's quarters in the Olympic village—wrote to Vogel in his favor.[59] And correspondents at the influential liberal newspapers, the *Süddeutsche Zeitung* and *Die Zeit,* championed his aesthetic.[60]

Besides the plaudits and prizes, Aicher had much to offer. The aversion of postwar architects and designers toward "gigantism," an article of faith most notably demonstrated by Schwippert's Bundeshaus, fitted Daume's notion that "the bombastic style of the Third Reich in 1936" would "rule itself out straightaway" in Munich.[61] Specifically, as cofounder of the Ulm College of Design in neighboring Baden-Württemberg, Aicher played a key role in the postwar revival of the Bauhaus. Developing a general aesthetic for architecture, photography, and design products that valued "the good, the beautiful and the practical," the influence of the school and the reputation of its collaborators extended far beyond the confines of its provincial Danube backwater. A broad educational remit attracted the support of distinguished guest lecturers, including Theodor Heuss, scientist Werner Heisenberg, philosopher Max Horkheimer, historian Golo Mann, and

FIGURE 5. Design commissioner Otl Aicher in front of his pictograms, 1970 (photo: Sven Simon, courtesy of Süddeutsche Zeitung Photo)

authors Heinrich Böll and Ralph Ellison. Like its Weimar predecessor, the school was "infused with a grand vision of social reform, based on the reconciliation of art, life, morality, and material culture," and sought to encourage a progressive industrial climate that would lead to spiritual renewal.[62] In reaction to the aesthetic of Hitler's artists and architects with their legacies of monumentalism and emotional manipulation, it rejected pathos and created a look that was "cool, functional, [and] rational."[63]

Moreover, Aicher was a man with a significant past. On the one hand, his membership of the White Rose resistance circle and marriage to the surviving sister of its leaders Hans and Sophie Scholl would insulate the OC from any future charge of repressing the past. Although not crucial in the decision to appoint him, "the name Mrs. Aicher-Scholl," as Daume noted, "[would] play well in terms of countering political propaganda from the East."[64] On the other, Aicher's balanced attitude—one that made him disinclined to indulge in the sometimes excessive memorialization of his brother- and sister-in-law ("this all too worthy remembrance")—ideally suited him to negotiate the event's complicated relation to 1936. The past might have rendered him "uneasy and uncertain, sensitive and on the alert"[65] but he was not insensitive in his treatment of it and would eventually propose an aesthetic marginalization rather than brutal eradication of Berlin.[66]

Finally, Aicher's intellectual radius swept the two main organizers up within its arc. Although not always appreciating Vogel's managerial manner, he published a series of articles from the early 1960s onward that echoed the mayor's concerns about urban development, one dealing specifically with Munich in *Die Zeit* of November 1967.[67] Aicher shared Vogel's vision of the city and its surrounding region as an inseparable entity, his *Strahlenkranz* (later spiral of fortune) emblem for the Games (modified by Cordt von Manstein) serving as a "symbol of shining Munich and the alpine foothill landscape with its light and flowers."[68] More importantly, Vogel's arts expert, Herbert Hohenemser (1915–92), assessor of culture at Munich City Hall and later chair of the OC's arts committee, had been accepted into the designer's circle after meeting in 1946.[69] And an instinctive understanding must have developed with Daume too when provisional discussions were held before the final bid in early 1966.[70] As in his relationship with Vogel, Daume will have discovered sufficient common ground and enough divergent interests to allow a successful working partnership to flourish. For instance, Aicher considered art a mere escape from the manifold demands of the postwar German present, a single semester at the Munich arts academy having led him to prioritize "the street" over "the museum."[71] But this clear difference of opinion created an organizational space in which Daume, with Aicher's approval, could indulge his passion for the high arts in Munich. At the same time, both men shared an eye for the visual and valued its impact. In Daume, Aicher found someone who, like himself, saw the world as an "Augenmensch:" "He thought with his eyes . . . comprehended by seeing. . . . He had a suspicion of things that could only be known cognitively. . . . For Daume the Olympics were not a task to be mastered through competent organization. . . . That was the job of experts. It was the event he planned, and the way it looked. What people remember when they go home afterward. Essentially he planned the physicality, the tangibility of the Games."[72]

Aicher's philosophy of design, moreover, chimed with Daume's concept of sport. Despite their inherent differences, Ludwig Wittgenstein, from whom the former drew his inspiration, could be made to form a convenient fit with the latter's oft-cited Johan Huizinga. For the Austrian philosopher, as for the Dutch historian and theoretician, all human culture was grounded in play and the rules of play. "Cultural and social programs," as Aicher expounded shortly before his death in 1991, "consist in the playing out of rules. Where there is conflict, contradiction and contestation, the definition of rules leads to play."[73] When it came to creating an aesthetic for the greatest games of all, Aicher and Daume's congruent philosophies converged and augmented each other: "the freedom of play," Aicher later noted when talking about Munich, was "not about leaving rules to chance" but ensuring "maximum variation" via "strict discipline and adherence to rules."[74]

But against Daume's fertile flights of fancy, Aicher regarded the Olympics pragmatically as "a task to be mastered through organization." In a groundbreaking presentation to the OC on the nature of visual images ("Erscheinungsbilder") in late 1967, he hailed design as an *Ordnungsaufgabe* that aimed at "unity" and "uniformity." Munich would evolve into a *Gesamtkunstwerk*—doubtless too Wagnerian a term for Aicher but one that perfectly captured his project—from the principle of "identity through relationality." Not unlike Gugelot's modular furniture with its standardized interchangeable parts, which was very influential at Ulm, uniformity would be achieved by a system that combined variable elements in a flexible but rule-bound and readily identifiable "relational grouping." This "all-encompassing visual appearance" went beyond the need to create a mere "ceremonial framework," of course. As Aicher clearly stated, it was imperative to deliver the "correction to Berlin" that the world was expecting.[75]

Set against the left-wing intellectual politics of the day, Aicher's further exposition on Berlin, however, turned out to be counterintuitive. Like many of the reactionary members of the IOC who had voted for Munich on the basis of its infamous predecessor, he had no hesitation in acknowledging the 1936 Games as "a high point in Olympic history."[76] A research trip to the Olympic Museum in Lausanne had convinced him that Berlin was the moment when the Olympics had blossomed from a "sports event" into a "world festival" *(Weltfest):* "In Berlin, for the first time, there was a separate campus that built the sports venues into a landscaped area, the bell that summoned the youth of the world, the cathedral of light, and a specific emphasis on decorative art."[77] This unprecedented degree of material and aesthetic engagement, Aicher noted, had provided the regime with a major propaganda coup, based on two interrelated strategies. Eschewing verbal means that "would have aroused suspicion," the Nazis had accentuated the "the new state's visual mode of expression, neo-classical architecture, enormity of scale, naturalistic sculpture, the colors red and gold, symbols and emblems of youth and power." Turning to the task in hand, Aicher asked the OC: "Will the world believe us if we say that Germany is different today to what it was then?" Responding himself, he said: "Trust cannot be gained through words, but instead only through visual proof and the winning of sympathy. It is not about explaining that this Germany is different, but about *showing* it."[78]

Aicher's simple answer would define the Munich Olympics, but it was far from innocent in its relation to the past. Like Berlin, Munich would rely on visual rather than verbal communication. Like Berlin, the formula of "shapes and colors" would be fundamental. And, like Berlin again—though not stated as a direct comparison—Aicher's innate sense of system and global structures would ensure that Munich presented itself as a *Gesamtkunstwerk.* In 1972, therefore, Berlin would serve both as a negative foil and an inspiration for strategy and technique. As Aicher put it pithily himself: "The look of the Munich Olympics" would have to "maintain the positive aspects of Berlin while at the same time eradicating its negative connotations."[79]

Simultaneously embracing and rejecting Berlin, Aicher projected Munich as its photographic negative:

> There will be no demonstration of nationalism, and no enormity of scale. Sport will no longer be considered an adjunct of, or preparation for military discipline. Pathos will be avoided, as will ceremonial awe. Depth is not always expressed through earnestness. Lightheartedness and non-conformity stand just as much for serious subjectivity. The Munich Olympics should have an unforced character and be open, carefree, and relaxed. It is clear that this will give them an emphatically celebratory character. Celebratory not in the traditional institutional sense but in terms of playful improvisation.[80]

This "psychological climate" and carefully "calibrated mood" would be created, in practice, by a combination of three basic elements: scripts, signs, and colors. Every Olympic text—from tickets and lunch vouchers to publicity brochures and the winners' certificates—was printed in Univers, an elegant sans-serif typeface created by Swiss designer Adrien Frutiger in 1957 and presented internationally at the Montreal Expo of 1967.[81] Directionally neutral but possessing the effortless ease of pen and ink, it was considered "inextravagant," "agile," "fresh," and "carefree." It combined "correctness and practicality with the stamp of youth."[82] Its inventor's foresight, moreover, appealed to Aicher's sense of discipline and order. Numerically quantified on a geometric grid, Univers was the first font to come with a listing matrix to help designers determine size and style.[83] In Munich it would be used, Aicher observed, without "imposing headlines," "bold emphases," or "aggressive font sizes," doubtless in homage to the democratic Bauhaus style of lowercase.[84] The words to which it lent visual form were laid out in long, thin columns to dismantle monumental blocks of information, a format that was later translated onto the distinctive elongated flags that adorned the Olympic site and the city's transport hubs in carefully choreographed groupings.

Visitors to the Olympic venues would be impressed by the overall *Erscheinungsbild,* but equally importantly, they would need to be guided by it to their destinations. Here too, Aicher was keen to avoid any sense of compulsion, preferring to regulate the massive additional flow of human traffic around Munich by "steering visitors indirectly with information that allowed them to choose themselves the way they wanted to go." Developing the pictograms invented by Masaru Katsumie to help tourists negotiate language difficulties at the Tokyo Games, Aicher designed a system of easily understandable symbols based on the twenty-one Olympic sports disciplines and a further hundred generic signs.[85] Obeying simpler

FIGURE 6. Olympic poster (Plak 006–040–021, courtesy of Bundesarchiv)

rules of grammar and interpretation, Aicher's pictograms were less abstract and subjective than their Japanese inspiration.[86] Bodies were reduced to their major component parts, and like the implementation of the Univers font, positioned within an exact grid of orthographical and geometric coordinates. Rules and grids determined the proportions of heads, torsos, limbs, the representation of sports equipment, and the distinguishing features of male and female athletes. Vitally, the pictograms gave a sense of flow and movement, and harmonized with the posters Aicher designed to advertise the sports events themselves. Hanging either

FIGURE 7. Olympic poster (Plak 006–040–011, courtesy of Bundesarchiv)

side of specially designed walls, the monochrome action shots overlaid with distinctive and contrasting colors produced a "flicker" effect when passed by vehicles and pedestrians.[87]

The bright Olympic colors, in which the posters and all other printed matter appeared, were the most striking feature of the 1972 look. Anticipating Desmond Tutu's notion of South Africa as the rainbow nation by some thirty years, Aicher painted Munich as the "Games under the rainbow." Avoiding the red and gold of the Nazi dictatorship (save some minor use of the former in a bright, strident hue), the core colors of light blue and green, supported by silver and white, and supplemented by yellow, orange, dark green, blue, and occasionally even brown, defined the Munich palette. The Olympic colors were omnipresent in ever-changing combinations—from the official guide to occasional bands on the pylons and masts that held the stadium roof in place—and, most dramatically, arched above the closing ceremony in the form of a luminous plastic rainbow crafted at considerable expense by sculptor Otto Piene. (The original idea of incorporating a "light show" in the final moments of the Games was dropped in case it aroused "bad memories of the so-called cathedral of light from 1936.")[88] For Munich's chief designer, the rainbow "symbolized aesthetics in their ultimate form and appearance without losing a sense of the fleeting and playful" and offered visitors the chance to "experience humanity as a unified whole, as a model of society without violence or borders."[89]

For all this, Aicher's eye was drawn primarily to light blue and its supporting cast of green, white, and silver—his original memorandum to the OC in 1967 making no mention of the rainbow at all. The sky-blue shade in which the pictograms were drawn and the ill-fated Olympic security force *(Ordnungsdienst)* clad on the day of the terrorist attack had much to recommend it. Not only did opinion polls confirm it as Bavaria's most popular color (it featured heavily in the Land's flag), but as "the color of peace" and "the color of youth" it exuded social and political significance as well. Despite the yellow-and-black of the city's coat of arms (the Münchner Kindl, a girl wearing a monk's habit), Munich was widely known as "the white and blue capital" *(weißblaue Hauptstadt).* Aicher attributed this less to the flag than the region's landscape. As "the color of a shining sky," of lakes and alpine silhouettes, light blue was the very essence of Upper Bavaria. Under certain climatic conditions, especially when warm winds blow northward from Italy, Munich enjoys "clear bright days und a deep blue sky," which bathe the Alps in light blue and create an illusion of close proximity to the city.[90] These colors, as the organizers were wont to repeat—not always without arousing cynicism in foreign listeners—contrasted with the other dominant hues selected for the Games: the silvery white and the light green of the region's lakes, hills, and meadows.[91]

Significantly, white and blue were central to the southern German baroque. Although Aicher neglected to mention it to the OC in 1967, the historical reference would feature prominently in the designer's justification of his choice over subsequent years. For one, the baroque accentuated the contrast between Munich and its 1936 predecessor. Ignoring the inconvenient location of Wagner's spiritual home in the north of Bavaria, Aicher claimed that the "powerful dark colors of Bayreuth," "the pathos of opera," and the "pompous metaphysics of the [country's] bourgeoisie" characterized Berlin, while Upper Bavaria's abundant baroque—"charming village churches," "organs and spinets"—offered Germany an alternative mode of expression and self-representation.[92] For another, the compositional techniques and effects of the period's music bore a striking similarity to the designer's guiding principles—an implication overlooked in even the most recent Aicher scholarship.[93] Contrary to the modern notion of individual genius as the necessary precondition for great art, baroque culture emphasized the ability of the craftsman to follow and apply strict rules. As in Aicher's own work, the lightness and cheerfulness of baroque music derived from discipline and regularity.

Finally, the baroque helped justify the designer's disapproval of the retreat of modernity into museums and theaters and enhanced his understanding of the relationship between culture and society as one marked by daily life, public spheres, and visual markers. "Compared to the baroque culture of visual design and open spaces, as still evident to some extent in the shop signage and house decorations of Bad Tölz," he observed, "the street culture of Munich [was] in a sorry state."[94] This was not irreparable, however, and the Munich Games offered the perfect opportunity "to demonstrate the Munich of today: an open, youthful, lively city."[95]

Breathing the spirit of the baroque and imbibing the lifeblood of the Bauhaus, Aicher produced a simple but all-encompassing concept for the Games. In his presentation to the OC in 1967, he had warned that "an unambiguous decision-making hierarchy" and "increased authority for the design chief" would be necessary "to prevent a variable system losing its potency and ultimately disintegrating."[96] He protected this ruthlessly across the whole Olympic enterprise, threatening to resign on the rare occasions any aspect of it came under pressure, twice controversially finishing a task himself when not satisfied with the result of an open competition: the emblem (with von Manstein) and the official poster. With these two notable exceptions, which received only lukewarm public approval, his vision achieved critical acclaim.[97] It determined every aspect of the Games' aesthetic. "Printed matter, posters, brochures, tickets, mastheads, short television slots, flag arrangements, . . . insignia" all appeared in his "colors and formats." Personnel were supplied with jump- and safari suits, cut by the Parisian fashion designer André Courrèges, who had already supplied new uniforms for the city police, which were color coded by Aicher according to function (e.g., orange for the Games' technical personnel, red for referees and judges, etc.). The traditional Bavarian *Dirndl* (dress, blouse, and apron) was given a modern revamp in sky blue with white trim and worn, with matching makeup, by thousands of hostesses around the Olympic venues.

At the same time, Aicher's concept was all-embracing in its political ambition. While sharing Daume's desire to return sport and the Olympics to some notional origin of play, he believed in the power of design to create a real social utopia. Such ideas drew from the technocratic belief in feasibility and broader "discourse of democracy" *(Demokratiediskurs)* that were widespread among the "1945ers."

Like Ralf Dahrendorf and other commentators, Aicher sought to address the political deficits in a society that in many other respects had been dynamic in its modernization.[98] Like Vogel, whose political creed revolved around the concepts of participation, individual fulfillment, quality of life, social justice, and human dignity, he endeavored to take the notion of democracy beyond the realm of the state and its institutions, rooting it firmly in society and increasing the freedom and participation of the individual within it.[99] Following Jürgen Habermas's famous statement—"democracy can only come about in a society of mature and responsible citizens; which is why it is not possible under any random social preconditions, or indeed even under specific ones; rather, this free society is the condition itself"[100]—Aicher viewed design as a means to reduce, or even eradicate, authoritarian structures in education, work, leisure, and recreation.[101]

This sweeping vision would turn the Munich Olympics into a huge playground, in which spectators and athletes could interact freely and regardless of nationality, race, or creed.

BEHNISCH AND PARTNERS

That playground would require considerable work, however, before becoming physical reality. Although the possession of a brownfield site in common public ownership made the Olympics viable in the first place, the transformation of the Oberwiesenfeld in the north of the city presented a major challenge. Munich was characterized by a historical north-south divide. Against the affluent suburbs of the south, which opened out onto a rising landscape of lakes and alpine foothills, the north was dominated by working-class neighborhoods where social housing, homeless shelters, and displaced persons' living quarters jostled with industrial and sewage plants, military training grounds, and the city's landfill site. In this milieu, the 2.8-square-kilometer site had served a number of purposes since the eighteenth century, functioning variously as an army camp, parade ground, horse-racing track, and airfield for zeppelins and hot-air balloons. In 1931, it began to provide space for the city's first civilian airport, most famously receiving Daladier and Chamberlain on their way to preserve "peace in our time" in 1938. After the war, it blended with its drab surroundings, taking on ten million cubic meters of rubble from the allied bombing raids, which altered its contours, most notably producing a towering hill (Schuttberg) at its southeastern perimeter. A grim reminder of the recent past, the "rubble mountain," a hill on which natural growth eventually developed, came to be used as grazing pasture for sheep and a practice slope for winter sports enthusiasts. While no stranger to play, the Oberwiesenfeld of the mid-1960s, however, could hardly be described as playful. By 1972 its terrain would have to house a stadium, swimming pool, multipurpose gymnasium, practice facilities, media center, housing for some seven thousand athletes, and all in stunning surroundings.

But as Aicher noted in his paper to the OC in November 1967, concurrent with but independent of his own initial deliberations, the organizers had made good progress toward deciding on an architectural concept that would serendipitously "harmonize with the overall design and its intentions."[102] In 1967, the committee realized the city's preexisting plans to build a sports stadium on the site and decided to run an open competition for a set of venues fit to host the Olympics. A month before Aicher delivered his presentation, the jury had selected a winner, but was still debating the feasibility of its central features. The emergence of the Stuttgart practice Behnisch and Partners (B+P) from a field of 104 competitors was a greater "stroke of luck" than Aicher might have realized. Popularly credited with the design's success, Günter Behnisch, another "1945er," attended only a few of the initial meetings and was less involved than his subsequent reputation suggests.[103] Were it not for the enthusiasm of his young partner architect Fritz Auer (b. 1933), who had followed the Olympics avidly since collecting cigarette card albums of the 1936 Games as a child, the company would not have entered the field at all.[104] Until that point, the firm had concentrated on schools and universities. But Auer, Cord Wehrse, and Karlheinz (Carlo) Weber (b. 1934)—another partner who later took responsibility for modeling the surrounding landscape—produced a concept of such breathtaking novelty that it swept to an overwhelming victory in the final round (seventeen votes to two).[105] Other than Daume and eight politicians from the city, Land, and state, the jury, chaired by Egon Eiermann, included expert judges such as city-planner Herbert Jensen and local architect and caricaturist Ernst Maria Lang.[106]

B+P's design was based on the concept of "non-architecture" and impressed the judges for three reasons.[107] First, it met the tender's demand for a stadium to hold ninety thousand spectators (a capacity later reduced to eighty thousand) while avoiding any hint of monumentality.[108] In 1936, Werner March had been forced to give way on his Bauhaus-inspired plan to leave the stadium's inner workings exposed under a skeleton of steel, glass, and cement when Hitler refused to welcome the world to a "modern glass box" and instructed Reichsbaumeister Speer to intervene.[109] March's design was clad in limestone dug from "native German soil," supplemented with 136 columns and imposing cornices, and surrounded by monumental statues that celebrated the cult of the body. Rising majestically above a level axis, the Olympic stadium of 1936 made unambiguous statements about Germany's resilience, power, and will to succeed.[110] Munich would need to strike a different note and the architecture of the most recent Games in Tokyo provided a useful starting point. While Japan's freestanding modernist centerpiece, complete with a shell-like, steel suspension roof, seemed an unrepeatable

FIGURE 8. Willi Daume and Avery Brundage inspecting the architectural model of the main Olympic venues with the Olympic village on the right in 1969 (in the middle, Olympic press chief Hans "Johnny" Klein) (photo: Fritz Neuwirth, courtesy of Süddeutsche Zeitung Photo)

achievement, Kenzo Tange's combined venue for the gymnastics and swimming events sparked the imagination.[111] Taking up the bid's commitment to spatially compact Games, B+P's design avoided the inherent monumentality of solitary buildings by bringing the sporting venues close enough to be connected by a common element.

The innovative nature of that element, which connected the main stadium, the gymnastics arena, and the swimming pool, formed the second point of appeal for the jury. Like the entire submission itself, it came about almost by chance. While working on the design, Auer and Wehrse noticed a newspaper photograph of Gutbrod and Otto's pavilion being built for Montreal. Sensing an immediate synergy between the see-through, cable-net tent roof and their own burgeoning concept, they famously borrowed a pair of nylon stockings from Auer's wife to stretch over tiny sticks on their model.[112] The sweeping roof that joined the main venues underscored the lightness and movement of the team's design: even in

1967, Aicher approved of the way it "gave the impression of being playfully improvised."[113] In keeping with the materials used for many public commissions after the war, its transparency transmitted important messages about the Federal Republic and the stability of its democracy.[114]

Third, the architects made a virtue of the site's uneven landscape. In stark contrast to the dramatic vertical landmark of the 291-meter-high television tower—begun in early 1965 before the Games were even considered—the sports venues, including the Olympic stadium itself, would be integrated into existing or freshly accentuated hollows on the Oberwiesenfeld and grouped around the foot of the Schuttberg. B+P took their lead from the so-called earth stadiums, commonly built in Eastern Europe in the interwar and postwar years. Structures such as the sixty-thousand-capacity Śląski Stadium of 1927 had not only proved cost-effective but, when integrated into the hilly landscapes of Katowice, appeared much smaller than their actual size. With the stadium constructed in this way, as Auer once noted, "you don't walk up to a wall that frightens or haunts you. The main stadium suddenly opens up in front of you like a huge bowl instead of something you have to climb up to."[115] In Munich, moreover, the landscape in which it was embedded would be transformed into an Olympic park, the Schuttberg turned into an Olympic mountain, and the site covered with fresh pasture from the surrounding region to chime with the Alps that were visible from several points within it. Resonant in itself, the landscape's concealment of the stadium's technical components enhanced its aesthetic, and—as Carlo Weber put it—"left only the symbolic visible."[116]

Despite the margin with which they eventually won, B+P were skeptical about their submission's chances. Munich in the 1960s was becoming a hotbed of architectural and urban planning debate. Progressive thinking was evenly balanced by the "Heimat groups," traditionalist citizens' organizations dedicated to preserving the city's cultural integrity against the leveling forces of modernity. Associations such as the Bavarian Unification (Bayerische Einigung), the Cultural Circle for the Protection of Munich's Cityscape and Cultural Legacy (Kulturkreis zum Schutz des Münchener Stadtbildes und Kulturerbes), and the Munich Citizens' Council (Münchner Bürgerrat)—the latter founded in 1968 and boasting some twenty thousand members—maintained close ties to the CSU and the Bayernpartei and gave full and critical voice on architectural matters.[117] Moreover, the recent experience of losing the competition to build the city's Neue Pinakothek gallery had convinced B+P that their design would have stood a better chance in forward-looking Berlin.[118] Vogel might have joked to Daume that "Munich is no Bedouin town," but it was actually the mayor's intervention that saved the firm from early elimination.[119] It also enjoyed the full backing of the jury chair Egon Eiermann. With an impassioned speech at a crucial moment, Eiermann, who built the German pavilion in Brussels and ran the jury that handed the task to

FIGURE 9. Street view in the Olympic village (photo: Carsten Schiller)

Gutbrod and Otto for Montreal,[120] ensured that the modernist look of West Germany's representative buildings would continue at the Games.[121]

Despite such prestigious support, B+P, like Aicher, would have to overcome the resentment of professional rivals and local traditionalists. When awarding the prize in October 1967, the jury's caveat about the expandability of Otto's modest roof across vast spaces in Munich played into their opponents' hands.[122] In December 1967, a report by two professors from the city's Technical University deemed the roof impossible to construct, and the following January, B+P had to threaten legal action when the Olympia Baugesellschaft (OBG)—the sister body to the main committee entrusted with developing the Olympic sites and properties—asked third-placed Erwin Heinle and Robert Wischer (among others) to develop an alternative roof on the basis of a replica model.[123] Given the clear breech of the Association of German Architects' (Bund deutscher Architekten) rules, an out-of-court settlement was reached, the OBG having to stop their search for simpler solutions and Heinle and Wischer going on—controversially, as no competition ever took place—to build the comparatively uninspiring Olympic village.[124] The communal planning bureaucracy, however, continued to place obstacles in B+P's way by delaying the necessary permits whenever it could.[125]

B+P's influential backers in the OC and beyond eventually won the day, however.[126] Barely a week after the jury's initial verdict, Eiermann, a constant champion of the firm's intentions, addressed Munich's planning committee and persuaded its members to vote, with only one dissenting voice, in its favor.[127] As with Aicher, the *Süddeutsche Zeitung* advocated the plan at critical junctures,[128] describing it as "captivating" and hailing the outcome of the competition as "one hundred Olympic ideas but one poetic vision."[129] International experts such as New York structural engineers Severud and Associates (who had build the St. Louis Arch) and French architect René Sarger overturned local specialists' advice, maintaining, with misplaced optimism, that the roof would be less expensive than conventional alternatives.[130] Vogel and Aicher voiced their support, and Daume lobbied Franz Josef Strauß at national level. In June 1968, six months after winning the competition, B+P were given final permission to proceed.

Over time, the roof would continue to be as controversial as it was stunning. Most conspicuously, the tenfold rise in costs added grist to its detractors' mill and attracted broad swathes of public opinion to their cause. More surprisingly, however, Frei Otto's relation to the project gradually soured too. Eiermann had supported B+P's design as a means of consolidating Otto's international reputation as a master of light structures, writing to the architect himself in this vein.[131] Otto had publicly supported the company through the period of delays and advised Auer about the technical adaptation of his Montreal designs.[132] But the common assumption in architectural literature that Otto managed the roof is inaccurate.[133] Ultimate responsibility lay with a group of structural engineers under Auer, with Otto, as he freely admitted in a 1973 interview, playing a subordinate role.[134] Moreover, Otto insinuated somewhat malevolently that B+P had exploited the success of Montreal to win a competition he had decided not to enter himself.[135] Several factors lie behind the architect's evident disenchantment. For one, while his Montreal design was intended to provide cost-effective shelter from the continental climate of North America, its Munich equivalent became expensive and, he feared, would deter future clients from employing anyone associated with it. For another, while Montreal represented a temporary solution for a temporary event, Munich—both contributing to, and arising from debates about rising costs—increasingly devoted itself to matters of durability: the semipermanent Plexiglas tiles used on the Oberwiesenfeld pushed it beyond the light membranes and variable materials normally employed in Otto's designs. And most importantly, Aicher and Behnisch's appetite for symbolism went against the grain of his philosophy. A strict functionalist, who maintained that a building and its components should be defined exclusively in terms of their practical value, Otto rejected his collaborators' "eyeing up eternity."[136]

It was exactly this symbolic value, however, and the sheer scale of the technical expertise required to create it, that secured the stadium's place in the affection of the city and nation. Using eight thousand three-by-three-meter Plexiglas tiles to cover almost seventy-five thousand square meters, and holding a roof structure in

FIGURE 10. Detailed view of the Alexandra Young Olympic roof (photo: authors)

place with 436 kilometers of steel cables attached to fifty-eight cast-steel pylons, the Munich stadium was the most ambitious building project in the history of the Federal Republic.[137] Unprecedented as an architectural and engineering feat, it required the help of glaciologists and bacteriologists to determine the likely movement of snow and ice and the impact of fungal growth upon the plastic bearings.[138]

Frei Otto might have been commenting ironically when he mused: "It is a wonder of the world. . . . From the 'little' man to the powerful citizen, everyone is proud of this roof."[139] But his sarcasm captures precisely the warmth with which most Germans came to regard the stadium. Initially disgruntled at the rise in costs, Vogel asserted in 1970, for instance, that the Olympic site amounted to only 0.2 percent of the world's annual expenditure on weapons of mass destruction.[140] And having maintained a discreet silence on matters of local politics after his promotion to national level, the former mayor openly opposed FC Bayern Munich's plan at the end of the century to convert the stadium into a dedicated soccer arena.[141] For Vogel and the majority of public voices thirty years on, B+P's architecture stood as a unique and unalterable symbol of West Germany's postwar commitment to peace and democracy.

GÜNTHER GRZIMEK

The same was true of the Olympic Park as a whole, which was shaped by one of the country's few progressive landscape gardeners of the 1960s, Günther Grzimek (1915–96).[142] Taken together, the bid's promise to deliver "Spiele im Grünen" and B+P's ambitious designs demanded an innovative relation of buildings to their environs. As the architects noted: "The main idea behind the design [was] the notion of a crafted landscape. The elements that make up a landscape [were] superordinate in significance. The roof [was] to protect parts of this landscape, while the landscape [was] to flow underneath it."[143] Grzimek was well placed to master the task: a close colleague of Aicher's, he had become Director of the Garten- und Friedhofsamt of the city of Ulm in the late 1940s,[144] served as a member of the advisory board of the College of Design,[145] and collaborated successfully with Behnisch on the city's School of Engineering in 1963.[146] Working in tandem with B+P's Carlo Weber, Grzimek breathed the spirit of Aicher across the Olympic site.

A functionalist, like Aicher, who eschewed ornamentation and the ethereal claims of grand art, Grzimek devoted his career to humanizing the everyday experience of individuals in modern industrial society.[147] Using the natural environment to provide physical and mental recuperation from the pressures of life, Grzimek's parks offered contrasting spaces for privacy and openness, movement and rest.[148] His work typically molded robust green idylls from a panoply of natural elements: mountains, hills, valleys, slopes, ridges, plains, water, marshland, lawns, meadows, trees, groves, and bushes.[149] Curved naturally around its existing gentle contours, the Oberwiesenfeld nonetheless presented Grzimek and the B+P team with a tabula rasa from which new life could take shape. The creation of an entirely fresh 14.4 square-kilometer landscape (Geländemodellierung) involved moving some 2.2 million cubic meters of earth, including 350,000 cubic meters of soil for forty tons of grass seed, 3,100 large trees and thousands of smaller varieties and shrubs.[150] The result was a space of flexible and multiple possibilities for groups and individuals alike.[151]

But like Aicher, there was an important political dimension to Grzimek's thinking too—Munich's new park being designed to create a utopia in which the city's visitors and inhabitants could interact and communicate across social and linguistic barriers. It represented, as he noted shortly before his death in 1996, "an object of use for a democratic society," or even, as he suggested in 1973, the very zenith of democratization.[152] Completing a series of city spaces stretching back through the bourgeois park of the eighteenth-century English Garden to the absolutism of the seventeenth-century Nymphenburg Palace, the Oberwiesenfeld of 1972 presented a model of open access and participation.[153] Although less Hegelian in its original concept—B+P playing it safe in 1967 with Greek antiquity as their major frame of reference—the site offered a physical conceit to Grzimek's teleology.[154] A small stream transected the terrain and was dammed up to form a symbolically resonant lake at the heart of the site. Running from the English Garden it formed part of the Nymphenburg Channel and provided a physical connection to the nearby city center and its historical development from absolutism to democracy.[155]

Yet Grzimek's landscape sought not simply to convey democracy but to liberalize it as well. His Olympic Park—in keeping with Aicher's views and ideas about participatory democracy—intended to "loosen the constraints of social relations and produce freer, more 'playful' forms of communication."[156] Translated into the green environment, this meant that visitors were conspicuously invited to walk on the grass and pick the flowers. Notices announced, "Please walk on the grass!"[157] Although in retrospect somewhat contrived, these ideas were ahead of their time: another decade would pass before Grzimek could entitle a book *The Appropriation of the Meadow* and the relaxing of boundaries between paths and lawns became the norm in public spaces.[158]

Aesthetically, as well as politically and philosophically, the undulating landscape of the Oberwiesenfeld, which invited visitors to relax within a fluid harmony of natural and architectural elements, stood in stark contrast to the Olympic venues of 1936. These had been created, in fact, by Grzimek's teacher Heinrich Wiepking,[159] a leading figure in German landscape gardening before the war who, as an official in Himmler's Reich Commissariat for the Strengthening of Germandom, suggested the draining of the Soviet Pripet marshes to create "German peasant land" *(deutsches Bauernland)*.[160] Wiepking's Reichssportfeld sought to generate feelings of awe and admiration, and did so largely by allowing architecture to dominate nature: a large plateau of trimmed geometric lawns separated by ample avenues gave little natural coverage, save for trees and shrubs planted in neat rows, and the gaze of arriving spectators panned naturally along these axes to the stadium rising imposingly in front of them. On three sides, however, artificially created woods linked with already existing parklands in the south to transmit subtle messages about the German nation. As in his other 1936 commission—the wooded parkland of the Olympic village at Döberitz just outside Berlin—Wiepking sought to overcome the disjuncture between Volk and nature in modern civilization and urban life. In keeping with the cultural pessimism of the time, he aimed to heal the "sick city-dweller" *(kranker Stadtmensch)* with a return to German "soil" *(Mutterboden)*.[161] To this end, large poplars, seventy-year-old oaks, and thousands of white beeches, birches, larch-trees, and other local species were planted around the edges of the Reichssportfeld to create the illusion of ancient German parklands.[162] In the Olympic village, the water course was lowered by seven meters to give the impression of a natural continuation with the landscape.[163]

Wiepking might have believed that "the spirit and energies of the human races are distinguished from each other in the landscape with the sharpness of a knife," as he put it in the official SS newspaper *Das schwarze Korps* in 1944.[164] But Munich's landscape architect had little qualms about following his techniques. Just as Aicher had drawn his own conclusions about the power of the Nazis' corporate design in 1936, so too his close collaborator employed a similar strategy when dealing with the Olympic Park. Unlike his early mentor, of course, Grzimek wished to affirm, not reject, modernity, and sought not so much to provide an escape from city life as to integrate the park into the heart of the city.[165] This was achieved by planting lime trees, familiar from Munich's boulevards, along the pathways that transected it. To optimize their natural appearance, they were arranged—albeit via the minute accuracy of a draftsman's grid—in irregular patterns.[166] A similar illusion was employed on the rubble mountain, another obvious connection between the park and the city. Elevated from fifty to sixty-three meters with earth excavated from the construction of the stadium, the Schuttberg was lent an even more imposing air by the planting of dwarf pines and oaks, cut specially to size to accentuate the height of its naked peak.[167]

PROBLEMS

Aicher, Behnisch, and Grzimek worked in harmony of purpose, their close cooperation throughout protecting a shared and all-encompassing aesthetic vision. On the whole, they did so with the overwhelming support of the committee, but on the few occasions their concept appeared to be compromised, they refuted alternative suggestions with unwavering severity. In two instances in particular, they crossed swords with powerful local interests in debates that opened out onto sensitive issues of regional and national identity. The first related to beer and Bavaria, the second to monuments and the memory of war.

Unlike the PR department, which exploited the outside world's positive image of Bavarian traditions, Aicher remained circumspect about the region's peculiarities. While Klein's team, intent on maximizing the Games' appeal to key tourist audiences, advertised the delights of imbibing the city's favorite drink, Aicher cautioned against over-indulgence.[168] In a critical paper delivered to the committee for visual design in 1967, he included the Germans' fondness for beer-fuelled sociability in a list of negative stereotypes the organizers should aspire to overcome: "Over-organization, emotive self-presentation, demanding to be recognized as a major power, military nationalism, intensification of the Cold War, beer-fuelled German *Gemütlichkeit,* sauerkraut and Beethoven, demonstration of national sporting prowess."[169]

Beer and the particular traditions surrounding it in Munich played a negligible role in the preparation of the Games. The Oktoberfest, for instance—mentioned briefly in the bid document as evidence of the city's ability to cope with large numbers of tourists—scarcely entered the organizers' mind in the subsequent years. In the same spirit, other Bavarian customs were also marginalized or modernized. The Bavarian state government had to fund its own folkloric festival, and the *Dirndl* was brought up to date. A national rather than local event, Munich's Olympics were to speak of a new Germany, one to which regional traditions were perceived as having little to contribute. Some, as Aicher noted, might originally have pictured the Games "framed by the cheery sociability that comes from having a world-famous alcohol industry, hemmed in by national costume, menus of earthy regional dishes from a pre-bourgeois age, and the insignia of peasant folklore nestling between pine green and the indigenous colors of an old royal house that still [lay] deep in the soul"—but the chief designer's stylization of local color in his own unique palette had an immeasurably broader remit.[170] The 1972 Games—as an official press release soon after Aicher's paper to the OC emphatically stated—were to be "neither a 'Veal Sausage Olympics' nor 'Munich Games,'" but rather "'German Games with Munich coloring.'"[171]

Aicher's vision and the advertisers' slogans could work in tandem, of course—the one shaped the Games, the other, a means to an end, simply ensured that enough visitors came to appreciate them. When beer and Bavaria impinged on Aicher's design, however, trouble quickly ensued. When budgetary cuts forced the organizers to sell permission to local breweries to erect a series of beer tents on the site, Aicher responded, typically, by tendering his resignation and preparing a strongly worded statement for the press.[172] Held to ransom by its chief designer, the OC had to renege and the food-and-drink industry was pushed to the margins, in two tents at the southern tip of the park.[173] Even then, Aicher refused to make the food and drink practical for customers and objected to signs that advertised their location. The companies involved lost considerable sums, which eventually cost the committee some DM 350,000 in an out-of-court settlement.[174]

Aesthetic integrity was at the heart of another more public controversy surrounding the Olympic site in 1970 and 1971. In the spring of 1967, several months before the conclusion of the architectural competition, Vogel and Hohenemser had chosen the top of the rubble mountain as a fitting location for a monument commemorating the first atomic bomb. Stemming from the mayor's original idea to erect a Hiroshima fountain or equivalent in the city on the twentieth anniversary of 6 August 1945, the plan had secured funding from the city hall and the German Trade Union Congress (Deutscher Gewerkschaftsbund, DGB), and gone into commission with Richard Belling (1886–1972), a surviving member of the Weimar avant-garde. The awarding of the Games to the city lent particular poignancy to the gesture, Vogel seeing an opportunity to connect the city's own former destruction with a monument that would "place a certain accent on the Olympic site, warn competitors and visitors of the unavoidable horrors of nuclear war, and encourage peace."[175] Behnisch begged to differ, however, and vigorously opposed both the form of Belling's *Schuttblume* (Rubble Flower) and the position in which the city proposed to place it. Producing "a series of contorted, intertwined curvilinear shapes that unfolded organically from a narrow stem at its base," the "rough, metal form hint[ing] at the tons of buried metal and rubble from which it sprang,"[176] Belling seemed over the hill to Behnisch.[177] (He would in fact die a few months before the Games.) Neither, in Behnisch's view, did the artist belong on top of the hill: not only would the size of his sculpture (eventually reduced from twelve to six meters) gain disproportional prominence on the site, but it would also destroy the illusion of height that Grzimek and Behnisch had built into the rubble mountain. Most importantly, the architects' shaping of the hill into a new sculpture in its own right defied the placing of a rival object on its crown. "The entire mound," as Behnisch never tired of arguing, was "a sculpture,"[178] and "drawing attention to it via other aesthetic means," as Aicher added, "contradicted the ideology of the site as a whole."[179]

Vogel, Munich City Hall, and the trade unions proved harder to defeat than the local catering industries, however, and Daume, as usual, had to broker an uneasy compromise. After protracted negotiations, the monument was placed twenty-five meters south of the mountain's eastern ridge, in a position where it could not be seen from the main venues.[180] Rarely defeated, Vogel retaliated by blocking Behnisch's alternative for the top of the hill—a "negative sculpture" in the form of a hole, three meters in diameter, drilled 120 meters into the earth and topped with a bronze disk. American artist Walter de Maria's *Thought Hole (Denkloch),* which Behnisch championed as "articulating the art of the age,"[181] represented the perfect complement to the park's carefully constructed landscape: "a monumental work that nonetheless didn't scream monument in your face."[182] Despite supporting statements from the *Süddeutsche Zeitung,* the German art establishment, and experts from around the world, this piece of "non-architecture" proved one step too far for the city administration, the conservative local press, and Bavarian representatives on the OC and the OBG.[183] Even Brandt expressed incredulity.[184] After six months' debate, the *Denkloch* was shelved—officially due to estimated costs of DM 1.5 million—and Vogel paid Behnisch back with a share of his own disappointment.[185]

CEREMONIES

The most important event to take place in the Olympic Stadium was, of course, the opening ceremony. As Vogel noted at the start of the torch relay in Olympia, this was—and remains—the only regular moment in history when almost the whole of humanity gathered (virtually) in an act of common celebration. After six years of planning and packaging, the Federal Republic would be granted two hours in which to impress itself on a captive worldwide audience of up to one billion viewers. Despite the Olympic Charter's strict attention to details, such as the lighting of the flame or the swearing of oaths and playing of anthems, local organizers enjoyed sufficient latitude to inflect these rituals, or at least the setting in which they unfolded, with their own particular vision.[186] Although the 1972 official report later emphasized a lack of room for maneuver in the IOC's statutes,[187] the opening ceremony in Munich stands out, along with those of 1932 and 1936 and later the Hollywood spectacular of Los Angeles 1984, as the most innovative in Olympic history.[188]

Recent experience gave the Munich team much to consider but little to go on, however. In the early 1960s, Carl Diem had organized a ceremony to celebrate the completion of the West German–sponsored dig at Olympia, an extension of Hitler's excavations from 1936 through 1941. The official handover to the Greeks offered Diem a touchstone with Olympic history, quite literally, as he would be in eager attendance when the memorial pillar encasing de Coubertin's heart was moved to a new resting place within the site.[189] Asserting Germany's inalienable right to a large share of the Olympic ideal, he set about organizing an event for representatives of one hundred National Olympic Committees and twenty-five international sports federations in 1961, at which gymnastic displays by one hundred German and one hundred Greek students would be followed by the joint performance of a Greek folk dance, a 400-meter race run by the top six placed athletes over the distance from the Rome Olympics, readings from Pindar, and a lecture by Swiss professor Carl Jacob Burckhardt.[190] Despite inviting Burckhardt to lighten the Teutonic tone, the proceedings represented one of the final, unadulterated acts of the "German Olympic imagination." Diem consulted music experts about playing the fanfare from the 1936 Games, either unnamed or transformed into a new composition, and strove above all to achieve a "simple, monumental form."[191]

The recent Olympics set equally inappropriate precedents for Munich too. Although the modesty of Helsinki 1952 ("an unforgettably dignified celebration"), the "open-air massed display" choreographed by Walt Disney for the Winter Games in Squaw Valley 1960, and the releasing of ten thousand balloons by schoolchildren at Tokyo 1964 pointed Munich's organizers in the right direction, opening ceremonies by and large lived off pomp and pathos.[192] Just years before Munich began planning, Rome and Tokyo had regressed toward the magnitude of Berlin, with an "overwhelming musical program of gigantic choirs" and "blaring military bands," and the 1968 Games did little to change the tone.[193]

As the Germans' exhaustive study of the final Games before their own clearly demonstrates, Mexico City was characterized by three factors, which held little appeal: monumentality, nationalistic enthusiasm, and disorganization.[194] Only half an hour before the opening, spectators were treated to the sight of lawnmowers moving at full pelt around the field and the sound of "marching music blasting out of loud speakers." The Mexican national anthem, announced by gun salutes, was sung with gusto by the home crowd, which broke into chants of "Viva Mexico" and rendered the music accompanying the entry of the teams inaudible. Although continually interrupted by mighty drum rolls, the marching music encouraged some teams to parade in step. As in 1936, a recording of de Coubertin's voice was played over the loudspeakers, and the Olympic flag was carried in by ten uniformed marines. Despite the distraction of gun salutes and balloons, the athletes grew restless with the symphonic-type recordings of Mexican folk music and unraveled from their ranks to take photographs of events around them. When the torch arrived, the final runner had to push her way through scrums of sportsmen, and after the lighting of the flame and the swearing of the oath, many of the ten thousand doves were unfit to fly.[195] The *Gazette de Lausanne* described it all as "*une fête froide dans un stade chaud*"—a "long-winded and wearying" ceremony, as Vogel commented to Damme—in which "no-one so much as dared to touch the sacrosanct protocol that was beginning to look very antiquated."[196]

Daume hardly needed Vogel's prompt, having begun to think about the Munich opening almost two years before Mexico. In that time, he had made excellent progress toward reinvigorating Olympic rituals for a modern audience. Meeting three times between January 1967 and March 1968, a working party ("Sport and Culture") of the DSB had set itself the goal of making Munich "a break with tradition that [would] lead the way for future Games."[197] Despite some mustiness—Daume still harbored hopes of inviting Nobel Prize winners to deliver lectures in the Olympic Stadium (like Sven Hedin in Berlin)—the group worked with progressive zeal toward articulating the bid's major pledges in ceremonial form. (Two years later, they would describe the arts program as "hopelessly outdated.")[198] Werner Körbs, Rector of the Deutsche Sporthochschule in Cologne, led the way, critiquing his predecessor Diem and stressing the need "to be modern and in touch with the times." Guido von Mengden, a leading member of Diem's original team who had managed, successfully if not uncontroversially, to rehabilitate himself under Daume's patronage in the Federal Republic (see chapter 3), agreed that "the cultural program could only consist of those Olympic ideas that retained some value in the world of today." And Kai Braak, senior producer at the Hessisches Staatstheater, argued, with one eye on the recent resurgence of the right-wing NPD, that the "Olympics [would] have to be decidedly anti-nationalistic (even anti-national)." The central ideas and phrases from these early meetings—"openness to the future," "cheerful playfulness"—would function as leitmotifs over the following years.

By early 1968, the parameters had already been set. Treading gingerly around elements of a nationalistic or militaristic nature, the ceremony was to be characterized by "traditional values adapted to the present," the "cheerfulness and joy of play," and "stripped of inappropriate pathos and pseudo-sacred elements that no longer sport to the youth of the [time]."[199] Although tame for the spirit of the age (see chapter 5), such ideas were revolutionary in Olympic circles, as evidenced by the reaction of the Greek NOC, to whom the words just cited were addressed. Asked by Daume in 1971 to remold aspects of the flame-lighting ceremony in Olympia in order to bring the tradition in-line with the forthcoming event in Munich, the Greeks took a year to reply and ultimately declined to alter a well-worn script that included a high priestess's prayer to Zeus.[200] But in Munich, plans for modernization met largely with unanimity as a series of committees and subcommittees were convened over several years under Daume's watchful eye. While it is neither possible nor desirable to detail every discussion here, it can safely be said that the opening ceremony in Munich was the product of broad cooperation and consensus.[201] On the whole, this process was built around interlocking and overlapping groups, working with a well-grounded understanding of what needed to emerge. Vitally, the tone was set not by national politicians or high-ranking artists, but by members of the national sports body seeking to bring Olympic protocol up to speed with the modern world. Conveniently, their deliberations harmonized perfectly with the overall strategy for the Games, and their early conclusions dovetailed with the established working processes of the OC. The DSB's recommendations fed into the arts committee, which in turn invited Guido von Mengden to give a paper.[202] With the board's blessing, a further group was established to concentrate on the ceremonial aspect of the Games (Working Party on the Opening and Closing Ceremonies), and was numerically and vocally dominated by the West German sports community.[203] Walter Umminger—not yet disgraced by the *Olympisches Lesebuch*—took the reigns from von Mengden.[204] Along with authors Günter Grass and Reinhard Raffalt and architect Paulo Nestler, Franz Baur-Pantoulier advised on choreography and was later joined on music by Wilhelm Killmayer, a former student of Carl Orff who was noted for his "rhythmic energy," "ingenious insights" and "fresh, innovative formulations."[205]

Although largely in agreement with the subcommittee's decisions, Killmayer found himself restricted by the agenda it had set itself, confiding to a colleague shortly after his appointment in 1970: "I don't have it easy here. A lot seems to have been decided already and everyone is trying hard, at all costs, to avoid causing offense."[206] His initial disquiet was certainly symptomatic of a broader unease about musicians. On the one hand, Daume hardly quailed at the compromised careers of established composers: in one of his first major articles on the Munich Games, he praised Richard Strauß's "musically outstanding Olympic hymn" from 1936, hoping that it might be played for the first time again in Mexico; and he valued Carl Orff and his pupil Werner Egk, who had assumed prominent roles under National Socialism (including Diem's Festspiel), but emerged largely unscathed in the new Republic.[207] On the other, he was wary of the music fraternity's reluctance to engage with the more popular feel the Munich festival hoped to engender. Meetings of composers and a regular working party on music (Arbeitskreis Musik), which included Orff, Egk, and von Karajan, pleaded strongly for national participation, a competition to commission "serious music," and the retention of de Coubertin's favorite classical melody, Beethoven's Ninth Symphony, which they envisaged performing with three Munich orchestras.[208] Daume played the musicians as he did the IOC with regard to the arts festival, allowing them to continue their deliberations while pushing ahead himself with the other committees and sending interim reports directly to the board. Given the large number of sports representatives at this highest level, he met with little resistance. Other colleagues, moreover, did not share his magnanimous attitude to the previous lives of certain composers. When it came to advertising an open competition for a new Olympic fanfare, a process, Daume argued, that should "minimize the intellectual side of things,"[209] the organizers considered placing an age limit of forty or requiring entrants to give their date of birth to prevent it being won by a "composer with an incriminating past."[210] (In the end, a fifty-strong jury on the weekly Second German Television sports program *Aktuelles Sportstudio* selected an erstwhile close collaborator of Bert Kaempfert, Herbert Rehbein, who later had to defend himself against the charge of plagiarizing the U.S. group Fifth Dimension's 1968 hit "Up, up and away.") Unlike design elites, therefore, who confected the look of the Games largely uncontested, music elites were treated with suspicion. Highbrow sounds were welcome and encouraged in the concert hall but not in the stadium, and dubious pasts could potentially cause international embarrassment.

"Easy and melodic," an "expression of middle-of-the road German tastes," Rehbein's winning fanfare was perfectly in tune with the score for the opening ceremony.[211] In principle, as the organizers decided at an early stage, Munich would overwrite the customary texture of the event with something akin to a "musical." Less operatic and militaristic, it would be "natural," "swaying," and "optimally integrated with the visual elements" of Aicher and Behnisch's design and architecture.[212] In practice, the organizers would need to apply for certain changes in regulation at the IOC and then drown out any elements that proved nonnegotiable with the exuberance of their own show. Their twofold approach was largely successful. Aicher's plan to break up the static blocks of parading teams by splitting them into spirals in the stadium field as well as his desire to rid the ceremony of doves were rejected by Lausanne. But many innovations made it off the drawing board.[213] Gun salutes were used more sparingly than in Mexico and cannon fire avoided altogether; President Heinemann would have been greeted by alpenhorn players had his early arrival not taken them unawares and prompted the playing of the national anthem; the last leg of the relay was completed by a little-known eighteen-year-old German athlete (Günter Zahn) in pristine white, supported by four international Olympians;[214] the oath was sworn for the first time by a young female athlete; the second rendition of the national anthem, which traditionally followed it, dropped; the great bell, a 1936 feature that had found its way into the architectural competition and the OBG's considerations for some time,[215] was replaced by a Dutch-manufactured *Glockenspiel* that entertained crowds arriving at the stadium with easy-listening classics such as "Kalinka," "Jingle Bells," and the German Volkslied "Muß I denn," sung around the time by Elvis Presley; and the program ended with Polish composer Krzysztof Penderecki's specially commissioned electronic version of Pindar's "Olympic Truce." Bookended, thus, by different shades of modernity and international reconciliation, the ceremony featured a performance by some 2,800 brightly clad Munich schoolchildren dancing in circles to a new Carl Orff setting of the Middle English "Sumer is icumen in" and "spontaneously" handing their toy bows and posies to the nearest athletes.[216] Nothing could have been further from the bombastic formalism of 1936 or the Eastern bloc's formidably drilled gymnastics displays, a comparison Daume had feared in the early stages of planning.[217]

As Orff's participation shows, the country's serious composers were not entirely neglected, even those who had contributed significantly to 1936. (Egk was also invited to write a version of the Olympic hymn but declined.)[218] But the overall sound of the event, determined by the melodies that accompanied the lengthy parade of nations, came from a different quarter. Realizing the need to lighten the tone, Killmayer approached Alfred Goodmann, an American living in Germany with a wealth of experience in the development of the modern music scene.[219] Goodmann sifted through North American college songs, musical hits, and melodies from Latin America, discarding tunes with political connotations, until Daume chose to contact Kurt Edelhagen, the leader of the Westdeutscher Rundfunk's eponymous "Light Orchestra," and was immediately wooed, not least by the station's willingness to cover costs. On hearing the news of Daume's independent actions, the working party on music threatened to resign en masse, but the OC president held his ground, winning his closest colleagues over to the notion that "the sound rather than the melody [was] the key" and that Edelhagen's musicians delivered "the [decisive] elements of color, rhythm, and cheerful play."[220] Plundering Goodmann's groundwork, three members of Edelhagen's band wrote "American swing" with a "subliminal effect," and on 26 August 1972, the conductor and a selection from his orchestra, dressed in Aicher's Olympic sky blue, provided the defining sound of the Games.[221] As the nations came in, they heard their national styles and characteristics gently stereotyped: Turkey to "Turkish Delight," Hungary to "Gypsy Love," Cuba to "Habana alegre." Edelhagen's light jazz and swing hardly caught the beat of the contemporary hit parade, nor did it reach the dizzying heights of Aicher and Behnisch's internationally renown design. It was, rather, a version of what middle-aged, middle-class men thought would appeal to the younger generation. (Daume's heart lay in an unrealized three-week festival, "The Most Popular Songs of the World," with Frank Sinatra, Bert Kaempfert, and Mireille Mathieu.)[222]

Nonetheless, it made massive strides in Olympic history and was readily accepted and praised as an integral part of the Games' fabric.

As with the design concept, however, certain Bavarian elements proved difficult to integrate. One reason for this was the chance employment of Edelhagen. From an early stage, the organizers had thought it desirable to include local folklore as a way of lightening the rituals, suggesting even that Egk might modernize suitable music from the region.[223] The working party on music had considered "profiling Bavarian folk music" and intended to discuss "involving traditional Bavarian groups" with the OC when Edelhagen was appointed without prior warning. Personal pique aside, their major objection to the light entertainment concerned "the complete withdrawal" of folkloric elements from it, and despite the backing of the Bavarian Ministry of Education and Culture, which pleaded the Land's case with Daume, their worst fears were realized.[224] Apart from the unfortunate alpine horns, the only overtly Bavarian aspect in the final script came from the Vereinigte Bayerische Trachtenkapelle aus Bernau und Ruhpolding and a group of Peitschenknaller (or "Goaßlschnalzer") which played and danced along with Mexican mariachis as the Olympic flag was passed from one mayor to the other. But even these had been controversial. The Trachtenkapelle had been inserted after Vogel, normally so willing to embrace Bavarian tradition, had objected to the participation of another traditional group, the Stadtpfeifer. When Vogel continued, without public explanation, to protest against the Peitschenknaller as well, choreographer Baur-Pantoulier sought support from confidants. August Everding (Intendant der Münchener Kammerspiele) speculated that the mayor might have misconstrued the whipping as a violent act, and author Reinhard Raffalt wondered if he harbored some strange association with concentration camps.[225] Neither of them—like Carl Orff who offered to raise the matter with him personally—shared the mayor's reservations, and the Peitschenknaller eventually made it into the stadium.

Given Vogel's continued refusal to discuss the issue, it is impossible to test his contemporaries' interpretations.[226] Even if motivated by concerns about personal image or professional ambition, the mayor's reluctance to surround himself with whipping and whistling points again to a residual aesthetic embarrassment about Bavaria's backward and/or militaristic image: at the 1958 World Fair, the Foreign Office had been sensitive about the adverse effect a Bavarian beer tent playing marching music could have on international audiences.[227] Certainly, both Bavaria and the Bundeswehr took a backseat in the opening ceremony. The Olympic flag was entrusted to the West German gold-medal-winning rowing team from Mexico City, and the band of the Bundeswehr only played the short Olympic fanfare. Nonetheless, early fears in the Ministry of the Interior that "excluding the army from its traditional role on the very first occasion the Games were being held in

FIGURE 11. Bavarian folk music at the opening ceremony, 26 August 1972 (photo: Sven Simon, courtesy of Süddeutsche Zeitung Photo)

federal territory [would] hinder its integration into society" proved exaggerated.[228] The army, without whose help no Olympics of the era could have functioned, was subtly but definitely visible throughout the Games. Quite apart from their massive contribution to the logistics of infrastructure and transport, soldiers accompanied hostesses to medal ceremonies and raised the flag for the victors. Dressed not in the standard, stylized *Dirndl* but in traditional varieties, chosen specially to reflect the diversity and customs of the region, attractive young ladies joined uniformed representatives of the national army, in outlying locations and in the Olympic stadium itself, to celebrate the ceremonial aspect of the Games at the end of each competition.[229] Bavaria and the Bundeswehr were not denied their rights in Munich. But at the opening ceremony, the single most important moment of the whole endeavor, their input was minimized.

. . .

The unique amalgam of performance, design, and architecture that characterized the Games proved an instant success, which few beyond the organizers had dared believe possible. In response to the opening ceremony, the West German sports-reporting agency *Sportinformationsdienst (sid)* wrote an editorial that captured the surprise and delight:

> For years Willi Daume has been promising everyone, the youth of the world included, cheerful Games. To do that took as much courage as it did to build the crazy roof, since, as we know, we don't do light-heartedness very well. The least skeptical response his plans provoked was: "That sounds great." *[Das kann ja heiter werden.]* Which can mean a lot of things in our language. And now, against all expectations, he has succeeded. . . . No—you have to hand it to Daume: he pulled it off. And if it wasn't good enough for some people, we'd have to say—we don't do more cheerful![230]

The contrast to Bonn's drab and worthy plans for Montreal 1967 could not have been greater, and politicians of all political hues (Genscher, Barzel, Kiesinger, Scheel) lined up to give euphoric sound-bites. Josef Neckermann confessed, "I didn't believe it was possible—but it really impressed me," and an Olympic hostess called Brigitte Maibohm, whose husband had delivered the radio commentary for the 1936 Games, simply dissolved in tears. Even potential cynics concurred. Eberhard Vogel, an East German soccer player and bronze-medal winner from the Tokyo Olympics remarked, "It was overwhelming. . . . It gave me a really warm feeling," and Richard Mandell, whose scholarly monograph on 1936 had only recently been published, confessed to being overcome with emotion against his better judgment.[231] The architectural ensemble and light-touch performances had achieved their desired effect. An Australian sailing competitor noted: "What host nation can better that in future?" Ludwig Erhard simply stated: "I'm glad today

FIGURE 12. Willi Daume applauding Avery Brundage at the opening ceremony (photo: Sven Simon, courtesy of Süddeutsche Zeitung Photo)

that I said yes to Munich's application in 1965."[232] And Willy Brandt, the beneficiary of his foresight, was grateful that the world had seen a "bit of 'modern Germany.'"[233]

However, Brandt was the only commentator, perhaps, to strike a discordant note as well. When asked if 1972 represented "a transformation in German nature," he shimmied around the invitation to compare Munich with Berlin, noting, as the *Frankfurter Rundschau* reported, that "attempts at comparative analysis like these" only meant something "in intellectual circles." The tenor of Brandt's reply, of course, sold West Germany's Olympic enterprise short. As this chapter has shown, the whole fabric of Munich, from design to performance, was the product—to a greater or lesser degree—of intellectual elites that took their cue from 1936. Design and architectural elites prepared the ground, artistic elites and sports functionaries (marginalizing the classical music establishment) brought it to life. In all their endeavors, 1936 was both foil and inspiration. Aicher, whose vision glued the concept together, informed himself of the Nazis' techniques to show the world they had long since departed; Guido von Mengden, a member of Diem's original team, drew on his experience again to capture the mood of the day; and Günther Grzimek lowered plains and planted trees like his teacher before him in 1936. From a quite different philosophical base, Aicher, Behnisch, and

FIGURE 13. Chancellor Willy Brandt receiving the painter Max Ernst in Willi Daume's villa near Munich, where Brandt resided during the Games (photo: Detlef Gräfingholt, B 145 Bild—F037597–004, courtesy of Bundesarchiv)

Grzimek produced a *Gesamtkunstwerk* that both rivaled Berlin and stood alongside it as the only Games of the modern era to fulfill the founder's original vision of an organic Olympic whole. Munich's modernist memory was hardly bought at the cost of a "declining consciousness of the Nazi past," as has been suggested.[234] Its architecture, design, and landscaping, rather, produced a sophisticatedly constructed site of reflection and self-reflection.

It would be wrong (as even in the latest scholarship) to assume that 1972 drew its lifeblood from the change of government 1969.[235] Sanctioned and encouraged by Daume, a member of the CDU, design elites all but sketched out perfect "SPD Games" before the end of the Grand Coalition. Brandt, one might even argue, had been fortunate. Through their various committees and expert panels, the Munich organizers remained faithful to the progressive industrial design culture that had served the country's image so well in the 1950s and 1960s, and eschewed the heaviness that dogged its presentation in Montreal. In conservative Bavaria, these were far from foregone conclusions. *Heiterkeit,* a term used by the DWB in Brussels, determined the day, and the national sports body, keen to revitalize an Olympic ritual fast running out of time in the modern world, readily accepted the challenge. By 1972, many elements had come together at the right time to fit the changing political climate. In the late 1960s, however, it was not just Bavarian reactionaries who sounded their disapproval of the organizers' decisions; young people around the world found their voice as well before the decade was out. Perhaps it was this critical constituency that Brandt had in mind when completing his side-step around 1936 in the *Frankfurter Rundschau:* "There was a time when we systematically aimed to make ourselves popular. But today there's no way we should conclude: 'Let's all be systematically cheerful now!' "[236] As the next chapter will show, in the years before the Games, the youth of the world wholeheartedly agreed.

5

After "1968"

1972 and the Youth of the World

If the smooth initial handling of Munich's Olympic project resulted from the consensual tone or "deideologization" that characterized West German national politics in the mid-1960s, its execution in finer detail would be troubled by forces of an unpredictable nature before the decade was out. The Mexico Games proved ominous. Were it not for the dubious decision of a thick-skinned government and the International Olympic Committee (IOC) to carry on regardless, the 1968 festival would have been ruined by radical politics. On 2 October 1968, just ten days before the opening ceremony, a summer of violent clashes between students and police culminated in the Tlatelolco Massacre, which caused 260 deaths and 1,200 injuries within a stone's throw of the Olympic sites.[1] Exploiting the presence of international journalists, the protesters chanted: "We don't want Olympic Games! We want a revolution!"[2] Once underway, the Games were dominated by politics and are remembered as much for the Black Power salute of the African-American medalists Tommie Smith and John Carlos as for the warmth of the Mexican people and the extraordinary altitude-assisted performances of athletes such as Bob Beamon.

In 1968, of course, revolution was not the sole preserve of Mexican students. Across vast tracts of the Western world, "the cultural eco-system," as Tony Judt has recently put it, "was evolving much faster than in the past. The gap separating a large, prosperous, pampered, self-confident and culturally autonomous generation from the usually small, insecure, Depression-scarred and war-ravaged generation of its parents was greater than the conventional distance between age groups."[3] In Western Europe, a rapidly expanding education system propelled huge numbers of young people into a tertiary sector hopelessly under-equipped for the speed of cultural change, fomenting discontent. When events came to the boil, they were sustained by a common, heady mix of theory, sexual liberation, and the justification of violent means, but marked as well by distinct local inflections. In Germany, specifically, nascent unease with the older generation's supposed amnesia about the recent past became acute. Not only did the Mitscherlichs' psychoanalytical account of the nation's unwillingness to recognize individual responsibility make it onto almost every student bookshelf (*Die Unfähigkeit zu trauern,* The Inability to Mourn, 1967), but radical campus leaders vehemently placed the blame on the young Federal Republic, a system they viewed as an anaesthetized, Americanized offshoot of the consumerist West. From the immediate perspective of the Munich organizers, this unexpected return of ideology transformed the 1972 Olympics into contested territory. How exactly were they to organize an event, defined famously since the days of de Coubertin as a celebration for the "youth of the world," when its chief participants had become distinctly disaffected? And how, in a national context, could "modern Germany" be adequately represented when the country was changing and challenging itself at a rapid rate? These were just some of the questions that faced the Organizing Committee (OC) as it entered its key phase of preparation in 1968.

In retrospect, as Judt also notes, "the political geography of the Sixties can be misleading," "the solipsistic conceit of the age—that the young would change the world by 'doing their own thing' "—proving ultimately "an illusion."[4] But this does not mean the mood of unrest was not keenly sensed by participants at the time, nor treated with any less urgency by those against whom their actions were directed. It is also clear that the demand for change, at first expressed with belligerent intent, was not immutable but changed itself over time, intensifying in some areas, modulating and dissipating in others. Even if many of the key decisions about the particular form the Games would take had been reached before the events of 1968; even if the mindset of influential organizers proved compatible with the emerging spirit of the age; and even if some of the most aggressive opposition to the Olympics among critical German youth had all but blown out by the late summer of 1972, the ways in which the organizers engaged—fully, partially, or in censorial fashion—with the intellectual and social climate over time is a crucial element in the narrative of the Games. Just as the Munich Olympics should not be reduced to a mere Social Democratic Party (SPD) pageant, it would be misleading to view their relaxed atmosphere simply as a reflex of "1968." Visitors to the Olympic Park might have been encouraged to "walk on the grass" and "pick the flowers" but, in actual fact, the "spirit of '68" stood in complex relation to the Games. The culture of 1968—like the SPD's election victory with which it was inextricably linked—certainly influenced them, but the ways in which it did so were not always obvious.

WEST GERMAN YOUTH

In the Federal Republic, as elsewhere, the unrest of 1968 did not alter the system of government. Rather, the experiences of those years condensed, radicalized, and accelerated cultural and lifestyle changes that had been evolving subterraneanly since the beginning of the "long 1960s" in the wake of social and economic developments brought about by the "Golden Age" of Western capitalism.[5] Rejecting middle-class parental values, young people espoused a range of alternatives, which invariably involved a renouncement of traditional worldviews imposed from above, the return of ideology in the guise of New Left thought, and increased political participation both within and outside the system of representative democracy.[6] Concurrently, the late 1960s witnessed the rise of hedonistic lifestyles among young people, which frequently clashed with the fundamental Olympic tenets *citius—altius—fortius* and challenged the performance principle *(Leistungsprinzip)* characteristic of men such as Daume and Vogel.

There is no need here to chart the development of the so-called extraparliamentary opposition (APO) that crystallized in protest against the perceived hyperconsensus of the Grand Coalition and its emergency laws between 1967 and 1969. But the effects of the troubles on the city of Munich are certainly worth noting. Though not a major theater of confrontation, the future Olympic city was no backwater either. While the frequency and scale of its demonstrations lagged some way behind those in Frankfurt and West Berlin, the "Easter riots," which erupted after the assassination attempt on Rudi Dutschke in April 1968, took a particularly unfortunate turn in the Bavarian capital. As more than fifty thousand protesters fought with twenty-one thousand policemen across the Federal Republic in the worst episode of civil unrest since the early 1930s, Munich, surprisingly, witnessed the only civilian deaths.[7] An Associated Press photographer and a student lost their lives in a street battle in front of the local newspaper distribution center of the right-wing Springer Press in Schwabing, half-way between the city-center and the Olympic venues.[8]

Although these events were to inform the OC's approach to the Games, and in particular the security measures surrounding them, the organizers' main task was not to deal directly with 1968 itself, but rather its complicated fallout among different categories of West German youth. The eventual collapse of the student movement and APO in 1969 led to a spectrum of new political and cultural developments within the younger generation. Generally, these came to be reflected in the Games, either in the concessions the organizers made or, more vaguely, as a result of their attempt to figure out the cohort's understanding of the Olympics. The developments with which the organizers had to wrestle included the emergence of the so-called K-groups on the fringe, the return of others to conventional political participation, and the readiness of others still—the majority, in fact—to combine a critical but nonradical habitus with the external trappings and hedonistic lifestyles exemplified by the 1968ers.

The organizers were troubled least by the K-groups—such as the KPD/AO, KPD, KPD/ML, and the Basic Workers' Groups for the Rebuilding of the Communist Party (Arbeiterbasisgruppen für den Wiederaufbau der kommunistischen Partei)—on the far left of the spectrum. Rather than rechanneling their energies into conventional politics or turning to terrorist action like the Tupamaros, the Red Army Faction, or the Movement 2 June—these small sect-like political cells adhered to a variety of views from Maoism and Stalinism to Leninism, Trotskyism, anarchism, and syndicalism, and drew their inspiration from the Russian and Chinese revolutions.[9] Devoting themselves to the establishment of authoritarian cadre parties, they waited in readiness for the violent overthrow of the government. While—as we shall see—their demonstrations kept the authorities on their toes during the Games, their overall impact on the shaping of the Munich event remained slight. Much the same can be said of the newly founded GDR-sponsored German Communist Party (Deutsche Kommunistische Partei, DKP) and its youth organization, the Socialist German Workers Youth (Sozialistische Deutsche Arbeiterjugend, SDAJ).

By contrast, a larger imprint was left by the section of the 1968 movement that, in Dutschke's famous phrase, embarked upon the "long march through the institutions." In the immediate aftermath of 1968, the SPD saw its ranks swell by tens of thousands of new members—particularly through its youth organization, the Young Socialists (Jusos)—who played an important role in sealing Brandt's election victory in 1969. Having involved themselves decisively in major political change, the Young Socialists sought to hold the chancellor to his promise of "daring more democracy." Swept up in this ever-enveloping discourse, the Olympic organizers increasingly inscribed the notion of wider public participation into the blueprint for the Games. In Hans-Jochen Vogel, this offshoot of the 1968 movement could ostensibly count on a sympathetic ear. He empathized with their discontent, reading it as a symptom of the problems of "affluent societies" in the West—a view which affected him throughout his time in office and, most notably, informed his agenda for urban regeneration. Typically, in a speech delivered to students on the Königsplatz a few days after the "Easter riots," he interpreted the unrest as an anxious reaction to the accelerated development of modernity. As a conservative and pragmatic Social Democrat, the mayor accepted the need for political and social reform while drawing the line at radical left-wing adventurism and the use of violence.[10]

Not long before the Games, however, this rejection of extreme leftist policies was to impact Munich City Hall directly. Nationally, the Young Socialists had been concentrating on shunting their party back to the unambiguous left-wing position of its pre-Bad-Godesberg days and forcing the newly elected Lib-Lab coalition to implement radical socialist reforms.[11] In early 1971, Vogel came under pressure to commit to a radical agenda before the 1972 council elections, when he was likely to secure a third term in office. When difficult negotiations between the left and right wings of the local SPD failed to reach a compromise, Vogel—perhaps with characteristic opportunism—declined to run again at the beginning of 1972, becoming leader of the Bavarian SPD instead and rapidly winning promotion to federal construction minister *(Bundesbauminister)* in Brandt's second cabinet after the general election in November.[12] He was succeeded in Munich by Georg Kronawitter, another pragmatic Social Democrat, who triumphed in the local vote in June 1972. Thus, just two months before the Games, radical politics were instrumental in removing one of the key architects of the event before his moment of glory. Although retaining his position as vice president of the OC, Vogel attended the Games as a guest rather than an official—and need not, after all, have fretted about appearing on the world stage with Bavarian folk troupes.

Like the K-groups, therefore, the Young Socialists occupied the organizers as the Games were taking shape. But neither formed the primary focus. The former were too marginal or dragonfly in lifespan, the latter, though important, were overshadowed by the sheer transformations in everyday life that were eagerly accepted and pursued by the majority of young people regardless of their political orientation. From the questioning of adult authority to pronounced sartorial and musical choices, a dominant mode of behavior emerged. This large amorphous group of newly invigorated and legitimated youth formed an essential audience for the Games. Without their support, the Olympics could not succeed, and the organizers felt obliged to make concessions, catering to their hedonism and setting up light and happy youth events such as the Olympic Youth Camp and the "Avenue of Games" (Spielstraße).

As with the difficult legacy of 1936, coping with the no less repressible present was far from straightforward. In key organizational phases, much remained unpredictable. "The youth of today is restless," Daume proclaimed to the annual organizers' assembly in 1969, "we find ourselves in an age of upheaval, sometimes of confusion and experimentation, an age without a binding framework. Our conception of the Games is not blessed with the equilibrium and calm it would have had in previous times. We don't yet know how things will be in 1972."[13] At the point of delivery, too, much proved contradictory. As a somewhat downcast PR department noted in its assessment of secondary school pupils in March 1972: "Our experiences in schools are depressing. Like almost all spheres of youth, this one as well is dominated by a minority, which is always geared to be 'against things.'"[14] Even if such negative feelings could be attributed to the influence of a small minority, it is clear that much had changed since 1966, when 93 percent of sixteen to twenty-one year olds had voiced unequivocal support for the Games.[15] At the same time, however, the PR team experienced little problem in enthusing teenage members of sports clubs and associations, and these became a natural and eagerly receptive group for ticket promotions. Many other young people who visited Munich were also swept away by the energy of the event. Werner Rabe, then a twenty-one-year-old reporter for the provincial *Waldeckische Zeitung,* now head of sport at Bayerischer Runkfunk, was overwhelmed by a feeling of his native country "at long last having arrived on the international stage," noting simply: "Everyone had a bloody good time in Munich."[16] Not all German youths, therefore, felt the same way. And this is what made the organizers' deliberations so difficult.

SPIELSTRASSE

Coming one after the other, the European spring and summer of 1968 and the loss of lives at the Mexico Olympics later in the autumn gave the Munich organizers cause for concern. Even though four years remained before the Olympic flame was due to arrive in Bavaria, Daume wrote to Vogel in December, voicing his anxiety and suggesting "the discrete establishment of a 'post for political planning' or some such" within the OC in anticipation of political disturbances. According to "absolutely reliable information . . . received from student circles," it seemed inevitable that the Games would attract the protesters' wrath.[17] In the event, no such post was created, but the passing of the watershed year in European history ushered in the OC's earnest and at times tempestuous engagement with its legacies. In April 1969, the topic plunged the organizers into probably the most explosive of their twenty-seven regular board meetings between 1966 and 1973. The minutes record an "in-depth, lively discussion"[18]—an elegant shorthand for a blazing row, which resulted in four prominent chairs and members of subcommittees offering their resignation within days.[19] The theme that caused such volatility was the relationship between art and politics and the practicalities of offering wider participation within the cultural program.

In one sense, these were not unfamiliar issues to the committee. Otl Aicher had addressed the notion of youth and its changing demands when he presented his initial thoughts as early as 1967, and the modern, light and democratic designs that he produced for the Games harmonized with the mood of the era.[20] To a large extent, it was possible to bring the ceremonial aspects of the Games into line with contemporary expectations too. In 1969, Daume had worried if it was at all possible "to carry out Olympic celebrations, which essentially elevate [the event] into the ceremonial mode, in nineteenth-century dress. The youth of the world no longer has any understanding for the sort of celebration that revolves around gun salutes, 'the parading of flags,' military marching and pseudo-sacred elements."[21] But as already shown, the OC eventually wrung concessions from the IOC and, to a certain degree, realigned the centerpiece opening. Yet Kurt Edelhagen's pastel-shaded, light Jazz orchestra hardly represented youth culture, and, as

Daume realized himself, the country's "intellectual heritage" could not simply be "hung from hooks on the tent roof."[22]

Much would depend on the relationship between sport and its cultural setting. Munich's bid had appealed to Brundage and the IOC by stressing the city's importance as a center for high classical culture (opera, theater, classical music), but had been broadened to include modernism and the avant-garde as well. More importantly still, popular culture was assigned a central role, the organizers desperate to avoid the impression their program amounted to little more than the "sum of European tailcoat festivals," as the *Spiegel*, unfairly, remarked at the end of 1971.[23] Quite the opposite was the case. While high culture was traditional at an event like the Olympics, embedded in the mental matrix of key organizers, and unavoidable in a city of Munich's stature, it was kept in the concert halls, theaters, and museums of the city center, at arm's length from the sports arenas. To achieve its promised synthesis of sport and culture, the OC privileged less elitist forms of art and brought these as close to the Olympic venues as possible. As Daume emphasized, in contrast to the gigantic, year-long program in Mexico City that had merely juxtaposed sport and the arts, Munich sought to produce a "harmonious accord of the two."[24]

The popular attraction at the Games, the Spielstraße ("Avenue of Games"), was placed in the Olympic Park itself. Initially brimming with optimism, however, the project became increasingly embroiled in controversy. The potentially explosive nature of the venture was immediately apparent when its prototype, "The Big Game" *(Das Große Spiel)*, was unveiled by the chair of the arts committee, Herbert Hohenemser, in a "Report on the Extra-sporting Functions of the Oberwiesenfeld" at the ill-tempered board meeting. The ambitious and—in terms of Olympic history—radical plan to allow an interactive, largely spontaneous array of performance arts to unfold within the Olympic precincts sought both to "bring about the desired integration of sport and the arts" and "to make conscious use of the now almost ubiquitous movement of youth, i.e., to involve young people actively in this part of the Olympic idea and to include them in the preparation of it."[25] Positioning this vital encounter between "youth, sport and culture" at the heart of the Olympic event, the paper aimed to find " 'a common language' . . . to reach a mutual understanding with the young" and create "a 'vent' for the youth movement and its unrest." In the early part of 1969, however, this seemed a high-risk strategy—even the authors could not "provide a guarantee that everything would go off without incident"—and the OC reacted with caution. While Beitz and the representatives from Kiel (Geib and Bantzer) opposed it on practical grounds, others—Bavaria (Köppler) and Munich (Vogel and Abreß) to the fore—attacked what they saw as an overt politicization of art. In short, it was considered inappropriate for the OC to provoke controversy or try to "solve problems by giving people the opportunity to 'act out' the symptoms of those problems." Hohenemser was furious, castigating his fellow OC members for fundamentally "misunderstanding the function of art in contemporary society" and doing little to engage with the "currents of the age." With Daume straddling both camps, the committee agreed to the plan in principle but expressed serious reservations about the details.

Given the OC's basic commitment and the president's essential approval, the project would go ahead, albeit revised and reduced in scale. Over the next three years, the committee's refusal to risk full engagement with youth culture condemned the "Großes Spiel" to a tug-of-war that pulled ineluctably toward what Hohenemser deemed the anathema of "the middle way." At the end of 1969, responsibility for the "Spielstraße" (as it became known in its second phase) was handed to Werner Ruhnau, an architect who had not only collaborated successfully with Frei Otto on the German pavilion at Expo '67 but, as an expert on modernist theater design and mobile theaters, seemed ideally suited to the task.[26] Ruhnau, however, was to be kept in check. The board reminded him at his first appearance that "improvised street theater, made up of external groups" was now off the agenda and that the whole program "should be coordinated centrally";[27] encouraged him at the next appearance to include more folkloric elements;[28] and obliged him by contract to obtain the written permission of the general secretariat before signing acts and accept the possibility they might be cancelled at any given moment.[29] In the end, he enjoyed much less room for maneuvering than he might have hoped for. Over "years of difficult negotiations"[30] the venture became shorter and less radical from one meeting to the next, ever more well behaved and conventional and, in the eyes of some critics, even something of a "museum piece" *(museal)*.[31]

The Spielstraße suffered because in addition to opposition from hypercautious or fundamentally unsympathetic political representatives, it attracted the disapproval of wider constituencies too. While it was supported by younger and more progressive members of the OC, it was obstructed by older sports functionaries, who had an important voice on many committees. General Secretary Herbert Kunze (b. 1908) and Max Danz (1909), the president of the West German athletics federation and a vice president of the NOC, attempted to sabotage it. Although it amounted to less than 2 percent of the Games' total budget, Danz considered it a waste of money, worrying not only that its raucous activities might disrupt the sports events but also that its ethos clashed with a traditional understanding of art and culture.[32] Typically for the old guard, art could assume a variety of roles and features, from the sublime to the decorative to entertainment, but it had nothing to do with sport or politics. These opinions were shared by colleagues such as Liselott Diem, who lambasted the Spielstraße in an article for the *Sportinformationsdienst.* In this influential information service for sports editors across the country, she cited the composer Carl Orff whose positive impressions of the modernist architecture and luscious green landscape contrasted sharply with his disdain for the avant-garde and popular culture on display around the park. Quoting Orff verbatim, Diem luxuriated in the opportunity to hail the Spielstraße an "insult to the Olympics."[33]

But the Spielstraße proved equally unpopular in quarters where it might have expected a modicum of solidarity. While Ruhnau later maintained his project had received "collegial support" from Behnisch and Grzimek, documentary sources tell a different story.[34] Bound contractually to conform to B+P's overall scheme, Ruhnau found himself on the receiving end of the company's exacting protection of its aesthetic vision.[35] Behnisch, in fact, censored Ruhnau's ideas the moment he sensed the merest threat to his own plans. In a memo of July 1969, he pledged to protect the Olympic Park from becoming a "repository for all different sorts of art and culture." As opposed to this grab bag of art, the brownfield site he and his collaborators were in the process of reshaping would transform the Oberwiesenfeld in its entirety into a "*work of art* three hundred hectares in size."[36] When it became clear that the Spielstraße could not be dispensed with, Behnisch proceeded to limit the damage. As with Belling's "Hiroshima sculpture," he ensured it would have no lasting impact on his masterpiece, with the exception of a small classical open-air theater (the Theatron), which in any case had formed part of his original plans.

In its final incarnation, the Spielstraße was located along stretches of the northern and southern banks of the artificial lake adjacent to the Olympic swimming hall and divided into five major areas: the Theatron, a peninsula with performing areas and art studios, a large show terrace on the slopes of the Olympic mountain, a media street with several performing platforms, and a multivision center. Artists including actors, musicians, dancers, and pantomime and circus acts performed on thirty stages spread along half a mile of pathways. In this ultimate version, the Spielstraße sought to remove the division between athletes and visitors to the park, wooing spectators to abandon their passive spectatorship, immerse themselves in play, and in so doing, eliminate or reconfigure the roles consumers normally assumed when they entered a stadium.[37]

This conceptual frame was informed by the theater architect's belief in the political nature of art and culture. While art had traditionally served as a tool for the powerful, he argued, at the very moment the division between artists and spectators is overcome, the latter are transformed into "citizens capable of acting with reason *(der Mitbürger, der mündig wird).*"[38] Giving voice to their opinion, they break free from the constraints and diktat of political power. As explained in an interview given for this book, Ruhnau's political philosophy and praxis were based on a literal reading of German etymology, the term *mündiger Bürger* ("responsible citizen") deriving from *Mund* (mouth/voice).[39] By addressing contemporary demands for greater participation, therefore, Ruhnau saw the Spielstraße as a necessary and positive response to the ideas of 1968. In this, he could count crucially on

FIGURE 14. Locals in Bavarian costume watching events from the top of the Olympic mountain (photo: Oswald Baumeister, courtesy of Süddeutsche Zeitung Photo)

Daume's backing. The president's benevolence stemmed less from political persuasion per se, however, than the deep-seated desire to widen participation and democratize access to sport (see chapter 1). Vitally, too, both men shared a great admiration for the Dutch historian and cultural philosopher Johan Huizinga, whose seminal *Homo ludens* (1938) shaped Ruhnau's philosophy of the Games and, with the exception of Karl Jaspers, tripped off the president's tongue more readily than the work of any other thinker. As with Aicher, Huizinga formed a bridge of sorts between the head of the OC and the creative talent gathered around him. For Huizinga, Daume, and Ruhnau, play made "life worthy of living," the ludique, "like music and painting, poetry and philosophy,"[40] forming "one of the main bases of civilization."[41]

This fortunate, if not altogether unslippery compatibility of viewpoints flourished in the Spielstraße's thematic focus on sport and the Olympics. On the one hand, the project attempted, in Daume's words, to offset the "deadly seriousness" of Olympic ambition and thereby contribute to the serene and relaxed atmosphere of the Games, which the organizers had set as their ultimate goal.[42] On the other, as he also noted, this counteraction could also explicitly criticize the demands and ethos of high-performance competition. For someone who normally extolled the

FIGURE 15. Section of the Spielstraße ("Avenue of Games") by the Olympic lake with provisional stage (photo: Marlies Schnetzer, courtesy of Süddeutsche Zeitung Photo)

value of top-level sport and justified the personal and financial sacrifices required to make it a success, the line he drew between mitigation and outright criticism could be dangerously blurred.[43] It was characteristic of Daume, however, to hold contradictory ideas in close proximity and nurture them productively for his own ends. His mediatory position certainly allowed the Spielstraße to retain an edge, although it also required him to issue certain warnings. Sport per se could be criticized, but individual athletes, whom he viewed as "intelligent partners" rather than "musclemen," were to be spared ad hominem malice. International guests of the Federal Republic, not least the IOC, were to be treated politely too, and all comments on East–West German relations strictly avoided.[44] A proposal by former East German Klaus Göhling to erect a "humane Wall" of inflatable PVC cushions as a "contribution to détente," having already been written to Erich Honecker, therefore, never progressed.[45]

For the main part, the Spielstraße laid on theater for all ages, from clowns and acrobats to pantomime and street performances. One popular example, which doubtless fitted Daume's agenda of satirizing high-performance sport without overtly politicizing it, was an Olympic hamster treadmill, in which the artist Timm Ulrich ran a marathon each day without making any progress.[46] But the venture, which comprised some two hundred artists and a further two hundred technicians and support staff from all over the world, afforded space to a variety of different art forms. Their activities ranged from multivision and multimedia art (photography, film, and video projections, and live-transmission from radio stations), to a sport photography exhibit, "free" jazz, and folk music, singer-songwriter composition, avant-garde painting and sculpture, "physical games" on which the public could play, inflatable air cushions, and installations for visitors to test their senses (e.g., Wilfried Mattes' *Haptic Way and Smell Events* and Goehl, Pichler and Price's *Metallophony*). Flower-arranging artists from Japan worked in harmony with the landscape to create idylls of calm among the hurly-burly.[47] And Klaus Göhling—despite not hearing back from Honecker—was hired for alternative projects such as his *Babbel-Plast* and *Schwabbelbrücke*, an inflatable bridge that spanned the Olympic lake.[48]

Although never repeated at subsequent Games, the Spielstraße proved a great success. In just ten days it attracted an estimated 1.2 million visitors[49]—almost twice the total attending the other cultural events[50]—leading Daume to hail it as "one of the highlights of the Games."[51] Documentary footage shows the majority of visitors fully enjoying themselves. Given the scarcity of tickets for the sports venues, the public welcomed the fact that the Oberwiesenfeld had more to offer than just sporting competitions, and complaints were few and far between.[52] Even when a male actor's trousers slipped and exposed his genitals while playing a female weightlifter in the Grand Magic Circus, the prompt arrival of security personnel had more to do with the zealously prudish OC than public outrage.[53] On the whole, the Spielstraße provided good-humored and easily consumable entertainment, which, despite the committee's worries, catered admirably for the relaxed mood of the times, a soft cultural offshoot of 1968.

Even if the Spielstraße was *museal* when compared with its original intentions, it was not *museal* enough for some. Despite the systematic cutbacks and censorship to which it had been exposed, it managed to retain some of its desired political potency. This was delivered primarily by a small group of international street-theater troupes: the City Street Theater Caravan from New York, ETEBA from Buenos Aires, Jérôme Savary's aforementioned Grand Magic Circus from Paris, the Marionetteatern from Stockholm, Mario Ricci's Roman Gruppo Sperimentazione Teatrale, the Tenjo Sajiki troupe from Tokyo, and the Mixed Media Company from Berlin. Aiming to overcome the fundamental opposition between actor and spectator, each ensemble worked in its own peculiar style, exploiting free theater forms and dealing flexibly with the space available to them by moving constantly between different physical locations on the avenue. The radical edge to these "main-act" groups, however, derived primarily from their subject matter. Commissioned by the organizers to address the theme of Olympic history, each had been invited to represent the Games of a specific year: 408 BC, Athens 1896,

Stockholm 1912, Los Angeles 1932, Mexico City 1968 and the future Games of the year 2000. This ambitious and provocative idea had originated from a basic scenario put forward by Berlin actor and avant-garde theater maker Frank Burckner, who had been involved with the planning of drama on the Spielstraße since the beginning of 1970. While Burckner set down broad guidelines, individual troupes could interpret the Games assigned to them as freely as they wished. By representing five previous Olympics as well as one from the future, Burckner's aim, simply, was to contrast de Coubertin's idealistic renewal of the classical tradition with negative aspects of twentieth-century history. "To act out the history of the Olympic Games," he observed, "is to represent the educational idea of sport *(Bildungsidee des Sports)* as refracted by reality." For Burckner that reality was dominated by "the constant threat to world peace by political, economic, religious and racial antagonisms."[54]

In their underlying message, however, the plays used the Olympics as more than a convenient backdrop for the portrayal of world events. As further elaborations to Burckner's basic scenario show, they criticized the Olympic movement itself and the perilous instrumentalization of sport by the political sphere. Thus the Athens and Stockholm Games of 1896 and 1912 came to stand for the imperialism, colonialism, and monarchical rule that marked their age. Backed by actors singing the "Internationale," the last Games before the First World War, for instance, would juxtapose the German Kaiser's imperialism with the communist pacifism of Karl Liebknecht. The 1968 Games, likewise, would reflect the force of Cold War tensions, the conflict between the "first" and "third" worlds, and the antagonism between contemporary youth and the older generation. Only the still distant Games of the year 2000, represented allegorically by Burckner's own Mixed Media Company working from an outline by Austrian futurologist Robert Jungk, offered any glimmer of hope. In 1972, the year 2000 represented a tipping point, when humankind would either cast aside the "three-headed monster of capitalism, militarism and politics" that overshadowed past and future Olympics or face "global catastrophe" *(Weltkatastrophe)*.[55]

When it came to the host nation, Burckner planned to confront its difficult past head-on. His original scenario envisaged Ricci's experimental theater group working on Berlin 1936 rather than Los Angeles 1932. The *mise-en-scène* was to include an Adolf Hitler puppet that grew and shrunk depending on communicative contexts. The stage directions called for the repeated uttering of Nazi phrases such as "A youngster must be tough as leather, fast as a greyhound, and hard as Krupp steel," and the action was to unfold before scenes from Riefenstahl's *Olympia* and audio triggers such as the noise from "competitions and frantic roaring, interrupted by recordings of Hitler's inflammatory speeches and victory announcements." The spectators were to be treated, further, to Beethoven's Ode to Joy interspersed with the sound of machine-gun salvos and bomber attacks.[56] However, these suggestions were too radical even for Ruhnau, who did his best to persuade Burckner and the theater troupes not to "speak in favor of a specific ideology" or "counter-act the open and tolerant spirit of the 'Spielstraße.'"[57] But decisively, Daume objected himself, arguing that reminding the world of 1936 was hardly the best way to represent the new, modern Germany.[58] Ricci duly obliged and presented an anti-capitalist play about Akron, Ohio, in the Depression instead.[59] Despite Ruhnau's claims to the contrary and Ricci's nonchalance at the time, it is clear that the 1936 sketch was censored. The excuse given to the artists—that the OC could not risk the GDR leaving the Games in protest—had a hollow ring, and the fact that Burckner was allowed to approve proposals from that point on without prior consultation with the OC, smacks of a deal.[60]

Sensitivities over 1936, therefore, paradoxically opened the way for others to exercise less critical restraint. One notable beneficiary was Japanese writer, filmmaker, and dramatist Shuji Terayama, who failed to submit his outline in time and had to develop one after his troupe, Tenjo Sajiki, arrived in Munich. While Terayama had been tasked with representing the Mexico Games of 1968, the end product bore little resemblance to the events of any Olympics hitherto. Although drawing on the Tlatelolco Massacre, his uncanny premonition of events about to happen in Munich's Olympic village remains chilling. Terayama's play provided stunning images of human brutality and violence, and could hardly have contributed to a mood of "serenity" among the audience. Spectators regularly left the performances in shock at the terrifying scenes of black-hooded actors blindfolding, whipping, and manhandling other members of the troupe onto a platform among the spectators in the middle tiers of the Theatron.[61] The victims—male and female—were stripped to the waist and hung over the guard rails by their elbows before dropping one by one, tortured and fatigued, into the audience from a height of several feet. Although ending with a large aluminum bird that flapped its wings but failed to fly—supposedly an expression of the hope that evil might one day be overcome—the play clearly emphasized merciless violence and the reign of terror.

The determination of most of the theater groups to make political statements galvanized the conservatives on the OC in their efforts to end the project. Here they had Black September to thank, whose actions in the Olympic village immediately brought about what years of agitation and the unfortunate actor's dropped pants had failed to achieve.[62] While every other aspect of the Games—sporting and cultural—resumed with the exception of a few official receptions on the afternoon following the attack, the Spielstraße shut for good on 6 September.[63] The move to close it came from Ludwig Huber, the conservative Bavarian minister of finance, during an extraordinary meeting of the executive board, and not surprisingly it met with no resistance from his fellow OC members. At the same time, by contrast, the OC voted unanimously to leave festive decoration around the city in place.[64] Daume was absent but did nothing to help the project survive. Protests by the artists, some of whom faced considerable financial difficulties, were to no avail. While Ruhnau, Burckner and representatives of the various troupes gave a press conference protesting their powerlessness and insisting their presence was now needed more than ever, the actors of Tenjo Sajiki expressed their displeasure by theatrical means. Three days after their last performance, they burned their props on stage before a full house at the Theatron.[65]

NEW LEFT CRITIQUES OF SPORT, THE OLYMPIC SCHOLARLY CONFERENCE, AND THE OFFICIAL YOUTH CAMP

The story of the Spielstraße is one that began with a basic compatibility, although not identity, of viewpoints between the world of sports and the mood of the age, proceeded toward a watering down of radical intent, and ended within the safe confines of the "soft" popular reaction to 1968. This basic process of accommodation, assimilation, and then resistance repeated itself, significantly, along several key interfaces between the Olympic organizers and the younger clientele so necessary to their project. In the years leading up to 1972, the Munich Games attracted criticism from all corners. In May 1970, for instance, the Catholic Countryside Youth of Bavaria (Katholische Landjugend Bayerns) passed a resolution condemning the unfortunate "gigantism," which despite the organizers' best intentions had come to characterize the public perception of the Games. Expenditure on the 1972 event, it was claimed, had literally gone through the roof, leaving a lamentable lack of funds for youth in the countryside.[66] More characteristically, however, less conservative quarters sustained the attack. As with many other institutions in the Federal Republic after 1968, high-performance sport came under fire from the neo-Marxist left that had informed the youth revolt. Critical theory determined the ways in which intellectuals framed radical thinking about sport and, by obvious extension, formulated a stinging critique of the Olympic Games.[67] The "rediscovery" of an alternative Marx to the disgraced variant of Stalinist communism and the renewed popularity of Frankfurt school thinkers such as Adorno, Horkheimer, and Marcuse turned Marxism into "the secular religion of [the] epoch."[68] In the long run-up to the 1972 Olympics, therefore, the organizers would find the materiality of their enterprise examined by a critical apparatus shot through with a disdain for the body and natural antipathy toward sport.

By the early 1970s, a relatively coherent philosophy of sport had established itself around a number of radical thinkers such as Bero Rigauer (*Sport und Arbeit,* 1969) and Ulrike Prokop (*Soziologie der Olympischen Spiele,* 1972). Focusing on the repressive nature of sport and its relation to Freud and Marcuse's dichotomy of labor and leisure, their arguments—as John Hoberman suggests—clustered around several main points.[69] Sport, in their portrayal, no longer functioned as an alternative to work but, in its high-performance variant, mirrored and replicated it. It was dominated by the performance principle and set targets and quotas, in the East even producing an island of "capitalism within socialism," and it served as an instrument of social control, depoliticizing by diverting attention away from the solution of social conflicts while simultaneously inculcating bourgeois values such as the primacy of the individual. Further, the asceticism and masochism demanded by training made sport a self-alienating activity, and the public's infatuation with its heroes, in East and West, came dangerously close to the adoration witnessed in dictatorships. Thus, for Rigauer, Prokop, and the rest, in a political and economic order characterized by "commodified relations" and "domination," sport "affirmed" the system, deflected natural impulses *(triebablenkend),* defused tensions, and generally depoliticized the masses.[70] As the Munich Olympics came into view, other arguments evolved as well. At a special conference *Olympic Games—Pro and Contra,* held in November 1970 at the Academy of the Protestant Church at Tutzing—an event closely monitored by Vogel's personal assistant Camillo Noel—Rigauer and other left-wing critics argued that the Games encouraged the implacable and increasing pressure to achieve *(Leistungsdruck),* while, worse still, creating the illusion of a harmonious and intact world.[71] For the radical theorists, the Olympics merely reinforced the "fetish character" of sport and "inculcate[d] technocratic behavior" in spectators and competitors alike.[72]

Criticism of the Games also emerged from the aptly named "Anti-Olympic Committee" (AOC), whose founders Dieter Bott, Güther Amendt, and Gerd Dommermuth had been active members of the extra-parliamentary opposition. Although less sweeping in their condemnation of capitalist society, their antiauthoritarian critique drew from a familiar reservoir of neo-Marxist and psychoanalytic arguments. In distinction to Prokop and Rigauer, however, the three conceded that sport might have its positive sides too, admitting, under certain conditions, it could generate happiness and well-being. In fact, the AOC never resolved this tension between sport's contribution to hedonistic lifestyles on the one hand and its dampening of the desire for revolution on the other. In contrast to the serious New Left theoreticians, however, the AOC typically expressed its viewpoints in jovial fashion. Despite the presence of left-wing luminaries such as Fritz Teufel, a former member of the Berlin Kommune I and well-known bogey of the bourgeoisie *(Bürgerschreck),* the formation of its Munich section early in 1970 had a touch of slapstick about it. In the techno-modern chic of the revolving restaurant at the top of the Olympic Tower, thirty activists declared the chapter open, before the manager called the police whose arrival was clearly visible from the 182-meter-high vantage-point, allowing the rowdy radicals to make their escape with comic timing. The AOC's plans for the Games themselves were no less farcical, consisting of a scheme to hold a "Layabout" or "Hippie Olympics" *(Gammler-Olympiade)* with new disciplines such as sandcastle building, a one-hundred-meters-in-two-minutes race, and competitions in distance spitting and head wagging.[73] Intended as a light-hearted provocation to attract the media to their antiperformance philosophy, the combination of left-inspired satirical protest and the Olympics proved highly successful. For reasons discussed in chapter 8, the Games enjoyed less than wholehearted public support after 1970, and newspaper journalists were only too happy to report on the AOC and its high jinks.[74] Certainly they captured and doubtless contributed to the mood of the popular mainstream: one installment of Barbara Noack's popular afternoon television series *Der Bastian* (1972) showed the eponymous hero—an attractive, apolitical "eternal student" with long blond hair—wandering the Olympic Park inventing the new discipline of "running backward" *(Sieger im Rückwärtslauf)*.

To a certain extent, therefore, the AOC's publicity schemes, popular television, and the public's favorite elements of the Spielstraße began to merge. They did so generally because of the common slide of radical critique into less pronounced modes of behavior and expression as it passed into the popular realm. But they did so also because of the broad-based humanist philosophy of sport that originated from Daume and underpinned some of the OC's more adventurous initiatives. As already noted, Daume hardly shared Brundage's blind and all-encompassing belief in the positive virtues of sport. For the pragmatic West German, high-performance sport was no longer an "alternative" *(Gegenbild)* to industrial society but its "mirror image" *(Ebenbild)*; it was hardly free of political abuse; and it most definitely found itself at the heart of the labor-leisure dialectic. To some degree, therefore, the OC president's views resonated with those of the New Left theoreticians. But Daume was no Marxist and, treating such topics in a cultured but decidedly unideological manner, nearly always came to conclusions that were diametrically opposed to theirs. If sport in general was now the "brother of work," the pure Huizingian effort *(zweckfrei)* required to play it remained essentially different from the "functional" variant *(zweckgebunden)* demanded by work; if competitive sport was a mirror-image of society, it should be modernized rather than abolished; and if international sport had been preyed upon by politicians, then it was the opportunists—such as Charles de Gaulle, whom Daume never tired of criticizing for his nationalistic remarks after France's poor showing at the 1960 Olympics[75]—and not the athletes who should be taken to task. Moreover, wherever sport led to division, the social, religious, or political barriers imposed upon it needed to be lifted. Whether demanding equal access to elitist sports (such as tennis, sailing, golf, or horse riding) for all members of West German society, arguing for the democratization of sport as a fundamental human right, or facilitating the participation of "third-world" athletes at the Olympics, Daume—as one of his most famous speeches was aptly titled—believed in "Sport for All."[76]

"Sport for All," not surprisingly, became the working title of an interdisciplinary scientific congress "Sport in the Modern World—Chances and Problems" held for over two thousand scholars from seventy-five countries (including the GDR) at Munich's Deutsches Museum on the eve of the Games. With panels on "Sports for the disabled," "Sport in middle and old age," "The theory and research of play," "The contribution of sports in the integration of world society," "The contribution of sport to social and economic development" and "Sport in Judaism/Islam/Hinduism," the organizers operated with a broad understanding of their subject in the hope of attracting a large gathering of international experts to set the future agenda of the discipline.[77] At the same time, the congress also sought to provide a forum to respond to the experience of "1968." As educationalist Andreas Flitner, a member of the conference organizing committee, put it, the event was intended to counter youth's suspicion that "the original meaning of the Olympic Games had been superseded by falsifying tendencies such as the self-representation of the host country, the national ambitions of teams and spectators, professional sportsmanship, the division of sport into artistic performances on the one hand and passive spectatorship on the other, [and] the commercial exploitation of the public."[78]

In addressing these topics, however, the organizers followed a familiar pattern, playing it safe and failing to invite the New Left critics. The inevitable Liselott Diem aside, the congress was attended mainly by younger liberal and reformist academics from the West German social sciences and humanities, ranging from philosophers such as Dieter Henrich to educationalists Ommo Grupe and Hartmut von Hentig. The performance principle was defended against the polemics of the absent New Left, most prominently by the liberal Karlsruhe sports philosopher, Hans Lenk. An Olympic gold medalist in the German rowing eight from Rome 1960, Lenk formulated his guidelines for a nonideological and undogmatic philosophy of sport around the voluntary nature of athletes' participation in training and competition. Stressing the libidinous character of sporting endeavor, Lenk turned the New Left's weaponry upon itself, comparing the athlete with the free-thinking, unalienated man of Marxist anthropology.[79]

Lenk was not entirely eulogistic, of course. Picking up the key political terms among moderate reformers of the era, he and others pleaded for greater participation and democratization in sport. As a result, the official report stressed that "many a critical word was heard" and the conference had "not become the cheering background for the Olympic Games."[80] Not everyone agreed, however. The West German delegation of university students, which had been invited on Daume's suggestion along with four hundred international sports students, was particularly scathing in its criticism.[81] In the words of the German University Sports Association (Allgemeiner deutscher Hochschulsportverband, ADH), which had selected participants and organized university visits for foreign students before the Games, the congress became a "stomping ground of apologists, who theologized and philosophized"[82]—an indictment indeed, given the moderate nature of their views compared to the New Left critics and the antiauthoritarian AOC.[83] It was less the content of the conference that upset the ADH so much as its tone. Having gone to great lengths to prepare workshop presentations, the delegation felt their efforts were not taken seriously by the organizers and found themselves being treated in an authoritarian, pre-1968 manner. Conference materials were not supplied in time, suggestions about making more time available for real discussion were ignored, and, finally, a protest motion was rejected. In the end, the West German students abandoned any hope of influencing proceedings and resigned to follow the example of many of their foreign counterparts. After the opening, most visiting students found better things to do in Munich and simply stopped attending.[84]

Strolling around the city's precincts they would have encountered a huge number of people their own age. Although precise numbers are impossible to establish, it seemed the youth of the world had indeed come for the Games. Many were housed in official and unofficial youth camps, which sometimes boasted the critical spirit of 1968 but more often than not provided a base to enjoy the hedonistic lifestyles the year had engendered. In total, the city and its surrounding towns and villages provided cheap accommodation for thirty thousand young visitors. The West German Sports Youth (Deutsche Sportjugend, DSJ) ran a camp that was larger than the Olympic village; twelve thousand youths were accommodated in Munich schools, which had closed early that year for the summer vacation; the Protestant and Catholic churches organized an ecumenical camp and opened all their community halls to provide a further 1,800 beds per night; and three thousand found lodging at a site organized by the federal minister of the interior in the Hasenbergl, not far from the Olympic Park in the north of Munich.[85] To prevent the Olympic venues and the city's other parks being transformed into spontaneous camping grounds, the city council also offered free emergency accommodation, the police willing to bus up to three thousand visitors to Ludwigsfeld in the northwestern outskirts.[86]

The most significant gathering of this type, however, was the official Olympic camp. Organized by the OC in Kapuzinerhölzl, less than a mile from the Oberwiesenfeld, it housed over 1,500 carefully selected seventeen to twenty year olds from fifty-three countries along with two hundred young leaders in temporary prefabricated houses.[87] Stockholm had inaugurated the official youth camp in 1912 and it became a regular feature within the Olympic program from the Berlin Games onward. As an extension to the Olympic village for athletes (from 1932), successive organizers had seen it as an opportunity to foster the "understanding between nations" that played such a central role in de Coubertin's philosophy. At Munich, this goal was achieved by inviting youths from around the world to live together for up to a month and providing them with opportunities to attend the Games and cultural events at the camp and around the region. In Munich,

Kapuzinerhölzl fulfilled an additional role. Inspired by Daume's vision, the OC came to view it as another way to compensate for the deficits of high-performance sport in the modern world. By bringing their own offerings of song, dance, and folklore, Daume noted at its opening ceremony, international delegations would establish an atmosphere of playfulness to counterbalance modern sport, which was "becoming ever more serious, sometimes even deadly serious."[88]

Camp regulations were very liberal and discipline lax. Although some committee members had proposed rigid rules, progressive voices won the day.[89] Although lights were supposed to be switched off at 11 P.M., participants effectively came and went as they pleased, many using Kapuzinerhölzl, at the bargain rate of twenty deutschmarks for board and lodging, as an inexpensive place to stay.[90] As far as the camp's program was concerned, the organizers decided to steer a safe course, avoiding controversial topics almost entirely.[91] For most participants casual sociability counted more than political discussion. The Russian delegation always had the samovar ready for visitors from the West in their impromptu "Café Katjuscha," and their first-class folklore performances led to invitations to participate in traditional summer fairs in local towns and villages.[92] Extramural events run at no addition cost also proved very popular. There was, naturally, great uptake for the Games themselves, but half- and full-day excursions to the highlights of the Bavarian tourist circuit also attracted healthy numbers. Local firms and businesses went out of their way to offer tours, some drawing more interest than others. Munich's breweries proved more attractive than the car manufacturer BMW or the waste incineration plant at Munich-South but—more telling about the low political appetite in the camp—drew almost three times the number of participants (1,315) than a trip to the memorial ceremony at Dachau on the eve of the Games (500).[93] Indeed, even the controversial decision to continue the Games after the terrorist attack seemed to have little effect on the camp, numbers only dropping significantly at the end of the fortnight.[94]

Some members of the West German delegation—selected by the ADH (students) and the Deutsche Sportjugend (teenagers)—were disappointed by the other guests' reluctance to engage in serious political activity. When they proposed a roundtable discussion to mark the "Day of International Solidarity with the Struggling People of Vietnam," for instance, the Russians suggested holding a cross-country run in their honor instead. To the Germans' chagrin, this softer proposal counteracted their own, and the day passed unmarked: "not even the Russians," the moderate *Frankfurter Rundschau* commented laconically, "wanted to discuss Vietnam."[95] Soon the disgruntled youth of the host nation lashed out at the organizers. Foreign youths, they argued condescendingly, had been given too much opportunity to enjoy themselves, the organizers having turned them into passive consumers of sport and cultural tourism and "deluded them into believing in a sugar-coated world."[96] Personnel were accused of manipulating events within the camp too. As "an expression of disdain for the political contrasts and conflicts between East and West, North and South," their emphasis on folkloric contributions had allowed the camp to degenerate into a "cultural Olympic Games" *(Kulturolympiade),*[97] and they had prohibited the distribution of flyers advertising demonstrations of one kind or another within the camp's perimeters.[98]

Undeterred by the lack of political activism displayed by the foreign delegates, some student members of the West German group took matters into their own hands. Two days after the beginning of the Games, they successfully sabotaged a live television show featuring an array of prominent guests, including Max Schmeling, Jesse Owens, and Emil Zatopek. Invited by ZDF to symbolize the youthfulness of the Games and their contribution to international understanding at its evening gala *Under the Tent Roof,* they mocked what they saw as the superficiality of the broadcasters' message by booing, chanting, whistling, and throwing paper airplanes at the cameras. Live interviews became impossible and the show was almost pulled.[99] Back in the camp, they began publishing an unofficial bilingual newspaper, *Olympix,* with the declared aim of unmasking Olympic hypocrisy. Criticism of the Games' commercialization featured regularly in the paper,[100] as did the fact the camp's housing had been provided by Munich arms manufacturer Krauss-Maffei.[101] Not surprisingly, the IOC came under heaviest attack for its decision to continue with the Games after the massacre of the Israeli athletes.[102]

The dissatisfaction of the West German participants and the politically relaxed atmosphere of the camp that so antagonized them offer an insight into the mood of the youth and organizers of 1972. Despite the unruly behavior, the West German cohort at Kapuzinerhölzl was hardly a hotbed of left-wing radicals. But sensitized by the critical spirit of 1968, they were no longer willing unquestioningly to accept anything offered them by Daume and Vogel's generations. At the same time, the camp turned out to be the least controversial of the OC's youth-orientated undertakings, the organizers' determination to promote a light and happy youth event at which serious politics were to be banished to the margins proving, in fact, a clear success. The camp leader reported "very good relations between all delegations" and received a postbag full of appreciative letters.[103] As one member of the British student delegation put it: "For most people here this has been the experience of a lifetime."[104] In this sense the organizers were right to claim the success of their enterprise: just as in the more difficult circumstances of 1936 (as argued by Christiane Eisenberg), the Olympic Youth Camp in Munich went some way toward creating mutual understanding among young people from around the world.[105] Setting aside its obvious winning formula—which provided young people, many from less prosperous nations, with inexpensive accommodation, cultural attractions, the buzz of Olympic competition, and the opportunity for liberal personal interaction in a safe environment—the Olympic ideal, for all its tarnished image, also triumphed on this occasion. As Kapuzinerhölzl 1972 showed, in the aftermath of 1968 the youth of the world did not always want to protest, they also wanted to have fun.

POLICING, POP, AND DEMONSTRATIONS

As well as arranging events specifically for young people, the organizers had to prevent their spontaneous activities from getting out of control or even off the ground in the first place. With mass youth participation at the heart of the Olympic ideal, the likelihood of large numbers of young people descending on the city gave the local authorities pause for thought. While no specific threat of major disruption emerged as 1972 approached (despite Daume's doomsday fears at the end of 1968), the OC operated on the premise that they should nonetheless prepare for every eventuality, the loss of life in Munich and Mexico in 1968 doubtless looming in their minds. Indeed, events show they were right to have readied themselves: during the Games hardly a day passed when some K-group or other did not organize a political demonstration, attracting anywhere from a small handful of diehards to several thousand. Events also show that the OC's cautious and meticulous planning paid off: with one major exception, Munich's streets and parks remained largely peaceful throughout the Games. The forces of law and order might have been criticized after the Palestinian attack for lapses in security and ignorance of counter-terrorist technique. But it would be historically inaccurate to mock the imputed naivety of the German police, patrolling the Olympic sites—as narrator Michael Douglas commented in the documentary *One Day in September*—in pastel shades, "armed only with walkie-talkies." Like the awful simplicity of September 11, the terrorist attack lay far beyond the conceptual horizon of the time (see chapter 7). But for those dangers and threats that lay within it, Munich was more than ready.

Responsibility for policing the Games fell largely to Manfred Schreiber, who became the OC's special commissioner for security in 1970.[106] Schreiber was an obvious choice, having served as president of the Munich force since November 1963. Born in the same year as Vogel (1926) and returning fifty-percent war-disabled after two years on the front, Schreiber's arrival on the OC added a further powerful voice from the 1945ers driven to rebuild a functioning democracy on German soil. The first chairman of the student body (ASTA) at Munich University after the war, his career also followed a similar trajectory to Vogel's—a degree in law leading to public administration in Bavaria's Ministry of the Interior, a major position in the city of Munich, and then (after twenty years serving SPD and CSU mayors) promotion to federal level as a high-ranking civil servant in the Ministry of the Interior during Helmut Kohl's chancellorship. Although an outsider on taking up office with the police, he rapidly adopted the force's esprit de corps and never publicly criticized his subordinates, even when they bore the brunt of public abuse after the disastrous outcome to the hostage crisis in 1972.[107]

Schreiber, like Vogel, approached reform with a distinctive mix of political progressiveness and steely pragmatism. As a right-wing member of the SPD in the early 1960s, he was aware of the police's traditionally reactionary stance. Indeed from the late 1960s onward, he became increasingly conservative himself, forcefully insisting on the state's monopoly of violence and largely rejecting the critical analysis of society emerging in 1968.[108] This creeping conservatism certainly informed some of his judgments on the Games, but his most decisive contribution owed more to policing reforms introduced in the early phase of his leadership in Munich. His predecessor Anton Heigl's tenure had been marred by the controversial Schwabing Riots *(Schwabinger Krawalle)* of June 1962, when a minor infringement by street musicians at an open-air concert in Munich's bohemian quarter escalated into violent clashes between (predominantly) young protesters and the city's *Schutzpolizei.* Serious civil disturbances ensued and continued intermittently for five nights. As a result, Schreiber drafted a much-needed change of policy, formulating a flexible concept to help large deployments of police officers deal with confrontation at massed events such as demonstrations, rock concerts, and major sporting occasions. Tested successfully for the first time at the Beatles' Munich concerts in June 1966, the "Münchner Linie," as it became known, entered the vanguard of West German policing in the 1960s.[109] Its distinctive emphasis lay on prevention and psychology. Overwhelming forces bearing the traditional armory of law and order were replaced, whenever possible, by smaller numbers using cognitive tactics. During demonstrations, channels of communication were kept open between organizers and participants, provocation was avoided, and physical force employed only when psychological means had been exhausted. While it would be wrong to see the "Munich Line" as a soft approach to public order offences, it often proved effective in stemming violent outbreaks before they gathered momentum. The "Easter riots" of 1968 were its one major failure.[110]

Schreiber's imprimatur on the 1972 Games was evident even before his appointment to the OC. After consulting his police president, Vogel addressed the committee on security at the end of 1969, noting two potential threats that would demand subtle methods of engagement: "militant, anarchic activists" attracted by the "extraordinary publicity" of the Olympics and—an oblique and ultimately unfounded reference to the GDR—countries seeking to prove their national superiority outside the sporting arena. In any such case, Vogel argued, "every time the organ of the state reacted forcefully, it would provide welcome proof that the Federal Republic was not in fact a peaceable country, its society based on aggression and repression" and thus put the "success of the entire Games at risk."[111]

In response to Vogel's worst-case scenarios, the OC considered a twofold solution. They determined, first, to implore the IOC to share responsibility for maintaining the serenity of the Games—an idea ridiculed as completely unrealistic by Daume but pushed through by Genscher—and develop, second, their own domestic plan of action. Without being identified as such, the rudiments of the plan were pure "Münchner Linie": "trying to redirect disturbances" and keeping "the forces of law and order away for as long as possible."[112] With the IOC predictably unimpressed by the suggestion it should guarantee civil obedience within a sovereign state, Schreiber, when appointed, pressed ahead determinedly. Early prevention and the avoidance of escalation were to become familiar topics at OC meetings over the next two years. Prevention was enshrined most prominently in the "Gesetz zum Schutz des Olympischen Friedens" (Law for the Protection of the Olympic Peace),[113] legislation that suspended the freedom of assembly, as codified in article 8 of the federal constitution, within a five-hundred-meter radius of the Oberwiesenfeld and other Olympic venues for the duration of the Games and, on specific days, along the routes of the torch relay, marathon, and cycle races. After initial hesitation at federal level followed by altercations over technicalities between Bonn and the Bavarian state government, Genscher managed to see the proposal through cabinet, with the Bundestag approving it in spring 1972.[114] The temporary law was supplemented by Munich City Council, which passed a further ban on political assemblies and demonstrations in the city center's pedestrian zone on 16 August 1972. On the whole, the legal prohibition—an aesthetically and politically more attractive alternative to the ring of thousands of soldiers thrown around the Olympic sites in Mexico City—achieved its intended "general preventative effect."[115]

Occasionally, however, it provoked rather than deterred. An event organized by the German Communist Youth Association (Kommunistischer Jugendverband Deutschlands) and their counterparts from another Maoist K-group (the KPD/ML) ended in violence, when marchers tried to force their way into the pedestrian zone. After the majority of demonstrators had dispersed, a core armed with motorcycle helmets, truncheons, and blackjacks attacked barriers manned by police at the Karlstor, resulting in (some severe) injury to fifty-eight officers.[116] Mostly though, the *Bannmeile,* as it was legally known, represented more of a lighthearted challenge. Following an anti-Vietnam War rally, for instance, in which two thousand demonstrators from all over Germany participated after the opening ceremony, some members of the Munich KPD decided to take the protest further into the heart of the city. Simply hopping one S-Bahn stop from Karlstor to the Marienplatz, they embarked on a brief illegal protest of their own. After unfurling banners decrying U.S. involvement in Vietnam and attracting the attention of locals and tourists, they made off quickly before the police could intervene. The scale of this peccadillo and the fact that the "Storming of the Karlstor" was never repeated will have amply justified Schreiber's methods, and the prohibition was loosened only for protests after the terrorist attack.

More controversially, however, the police president allowed the growing conservatism that marked his attitudes from the late 1960s to bear on aspects of the cultural program—the ill-starred Spielstraße becoming the main focus of his prevention-first mentality. By the eve of the Games, he was convinced that light entertainment in the Olympic park would be "hijacked by the public," and remained adamant the police would be forced to shut it down at the first sign of trouble.[117] Such anxieties and threats—which proved greatly exaggerated—formed the logical conclusion to long-running skirmishes over Ruhnau's plans. Concerns about visitors' safety, ostensibly, caused Schreiber to forbid the selling of beer on the Spielstraße, deny artists access to the majority of paths and roads in the Olympic park, and prevent the Olympic mountain from being transformed in the evenings into a "Mountain of Kinetic Pleasure" *(Berg des kinetischen Vergnügens)* with huge mobiles, a labyrinth, and light show. On his orders, this potential mecca of youth and alternative culture had to close at 10 P.M.[118] Moreover, he contributed significantly to the downsizing of the artistic enterprise as a whole. Of the forty-eight original acts, twenty were rejected on aesthetic or financial grounds, while ten fell foul of the police president's veto. Düsseldorf painter Günther Uecker, for instance, was prohibited from creating spontaneous works of art by letting the public fire differently colored arrows into wooden canvases—an act no more dangerous than the traditional shooting galleries at the Oktoberfest. More incomprehensibly, Schreiber cancelled a surreal wardrobe in which members of the Westfalian Landestheater were to perambulate across the Spielstraße discussing events of the day.[119] Despite approval from noise-pollution experts,[120] street musicians were forbidden from using amplifiers on the first three days of the Games, a ban that would be lifted, paradoxically, if they did not attract large crowds.[121] Given Schreiber's sanctions, it is hardly surprising that the Spielstraße organizers dedicated no more than 4 percent (DM 100,000) of their budget to pop music.[122]

Pop music—perhaps *the* common language of an emerging global youth culture—had concerned Schreiber for some time. By 1972, open-air festivals were a regular feature in West Germany, and Munich had established itself as the country's hippie capital, the scene gathering regularly in the English Garden in Schwabing just a few kilometers from the Olympic venues.[123] Although audiences often "got high," rock concerts were not always unruly or illegal affairs: during the Games (30 August), for instance, the famously strident British band The Who performed their rock opera *Tommy* in front of an audience of two thousand at the Deutsches Museum, with the police reporting "no disturbances and no indications of drug consumption."[124] The idea of organizing a massed open-air concert as part of the cultural program of the Games, however, struck fear into the hearts of the authorities, who immediately pictured thousands of young *Gammler* (as hippies were known in Germany) and *Hascher* (marijuana smokers) milling around the city.[125] Moral issues aside, the mere presence of drug users in the Olympic precincts would have obliged the police by law to intervene and created the scenario Schreiber was determined to avoid.

Schreiber's insistence on avoiding awkward situations rang the death-knell on an event that might have written Munich into the annals of rock history. Inspired by Daniel Spiegel, who enjoyed close links with the British pop industry and was responsible for music on the Spielstraße, the art and culture department of the OC considered staging a massive music festival. Featuring many of the biggest names of the day—Led Zeppelin, the Rolling Stones, Frank Zappa and the Mothers of Invention—the "Rock Olympics," as one London promoter put it, might easily have surpassed the Games themselves.[126] In September 1971, *Melody Maker* and *New Musical Express* began announcing that the Olympic park was to host the largest series of rock and pop concerts ever held, a two-week mega-event to put Woodstock and other festivals in the shade. Spiegel's vision depicted tens of thousands of music fans sitting on the slopes of the Olympic mountain, listening to music coming from the Theatron amphitheater through amplifiers and loudspeakers.[127]

When Schreiber discovered the plan—uncharacteristically late, in spring 1972—he was horrified at the prospect of an additional forty thousand to fifty thousand visitors swarming over the Oberwiesenfeld without tickets to the sports events. After meetings between Spiegel and his deputy Reinhard Rupprecht failed to resolve the situation, he used his powers of persuasion on the OC.[128] Doubtless with images of Woodstock and the Rolling Stones' 1965 and 1969 concerts in Berlin (Waldbühne) and London (Hyde Park) in mind, he argued that hoards of drug-consumers would refuse to leave the Olympic Park in the evenings, turn it into a camping ground, and impede the Games. Invoking a familiar topos of the time, he conjured up the "very unsightly image" of massed events and "the danger of epidemics."[129] Daume and the Bavarian ministry of the interior were of a similar mind, and Spiegel was instructed, with the help of "Johnny" Klein's PR department, to ensure that his potential clientele stayed well away from Munich.[130] When he attempted to salvage his project, suggesting that an alternative festival *(Ausweichfestival)* in the surrounding countryside might draw young people with little interest in sport away from the Oberwiesenfeld, he met with continued skepticism.[131] The Bavarian Ministry of the Interior buried the project completely by instructing communes across the state to rebuff Spiegel's approaches.[132]

The first tenet of the "Münchner Linie"—prevention at the earliest stage—was, therefore, fully activated for 1972.[133] The second—stemming escalation with psychological rather than physical methods—was also much in evidence. Although apparently more liberal and relaxed, the latter formed a piece with the former. To ensure calm around the Olympic sites, Schreiber had them policed in innovative fashion. In the Olympic precincts, the normal forces of law and order were replaced for the duration of the Games by the Ordnungsdienst—comprising two thousand young police officers and federal border guards from all over West Germany who were active members of sports clubs and had volunteered to serve in Munich on paid leave of absence. Kitted out—indeed—in pastel shades, the Olys's task was to keep the peace in a gentle and unobtrusive manner.[134] As they were instructed in special training: "calming, relaxing and easing takes precedence over 'ominous resoluteness.'"[135] To this end, they benefited from the expertise of the Munich police's in-house psychology department.[136]

Moreover, an internal police working group had assessed every potential threat. Based on scenarios that spanned from sabotage (e.g., soiling the water in the Olympic pool) to assassination, a range of flexible responses was envisioned.[137] Among others, a so-called gag-commission developed a series of tactics to counteract the least serious disturbances. Political demonstrations in the Olympic stadium, for instance, would activate members of the Ordnungsdienst, who would march in wearing spiked helmets and carrying flashlights and hand sirens in an attempt to diffuse the situation through hilarity. If the humor of this scene and the well-scripted witticisms of the stadium announcer were not infectious enough, the security service would have opened fire on the demonstrators—with a specially constructed cannon shooting sweets instead of bullets.[138]

Such measures proved unnecessary, however. And while in retrospect their superficial levity sits uncomfortably with the tragic mistakes made during the hostage crisis, the training was generally effective. When a group of two hundred protesters defied the ban on demonstrations within the Olympic precincts and approached the stadiums waving red banners and singing the "Internationale," they did not encounter the physical resistance they had been expecting. Instead, they were infiltrated by members of a special unit of the Ordnungsdienst (Verfügungstruppe) in civilian clothes, who engaged them in discussion and quickly persuaded them to disperse.[139] Like the *Bannmeile,* the Ordnungsdienst worked well. Its dual role as a police force and international PR opportunity contributed in no small part to the relaxed atmosphere on the Oberwiesenfeld. Conservative and/or visionary, Schreiber's policing decisions were in harmony with the buzz that hummed around the "natural" surroundings and breathtaking architecture of the park.

. . .

As the policing policy shows, the culture of 1968 had a complex effect on the Games. On the one hand, the Munich force's experience of bloodshed in 1968 led it to develop Olympic guidelines that verged on the puritanical. On the other hand, however, its tactics tapped into the mood of the times in order to counteract its more radical offshoots. Both facets, importantly, stemmed from a philosophy of policing that had evolved not as a reaction to the revolutionary year itself but had already begun before it. Such complexities were evidenced across the OC's 1968-friendly planning for the Games and indeed in the various and unpredictable ways that youth reacted to those emerging projects. The times, to paraphrase Bob Dylan, were changing constantly and throwing up unforeseen difficulties and pleasant surprises as well as quirks of interpretation for the later historian.

In 1971, at a time of financial pressure, the OC fretted about a proposal from Vogel to allow students to take up residence in the women's quarters of the Olympic village temporarily before the Games. Daume and several members of the executive board worried the students might refuse to vacate their accommodation out of some sense of protest, and press chief Klein pondered the international PR disaster that images of their forceful eviction would send around the world.[140] But in the event, the OC's concerns were unfounded, the students leaving the village, at an inconvenient time in the academic calendar, without a whimper. The radical cells too—notwithstanding the achievements of the Munich police and the internal security services in controlling them—created far fewer problems than expected. Most of them caused little more trouble than the Christian hippies "the Jesus People," who came in their hundreds to Munich to spread their message and participate in a rally organized by the German YMCA.[141] When Richard Mandell, the U.S. historian of the 1936 Games, ran into the Basic Workers Groups *Olympic Exhibit 1936–1972: Development of the Class Struggle in the Federal Republic,* he was struck by the friendliness of its young members, who tried to persuade him that they shared similar worldviews.[142] Not least, the shared outrage at the slaughter of the Israeli athletes had a dampening effect on radical intent halfway through the Games.

Leaving aside the rumors and threats that framed a great deal of the OC's preparations, the most striking feature of 1968's impact on the Games is its (often rather hollow) translation into the mainstream. This is perhaps most clearly exemplified by Heide Rosendahl, the darling of the West German track-and-field team. Much photographed in her hooped socks and John Lennon glasses, the sprinter, long-jumper, and pentathlete became the female equivalent of Mark Spitz, adorning the bedroom walls of the nation's teenagers. Relaxed but confident, performance-orientated *(leistungswillig)* yet undespairing in defeat, Rosendahl stood as the embodiment of Brandt's young and "modern Germany." Losing the pentathlon gold by a fraction of a second to Northern Ireland's Mary Peters, she was presented in the popular press as "a victor who refused to be a loser."[143] Yet, although her fashion sense and external appearance represented the cultural changes brought about by 1968, Rosendahl seemed otherwise untouched by the gravity of events around her. At the height of the student unrest in 1968 and 1969, her senior dissertation at the Deutsche Sporthochschule in Cologne on the sub-

FIGURE 16. Heide Rosendahl celebrating her victory in the long jump, 31 August 1972 (courtesy of Süddeutsche Zeitung Photo)

ject of Olympic youth camps from Helsinki to Tokyo expressed apologetic ideas about the 1936 Games, their chief organizer Carl Diem, and his thoughts on a sporting Europe after the war.[144]

While it is uncharitable to draw on an athlete's college assignment that was never intended for publication, it underscores our main point: in sport and the Olympics, as in many other areas of West German and indeed European life, the cultural effects of 1968 impacted the popular mainstream without necessarily restructuring its deeper mentalities. Rosendahl's unreconstructed thinking about the German past and the role of a supposedly apolitical Carl Diem within it certainly chimed with the views of certain older sports functionaries such as Diem's widow Liselott, who was director of the Sporthochschule when she was completing her degree. Diem proposed Rosendahl carry the Olympic flame, her husband's invention, into the stadium in 1972.[145] The K-group members who ran the critical Olympic exhibit, one imagines, would have seen it quite differently. But although such groups might have lain closer to the original motor of change in 1968, Rosendahl—like Barbara Noack's dreamer *Bastian* and the less controversial acts on the Spielstraße—was now its accepted and acceptable face.

The return of ideology might have haunted some aspects of the preparations for Munich. But the real specter at the feast came from across the border. After winning gold in the long jump, Rosendahl was to complete her medal haul with a victory over the GDR in the women's 4x100 meter relay. Starting the final leg with a slim advantage over Renate Stecher, the individual 100- and 200-meter champion, she held on to break the tape. To the delight of the home crowd, the "good girl" with the hippie image had taken the sting—as her opponent's name implies in German—from the GDR's assault on the Games. It was to be a rare victory in a battle that lasted almost two decades.

6

East versus West

German-German Sporting Tensions from Hallstein to Ostpolitik

Nineteen seventy-two was an extraordinary year for the Federal Republic. Within months it not only staged an outstanding Olympics, but via an agreement with wartime allies over the status of West Berlin and a series of treaties with Moscow, Warsaw, Prague, and East Berlin, succeeded in bringing the spirit of global détente to bear on relations with its Eastern neighbors. Although most difficult to conclude, the final negotiations with the German Democratic Republic (GDR) contained an essential vagueness that allowed both sides to claim real gains and symbolic victories. While the GDR understood the treaty as a repudiation of German unity, the Federal Republic believed it had found a substitute for it. The former won "recognition" from the Federal Republic, entry alongside it into the UN in 1973, and, in the same year, a dramatic increase in diplomatic relations (up to seventy-nine states from only seventeen in 1969). The latter recognized the independence but not sovereignty of its Eastern rival, secured the status of Berlin, freed itself from cumbersome foreign policy constraints, and created a more open environment for trade and exchange.

In the second week of the Games, Brandt's closest advisor on Ostpolitik, Egon Bahr, went to East Berlin for a crucial meeting with Honecker, and just two months later the chancellor led his party to its best ever election result in what was effectively a hard-fought referendum against the Christian Democratic Union (CDU)/Christian Social Union (CSU) on the topic.[1] It would be misleading, however, to read sport in 1972 and the immediately preceding years as a simple cipher for identificatory politics and emotions. The Munich Games might have coincided with the conclusion of Ostpolitik, but they were not a straightforward "Ostpolitik Olympics." There are several reasons for this. First, although opinion polls in

1972 showed strong support for an acceptance of the fact of German division, they registered an equal unwillingness to recognize the GDR. Brandt drew this distinction punctiliously, even in the realm of sport and the Munich Games.[2] Second, a long tradition of sports-political enmity between the Federal Republic and the GDR led to ingrained attitudes and modes of behavior which set their own agendas in the international arena. And third, the Federal Republic's rapprochement with the GDR's allies after 1969 threw East Berlin severely off course for the Games. These second and third factors rendered the relationship between sport and inter-German politics decidedly labyrinthine, and it is only when set against the background of almost two decades of feuding that they can be fully understood.

THE GERMAN QUESTION AND THE IOC

From as early as the 1950s, the two Germanys and the Olympic movement triangulated in a relation of angst and provocation. From the foundation of the Republic, Bonn was convinced that any recognition of its Eastern rival would delay reunification, and set out its stall as the sole representative of the German nation *(Alleinvertretung)*. Diplomatically, it enforced its will around the world via the Hallstein doctrine, a Foreign Office policy (from 1955 onward) that threatened to break off relations with any country (bar the USSR) that recognized the GDR. States in need of trade and development aid proved particularly open to such reasoning and keen to enter financial bargaining. At the same time, the GDR pushed representational issues to the limits—provoking Bonn's representatives over symbols and nomenclature wherever possible—and in the Middle East in particular, it became increasingly necessary to turn a blind eye to keep the scheme intact.[3] Nonetheless, despite its growing expense and inherent contradictions, Hallstein remained a potent weapon of defense until the Social Democratic Party (SPD) came to power with its new agenda in 1969. With the exception of Cuba (1963) and a number of Arab states (after 1965), no third-world country assumed official relations with East Berlin until that point.[4]

It proved altogether more difficult, however, to transfer the success of Hallstein to the NGO world of international sport. Here, the visual ritual of competition supported by emblems, flags, and anthems accentuated the problem. It was one thing for West German diplomats to debate—and choose, if necessary, to ignore—the latest GDR peccadillo at a trade fair thousands of miles from home, but quite another to remain indifferent as East German colors glided up flag poles in stadiums around the world. Bonn insisted on the regulation of international paraphernalia—down to the size of badges on tracksuits—and viewed any flaunting of the rules as the thin end of the wedge. NATO lent support, particularly after the erection of the Berlin Wall, by threatening and imposing travel restrictions on GDR athletes as a deterrent against breaking the West's strict protocols, while the Federal Republic kept its own house in order by declaring the flying of GDR flags and insignia a public order offense (1959). Host nations around the world came under pressure to exclude East German sports teams for minor breeches of convention, and the GDR often obliged by withdrawing, sometimes with their Eastern allies in tow, to great publicity effect.

Oddly, Bonn's general obsession with symbols seemed to function positively for both parties: while the GDR manipulated them to "advance in tiny increments," minor infringements permitted the Federal Republic to "register complaints with local governments . . . to demonstrate earnestness without invoking any heavy-handed threats about breaking diplomatic relations."[5] In other words, the fine print of Hallstein allowed both sides to articulate Cold War politics while keeping them in check. Sport, paradoxically, was a different kind of game—one in which the Federal Republic's fixation with symbols left it exposed on two flanks. First, it was vulnerable to the "cat-and-mouse game" of permissible national emblems at international events, the GDR reveling in the ever-changing minutiae of the regulations and switching its badges, vests, and tracksuits to maximum annoyance at the eleventh hour.[6] Second, it fell increasingly foul of decisions taken by NGOs that were beyond the reach of governmental influence.

While sports events of all kinds—from skydiving to junior table-tennis—in all parts of the world were affected by feuds over German representation, the symbol-laden arena of the Olympics provided the main theater of contestation. The International Olympic Committee (IOC) struggled with the "querelles allemandes" for over a decade and a half. In 1951 in Vienna, it recognized the National Olympic Committee of the Federal Republic as the "NOK für Deutschland" and rejected the GDR's application for membership. Only the West Germans, themselves excluded from the first postwar Games in London 1948, were allowed to compete at Helsinki 1952. The IOC revised its decision in Paris in 1955, provisionally recognizing the GDR as the "NOK für Ostdeutschland" on the condition that it form a joint team with the West Germans—an arrangement that lasted for three Games from 1956 to 1964. In Madrid in 1965, the IOC crossed the Rubicon and granted the GDR full rights as a geographical area with a separate team for Mexico 1968, albeit still within the joint framework. At the session held immediately prior to those Games, it completed the process, finally redesignating the GDR as the "NOK der DDR" (or "Deutschland-DDR" for the purposes of competition) and permitting a fully independent team for the next Olympics in Munich.

In the course of this complicated process, long-suffering West German sports functionaries were torn between the contradictory visions of their governmental sponsors in Bonn and sporting masters at the IOC. NATO reacted indignantly to the notion of a joint team for 1956, and Adenauer and his foreign minister, Brentano, were equally opposed, not least when the GDR changed its flag in 1959

FIGURE 17. GDR team at the opening ceremony (photo: Friedrich Gahlbeck, Bild 183-L0827–207, courtesy of Bundesarchiv)

and the IOC forced both sides to accept a neutral replacement (the five Olympic rings superimposed on black, red and gold) and a nonpartisan anthem (from Beethoven's Ninth Symphony).[7] Paradoxically, the erection of the Berlin Wall forced Adenauer into a volte-face on the Olympic issue. As the German Sports Association (DSB) responded to Berlin mayor Willy Brandt's call to retaliate by banning bilateral competition (Düsseldorf Decree 1961), the joint team, which was unpopular with the West German public, ironically grew in importance for the government. Daume's proposal of separate teams for the 1964 Games under one flag (which previously would have gone some way to placating Adenauer) was flatly rejected by the Ministry of the Interior.

The pragmatist in Daume quickly tired of the niggling controversies that plagued the united team. The Summer Games in Tokyo (1964) and their winter equivalent in Grenoble (1968) required fourteen rounds of negotiation between the two NOCs, ninety-six conferences between individual federations and sixty play-off tournaments to determine which athletes would participate.[8] Perhaps more than any other sector of public life, Olympic sport confronted its functionaries with the unadulterated fact of German division and the difficulties of dealing with governmental tensions on both sides of the border. Daume often quoted Karl Jaspers, the philosopher who a year before the Wall controversially stated that the Germans should renounce their futile hopes of coming together as one nation again.[9] But such progressive ideas cut as little ice in Lausanne as they did in Bonn. At the IOC, Brundage's love of all things German and vision of Olympism as separate from politics, but contributing to the solution of political problems, gave him grand designs of bringing about reunification single-handedly. When approached about the possibility of Berlin's hosting the 1968 Olympics, for example, he gushed with world-political ambition: "This would really be sensational and might do more than Kennedy and Khrushchev, together, for the peace of the world."[10] On another occasion, he claimed: "The creation of a United German Team and its continuance through six Olympic Games . . . has been a great victory over politics that illustrates the power of the Olympic Movement dramatically." For good measure, he would underscore such arguments by citing the thwarted boycott of 1936 when "the Olympic idea proved itself stronger than the forces which afterward led to the great World War."[11] It would take a massive shift in world opinion and a serious threat to his own hold on power for Brundage to abandon his apodictic position on the German question.

After the building of the Wall, the adherence in Bonn and Lausanne to the chimera of East-West cooperation in sport placed Daume in an awkward double-bind. Contributing greatly to this was the East Germans' rapid mastery of Olympic discourse. The GDR had entered the movement in the early 1950s on the coattails of the Soviets, who embraced international and Olympic competition for the same reasons as other totalitarian regimes before the Second World War: a belief in "modernity and social improvement," which they shared with the IOC, and the desire to showcase the superiority of their system through athletic prowess.[12] The Soviets soon perfected the language of Olympism, their representative Konstantin Andrianow railing at the IOC Executive Board against "the forces hostile to sports traditions and friendships among athletes," which he deemed to be "turn[ing] sports into a political weapon."[13] Soviet adherence to the Olympic creed was absolute. While by the 1960s the West Germans cherished the Olympics merely as one of those "islands of peace where political calm is maintained as much as possible," the Soviets remained true to the totalizing vision of the founder and his loyal successors.[14] As late as 1980, at the opening ceremony of the Moscow Games, this idealizing notion of Olympic tradition was writ large when "a group of marchers dressed as ancient Greeks, some astride a chariot, entered the stadium, [a] giant card section presented a picture of the Parthenon, [and an] announcer offered a thoroughly positive reading of classical history" quite alien to Soviet historiography of the time.[15] In the 1960s, Brundage's selective reading of world history led him to tell Andrianow that Karl Marx offered "an excellent summary of Olympic philosophy."[16]

The GDR was never far behind. Realizing the need to play the old-boy networks of the IOC, it replaced Kurt Edel, a former KGB agent, at the head of its

National Olympic Committee with Heinz Schöbel, an urbane Leipzig publisher who proved more to Brundage's liking. In 1966, Schöbel composed a history of the Olympic Games that, like the Soviet model from which it took its lead, was replete with ideological inconsistencies.[17] In this account, the ancient Olympics represented "highpoints in the glorious development of culture and democracy" for "free citizens" imbued with a "basic humanistic conviction," and formed the ideal forerunner of modern sport "in the realization of its humanistic form in socialist society." De Coubertin's legacy, Schöbel noted, had been to preserve these ideals for the sake of "social change" and to make sport "democratic and international."[18] Brundage supplied a preface for the first, and indeed several subsequent editions, and the work helped earn Schöbel the GDR's first, much-coveted seat on the IOC in 1966.

On a personal level, the East Germans could curry favor with Brundage as well as their Western counterparts. They appealed to his tastes by stressing "the close connection of sports and art" in the GDR, flattering him with requests to show a film on his art collection at the Pergamon Museum in East Berlin.[19] In 1968, Schöbel presented the IOC president with a leather-bound Festschrift (*Die vier Dimensionen des Avery Brundage,* The Four Dimensions of Avery Brundage), quite possibly one of the most hypocritical works to come out of the GDR. In it Brundage, like de Coubertin and the ancient Greeks before him, emerged through a kaleidoscope of propaganda as "a talented youngster characterized by [his] ability to work hard, tenacity, determination"—as someone who had overcome the odds, practicing by "adapting an iron ring" and throwing "heavy stones."[20] Most strikingly, this latter-day Siegfried's insistence "on strict respect for Olympic principles in [the] Berlin Olympic Games in 1936" was equated with his "remarkable" support for the "affiliation of the Soviet Union with the IOC." Brundage, who had actively followed the book's progress, ordered 750 copies from Leipzig to distribute to admiring former classmates from the University of Illinois.

The Soviet bloc's charm offensive put Daume under pressure. The West Germans matched or bettered the GDR, present for present,[21] publication for publication.[22] But with the East Germans playing a shrewd game and his own government showing an inflexibility that was going out of fashion in the international arena, Daume needed to draw on all his diplomatic skills. Portrayals of the West German NOC president have often depicted him both at odds with the federal government's determination to maintain a united German team in the 1960s and at the same time devastated at the GDR's eventual recognition by the IOC in 1965.[23] There has been little reflection on the inherent contradiction in these positions, but, on closer inspection, they give the lie to Daume's tactics during the course of the decade. Daume was no stranger to well-meaning duplicity on the German question. At the turn of the year 1956, he had confidentially informed the minister of the interior, Gerhard Schröder, that in sports terms the GDR had "in effect unfortunately already" become "a sovereign state."[24] On his election to the IOC a year later, however, he assured Brundage of his continued support on the "great task" of the united team, noting how the Olympic idea had "broken through iron and paper curtains" and forced men "to look into their brother's heart."[25] While Daume's stance was basically incompatible with that of Brundage and the West German government, he paid lip service to both to maintain his personal platform. Faced with the almost certain prospect of his two powerful masters eventually losing the struggle to contain East German ambitions, his twin strategy of protest and compliance, although exhausting, left his power intact.

In the particularly fraught run-up to the 1964 Games, Daume's dual approach was much in evidence. On the one hand, the West German sports establishment was growing increasingly disheartened at Brundage's implacability over the German issue. Daume's desire for separate teams caused dismay at IOC headquarters,[26] with Brundage—as described even by his old friend Liselott Diem on her return from a visit to Chicago—behaving as a "jock" who "had no interest in anything else."[27] On the other hand, Daume went out of his way to assure the president of his commitment to a united squad.[28] These contradictions continued in Tokyo itself, where—distancing himself from the West German embassy and carrying a handgun after threats on his life—he announced to anyone willing to listen, "that it was all over for the unified German team."[29] At the IOC session just before the Games, however, he proclaimed—in contradiction of the actual experience of those concerned—that "the athletes from both parts of Germany got on famously," and lavished praise on the joint team as a resounding "triumph for the Olympic idea."[30] Back in Bonn, he also convinced the Ministry of the Interior of his continued belief in the all-German cause.[31]

Despite confessing that the IOC, given the opportunity, would recognize the GDR by a margin of four to one,[32] Daume covered his back by inviting the federal government to set up a steering committee in preparation for the decisive ballot in Madrid in October 1965.[33] As before the 1964 session, when Andrianow had been expected to force a vote,[34] the Foreign Office (supported by representatives of the DSB, the NOC, the national sports press, the Ministry of the Interior and the government's press and information office) went into overdrive, instructing forty of its embassies to exert pressure on IOC members via the highest possible authority in their host countries.[35] At the same time, East Berlin pursued a similar course of action.[36] The West Germans flew Alfredo O. Inciarte (the IOC member from Uruguay) to Europe on full expenses and provided a personal budget of DM 2,000 to exert his influence;[37] Daume was granted DM 150,000 to finance an extensive "invitation campaign" and traveled himself, just weeks after Schöbel, to Mexico, where he presented President General Clarke Flores with an antique Bierkrug and the original score of Richard Strauss's Olympic anthem from the 1936 Games.[38] A month before the vote, despite the Foreign Office's studied optimism,[39] Daume knew there was little chance of victory.[40] Secure in this knowledge, he went through the motions of pleasing the government, sending a legal expert's report to all IOC members and honing a speech for Madrid that would surpass the rhetorical brio of his efforts in Tokyo.[41] In the event, the IOC listened, complained about the overt politicization of sport on the part of the West German government, and—relieved at last to rid itself of the endless "querelles allemandes"—voted by an overwhelming majority to grant the GDR a team of its own.[42]

BOUNCING BACK WITH THE BID

Within three weeks, Daume had approached Hans-Jochen Vogel with a proposal to bring the 1972 Games to Munich.[43] The astonishing rapidity of the West Germans' decision led their East German counterparts to surmise that Bonn had demanded immediate action to "regain lost prestige."[44] While entirely plausible, the GDR's analysis was nonetheless incorrect. Daume was later wont to recount that he decided to bid in Madrid, realizing how much the country now needed to cement friendships and allegiances.[45] There is certainly some truth in this explanation, but it neglects the important fact that the idea of hosting an Olympics in Berlin was still circulating in the course of 1965. Brundage had been "questioned about the possibility" while in Europe that May,[46] and had irritated the East Germans in August by dangling the prospect to dissuade them from pushing for independence.[47] It is also likely that—even indirectly—a good deal of Daume's pre-Madrid campaign was devoted to the Munich "plan B." Ambitious to climb the IOC ladder, hosting the Games in Germany would have featured strongly in his long-term strategy. Appearing to have lost on an apparently cherished point of principle in Madrid, thus, did no harm in amassing a potential sympathy vote when it came to bidding for the big prize itself.

When considering the viability of the bid at home, the German question did not overly trouble the initial discussants. Vogel raised it with Daume (along with finance),[48] but was advised by his party leader Brandt that awkward questions of protocol might well be resolved by 1972.[49] Chancellor Erhard, at his first meeting with the two lead organizers, made no mention of the issue,[50] and the prospective bid went through the cabinet meeting of 2 December 1965 equally unimpeded.[51] Six days later, minister of the interior Paul Lücke assured the burgeoning bid team "the federal government [would] do everything in its power to support the realization of the 1972 Olympics [and] create all prerequisites for their undisturbed hosting."[52] Yet this soon transpired to be a rash promise, one that would jeopardize the Games during and after the bid. In November and December 1965, Erhard might have prioritized the prestige-bringing benefits of the Olympics to the Federal Republic's worldwide image above the intricacies of the German question. But by Easter the following year, with the government struggling to keep its pledge and the Eastern bloc agitating against the erstwhile "capital of the movement," he would find himself backed into a corner.

Munich's bid and the political problems that trailed in its wake might not have arisen at all if two key ministers—Vice Chancellor Erich Mende (FDP, Intra-German Relations), and Gerhard Schröder (CDU, Foreign Office)—had been present at cabinet on 2 December. Neither, as their general record and subsequent interventions suggest, would have shared the chancellor's enthusiasm. Both had introduced important policies toward the East, but retained vital caveats in their outlook. In his first three years in office, Mende had begun what would become the "policy of small steps" under Brandt and Bahr, implementing a number of measures that improved relations between Bonn and East Berlin and alleviated some of the impact of the Wall on the German population. Yet despite the FDP's general hostility toward Hallstein, he advocated it fiercely for the hosting of international events on home soil. Schröder, one of Erhard's closest allies in the cabinet, followed an even harder line. Although his "policy of movement" established trade missions in Warsaw, Budapest, Bucharest, and Sofia, these advances were underpinned by a strict rejection of negotiations with the GDR, even at subgovernmental level.[53] Although remembered for steering a new direction in foreign policy, unlike Brandt and Bahr, he was not yet ready to accept the status quo of German division. For Schröder, this relationship represented a zero-sum game, in which each side's gains were bought at the cost of the other.[54] In the aftermath of Madrid, it is unlikely the foreign minister would have considered the prospect of an independent East German team in Munich a price worth paying.

As early as January 1966, when the IOC began to seek assurances about the rights of East German athletes, it became apparent that the cabinet had bitten off more than it could chew. The Ministry of the Interior dragged its heels until March and then formulated an evasive reply, stating that it would "do all in its power to . . . create, in every respect, such conditions as [would] make it possible to arrange [the 1972 Olympics] without disturbance and . . . endeavor fully to meet all the requests of the IOC *on the basis of the regulations of the IOC presently in force.*"[55] The IOC was immediately wise to Bonn's get-out-of-jail card, which aimed to protect the Federal Republic against any enhancement of the GDR's status before 1972. In line with the Olympic Charter that forbade discrimination on grounds of race, religion, or politics, and indeed in keeping with similar assurances in Munich's bid document,[56] Lausanne pressed for specific guarantees.[57] The issue had become acute again after the GDR's dramatic withdrawal from the World Biathlon Championships in Garmisch-Partenkirchen in early February 1966, when Bavarian police surrounded athletes for wearing state insignia on their training uniforms.[58] Having been made to look "like the last cold warriors"—as Daume wrote to Lücke—the bid team sensed its chances "ebbing away."[59] Certainly, the Eastern bloc's anti-Munich campaign had gone into overdrive. Rumors circulated that

Andrianow would be attacking the fragile sporting status of West Berlin at the IOC session in Rome, and—in stark contrast to their cordial discussions over bilateral sports relations the previous year in Moscow—the Soviets ignored Daume's attempts to arrange a private meeting.[60] While Daume waited in vain for a visa,[61] Andrianow highlighted cases of West German discrimination in the press.[62] The East German Communist Party's (SED) secretariat for international relations also planned to publicize details of the Garmisch incident around the world.[63]

The bid team waited in vain for an unambiguous letter from the government, but it did not arrive. With several ministries—Mende's and Schröder's to the fore—holding fast to the temporal qualification,[64] the Foreign Office fretted that the Madrid formula (separate teams with common insignia) could entail "a form of national surrender" with "far-reaching psychological consequences."[65] While the government would gladly insist on Madrid regulations when persuading the organizers of international competitions to remove GDR paraphernalia from their stadia, the idea of flying the neutral German Olympic flag at its own showcase event six years later was hardly appealing. By April, a clear gap was opening up between the concessions that the Land of Bavaria and the city of Munich were prepared to make and policies the federal government continued to view as nonnegotiable. While Munich and Bavaria conceded to demands from the Eastern bloc about the behavior of populous émigré associations in their region,[66] the Ministry of the Interior refused to expunge the critical caveat from its second guarantee.[67]

With "the Russians firing from all barrels," Daume became frantic. In a telex to Erhard he contended that Canada and the United States, both members of NATO, had previously provided such guarantees—and passed on, "for its oddity value," Brundage's remark that even Hitler had given written assurances in 1936 "that Jews would be admitted to the German Olympic team."[68] The cabinet remained unmoved—Lücke stressing that the Madrid ruling represented the utter limit of acceptability, and Mende arguing he was unwilling to concede "even if Munich's bid failed on this account."[69] Erhard was hemmed in and had little choice but to ignore Daume's pleas from the Italian capital.[70]

However, the loophole in Olympic protocol and gnawing concerns in some ministries about a likely public backlash were to save the day. Exploiting the fact that governments communicate with the IOC via prospective host cities and that the German declaration required a translation, Vogel and Daume prepared to doctor the English version of Lücke's blanket statement from 8 December.[71] Following Mende's advice,[72] the chancellery telexed Daume with a statement that continued to underline the federal government's "unqualified right to assert its sole right to speak for the entire German people,"[73] although this was withdrawn on the advice of the Foreign Office and the German ambassador in Rome.[74] At any rate, Lücke's ministry had been softening since the cabinet meeting, and after several frenetic days of negotiation, Daume and Vogel were finally permitted to utter the necessary guarantee orally.

To the surprise and delight of the West German public, Munich won the Games. But the government was having serious doubts and would come under intense pressure from the Eastern bloc to repeat its reluctant promise in writing. Over the next two and a half years, the letter required by the IOC and the GDR's final thrust for full Olympic recognition would push Bonn to the brink.

RECOGNITION AND DIPLOMATIC DEFEAT

The IOC sessions in Madrid and Rome—to borrow Schröder's analogy—had created a zero-sum game. It was not just that the Federal Republic's victory in Rome cancelled out the GRD's in Madrid. Rather, each country's triumph now contained the seeds of its own undoing. The Federal Republic had won the right to project itself via the 1972 Olympics, but also had more to lose should it go to the line to beat the GDR's lunge for status. Similarly, East Germany had gained the right to compete with a separate team at the 1968 Games, but the proviso that this team share a flag and anthem with the Federal Republic gave the West Germans a neatly defined default position to which they would refer if event organizers could no longer be persuaded to ban the GDR flag outright. Despite the bitter blow, the West German cabinet had soon capitalized on the opportunity even before the end of 1965, recommending the adoption of the "Madrid solution" in all cases "in which [their] claim to sole representation . . . [could] not prevail."[75] The GDR interpreted the new situation in exactly the same fashion, putting plans in place to counter any move by the Federal Republic to turn the "great progress" made in Madrid to its disadvantage.[76] Thus, Bonn and East Berlin were set for a further round of controversial encounters over Hallstein, with Madrid providing the rules of engagement and Munich as a vulnerable collateral asset. Only the DSB took the Madrid decision at face value, voting within weeks to lift its Düsseldorf Declaration of 1961 and normalize intra-German sports relations. Having achieved its goal of (at least partial) Olympic recognition, however, the GDR had little interest in playing real games with its neighbor—and the number of contacts remained a fraction of their pre-1961 total.[77] While West German sport representatives genuinely wanted a fresh start, neither government was remotely bothered.

Despite the global thaw of the mid-1960s, a deeper freeze had set in between East and West Germany. Erhard's inaugural speech, a diplomatic disaster in the Middle East in the winter of 1964 and 1965 (chapter 7), and fears among conservatives about the potential consequences of the GDR's economic upturn had led to an increasingly zealous implementation of Hallstein policies.[78] In early 1966, the state secretary in the Foreign Office, Karl Carstens, deemed the GDR—incorrectly, as it turned out—to be "progressing unstoppably" and urged the government to "continue the struggle" for "every partial victory."[79] The year continued, therefore, in a blaze of activity designed to show the Federal Republic "was not becoming reconciled to the existence of a second German state."[80] Complaints were made on petty issues, such as the diplomatic plates on the East German consul's car in Yemen and the flying of GDR flags at the Algiers trade fair. In this climate, the DSB was also to feel a chill wind. Although its willingness to engage with the East was in keeping with the public mood—a survey in early 1967 found 83 percent of the population in favor of intensifying cross-border sports relations, 67 percent stating that the GDR should be allowed to fly its flag and sing its anthem in Munich's Olympic Stadium[81]—cabinet discussions in the autumn of 1966 put the national sports body under greater pressure than before.

Flag and anthem protocol at the European track-and-field championships in Budapest in August lit the government's touch-paper.[82] Despite assurances from the International Amateur Athletics Federation (IAAF) that the Madrid formula would be applied, winning athletes from the GDR were honored with full national colors. With the West German team refusing to boycott the event as requested, the government had been forced to look on impotently. The cabinet was gravely concerned that such incidents could multiply and force the Federal Republic into accepting the GDR flag in Munich. Some argued the Games should be given back immediately (under the pretense of financial strain), others that funding be withheld for the foreseeable future. Although neither suggestion was pursued, a feeling took hold that sports resources should become dependent on their recipients' support for "the Federal Republic's vital political interests." Word spread of CDU discontent and rumors circulated that the IOC might transfer the 1972 Olympics to Stockholm.[83]

In subsequent weeks, the Foreign Office drafted a perspicacious paper on the problems of enforcing Hallstein in international sport. This recognized, first, that despite NATO's recent commitment to flag and anthem codes, member states were already applying regulations less strictly than desired. Second, it noted the unwillingness of Western governments to interfere with international federations, sport being considered separate from politics but valued for its galvanizing effect among those levels of society "particularly inclined to emotional forms of response and with little grasp of political matters." And third, it lamented, while sports officials in the Eastern bloc were nourished on a direct political drip, Bonn held little sway over its own representatives who viewed the political aspect of international sport as the prerogative and duty of governments alone.[84]

The most intriguing aspect about the Foreign Office's analysis—apart from its envy of "totalitarian states"—is its failure to register any notion of success. Neither the Federal Republic's victories in keeping the GDR at bay diplomatically, nor the GDR's advances in the world of sport play any part in its interpretation.

The first absence explains the narrow line the West German government continued to take generally in 1966. In retrospect, as scholarship has shown, Hallstein (although frayed at the edges) clearly permitted Bonn to keep the "East German regime . . . on the fringes of international life precisely as long as [it] wanted."[85] At the time, however, the government remained uncertain about its own success and increased its Hallstein measures out of a sense of desperation. The second absence—that of the GDR's athletic triumphs—displays a fundamental lack of understanding of how sport worked, and would ultimately cost the Federal Republic this prominent episode in the Hallstein war.

Sport functioned differently from international politics. Worldwide—not just in Western democracies—it viewed itself as nonpolitical and universalistic. By 1966, the Federal Republic might have gained membership to 1,121 NGOs compared to the GDR's meager 252 (out of a total 1,470),[86] but the latter had become a full member of every sports federation in the world (fifty-two) with the exception of FISU (student sport) and FIBT (bobsleigh).[87] Between 1956 and 1965, it had taken part in eighty-five world championships in twenty-four Olympic disciplines and had been forced on only five occasions to compete in a joint German team.[88] Sport, moreover, respected winners and indeed required their participation to make its championships valid. In the diplomatic sphere, the West Germans kept the East Germans on the margins (even at times of political vulnerability) because they were able to out-punch them economically. In the world of sport, however, the growing accomplishment of East German athletes in the course of the 1960s meant that their absence devalued the currency of international meets. Some federations even downgraded events from championship status if pressured to exclude the GDR.[89] In sport, therefore, athletic capital replaced financial incentives and reversed the normal poles of Hallstein.

The Foreign Office's failure or unwillingness to grasp this difference proved its undoing. In September 1966, Bonn wagered that its athletes needed only to assert their rights as stubbornly as the East Germans for event organizers to accede to their wishes. The government's renewed resolve was soon put to the test in October 1966 at the Mexican "Pre-Olympic Weeks," a meet organized annually in the mid-1960s to allow the 1968 Organizing Committee (OC) to test its stadia and give athletes a chance to gauge high-altitude conditions. At the same meet in 1965, the West German team had walked out at the sight of the East German flag and refused to return until it was removed. Since the Federal Republic enjoyed good relations with Mexico, the offending item had been taken down to allow the event to continue.[90]

In the late summer of 1966, however, the new West German ambassador, Dr. Carl August Zapp, was given a baptism of fire even before his ceremonial welcome in Mexico. For the 1966 event, the organizers—doubtless seeking a compromise—proposed to eliminate national flags from the opening and medal ceremonies but to fly them nonetheless around the eight stadiums and play the national anthem for East German gold medalists (as in Budapest).[91] The Foreign Office was incensed and, under instruction from the cabinet (14 September 1966), sent its ambassador to inform the Mexican foreign minister that its team (under threat of losing DM 300,000 of governmental funds) had reserved an early flight home for all eventualities. To strengthen his hand, Zapp requested assistance, which duly arrived in the form of Werner Klingeberg, an experienced member of the diplomatic corps. Having served in the ranks of National Socialist sport and accompanied Leni Riefenstahl on her controversial film tour to the United States in 1938, Klingeberg was well connected and jetted in from Washington with assurances of support from the U.S. State Department, his old friend Avery Brundage, and Douglas Roby of the U.S. NOC. Despite hefty protests from the GDR, the event went ahead under a blanket ban on all national paraphernalia, a result celebrated as a triumph at the Foreign Office, with its enforcer bullishly exclaiming: "Mr. Daume told [the Mexicans] that he found himself in a situation he 'couldn't get on top of.' If he couldn't, then the Foreign Office seemed to be able to get on top of it."[92]

Zapp, however, struck a more sober note, observing that such interventions left an unpleasant aftertaste and predicting the West Germans would not always be able to turn events to their advantage.[93] The diplomatic machinations and their consequences in Mexico bear witness to the prescience of his statement. Most noticeably, a general slipperiness and confusion pervaded the conduct of leading functionaries in their dealings with the federal government. The Mexicans, who were obviously divided, passed Zapp and Klingeberg from one person to the next. Brundage was full of contradictions, obstinately refusing to classify the meet an Olympic event (which would have activated the desired Madrid formula), suggesting that only the Mexican and Olympic flags should be flown, and pedantically agreeing that the GDR should compete under the title "Ostdeutschland," except in the three sports (boxing, swimming, and cycling) whose international associations had already approved the title "DDR." Daume, who had originally tried to bring about a fait accompli by not informing the Ministry of the Interior about the Mexicans' unwillingness to change the protocol, sent his own envoy to clarify the issue of designation (Klingeberg having omitted to do so!), whereupon the GDR withdrew in mid-competition. Despite Klingeberg's triumphalist tones, the West Germans had done themselves no favors.[94] Their actions had deprived athletes from around the world of the honor of wearing their national colors, invoked the ire of the IOC, and projected an image of the Federal Republic as international spoilsport.

The fracas in Mexico has been recounted here at some length, because in these years it was repeated in one form or another at innumerable events around the globe. Zapp was instructed to assuage the hosts on this occasion, reassuring them they had not been singled out for special treatment.[95] But organizers and governments were beginning to take offense, and, increasingly, Bonn's actions were playing into the GDR's hands. As the East Germans deduced from the Mexico incident, the Federal Republic's renewed offensive could be simply countered with a plea to organizers to act "in the spirit of peace and mutual understanding, according to the statutes and regulations of the international sports federations." With Brundage and the international sports world now almost unanimously voicing their opposition to any form of discrimination, the GDR needed only to play the innocent and claim that "sport [should] never be allowed to become an extension of the Cold War or medium for the aggressive politics of the West German government."[96]

In sport, therefore, in distinction to the world of trade or diplomacy, the GDR went with the grain of international opinion and mores, the Federal Republic against it. In West Germany, sports functionaries continued their efforts to reverse the government's stance and bring their country into line with accepted practice. Daume even employed the same legal expert he had used to "oppose" the GDR's advancement in Madrid in an attempt to persuade Bonn that competing in the presence of GDR insignia did not imply recognition.[97] The Ministry of the Interior could not fault the juridical argument,[98] but as the world increasingly accepted the GDR's athletic rights, the government remained unmoved.[99]

Daume had hoped the change to the Grand Coalition in December 1966 might create a more relaxed atmosphere, but even Brandt's arrival in the Foreign Office brought only slight relief.[100] Some minor changes were wrought from Bonn in response to what was becoming an international landslide. For instance, just as the GDR had realized the need for flexibility in the pursuit of its goals,[101] the West German government (privately) agreed in 1967 to allow its athletes, after due protest, to remain at events where GDR symbols were in evidence.[102] On the whole, however, the Grand Coalition's sports policy differed little from that of its predecessor. For although the new government embraced East-West détente, and the SPD leadership at the Foreign Office found some of the isolation campaign wearisome, Bonn still regarded Hallstein "as a form of leverage over the GDR, a 'trump card' that could be bargained away in exchange for concrete arrangements with the SED regime."[103] This tactic also shielded Kiesinger against criticism from ultraconservatives within his own party.[104] Moreover, the Foreign Office was split internally, its two state secretaries representing opposite ends of the spectrum.[105] Despite Brandt's desire to open up sports relations with the East, uncertainty about the overall political climate encouraged caution and led to a virtual standstill. Furthermore, Bonn believed that the longer it held onto the Games the more difficult it would become for the IOC to find an alternative venue.[106] The notion that this temporal card increased the Federal Republic's chances of calling the shots was a grave miscalculation.

The IOC and the Eastern bloc were on the move: the former over written confirmation of the government's commitment for 1972, which had not materialized since Vogel and Daume's verbal assurance in Rome; the latter in its attempt to have the Madrid ruling changed to one that sealed complete independence for the GDR even before the 1968 Olympics took place.[107] The two issues became interwoven in the run-up to the Mexico Games. With Interior Minister Lücke refusing to furnish Daume with the requisite letter[108] and Brandt declining Vogel's admonitions to intervene,[109] the 1967 IOC session in Tehran was set to be a tense affair. Only a long and rancorous debate over the recognition of North Korea, which left the plenum reluctant to enter any further discussion, prevented the Soviets from advancing the GDR's case.[110] But the mood in Tehran was clear, one member making "the macabre comparison to 1936, when Hitler, without hesitation, had tolerated Jews in the German team."[111] The 1968 Mexico Olympics, therefore, at which the next IOC session was scheduled, would form the backdrop for the Soviet bloc's next assault. Under mounting pressure from Lausanne, the Munich OC (with governmental representatives abstaining) supplied its own promise of fair conduct, but not surprisingly the IOC continued to insist on a federal guarantee.[112] In the autumn of 1968, the Ministry of the Interior proposed Daume be given a secret undertaking, which he could use in an emergency to forestall or derail any recognition debate.[113] But given residual tensions between government departments and assurances from Brundage that the German question would not appear on the IOC agenda, neither Daume nor the ministries supporting him pursued the matter further.[114]

Expecting no major trouble in Mexico, Daume arrived to find business as usual.[115] Resolutely ignoring world events, the IOC was allowing the Games to proceed as normal despite the student massacre and a plea from multiple gold-medalist Emil Zatopek for the Soviets to be banned in the wake of the invasion of Czechoslovakia. The GDR and the Federal Republic were indulging in familiar rituals too. The East Germans lodged a complaint about the hoisting of the West German flag in the Olympic village to the strains of the national anthem rather than the neutral Beethoven,[116] and—acting on a tip-off from a defector from the GDR cultural program[117]—the West Germans stopped their rivals parading into the Olympic stadium behind the forbidden nomenclature "DDR."[118] The Mexican police swooped at the stadium entrance and, despite East German Sports Association (DTSB) chairman Manfred Ewald instructing his athletes and officials to surround their sign, managed to cover it clumsily with the label "Alemania Este."

But within hours of this incident, the IOC had granted the GDR full recognition. Although it had agreed to postpone the issue until its 1969 meeting in Warsaw, Brundage became a victim of his own scheming. Facing reelection in Mexico, the president had sought to retain the support of both Germanys in the course of 1968. He had assured the West Germans that the recognition issue would not be discussed in Mexico[119] while simultaneously instructing their rivals that a technicality of the Madrid agreement—which became null and void after the 1968 Games—meant they only needed confirmation from the executive board rather than a full discussion in the plenum.[120] Whether Brundage would have made good on his promise is a moot point. In any case, the East Germans became nervous and threatened to withdraw support for his reelection and expose his connivance to the membership.[121] Brundage reopened the issue the next day with a gusting speech against discrimination in sport.[122] Against the run of play in NGO politics—in May 1968 the GDR was turned down for membership to the World Health Organization by a vote of fifty-nine to nineteen[123]—the GDR gained full recognition by a margin of forty-four to four. West German IOC member Prinz Hannover's motion to rid the Games entirely of national insignia narrowly failed to reach the required two-thirds majority, so the GDR could look forward to trooping its colors in Munich. Brundage, with Soviet backing, was reelected president.

In Mexico a Foreign Office observer, charged with monitoring the loyalty of the West German sports representatives,[124] registered their lack of effort to influence African and Latin American IOC members.[125] In the immediate aftermath Vogel was unperturbed, Daume and his colleagues relieved. Reaction in Bonn, by contrast, bordered on the hysterical: amid calls to give the event back, the CDU/CSU parliamentary caucus discussed declaring Munich an extraterritorial city for the duration of the Olympics.[126] The cabinet, however, kept its cool. With Montreal eagerly waiting in the wings to snatch the 1972 event,[127] Minister of the Interior Benda believed it impossible to return the Games,[128] and the chancellor "establish[ed] that the preliminary consultation [had] shown that the IOC decision had no consequence in international law and should therefore be taken calmly."[129] Since the GDR's flag would appear in fulfillment of another body's statutes, since the IOC did not recognize states but rather geographical areas represented by NOCs, and since by declaring so in advance the Federal Republic would not even be granting a de facto recognition *(stillschweigende Anerkennung),* the GDR's insignia, so the logic ran, could be tolerated in Munich. Forced to accept the new situation for fear of public outrage,[130] the federal government eventually put its differences aside and simply reversed its earlier arguments.[131] Not for the first time in the history of the 1972 Games, the paradox of sport's "nonpolitical" nature came into play, the cabinet's statements in subsequent months essentially mirroring those formerly made by the GDR and Daume's legal expert in 1967.

In victory, the GDR switched tack as well, adopting the Federal Republic's familiar line from previous years. Amid jubilation in the East German press, Ulbricht proclaimed "the decision once again underline[d] the fact that the presumptuous claim to sole recognition *[Alleinvertretungsanmaßung]* [had] been rejected."[132] Four days later a plan had already taken shape to exploit the opportunity to the full: IOC members who had voted for the GDR were to be sought out and the Mexico decision used to formulate steps toward diplomatic relations in carefully selected countries.[133] In this area, there was indeed a rapid breakthrough in 1969, with a record six noncommunist nations recognizing the GDR in one year. But only one of them (Sudan) had an IOC member at the time of the Mexico vote. In other words, diplomatic success in the realm of sport had no direct effect on the world of politics. In this sense, Joachim Scholtyseck was correct to note how "insignificant cultural relations ultimately were when seen against the backdrop of major political disputes."[134] This does not alter the fact, however, that at the time both German governments treated sport with the utmost seriousness, fearing its defeats and cherishing its triumphs. Scholtyseck's maxim would have been anathema to most German politicians of the 1960s. Furthermore, sport in that period—albeit in a relation of complex contingency—ran ahead of politics. Hallstein might have been the Realpolitik of its age, but sport proved a truer barometer of the future.

THE MUNICH OLYMPICS IN THE AGE OF OSTPOLITIK

From late 1968 onward, the mercury began to fall. Pressed again by Brundage and Daume, the cabinet finally agreed to supply the IOC with a letter before the end of the year.[135] It still balked at lifting the 1959 restrictions on the GDR flag, despite strong encouragement to do so by the interior ministers of the Länder[136] and vocal agitation from many MPs.[137] Notwithstanding some minor governmental triumphs at sports events, the interior ministers had pressed their case further by June 1969, and NATO relaxed its regulations. Thus, long after they had in any case become ineffectual, the final impediments to the smooth running of international meets were removed. The government could do little but echo NATO's guidelines and permit the organizers of events in West Germany to fly their rival's flag if required to do so by their federation.[138] When Brandt came to power that year, there was little more to do. In the short term, the new chancellor and his secretary of state, Egon Bahr, "found it expedient" to continue Hallstein generally.[139] But in March 1970, they acceded to the Länder's wishes by lifting the 1959 restrictions and instructing their embassies—albeit without public announcement—to take no further steps against insignia at sports events, trade fairs, and exhibitions.[140]

Three years before the Munich Olympics, therefore, a particular phase of Cold War feuding drew to a close. But a new one simply took its place. The GDR might have won the flag wars, but Munich provided a unique opportunity for both Germanys to transmit particular messages to the world. While the West Germans had to attend to the Herculean task of hosting the most modern Games in Olympic history, their Eastern counterparts could focus on a local ideological derby. In contrast to the period up to 1969, sport and politics in the Federal Republic largely pulled together.[141] Sport saw itself as contributing to Ostpolitik, while the government fostered greater athletic contact with the Eastern bloc.[142] However, since the sports-political apparatus across the border was raising its game, there would be much for both to absorb and deflect.

The GDR was to pursue two goals at Munich: the establishment and increase of its own status, and the prevention of the Federal Republic's attempts to do the same. It was to enjoy the party to the full while simultaneously destroying it for the hosts. The first aim had been broadly met by the IOC's decision in Mexico. It was to be completed by the vigorous production of medal-winning athletes (a subject about which much has been written already).[143] Having humiliated the Federal Republic on the track in Mexico, coming in fifth to its eighth, East Germany continued its meteoric rise in world sport via a system of talent-spotting and drug-fuelled training programs. It placed third at Munich and second four years later in Montreal, ahead of the United States. As widely signaled in the Eastern press, in 1972 the GDR intended to "let the West pay for the Games while getting on with winning them themselves."[144]

The second aim—to spoil the Federal Republic's positive self-image—was to be delivered via an equally prodigious propaganda campaign. Well-worn themes in the East's critique of West German sport and society in general were to be repackaged for a broad international audience, the Federal Republic being portrayed as a hotbed of revanchism and neo-Nazism and the world being told of one Germany's devotion to and the other's dereliction of Olympic duty.[145] The central committee of the SED passed its first Munich-related "decree" barely two months after the Mexico Games in January 1969 and segued swiftly into an orchestrated campaign of newspaper articles across the Eastern bloc.[146] In the same year, the Gesellschaft zur Förderung des olympischen Gedankens in der DDR (Society for the Promotion of the Olympic Ideal in the GDR) published *München 1972 Schicksalsspiele?* (Munich 1972 Games of Destiny?), a work that manipulated Daume's concern about the critical juncture 1972 represented in Olympic history.[147] While none of the arguments were new, their compression into a loudly trumpeted, hard-hitting book, capped with the infamous and oft-repeated equation "$2 \times 36 = 72$," heralded three years of heavy bombardment.

At the same time, the GDR could normally rely on support from its socialist allies, who mercilessly countered perceived acts of discrimination against one of its group and denounced the inevitable faux pas committed by the OC in its implementation of complex Olympic law. The incorrect wording on the first Olympic coin, the appearance of Walter Umminger's *Olympisches Lesebuch,* and the presence of emigrant organizations and U.S. propaganda radio stations (Radio Free Europe and Radio Liberty) in Munich and Bavaria allowed them to embarrass the Federal Republic with robust responses on the world stage. Specifically targeted by the GDR as "counterrevolutionary organizations" and "international spy- and agent-rings," campaigns against the latter two enjoyed unwavering and enthusiastic support from the Soviet Union and its satellites closest to the West German border (especially Czechoslovakia).[148] Amid rumors about the gathering of right-wing groups in Munich, the Federal Republic was forced to broker "an Olympic truce" that entailed moving the expellee organizations' annual congress away from Munich. The considerable domestic complications of this deal were matched by the friction generated in reaching a compromise between Munich/Bonn and the high-profile presidents of the American stations (General Lucius D. Clay and former U.S. president Harry Truman).

Agitation against Munich was an iterative process. When one topic burnt out, the Soviet allies let it smolder[149] while lighting the next fire.[150] On the surface, therefore, events might have appeared to be unfolding according to predictable patterns, one side drawing from a familiar inventory of irritations, the other parrying with weary but wary exasperation. This was certainly a vital aspect of the Eastern bloc's approach to the Munich Games but it was not the most important. During this period, the new political situation made the GDR's position less stable. Ostpolitik was opening up fresh channels of communication between the Federal Republic and individual socialist states and providing the medium through which incentives could be offered and deals brokered to the potential detriment of its rival. Amongst the four wartime allies, the Soviets had perhaps most to gain from Brandt's policies. The USSR had seen its international reputation plummet after the invasion of Czechoslovakia in 1968 and felt increasingly under threat from China. Domestically too, it needed trade and technological input from the West to support an economy that was struggling to feed its own citizens. Although standing to achieve international recognition, the GDR was concerned. Even before the SPD came to power, East Berlin sensed in Bahr's "Wandel durch Annäherung" (change through rapprochement) the danger of Western infiltration and isolation from its allies.[151] Brandt's election victory had little effect on the GDR's uncompromising sports-political line, and seemed, in fact, to reinforce it. Fearing the Federal Republic would use the Games to push its claim for "Alleinvertretung" and increase its influence in international sports federations, the East German leadership became more vigilant—indeed paranoid—than ever.

Recent historiography has shown that the East Berlin was right to watch its back in the new political climate. Generally, the Soviets were not prepared to buy its recognition at any cost, and in keeping with Brezhnev's desire to maintain the subsidiarity of his satellites, would neither relinquish their strategic rights on GDR soil nor sacrifice their victor's say over Germany as a whole. The complicated mechanism of Ostpolitik—which bundled four individual treaties with Moscow, Warsaw, East Berlin, and Prague and an agreement between the four wartime allies over the status of West Berlin—only served to consolidate Moscow's control. Cascading so that it ensured no agreement could be signed until the Soviets had first secured the deal that suited them best, three years of negotiations allowed the USSR to consolidate its postwar suzerainty in Eastern Europe. The considerable time-lag between the promulgation and ratification of treaties in the West German parliament allowed, and forced, the Soviets to exert considerable influence on discussions over the other treaties. This complex mesh of diplomatic activity affected the GDR in particular. In contrast to the relative freedoms afforded the Federal Republic by the West, East Berlin was micromanaged by the USSR, which demanded by turns a cooling or intensification of inter-German talks. Moscow showed little compunction in disappointing its ally's expectations either, decoupling its satellite's interests at various junctures. Moreover, it skillfully exploited a rift between Ulbricht and his deputy Erich Honecker, keeping both in play until it was convenient to let the latter usurp the former.[152]

If political relations were typified by suspicion, frustration, and the desire to exert and evade control, the course of sporting diplomacy hardly ran more smoothly. In sport, in contrast to politics, however, it was the imperial master that felt exploited by its satellite. Three months before Brandt's election victory, Sergei Pawlow, the chairman of the committee for physical exercise and sport at the council of ministers of the USSR, sent a letter to the Soviet ambassador in Bonn, presenting a catalogue of grievances, which corresponded to the GDR's general attempts to emancipate itself from the USSR in the late Ulbricht era. From the perspective of the Moscow sports establishment, the GDR had failed to play ball since its full recognition by the IOC in 1968. It bragged about its diplomatic breakthrough without acknowledging the decisive contribution of the entire Eastern bloc. "Seeking only its own advantage," it had taken to tactically removing its top athletes from all but medal-rich events and, worse, to tricking its way to victory over the USSR (for instance by sending its national squad unannounced to play the Soviet youth team). While the Soviets had generously shared the results of their sports science research, the GDR had teasingly gone to ground with its newly acquired knowledge.[153] And while the Soviets had sponsored the election of GDR colleagues onto the committees and executive boards of international federations, the East Germans had reneged on mutual commitments. At the Mexico session of the IOC, the Soviets had forced Heinz Schöbel to confront Brundage and prevent the recognition issue slipping off the agenda for another year. Thus in the late 1960s, although the sports rivalry between the USSR and the GDR had not yet reached the heights of acrimony of the late 1970s and 1980s, distrust and discontent had already taken root.[154]

In contrast to Ostpolitik, sport represented a sphere in which the GDR could express semiautonomy from the Soviet Union. Both realms would turn in on each other, however, as the socialist states began to consider their approach to Munich against the unfolding political process. This preparation for the Olympics interacted with the broader developments but—not surprisingly given the looser coordinates in sport—reflected them and deviated from them in equal measure. The most significant difference lay in the scope given to East Berlin by Moscow to assume a defining role in the Eastern bloc's plans for 1972. While the Soviets directed events on and behind the political stage, they were content to let the East

Germans take up the running for the Olympics. In fact, the lengths to which the GDR went to influence its allies and disseminate its Olympic policies represented the largest public and diplomatic operation in the country's history, exceeding even the political fallout from the Prague Spring of 1968.

Shortly after Ulbricht replied abrasively to Brandt's declaration of government in December 1969, the Sekretariat des ZK confirmed the formation of "AG 72," a Party Commission for the Political and Ideological Preparation of the Olympic Games.[155] This commission, which remained unknown to Western sources, assumed responsibility for coordinating and implementing Munich propaganda.[156] The stellar constitution of the twenty-three-man committee underlines the importance of the Games to the GDR. Reporting to the Politburo, it was chaired by the assistant head of the Westabteilung, Albert Norden, and included Michael Kohl, who became the GDR's chief Ostpolitik negotiator.[157] Alongside members of the DTSB, the State Committee for Physical Exercise and Sport, the Free German Youth (FDJ), and the Free Federation of German Trade Unions (FDGB), it contained several assistant ministers and the heads and/or assistant heads of all central committee departments necessary for the swift implementation of any of its directives.[158] As one insider noted, it was "the only GDR institution . . . in which four qualified political functionaries [were] chiefly concerned with the question of the 1972 Olympics."[159] Its tasks fell into three main areas: liaison with the socialist brother states; the regulation of the GDR's interaction with the Games (tourists, youth and student camps, cultural programs); and the production of a unified message to counteract the Federal Republic's attempts to use sport to "unleash a broad wave of nationalism and gain ideological influence over the population."[160]

Its furthest-reaching measures resulted from decisions to arrange a meeting of the foreign ministers, government sports representatives, and leaders of sports bodies from every socialist country (with the exception of China and Albania); to enter bilateral agreements with each of these; and to take soundings from and provide and exchange information with friendly and selected neutral countries. The net was to be cast wider afield to liaise with familiar socialist partner states such as North Korea, Cuba, and Yugoslavia; to exploit already existing political, trade, and cultural contacts in Algeria, India, Ceylon, Mexico, Chile, Colombia, and Ecuador; to sound out Iraq, Cambodia, Sudan, Syria, the United Arab Republic (of Egypt and Syria), Burma, India, Guinea, Mali, and Tasmania; and to seek out left-wing sympathizers in Finland, Sweden, Denmark, France, Italy, and Austria.[161] The unfolding of the political negotiations in 1970 only served to confirm the basic tenets of the GDR's Olympic plans. After the first meeting with the Federal Republic in Erfurt in March 1970, an SED commission charged with assessing the possible outcomes of German-German talks concluded that recognition was unlikely before 1975 and that "strengthening the alliance with the Soviet Union and other socialist states and furthering the international recognition of the GDR" should take top priority.[162]

Accordingly, the East Germans' massively ambitious sports-political concept for the Games was executed to the letter. From the early 1950s until 1969, East German sports functionaries had met with their allies at annual meetings of the sport leadership of socialist countries *(Sportleitungen der sozialistischen Länder).* From 1969 onward, however, they took up the running themselves. At a special meeting of deputy foreign ministers and sports leaders held in East Berlin in May 1969, the hosts were able to sign up their allies to a detailed political road-map for Munich.[163] After particularly vocal support from the Poles and the Soviets, the deputy ministers—including the normally reticent Romanian representative—agreed in general to uncover and counter the "underhand politics" of West German imperialism and to form a united and decisive front against discrimination.[164] Practically, they were to argue for the maintenance of the ceremonial aspects of Olympism; to stress its internationalist character; to uphold the notion of West Berlin as a separate political and cultural entity; to coordinate a response to invitations to the Olympic cultural festival; and to keep sports and sports-scientific contact with the West to a minimum. The meeting agreed to manage these initiatives via vibrant mutual exchange and further bi- and multilateral consultations.

Buoyed by this early success, the GDR nonetheless realized it would need to work hard to maintain the initial momentum. By June the following year, it had met at the central committee and ambassadorial level with the Soviet Union, with the foreign ministries of the other Warsaw Pact allies, and had established contact with a string of other countries from Cuba to Mongolia.[165] Olympic contact persons had been identified in GDR embassies across the Eastern bloc and in reciprocal embassies in East Berlin.[166] On the surface, the GDR found its allies politely obliging. With the exception of Romania, they all agreed to the future establishment of multilateral agreements on key individual matters. But in reality, they were already going their own way. The East Germans had originally argued for complete rejection of the relay and—after disapproving comments made to the Munich organizers by the IOC at its session in Amsterdam in May 1970—of the youth camp and cultural festival as well.[167] Nonetheless, the Soviets, Hungarians, and Romanians had established informal links with Western youth organizations; Bulgaria, Hungary, and Romania looked likely to join the torch relay;[168] and the latter two with Poland were opting into the cultural program.[169] This was being organized mainly via the usual commercial channels that regulated such forms of East-West exchange during the Cold War, and clearly the prospect of Western currency and Olympic capital provided more luster than the GDR's ideological smear could tarnish.[170] According to Western media sources, the Soviets and Czechs, who were keeping the GDR in the dark about their intentions, had also entered negotiations.[171]

On a more general level, however, the GDR was concerned that its allies were underestimating the inherent dangers of rapprochement. Some—correctly as it turned out—denied there would be problems with the GDR flag and anthem in Munich. Others argued that Brandt's government had adopted a more realistic approach to the socialist states and therefore would hardly seek confrontation in Munich. Even the normally obliging North Koreans withdrew at short notice from organizing the annual conference of sports leaders.[172] All in all, the GDR's assessment of its partners' political preparations for the Olympics was withering.[173] Concerned at the turn of events, the SED central committee asked Moscow to call an emergency meeting of European brother states at party level in December 1970.[174] In the Russian capital, the GDR found itself forced into softening its initial vetoes in order to stay in touch with its allies. With prior Soviet consent, it gave way on culture and youth issues, but was able to reinforce its ideological agenda at length and reach a new consensus on central issues.[175] Only the Romanians dissented.

In this first phase, the GDR, albeit with limited success, acted as the policeman of the East. At a time when its shackling by the USSR prevented it from free negotiations with the Federal Republic on the grand political stage, it was allowed to patrol the socialist sports world with strong intent. Doubtless its relative freedom to wander resulted from the conservative sports-political line it was propagating, one which matched the one imposed by Brezhnev on the GDR in its relations with the Federal Republic and wholeheartedly supported by Honecker. In the GDR, sport traditionally fell under the remit of the deputy leader of the SED, and certainly Ulbricht was out of the loop.[176] He was not informed of the Moscow meeting and, as his hold on the reigns loosened further, the GDR's Olympic politics were to ferment implacably around "Abgrenzung" (demarcation) and the rejection of any West German "Alleinvertretungsanmaßung" (presumptuous claim to sole representation). As Ostpolitik developed and Honecker came fully to power, the East Germans' line on the Olympics hardened. Their implacability set them apart from their Warsaw-pact allies. While the Soviets were bent on extracting the maximum gain from both Germanys, the satellites wearied of the German question in sport as much as the Federal Republic's allies had from the mid-1960s onward. In the course of 1970, polemics in the Eastern-bloc press against Munich subsided and in some cases even displayed some "benevolence": West German analysts noted that (with the exception of the GDR) Olympic coverage in the Eastern bloc had become "detectably more objective" after Brandt's meeting with Stoph in Kassel.[177] At the Moscow meeting, moreover, the GDR overplayed its hand on the Nazi legacy and underestimated the positive effects that Ostpolitik was having on its allies. As one representative lamented on his return to East Berlin: "The Olympics can't just be compared to the Games of 1936. For all its flaws and weaknesses, the Federal Republic is not a fascist state. . . . We must therefore desist from the political strategy of throwing insults and making out that it is only a matter of unmasking our opponent."[178] Both stances—the Soviets' general slipperiness and the unwanted positive reception of Ostpolitik among the satellites—were to complicate the GDR's diplomatic preparations immeasurably.

It suited the Soviets to be called upon by the GDR as the highest authority in cases such as the perceived crisis of December 1970. Such instances allowed Moscow to reassert its own position of hegemony and reassure East Berlin of its loyalty. They also gave it the space to pursue its own goals. For its part, the GDR was not blindly naïve and kept a firm, suspicious eye on its ally, especially as the latter produced a series of contradictory statements in the course of 1970.[179] It watched on with regret as Daume, Mayor of Kiel Günther Bantzer, and Klein were given a harder time from sympathetic socialists in Helsinki than the Soviet press in Leningrad.[180] And it felt left out in the cold when its proposal for a bilateral high-altitude training center in one of the Soviet republics met with barely lukewarm enthusiasm.[181] Most significantly, the GDR was humiliated as the Soviets failed to enforce the decision not to participate in the Olympic Torch Relay. Despite the agreement to boycott this symbolically resonant prequel to the Games, Hungary and Bulgaria were allowed to break ranks, with the Soviets turning a deaf ear to pleas for them to intervene.[182] The GDR's plans for the Eastern bloc to abstain completely from cultural aspects of the Munich event lay in ruins.

In 1970, quite apart from the master narrative of Ostpolitik, Moscow's bid to host the 1976 Olympics provided the Soviets with another reason for veering as much to the West as to the East on the German issue. Explaining the importance of a "flexible strategy" to win the event, the Soviets had counseled the East Germans that their public support for them would temporarily wane.[183] Indeed, Soviet press coverage of Munich's preparations remained "reserved" in the period, and Andrianow conspicuously abstained from abusive comments in a high-profile interview with *Die Zeit*.[184] Despite such favorable conditions, the competition to host the 1976 Games proved diplomatically complex for the Federal Republic, as the United States also proposed Los Angeles as a candidate city. Keen to host the Games in their bicentennial year in a city that enjoyed the warm support of California-born President Nixon,[185] the United States informed the Foreign Office in Bonn that it would appreciate the votes of the West German representatives.[186] Daume, however, had already given assurances to Brandt that the three West Germans on the committee would follow the chancellor's desire to support Moscow,[187] a message that had been passed back through official Soviet channels by the Federal Republic's ambassador in Moscow.[188] Whether deliberately concealing Brandt's approval or genuinely preferring to view matters in Olympic rather than world-political discourse, Daume argued that the Federal Republic would support the USSR not only because the Games had never been held in a socialist country but also—with some cynicism—because the poor standard of living in the Soviet capital would give Munich, four years on, retrospective sheen.[189]

In the end, either neutralized by the worldwide campaigning of the superpowers or shying away from an awkward decision, the IOC opted for the compromise candidate, Montreal, a city few had given any chance before the vote. The Soviets lost in such bad grace that many were relieved they had been defeated.[190]

By 1971, however, the Soviets had the broader political jigsaw on which to concentrate again. For the GDR, it was a time of increased concern as their Soviet allies drew closer to fuller agreement with the West. Despite Soviet assurances to the GDR that sports contact with the Federal Republic would remain at its current low level, the political rapprochement brought with it an increase in official dialogue between sports leaders.[191] In the space of just over one year, two West German parliamentarians made a sports-related trip to the USSR;[192] Willi Daume and Hans-Jochen-Vogel, followed by representatives of the DSB, visited Moscow; a delegation from the Munich OC attended the Spartakiad; and Sergei Pawlov became the first Soviet sports functionary at minister level to travel to the Federal Republic. This upturn in activity was significant, since cultural exchange, first institutionalized in the German-Soviet cultural treaty of 1959, had previously been nothing more than dutifully measured.[193] However, at the same time as the ink was drying on the Moscow treaty, the Soviets began canceling cultural events—including the Munich OC's Olympic exhibition scheduled for Moscow—to hasten its ratification.[194] As the negotiation of a Berlin agreement came onto the agenda too, the symbolic capital of the West Berlin sports issue rose dramatically in stock. Soviet press criticism of Munich increased significantly,[195] and in the weeks before the signing of the Four Powers Agreement in September 1971, the USSR created havoc for the SPD by refusing until the eleventh hour to issue visas for West Berlin athletes competing at a Soviet-West German track-and-field meet in Kiev.[196] Such brinkmanship and the denial of rights that were about to be conceded,[197] Bonn concluded, were aimed at inflating issues so that the Soviets could appear to be giving away more at the negotiating table.[198]

The Berlin-Kiev incident, however, proved to be the final West German–Soviet sports political crisis. As attention turned to the final inter-German stages of the negotiations and to saving Brandt's government in 1972, the sting was drawn from direct German-Soviet confrontation. In March 1972, the cancelled Munich exhibition eventually went ahead in Moscow, the Soviets using this position of generosity to insert an art exhibition extolling the virtues of Soviet sport into the official cultural program of Munich.[199] Despite the unavoidable political nuancing of such events, cultural exchange was essentially reharnessed to the goal of political progress.

In 1972, therefore, the Soviets settled back into the natural rhythms of playing the East and West Germans alike for all they could get. On the West German side, this meant a rush of sporting visitors to Munich and its political environs. In March, the mayor of Moscow, Promyslow, traveled to Bonn, Düsseldorf, and

Munich and paid a special visit to the technical suppliers Siemens.[200] The constitution of the next delegation to come calling underlined the Soviets' vital interest in Western trade. Just two days before the Bundestag vote of no-confidence in Brandt's government, the OC in Munich was visited by a fourteen-strong group from the USSR under leading politician Nowikow. The group included the deputy chair of Gosplan (Lebetew), the deputy minister for the Radio Industry (Pankratow), the minister and leader of the Department of Foreign Trade (Simakow and Nikitin respectively) and representatives of the State Committee for Science and Technology.

In May, Pawlow accompanied the USSR soccer team to their match against the Federal Republic to mark the official opening of the Olympic Stadium, and lauded the ratification of the Moscow and Warsaw treaties, underscoring the importance of sport in the popular political imagination.[201] As well as sending a full squad that would "present the world with an array of superlative sporting achievements," he confirmed the USSR's full participation in the cultural and scientific program. One hundred and twenty young people (50 percent more than originally agreed with the GDR) would attend the Youth Camp, representing "the entire multi-national family of the peoples of the Soviet Union." The West Germans spared no expense in sealing the mood of cooperation.[202] The Soviets were given coffee with Genscher and taken to the opera at the National Theater and Daume's private birthday party in Ruhpolding. They planted a tree on the Olympic site and were flown by helicopter to the Adidas factory in Herzogenaurach on the way to lunch at the top of the Zugspitze.

These exchanges fitted snugly with the general political mood of the summer of 1972. On 3 June, the Moscow treaty was implemented. Ten days later, business followed a reassuringly unspectacular course, trade-offs being offered, exchanged, and delayed. When a delegation of Soviet parliamentarians visited Bonn, they were scarcely perturbed by the CDU/CSU caucus's attempts to lure them into jaundiced interpretations of the treaty, and enjoyed the generally improved and relaxed atmosphere.[203] The West Germans requested equal access to publicity in the USSR, while the Soviets, buoyed by Nixon's recent visit to the USSR, were keen to forge ahead with a conference on European security.[204] The Federal Republic, now in a position to concentrate on its negotiations with the GDR, was able to stall without impunity, claiming that the American energies necessary for such a task would be channeled into their own election until November. The time was almost ripe for "putting flesh on the bones of the treaty," but in Brandt's own words, patience was the order of the day.[205] The Olympics allowed the West Germans to sweeten such patience with hospitality and good intentions, and the Soviets to accept it with apparent grace.

The East Germans, deep into negotiations of their own treaty at last, had good reason to be concerned about their ally's Olympic dalliance with the West. It was obvious that the Soviets' contact with the Federal Republic had gone far beyond the low level they had originally promised the GDR.[206] It was equally clear that they were negligent in informing their ally about their contact with the West. At the 1971 Spartakiad, for instance, the East German delegation had been startled to read press reports of the West German Olympic exhibition to take place the same year.[207] And when the GDR delegation went to Munich to discuss the logistics of their team's accommodation, they were disconcerted to find the OC buoyed by the personal backing of the Soviets. By the end of 1971, the GDR was well aware that energy was draining from the Eastern bloc's coordinated attack. The IOC session in September 1971 satisfied the Soviets and their satellites that there would be no downscaling of the prestige-conferring Olympic victory ceremonies at Munich and undercut the credibility of the GDR's propaganda.[208] Information gathered from its allies in subsequent months suggested a distinct mellowing of stance toward the Games. By this stage, most socialist countries judged the preparations for the 1972 Olympics as perfectly normal and in keeping with the scale of the event, forcing the GDR—ironically at a point when for different reasons the topic remained contentious in the Federal Republic and the IOC—to relativize its own stance on the Munich Games' "gigantism."

• • •

At Munich the sports clash between the two German rivals retained the quality of a highly condensed and rarefied version of Cold War enmity. But between the Olympic years of 1968 and 1972, many changes had occurred to the political and sports-political contexts in which this contest was embedded. At Mexico 1968, the GDR defeated the Federal Republic both on and off the track. By the time it marched into the Olympic Stadium four years later, however, the best it could manage was a draw. Once again it defeated the Federal Republic in the medal table, but both countries nestled side by side in places three and four, the West German athletes turning in the only significantly improved performance of any Western nation since 1968. Diplomatically too, large cracks had developed in the socialist states' united front of 1968. Determined to meet Brandt's rapprochement with demarcation, the GDR instructed its team to isolate itself from all contact with the West. Famously, its athletes blanked President Heinemann on his visit to the Olympic village. At the same time, however, its allies were embracing the advantages of Ostpolitik and the Olympics more warmly. As the torch relay meandered across socialist southeast Europe, it was greeted with unalloyed pleasure by hundreds of thousands of athletes and ordinary citizens in Bulgaria, Romania, and Yugoslavia. In Hungary, hot-air balloons embossed with the five Olympic rings rose into the air as flowers were thrown over the runners from a helicopter amid repeated cries of "München! München!" and "Auf Wiedersehen!"[209] Those countries that had declined to participate now also featured strongly in other ways. The Czechs presented the OC with a highly valuable statue to enhance Munich's Olympic landscape—a gift that the Ministry of the Interior interpreted as a "gesture of reconciliation with regard to the Munich Agreement of 1938."[210] Polish music rang out at the opening ceremony, and the Soviets, as chief guests of honor, were whisked to it by helicopter after a lavish lunch at the city hall.[211]

The Cold War, of course, was far from over, and modes of behavior more akin to its normal habitus also still pertained. Often—particularly where the Soviets were concerned—several apparently contradictory tactics were employed simultaneously. Within a ten-day period in April 1972, for instance, the Russians sent a delegation of significant rank to Munich and pushed themselves and the GDR to the limit to ensure Brandt's survival in the Kafkaesque vote of no-confidence in the Bundestag.[212] At the same time, however, they called a special meeting with the SED's Rudi Hellmann to reaffirm plans for tough action against abuse and discrimination at the Games.[213] Two points become clear here. First, when the Soviets had allowed the GDR to police the Eastern bloc in preparation for Munich, they had done so on their own terms. At the beginning of the Ostpolitik process, it doubtless suited them to let the East Germans run the Olympic project while they gauged the distance they needed to maintain while pursuing their political goals. Part of that distancing actually consisted in permitting the satellites a considerable amount of latitude in dealing with the GDR's strict instructions. When the Soviets had achieved their goals and, to East Berlin's chagrin, allowed the satellites to involve themselves substantively in the Games' cultural programs, it suited them to close ranks again with the GDR.[214] Two days after the implementation of the Moscow treaty on 3 June, Soviet foreign minister Andrei Gromyko was in East Berlin scaremongering that the Federal Republic was almost certainly aiming for a united Germany. A series of hard-line meetings of the socialist states' sports representatives in the second quarter of 1972, at which the Russians took the leading role, falls conspicuously into the general pattern of the Soviets' Ostpolitik tactics: engagement with the West invariably balanced by discouragement to the GDR to follow suit.[215] Second, for the Soviets in comparison to the East Germans, sports diplomacy in the final years before the Munich Games occupied a lower level than the major political themes of the day. As their Sports Minister Pawlow told Daume in the summer of 1971, when the West Berlin crisis seemed to be brewing: "Die Hunde bellen, die Karawane zieht weiter" (the dogs bark but the caravan moves on). The Foreign Office's interpretation of this Russian proverb perfectly sums up the relatively minor effect of the niggles that accompanied much East-West interaction in sports at the time: "the attacks will continue without really threatening future dealings."[216]

Throughout the run-up to the Games, the West Germans met the GDR's provocation with great restraint.[217] The resolution of difficult situations was left mainly to sports functionaries such as Daume, whose excellent relations with counterparts in the Eastern bloc could often be exploited.[218] Failing that, Daume was not adverse to splitting Eastern bloc loyalties on the committees and subcommittees of the IOC.[219] The federal government, apart from dissuading its sports functionaries from involving themselves in overtly political discussion on trips behind the Iron Curtain, usually kept its distance.[220] In fact, it was not until April 1972 that an interdepartmental "Arbeitsgruppe für innerdeutsche und außenpolitische Fragen" (Working Party for Internal and External Affairs) began to meet.[221] The appearance of this official working party so late in the day confirms the West Germans' underlying confidence in their Olympic project. Although wary all the while of the GDR's propaganda, the organizers increasingly enjoyed the positive mood engendered by Ostpolitik. They could also count on the Eastern bloc's long-standing investment in the Olympic ideal and reluctance to relinquish its benefits on behalf of the GDR. Off the track, the GDR certainly scored some victories. But they were small in scope and paled beside the Federal Republic's production of an Olympic spectacle, which intellectually, culturally, and aesthetically surpassed all that had gone before it. Besides, events of an altogether different magnitude were about to steal the show.

7

The End of the Games

Germany, the Middle East, and the Terrorist Attack

On 5 September 1972 terrorism made its first major impact on global television. As hooded heads stood sentry with combat rifles on the balcony of the Israeli team's accommodation at 31 Connollystraße, the terrorists, "'super-entertainers of our time,' offer[ed] . . . irresistibly dramatic bait which [the world's media could not] help but swallow."[1] After almost twenty hours in the studio, ABC sports broadcaster Jim McKay broke the news to late-night viewers in the United States with the famous words: "When I was a kid, my father used to say our greatest hopes and our worst fears are seldom realized. Our worst fears were realized tonight. They're all gone." Thirty years later, McKay recalled: "It was the end of innocence for all of us."[2] ABC's legendary sports director Roone Arledge added: "It was a day like no other in sports. . . . The change in our universe was total."[3] The Olympic Games and other sporting mega events had been plunged into the age of high security.

Ten days earlier, the Games had started quite differently. Observers sensitive to historical burdens and geopolitical tensions were pleasantly surprised at the warm welcome extended by the home public to all its guests and the ease with which political rivals shared unusual proximity at the opening ceremony. The United States, unabused for once by Vietnam War protests, followed the USSR into the stadium without incident, and the German Democratic Republic (GDR), dressed in a range of pastel shades, was greeted with polite, if slightly muted appreciation.[4] To the relief of many, the small delegation from Israel too was swept up in the benign enthusiasm generated by the carefully choreographed festival. Dan Alon—an Israeli fencer who was woken on the morning of 5 September by the dull thud of bullets from the next apartment entering the wall above his bed—recalled in an interview with the authors in 2006: "Taking part in the opening ceremony, only thirty-six years after Berlin, was one of the most beautiful moments in my life. We were in heaven." In the commentary box, Jim McKay did not let the moment pass either: "There was a great applause when the nation of Israel walked in here, and of course, you couldn't be in Germany and not remember. We're just about fifteen miles here from the concentration camp of Dachau. But it is perhaps a measure of the fact that peoples and times change and nations do change that Israel is here. The Germans are cheering the Jewish athletes."[5]

McKay might have articulated what many were thinking, but his historical gloss did little justice to the complex relationship between the Federal Republic and Israel. On the one hand, isolated incidents testified to the inordinate prejudices on both sides. When Vogel was preparing to visit Israel in December 1971, he was briefed about the "rejection" Germans "still [had] to face in certain Israeli circles and how carefully one [had] to tread when entering bilateral relationships."[6] On the other, from the late 1960s public discourse in Israel suggested that relations between the two countries "had already completely normalized," and by the early 1970s ties had reached their most cordial.[7] After nearly two decades of "inherently asymmetric, volatile, and shallow" relations, in which the Israelis accepted reparations while reminding a resentful Germany of its guilty past, Vogel could undertake his public engagements in Tel Aviv and advertise the Olympics in full assurance of growing friendship.[8] Embarking on his third visit, the mayor was known in Israel for his promotion of German-Jewish reconciliation, not least with youth exchanges between Munich and Israeli communes since the early 1960s.[9] More generally, moral support offered by the West German government and population during the Six Day War had eased an "increasingly fractious relationship."[10] While the GDR was still despised for its unquestioning, Soviet-inspired support for the Arab states, anti-Zionist campaigns in the 1950s, and its refusal to acknowledge Jewish claims for reparation, the Federal Republic had extended the statute of limitation on war crimes, seen off the specter of right-wing extremism (NPD), played a key role in securing a trade preference treaty for Israel with the European Economic Community (EEC) in 1970, and the same year welcomed Foreign Secretary Abba Eban, the first official visitor from the Israeli government.[11]

When the Israeli athletes marched into the Olympic stadium in Munich, their country's relationship with the host nation was diplomatically solid but emotionally fragile. Their parliament, for instance, would gladly welcome a friendly visit by a soccer team of German MPs, but pounce when one of its members commented that sporting events might help overcome the past.[12] This delicate balance between mutual support and deepest hurt provided the frame for the Israeli team's entrance in Munich. In August and September 1972, the picture within that frame was subject to further national and international complications. To understand the fuller context of Israel's Olympics, the attack on its team, and the considerable detritus that trailed in its wake requires an appreciation of sporting relations between the two countries and the Federal Republic's diplomatic tango between Israel and the Arab world from the mid-1960s onward.

GERMAN-ISRAELI SPORTS RELATIONS AND THE MUNICH GAMES

Although contact between West Germany and Israel was deemed adequate, limitations imposed by Tel Aviv in 1961 placed the prospect of an official cultural treaty some way off. Against this background, sport proved particularly useful as "an important way of winning sympathy."[13] Not only did it guarantee good press coverage, but it reached young people with little interest in high culture. By 1972, in fact, the Federal Republic's youth sports exchange program with Israel outstripped those maintained with any other country.[14] Contact had become easier since the Israelis lifted their ban on senior teams competing bilaterally against West Germany in 1969.[15] Shortly afterward Josef Inbar—president of the Israeli National Olympic Committee and Hapoel, the country's largest individual sports association—requested support, and the Federal Republic took willingly to its donor role.[16] In 1971, when Hapoel invited West Germany to send ten to twenty top athletes to compete for the first time in its anniversary Games, the Foreign Office sponsored sixty stars (including Heide Rosendahl) to attend.[17] Borussia Mönchengladbach—the glamour soccer team of the 1970s—were greeted rapturously on the several occasions they traveled to play the Israeli national team[18] and in 1970, when a terrorist attack on an El Al airline complicated arrangements, they were even transported by the Bundeswehr.[19] Countless teams followed the club's example, and the Foreign Office paid to train Israeli sports coaches in Germany and monitored the sending of experts to Israel.[20]

It was not just the athletes who enjoyed close relations. In 1957 Daume persuaded the DSB to donate DM 50,000 toward a sports hall for the new village of Kfar Makkabiah and accompanied a young Werner Nachmann (by 1972 the Chairman of the Zentralrat der Juden in Deutschland, National Committee of Jews in Germany) to deliver the check.[21] Traveling to Israel half a decade before the first German politician in office, he met key Israeli personalities and later became cofounder, partner, and board member of the Feuchtwanger Bank in Munich.[22] In 1962 and 1963, he encouraged the Deutsche Sporthochschule to cultivate connections, started by the Diems, with its Israeli equivalent, the Wingate Institute.[23] Several visits supported by the Ministry of the Interior led to the first official partnership between a German and Israeli university in 1971 and joint Olympic training camps in the environs of Cologne before the Munich Games.[24] Having cooperated with Nachmann again in 1965 over the refounding of the Makkabi Deutschland e.V. (disbanded in 1938), Daume finally persuaded the German government to honor the association's reparation claim for confiscated funds in 1971.[25] It is hardly surprising, therefore, that both the Bavarian Landesverband of Jewish religious communities in Munich and the Israeli Foreign Office supported the West German bid to host the Olympics, the former even writing to sympathetic IOC members around the world.[26]

In turn, Daume lobbied Lausanne to grant Israel a seat on the IOC. Attempts had failed in the early 1960s, when Brundage simply stalled Daume's initiatives on administrative grounds,[27] but in 1969 he solicited the support of twenty members, impressing upon them the Federal Republic's desire to secure Israel's representation before the Munich Games.[28] Despite a host of affirmative replies and Daume's willingness to fight Arab opposition if necessary, Brundage used technicalities and delaying tactics again to frustrate the Federal Republic's good intentions.[29] Thus, despite participating in every Games since 1952 and enjoying warm support from most Western nations, the Israelis felt isolated in 1972. Controversially, they had been barred from the intermittent Regional Games by their Arab rivals, a bitter experience which led them, ironically, to support Brundage in opposing the exclusion of Rhodesia.[30]

Nevertheless, if the Federal Republic needed the Games to cement its improving image around the world,[31] then Munich would provide Israel with an international stage "on which the little country would have a welcome opportunity to fly its flag" and connect directly with the European continent to which it aspired to belong.[32] The location of the Games had not been an issue for the Israeli press, and while many were wary about a team representing them in Germany, such sentiments remained below the surface.[33] Munich was presented in much the same way as in other "friendly countries," and even a television screening of Leni Riefenstahl's *Olympia* just before the Games failed to elicit a single commentary or public reaction.[34] Due to a freshly installed satellite receiver that allowed the country to enjoy live coverage of an international event for the first time, "Olympic fever" gripped Israel in a way that "no-one could have predicted."[35] The opening ceremony made an enormous impression, inducing the *Jerusalem Post* to print a front-page editorial so effusive in its readiness to contrast Munich with Berlin 1936 that the organizers could scarcely have written it themselves.[36]

Almost simultaneously, however, an event beyond the organizers' control caused the commemoration of the past to rub salt into open wounds. When only three of Israel's twenty-eight-strong delegation attended the official memorial service in Dachau on the eve of the Games, there was public outcry at home.[37] deputy prime minister Yigal Allon demanded a detailed explanation, although the team had already planned its own event at the site several days later (along with twenty-nine young people from the youth camp and eight Israeli mayors who had come to the Games) to commemorate the outbreak of the Second World War on 1 September.[38] It is this event, shorn of its unfortunate context, that opens

Kevin MacDonald's film *One Day in September.* The embarrassment induced the normally restrained and pro-German sections of the press to criticize the host nation.[39] *Al Hamishmar* commented that the Games had returned to Germany too soon, and orthodox members of the Knesset, who had earlier complained about the Star of David being paraded at the opening ceremony on the Sabbath, now went into overdrive.[40] National television was generally sensitive to the orthodox position, and the German embassy soon noticed a change in its coverage. Although the daily shows were proving a great success, many viewers were irritated by the impression that they "might as well be taking place on the moon, but [were] nonetheless very close to Dachau."[41] Despite the warmest of sporting relations and the technology-fuelled enthusiasm for the Munich event, the fragile skein of public friendship had snagged on the first object to protrude from the Games' careful construction.

POLITICAL BACKDROP

Despite the upturn since 1967, diplomatic relations could be equally spiky. In the mid-1960s, Germany's delicate balance between its moral responsibility to Israel (a vital factor in persuading the Western allies of its new democratic pedigree) and economic and foreign policy interests in the Arab states was toppled over clandestine weapons deliveries to Israel, Egypt's threat to formalize ties with the GDR, and the Federal Republic's full recognition of Israel. "Having sailed along in the slip stream of the Western allies for the first ten years since gaining sovereignty, the Federal Republic's first independent encounter with international politics" went badly awry and the Erhard government's widely criticized mishandling of the crisis led to ten Arab states breaking off diplomatic relations in May 1965.[42]

Bonn's initial assessment that the estrangement could be resolved in a matter of months proved unrealistic, the crisis becoming its greatest "foreign policy debacle since the end of the war."[43] In 1967, the GDR made capital out of the disastrous Arab collapse in the Six Day War, and while the Federal Republic's star rose in Israel, it plummeted elsewhere in the Middle East. When the Arab world became uncomfortable with the Soviets' tightening grip in the early 1970s and frustrated by the GDR's inability to underwrite its rhetoric with serious financial backing, Bonn was keen to listen. By the end of 1971, Yemen, Algeria, and Sudan had reopened diplomatic relations, and in March 1972 the Arab League was due to discuss the stance of Lebanon, Egypt, Saudi Arabia, Iraq, and Syria. Brandt's new Eastern policies played a critical role in German-Arab détente.[44] Since the mid-1950s, the Federal Republic had resigned itself to countries such as Egypt equating its recognition of Israel with the status of their own ties with the GDR, but Ostpolitik effectively removed that bargaining chip and allowed Bonn to negotiate without putting its other relationships up for discussion.[45] Given the upturn, it is not surprising that Daume was strongly encouraged to make time just two months before the Games to join foreign dignitaries at the opening of the "Stade de la Révolution" in Algiers.[46]

Israel, however, was deeply anxious—first, that Brandt's unblemished war-record might diminish German moral responsibility toward Israel; and second, that his desire to embrace the Arab-supporting Soviet bloc would weaken bonds with Tel Aviv. Both worries were unsubstantiated. Brandt's gesture in the Warsaw ghetto largely assuaged the Israeli public's concerns,[47] and constant reassurances from governmental visitors allayed fears about the effects of Ostpolitik.[48] Nonetheless, it was clear that the Federal Republic had begun to shield behind the increasingly pro-Arab stance of oil-conscious institutions such as the United Nations and the EEC,[49] at the same time strengthening its case for entry to the United Nations and nurturing bonds with its European neighbors, in particular France.[50] The Israelis were more sensitive than ever when West German politicians talked about "normalization." Doubtless with an eye to reconnecting with the Arab world, Brandt's declaration of government in 1969 omitted his predecessor Kiesinger's reference to Israel, and soon after, the new coalition foreign minister Walter Scheel (FDP) went further, stating "We have the same relationship with Israel as we do with other countries."[51] The FDP had maintained a cooler stance on Israel throughout the 1960s, and in distinction to Brandt's more reserved tone, the Foreign Office would continue to press for an unburdening of German-Israeli relations in subsequent years for the sake of overall balance in the region.[52] With Egypt and Israel prepared to resume hostilities in late 1971,[53] the brief given to Vogel by the Foreign Office before his Israel trip left little room for ambiguity.[54]

Israel, however, was not prepared to sit idly by. In the course of 1972, its government undertook two distinct spoiling motions. Both used praise to accentuate West Germany's special historical ties and to complicate its efforts to embrace the Arab world.

The first of these attempts came a month before the Arab League was due to meet in March 1972. In late November 1971, while heading an FDP delegation to Israel, Party Chairman Wolfgang Mischnik had reassured his hosts that "the resumption of diplomatic relations with the Arab states [was] not yet imminent."[55] The same week, Golda Meir, acting on advice from Günter Grass, had written warmly to Brandt, suggesting a meeting of socialist leaders to discuss matters of common interest.[56] Brandt had shown willingness in the new year,[57] but before any gathering could be organized, Meir raised the stakes by inviting him to become the first West German chancellor to make a state visit.[58] A week before his arrival, reports of the invitation were circulating in the Arab press and alarm bells were ringing around the Federal Republic's diplomatic missions.[59] Bonn's representatives concurred that any visit would destroy Brandt's standing in the Arab states, unleash a range of disastrous consequences for the Federal Republic in the region, badly affect exports, and "in view of the well known Arab tendency to react emotionally" lead to possible attacks on German property and citizens.[60]

Coming just weeks before the Arab League meeting, the "badly timed" invitation was interpreted by Bonn and the Middle East as a deliberate move to torpedo West Germany's diplomatic progress with Israel's enemies.[61] Brandt announced that a suitable date would first have to be found, but the holding tactic failed to diffuse the situation.[62] While the Israelis welcomed the statement as a sign of strong relations,[63] left- and right-wing opinion in the rest of the Middle East called for a reassessment of Arab-German ties.[64] On the official level, however, no one had any appetite to let Meir disrupt their plans. The Egyptian government spokesman noted, "We know the other side's tricks," and the Tunisian ambassador reiterated the Arab distrust of Israeli motives but utter confidence in the chancellor's integrity.[65] Brandt, for his part, confirmed the visit would be postponed until relations with the Arab nations had been regulated and not take place in any case without further consultation with the Arab states.[66] Both sides seemed satisfied. On 9 March, a month after the invitation was received, Brandt thanked Meir for the "important initiative in the development of relations between [both] countries" but cited difficulties over the ratification of the Polish and Soviet Ostpolitik treaties as grounds for delaying.[67] Two days later, the League voted to enhance its links with the Federal Republic, and on 8 June 1972, Cairo, the unofficial capital of the Arab world, resumed diplomatic relations.

Just two weeks later, Israel registered grave disappointment at a perceived lack of German support over new import tariffs in the EEC and, on the same day, launched its second spoiling action.[68] Once again it sought to highlight its special relationship with West Germany, surprising Bonn with plans to mark the twentieth anniversary of the 1952 Luxemburg Treaty. Although the reparations deal that guaranteed Israel DM 3.5 billion over fourteen annual installments had expired in 1966, it still rankled in the Middle East as a symbol of West Germany's ties to Israel. With Meir proposing to make a public statement to the cabinet and former Israeli ambassador in Bonn, Felix Shinnar, exploring the possibility of a parallel program on the Westdeutscher Rundfunk, Brandt had little choice but to find a suitable reply.[69] The Foreign Office worried that the Israelis would use the occasion to pressure Germany into further payments (in particular to cope with the stream of immigrants from Eastern bloc countries since 1965), but urged a robust response.[70] A speech was drafted, but it was hardly the ideal text to be delivered on 10 September, the scheduled close of the Munich Games. While the organizers and government had hoped the Olympics would allow the world to *see* a new Germany, they had not planned for this transformation to be *enworded* via a heavy turn to the past. The Federal Republic's finest showpiece since 1945 was not supposed to end with the chancellor reminding the world of "the horrors of war and the inhuman persecution under the National Socialist tyranny," "the consequences of that unholy past," or even "Germany's renunciation of its Nazi past." The Foreign Office was troubled, redrafting Brandt's speech several times over the summer[71] and pondering deep into August the possibility of simply letting the occasion pass in silence.[72]

On 4 September, however, news broke that the Israeli government had decided to cancel its celebrations after all.[73] Sources close to the cabinet noted that Israel had not wished to "embarrass" the Federal Republic and "the social-democratic sister party in particular," but almost certainly other factors were also in play. For one, it was felt an unpropitious moment "to let Bonn believe it had done enough for Israel"; and for another, Meir was anxious not to incite Menachem Begin's right-wing Cheruth Party before the forthcoming elections. Twenty years earlier, the signing of the treaty had caused the heaviest demonstrations in the nation's short history, with Begin serving a three-month ban from the Knesset after an incendiary speech before the plenum. For whatever reason, on 4 September the Federal Republic was spared another difficult moment in its troubled triangular relationship. It was to be a very short reprise indeed.

THE ATTACK

On the evening of 4 September, the Israeli delegation went to see the musical *Fiddler on the Roof* in Munich's city center, returning mostly to the Olympic village around half past midnight. A mere stone's throw from the theater, eight members of a Palestinian terrorist commando, all in their late teens and twenties, were receiving final instructions in a restaurant at the main station. After mingling with tourists for several days and even attending the Olympic volleyball tournament, they were about to begin Operation Ikrit and Biram.[74] Little over twenty-four hours later, eleven Israelis, one West German police officer, and all but three of their number would be dead.

The operation was named after two villages from which Palestinians had been expelled in 1948 to make room for Jewish settlements, but the group derived its *nom de guerre,* Black September, from the events of September 1970, when King Hussein of Jordan's army attacked the Palestine Liberation Organization (PLO) headquarters in Amman, killing some three to five thousand guerrillas and capturing four camps in ten days. Surviving activists regrouped in Beirut and Black September emerged as an important element in a new terrorist infrastructure. Led informally by high-ranking PLO commander Abu Iyad, the group functioned without offices or spokesmen, and allowed Yasser Arafat to build a façade of political respectability while enhancing his credibility as a hard-liner within the organization.[75] The Munich attack was a case in point: although he denied all knowledge of it, Arafat personally approved it[76] and—as he admitted to Ion Pacepa, the Romanian foreign intelligence chief, as early as October 1972—permitted one of his aids, Hani Al-Hasan, to be involved in its preparations.[77] Years later, insiders would claim the operation was motivated by revenge on the IOC for ignoring requests from the Palestinian Youth Federation to compete in its own right at the Munich Games, but the IOC archive does not bear this out and more plausible arguments have been advanced elsewhere.[78] It is possible that the attack was intended to help Arafat arrest an incipient revolt among second-rank commanders dissatisfied with his running of affairs since the PLO's ignominious defeat in Jordan.[79] Related to this, it might also have sought to redress the balance of power with its left-wing rival, the Popular Front for the Liberation of Palestine (PFLP).

Since 1970, a number of hijackings and international terrorist strikes had allowed the PFLP under George Habas and Waddi Haddad to grow.[80] Most spectacularly, it attempted in September 1970 to simultaneously hijack four Western airliners bound for New York. Succeeding with three, it flew two to Dawson's Field, a former Royal Air Force landing strip in Jordan, where after the release of all the hostages, the planes were blown up in front of a world television audience. It was Dawson's Field that triggered King Hussein's assault on his unruly Palestinian minority and ultimately caused the formation of Black September. This new PLO group in Lebanese exile first came to attention with revenge attacks on Jordanian targets, ranging from the attempted sabotage and hijacking of Royal Jordan Airlines planes to the failed assassination of the country's ambassador in London and, in November 1971, the murder of prime minister Wasfi Al-Tell in Cairo.[81] But by 1972, the group was broadening its focus. A few months before the Olympics, it hijacked a Sabena flight from Brussels, forcing it to land in Tel Aviv and demanding the release of 315 prisoners from Israeli jails.[82] The hostage-taking came to a dramatic conclusion, when after ten hours of fruitless negotiations, Sayeret Matkal, an Israeli Defense Force special unit commanded by future prime minister Ehud Barak, overpowered the hijackers. Although deadly, Black September's activities on German soil had been less conspicuous. On 6 and 7 February 1972, the group shot five Jordanian workers in their beds in Brühl near Heidelberg on suspicion of collaboration with the Israeli secret service, and caused DM 1.2 million of damage in an attack on the Stüver company in Hamburg, which exported power generators and relay stations to Israel.[83]

On 5 September 1972, however, Black September's efforts would eclipse the PFLP's actions on Dawson's Field and raise world consciousness of terrorism to an unprecedented level. Shortly after 4:00 A.M., the Munich commando took eleven Israelis hostage in their apartments in the Olympic village, killing two in the initial struggle. In all likelihood, the gunfire alerted those not yet captured to escape. Realizing they were in mortal danger, the rifle shots—as revealed by Dan Alon—considered eliminating a terrorist sentry with the weapons they used for

FIGURE 18. Member of Black September commando, 5 September 1972 (photo: W. Schmitt, courtesy of Süddeutsche Zeitung Photo)

competition, but concluded this action would only risk the lives of their unfortunate teammates, and fled to safety with the others over the next three hours.[84] As earlier that year at Tel Aviv's Lod Airport, the terrorists demanded the release of 234 Palestinian prisoners from Israeli jails as well as foreign comrades such as Andreas Baader, Ulrike Meinhof, and Okamoto Kozo (who had taken part in the Japanese Red Army's own attack on Lod in May 1972). After being flown to a destination of their choice in the Middle East, they would free the hostages in stages.

The terrorists' two-page communiqué stressed the Federal Republic's responsibility to resolve the situation, threatening to "teach the arrogance of the Federal Republic a severe lesson" should their ultimatum not be met. But there was little the West German government could do. On the one hand, the terrorists laughed off repeated offers of "unlimited sums of money" or political asylum, pointing out that as soldiers they would be executed if they disobeyed orders.[85] Moreover, the group's ethos of ultimate annihilation had been witnessed in Tel Aviv, when the hijackers threatened to blow up the plane and kill themselves in the process should their demands be ignored. On the other hand, the politicians were of little help either. Not only did Meir quickly tell Brandt that, unlike her predecessors (and indeed successors), she would not release the prisoners, but attempts to influence the terrorists via third parties proved equally frustrating.[86] Egyptian IOC Member Ahmed Eldemerdash Touny's efforts to negotiate with the unit in the Olympic village were as fruitless the Foreign Office's appeals to Middle Eastern governments. Even Brandt, who traveled to Munich in the afternoon, saw his plea to the Arab states go unheeded.

A week later, Manfred Schreiber would tell the *Spiegel* that the nine hostages who survived the initial attack had been all but dead from the outset.[87] But this remark was made in hindsight, and on the day itself, when the unreal quality of events plunged the authorities into a dysfunctional stupor, little such clarity was displayed. Six members of the Hong Kong delegation, who were living in the penthouse above the Israelis, went to breakfast only for two of them to be allowed to return and be instructed by a terrorist which staircase to use.[88] The media on surrounding vantage points and ABC's telescopic lens on top of the Olympic tower captured every movement on the balcony and negotiations in the immediate vicinity.[89] And although Schreiber had cordoned off Connollystraße, ABC's John Wilcox secreted himself almost directly opposite the siege in the offices of the Burmese soccer team,[90] and Gerald Seymour, who later made his living as a writer of terrorist thrillers, reached the Puerto Ricans' accommodation at the eastern end of the street with a crew from London-based ITN.[91] As Dan Shilon of Israeli television admitted: "This was a bizarre, surrealistic situation in which we journalists surrounded the event with every possible camera."[92] Audiences around the world watched life in the rest of the village continue, with athletes sunbathing and playing ping-pong. Thousands of onlookers congregated at the perimeter fence[93] and were joined by a further seventy-five thousand when the Games were suspended in the afternoon and the stadium emptied into the surrounding park.[94]

In this context, the West German authorities were strangely paralyzed. Although an investigation by the Bundestag's Committee of the Interior (Innenausschuß) concluded there "had at no point been complications of hierarchy" and that "in the situation everything possible was done, appropriately handled and the correct decisions made," its findings bear little scrutiny.[95] Ignoring the rules of federalism, national minister of the interior Hans-Dietrich Genscher joined his equivalent at Land level, Bruno Merk, as well as Manfred Schreiber at the core of the crisis

FIGURE 19. Improvised protest against terrorism in the Olympic park, 5 September 1972 (photo: Rue des Archives, courtesy of Süddeutsche Zeitung Photo)

committee (Krisenstab). Sigismund von Braun, state secretary in the Foreign Office, and Franz Josef Strauß, the CSU leader and second-most powerful member of the opposition, were also present. Throughout the day, they received advice from sports functionaries and Arab and Israeli officials of various rank and standing: Vogel, Daume, and Walther Tröger, mayor of the Olympic village; Brundage who twice insisted the IOC would not countenance the removal of Olympic athletes against their will;[96] the Israeli ambassador (Ben-Horin), head of Mossad (Zvi Zamir), and a member of Sayeret Matkal (Victor Cohen); the head of the Arab League in Bonn (Mohammed Khadif), the Tunisian ambassador (Mahmoud Mestiri), the leader of the Egyptian team (El Chafei), and the aforementioned Ahmed Eldemerdash Touny. Quite apart from the delicate hierarchy of city, Land, and state, a "tangled web of responsibilities and competences," as Matthias Dahlke recently put it, developed, hindering effective decision-making.[97] Moreover, the level of trust in the Arab negotiators was so low that they were not informed of the Israelis' unwillingness to negotiate.[98]

This melee and the unreality of the situation it sought to master produced a number of impractical suggestions as to how the hostages might be liberated. These give a good insight into the psychological state of those who made them or listened to them. Brundage wasted valuable time having the crisis committee investigate knockout gas, which he erroneously remembered being used by the Chicago police in the 1920s to overpower the mob.[99] The group also received fantastical schemes sent in by members of the public: a Bremen resident and Knight's Cross holder from the Second World War offered to free the hostages in a surprise attack; a man from Landau proposed to go in with local friends; and another wanted to "overwhelm" the hostage-takers with one hundred thousand demonstrators.[100]

As one deadline after another slipped (from 9:00 A.M. to noon, 1:00 P.M., 3:00 P.M., and 5:00 P.M. respectively), the terrorists tired of the obvious delays and at 4.30 P.M. changed their strategy, opting to leave Germany before the prisoners had been released and demanding to be flown to Cairo straightaway, where the exchange of hostages could take place the following morning.[101] Genscher and Tröger were allowed into the apartment to talk with the hostages, who assured them twice of their willingness to leave provided their government released the Palestinian prisoners. However, the Israeli position remained unchanged,[102] and in the evening the Egyptian president Anwar El Sadat refused to take Brandt's phone call, his prime minister Aziz Sidky simply stating: "We do not want to get involved."[103] For obvious reasons, the West Germans felt bound to resolve the matter by force. Genscher, like the chancellor's son Peter, offered himself in exchange for the hostages, later recording in his memoirs: "In my concern for the frightened, terrified, and desperately hoping people in the hands of the terrorists, I felt the burden of our history with Israel and the Jewish people more strongly than ever before."[104] Moreover, even if the Egyptians had agreed to intervene, there was no guarantee the terrorists would actually fly to Cairo,[105] an imponderable that endangered the lives of both hostages and the Lufthansa crew.[106]

From the outset, military solutions were considered too dangerous, although contingency plans had been put in place should the terrorists begin to execute the hostages or try to escape.[107] From late afternoon, three attempts were made or considered. Shortly beyond the last ultimatum at 5:00 P.M., the police decided to storm the building with over three dozen officers. But the operation had to be abandoned since, due to a failure to order a news blackout, the terrorists were able to join the worldwide television audience in watching inexperienced volunteers in tracksuits dropping equipment and ammunition on the gravel roof above their

FIGURE 20. Burned-out helicopter guarded by police at Fürstenfeldbruck airfield, 9 September 1972 (photo: AP, courtesy of Süddeutsche Zeitung Photo)

heads.[108] A second plan to shoot the Palestinians as they walked to the helicopters waiting to take them to the plane ended in an equally undistinguished manner, when the group's leader who decided to walk the underground route first was alerted to the presence of machine-gunners and precision marksmen.[109] And finally a farrago of errors at Fürstenfeldbruck military airport twenty kilometers to the north of the site brought Black September's ultimate sanction and Schreiber's worst fear to realization.

Untrained in close combat and fearing for their lives, a special commando of twelve volunteer police officers, posing as flight assistants on the waiting Lufthansa plane, abandoned their mission to overpower the terrorists shortly before the helicopters bringing them to the airport landed.[110] When a shootout started, police marksmen were ill-positioned, badly lit,[111] and scandalously under-equipped;[112] support from armored vehicles took an age to weave through the heavy traffic and onlookers clogging the city center.[113] After the lengthy gun battle claimed the lives of the nine remaining hostages, five of the eight terrorists, and Munich police brigadier Anton Fliegerbauer, in addition to leaving one of the helicopter pilots seriously injured through friendly fire, government spokesman Conrad Ahlers made a late-night announcement—based incredibly on a mysterious, unknown source—that the Israelis' lives had been saved. Newspaper first editions around the world rushed to publish a happy ending its readers would already know to be inaccurate.

Two systemic flaws outweighed the basic negligence: the police sent too few marksmen, and those they did were reluctant to kill. Quite apart from failing to ascertain the number of terrorists until inexplicably late (and then passing on the information incorrectly), the police chose to operate with an inaccurate one-to-one ratio of marksmen to terrorists.[114] The previous year, a siege at the Deutsche Bank in Munich's Prinzregentenstraße had been resolved by overwhelming the perpetrators three to one, but the police had been criticized when a hostage was believed to have died as a result of friendly fire. Statements by Schreiber and Wolf after the Olympic debacle suggest the earlier tragedy had led to excessive caution.[115] More importantly, the marksmen's training had prepared them to incapacitate but not eliminate their targets. Despite being told they were acting under emergency legal cover *(Nothilferecht)*, one later admitted to having scruples *(Beißhemmung)* about taking the Palestinians' lives.[116] Psychological fears, individual and collective, contributed as much to the disaster as practical errors.

Only fourteen years after an air disaster at Riem claimed the lives of eight Manchester United soccer players, the world turned again to images of destruction and the end of a sporting dream at a Munich airport. In their communiqué the previous day, the terrorists had warned that "any attempt to interfere [would] lead to the liquidation of all the Israeli prisoners, with the Federal Republic being held responsible." Both parts of their statement proved prescient, the second somewhat strangely so. For while the crime was Black September's alone—the damning response in the West convincing the PLO (although not the PFLP) to cease all terrorist activity outside Israel and the occupied territories—the responsibility for the outcome came to settle on the Federal Republic and, in particular, Munich's police force.[117] Decades of campaigning for compensation by the families of the deceased and recent filmic treatments have consolidated a certain easy castigation of the West German authorities. It is worth pausing, however, to place the attack in a number of important security contexts. These will serve both as a corrective to simplistic but widespread assumptions of German culpability and as the background to the diplomatic aftermath that plunged Arab-German-Israeli relations into deep crisis.

Intelligence

The first context is the lack of specific intelligence information in the months prior to the attack.[118] This stark shortcoming, however, is mitigated by three considerations. First, the Germans expected politically motivated disturbances to emanate from domestic rather than international sources, either from left-wing groups or eastern and southeastern European émigrés clustered around Munich. Both potential hazards had been so successfully countered before the Games began that the authorities might even have been lulled into a false sense of security.[119] The Law for the Protection of the Olympic Peace had been passed, after some hesitation, by the Federal Parliament (see chapter 5). And after its "May offensive" (which included an attack on Munich police headquarters), the "first generation" of Red Army Faction (RAF) leaders had been arrested.

Second, the West Germans were not alone in being taken unawares. Neither Britain's MI6, the CIA, nor the French DGSE had any inkling and, as recently evidenced by Aaron Klein's analysis of previously undisclosed Israeli papers, the Mossad and other Israeli services were in the dark as well.[120]

Third, the intelligence community did not so much fail to register the terrorists' preparations as focus intensely on their customary modes of behavior. Like the events of September 11, 2001, Black September's operation in the Olympic village was a first: hostage-taking had become common since 1970, but it normally occurred in planes. In February that year, the PFLP seized the first German aircraft, claiming a US$5 million ransom, but in Western Europe Palestinians had never taken captives in buildings. In June 1971, the head of the Staatsschutz in the Bavarian Interior Ministry took seriously Israeli warnings about hijackings[121] and in its last paper before the Games, in June 1972, the Bayerisches Landesamt für Verfassungsschutz noted the threat of Black September and the PFLP to charter flights.[122]

According to available sources, only one figure within German security circles anticipated what might occur. As part of a range of training scenarios, Munich's police psychologist Georg Sieber—who specialized in finding peaceful solutions to crisis situations and was appointed by Schreiber to assist the progressive and psychology-based agenda of the Münchner Linie—envisaged a so-called "PLO-Modell," which described in some detail what eventually happened on 5 September.[123] In such an event, Sieber suggested, the terrorists could be unsettled and forced to end the siege by using specially controlled smokescreens to simulate a fire in the building.[124] When fiction became fact, however, Schreiber excluded his psychologist from operations, later claiming that only leading police officers possessed the professional and life experience the situation demanded.[125] Joachim "Blacky" Fuchsberger, the famous Munich stadium announcer, remembers Schreiber commenting on Sieber in less charitable fashion: "Police psychologists ought to be clobbered to death." Leaving issues of personal animosity aside, it is clear that Sieber's solutions would have proved ineffective in Munich, since they were based on the flawed assumption that the terrorists would consider alternative endings to their operation.

Terrorist Structures

Beyond the unfamiliarity of the situation, Black September was notoriously difficult to penetrate. Representing a break with traditional PLO structures, it operated around hermetically sealed cells, to which instructions were passed by intermediaries.[126] In the case of Munich, two high-ranking Black September functionaries—the organization's senior operations officer Abu Daoud (real name Mohammed Daoud Oudeh) and Abu Mohammed (Fakhri Al-Omri), the right hand of the unofficial leader Abu Iyad (Salah Khalaf)—played a prominent role. The West German investigation later assumed both must have been in Munich immediately prior to the attack,[127] the commando probably receiving its weapons and instructions from Daoud (who, independent evidence suggests, also helped the last man over the perimeter fence of the Olympic village)[128] and trying, unsuccessfully, to contact Mohammed at a number in Tunis from the Israelis' apartment in the course of the day.[129] The unit itself consisted of six young men and two leaders.[130] The six footsoldiers came originally from Palestinian refugee camps in Lebanon, received military training in the Libyan desert, and flew in on the eve of the Games in groups of three from Tripoli via Rome and Belgrade with forged Jordanian passports. While aware they had been chosen for an important operation, they had no specific details and met their leaders—Issa (real name Muhammed Massalha, age twenty-seven) and his second-in-command, Tony (Yussef Nazal, age twenty-five)—for the first time on the evening of 4 September. Although the latter's whereabouts in the weeks before the mission were never firmly established, circumstantial evidence suggests they started making the necessary preparations only four to five weeks in advance, using short stays in Munich to familiarize themselves with the Olympic village.[131] Both would have blended in easily, Issa having lived in West Germany for a decade where he completed an engineering degree.[132]

Meager German Contacts

In this operation, Black September kept contact with other organizations to a minimum. While RAF leaders Andreas Baader and Ulrike Meinhof were known to the highest echelons of the PLO and attended an Al Fatah training camp in the Jordanian desert in the summer of 1970, there is no evidence of cooperation over the attack. Meinhof might have responded to the Munich commando's demand for her release—with a hunger strike and pamphlet that celebrated the strike as "anti-imperialist, antifascist, internationalist"[133] and compared Israeli defense minister Moshe Dayan with Heinrich Himmler—but her response is best read as a combination of international terrorist solidarity and the phenomenon of anti-Semitism in the New Left.[134] The same can be said of Horst Mahler's support at his RAF trial in December 1972.[135]

A similar pattern emerges around the Tupamaros West Berlin, another violent offshoot of the 1968 movement, which tried to blow up the Jewish Community Center in Berlin on the anniversary of Kristallnacht in 1969. In October of that year, one of their members, Georg von Rauch, returned from an Al Fatah camp in Jordan, claiming that "something would go down at the Olympics *[Auf der Olympiade passiert was].*"[136] Given the harebrained nature of a subsequent plot hatched by the German himself, however, it is unlikely the terrorist would have been able to furnish the German authorities with important information had he survived a hail of police bullets in 1971. Discovered by security forces when group leader Dieter Kunzelmann was arrested in July 1970, von Rauch's scheme consisted of a thirty-six-page dossier detailing how to "explode" the Olympic Games. A volley of shots at the opening ceremony would signal the storming of the Olympic village, the outbreak of chaos all over the city, and the advent of "new communes everywhere."[137] Judged as "somewhat utopian" by a senior Munich police officer, the plan was hardly taken seriously.[138]

Nor did Black September receive any assistance from the GDR—an unsubstantiated claim in the film *One Day in September* that has migrated into historiography as fact.[139] While three journalists reported to the Stasi from their men's team's accommodation less than fifteen meters from the action[140] and the archive shows the East Germans to have been generally well-informed—both about efforts to resolve the situation and the search for collaborators among the local Palestinian community[141]—there is little doubt they were nothing but passive observers. Shortly after the Games, West German investigations quickly ruled out any GDR involvement, an assessment that has stood the test of time and required no revision after the release of Stasi documentation.[142] Indeed, in an interview for this book shortly before his death in 2007, Markus Wolf, the former head of the Stasi's international operations (Hauptabteilung Aufklärung, HVA), confirmed this position.[143] Rather than supporting the attack, those in charge of state security, including minister of state security Erich Mielke, feared that similar incidents might spill across the Iron Curtain, not least at the Tenth World Youth Festival in East Berlin in 1973. Two anonymous letters threatening a Black September attack on the Israeli delegation were taken extremely seriously,[144] Mielke issuing explicit instructions on how to deal with hostage situations.[145] Stasi operatives responsible for the security of foreign delegations also received special training in urban warfare and, in contrast to the Ordnungsdienst (OD), the "Olys," in Munich, were heavily, if inconspicuously, armed.[146] Moreover, all Palestinians in the GDR, including fifty who took up residence in East Germany after Munich, were put under increased surveillance.[147]

If Black September relied on logistical support outside its own network, then it is likely to have come from individuals within the Palestinian diaspora in West Germany. Strong evidence points to members of the General Union of Palestinian

Students (GUPS), an organization close to the PLO.[148] During the hostage crisis the commando tried to phone the former high-ranking GUPS functionary Abdallah Al Frangi, a thirty-year old Palestinian who had been resident in Germany since 1962 and lived with his German wife and son in Langen near Offenbach in Hesse.[149] Al Frangi had been leader of GUPS from 1969 to 1970, secretary of its Frankfurt chapter in 1970, and editor of *Palästinensische Revolution,* a publication of the Palestinian community in West Germany, which championed the armed struggle against Israel. Carrying an Algerian diplomatic passport and acting under the cover of Botschaftsrat at the Arab League in Bonn, Al Frangi served as Al Fatah's representative in West Germany.[150] Although two judicial inquiries were opened against him the previous year for unlawful possession of weapons and bomb-making materials, nothing had come of them. In the absence of further intelligence clues, Al Frangi's undertakings on behalf of Black September (if any occurred at all before the attack) would have been difficult to detect.[151]

Contemporary Security Measures

Faced with a highly professional unit that left virtually no intelligence trace, the organizers would have required a heavily armed police presence to prevent it reaching its target. Such protection would have compromised the serenity of the Games, Schreiber explicitly acknowledging the increased risk its absence would cause in his security report over two years before the event.[152] The choice of an Ordnungsdienst specially schooled to charm the public and execute its duties with a light touch certainly assisted the terrorists in the first instance. Although the athletes complained about tight security—an article on the issue appearing on the front page of their daily paper *Village News,* ironically, on the eve of the attack—the Olympic village was easy to penetrate.[153] On one occasion, journalist and academic Richard Mandell simply jogged through the gates, pretending to be a member of the Peruvian athletics team.[154] In the same way, Abu Daoud entered several times posing as a Brazilian, making it into an Israeli flat with Issa and Tony on 28 August by convincing a female member of the delegation that they were keen to visit the Holy Land.[155] But beyond presenting simple reconnaissance opportunities, lax security made little difference to Black September's plan. They did not need the gaping hole in the fence—left deliberately unrepaired despite members of the OD alerting their superiors—simply scaling the least manned perimeter gate in the night-time hours instead.[156] Nor did they necessarily benefit from the fact that the third, lightly armed shift of the OD[157] on 4 September was reduced by around a quarter due to sickness and leave—heavily equipped, they would simply have shot their way to the Israelis' apartment.[158]

Against the calculated risk of relaxing their guard, the West Germans implemented measures in keeping with contemporary practice. Schreiber undertook a close examination of security at the previous three Olympics and went on a study trip to Peru, Argentina, and Brazil in November 1971. According to what he learned, prominent visitors to Munich were allocated specific security grades *(Sicherheitsstufen).* While no foreigner was assigned to the highest category, extra protection was given to grade II luminaries such as Brundage (who had received abduction threats from the South American Tupamaros), the emperor of Ethiopia Haile Selassie, the Queen of England, British prime minister Edward Heath (IRA), French president Georges Pompidou, and Indian prime minister Indira Gandhi. Telling for the time, however, is the list of grade III and IV visitors who did not receive additional cover because they were judged at minimal risk: the queen's husband Prince Philip, Carl Gustav of Sweden, Constantine of Greece, Nixon's national security advisor Henry Kissinger, Austrian chancellor Bruno Kreisky, Swedish prime minister Olof Palme, and United Nations general secretary Kurt Waldheim.[159] Antiterrorism policy, in fact, seemed to suggest that the police could only do their best against opponents who invariably had the upper hand. In his report on the South American trip, Schreiber commented laconically on the abduction of the German ambassador to Brazil in 1970: "Preventing such attacks is extremely difficult."[160] Statistically, he was right: in the early 1970s, hijackings and hostage situations tended to end in the terrorists' favor.[161]

Israeli Negligence

It should not be forgotten that the Israelis made misjudgments of their own. The team had been treated no differently in the Olympic village from other countries traveling with small squads, and were offered five flats extending over the ground and first floors of a midsize building rather than a high-rise that would have greatly enhanced their security. In fact, even within their complex, the delegations from Hong Kong and Uruguay were assigned the second and penthouse floors, all but one of the Israeli flats being reached via a direct entrance from Connollystraße. As Abu Daoud, Tony, and Issa also discovered on their forays into the village, the building could be entered by an unlocked door on the service level below.[162] Although the Kopel report (still classified in Israel) is believed to indicate that these issues were raised by the Israeli *chef de mission* Shmuel Lalkin at a number of meetings with German and Israeli officials,[163] the record shows that neither country was perturbed.[164] Perhaps Tel Aviv labored under the same illusion as Daume, who a few years earlier answered a journalist's question about the possibility of Arab sabotage on the Israeli team with a categoric: "No, absolutely not. That would go against the Olympic spirit. In Tokyo and Mexico, Arabs showed too that they respect the Olympic peace."[165] At any rate, the Israeli team came to Munich without its own security detail: team doctor Mattiyahu Kranz might have liaised with the German authorities but was not an agent. Neither was additional protection sought from the hosts for team members, either in the village or for outings such as the theater trip on 4 September. The sacking of high-ranking security officials shortly after the disaster was a tacit admission of Israeli negligence.[166]

Contemporary Military Potential

Finally, once pressed into action, the West Germans were systemically underequipped for the task. However, no other country in the world, with the exception of Israel itself, could have freed the hostages with confidence. The terrorists dug into a secure position that could only be attacked from a narrow spiral staircase or a small and well-guarded garden-side balcony. Sayeret Matkal's liberation of the Sabena airline in Tel Aviv for the loss of only one hostage proved that it could defeat Black September, but that extraordinary operation had been the first of its kind and was beyond the powers of the Western security forces at the time.[167] Not only did the West German Ministry of the Interior swiftly create the GSG9, an elite counterterrorism unit, in response to events at the Games, but Munich also triggered the British and the French to establish elite counterterrorism teams of their own. The United States took even longer with its Delta Force.[168] The liberation of hostages from a Lufthansa jet hijacked by RAF terrorists in Mogadishu (1977) and the Iranian Embassy siege in London (1980) were, in this sense, direct consequences of the Olympic massacre.

Meir offered Brandt her special unit at an early stage in the siege, but for national and international reasons the chancellor obviously had to refuse.[169] Moreover, domestic legal considerations weakened the Germans' hand further. Strictly dividing peace-time security along federal lines, Article 35 of the Basic Law forbade the deployment of the national army (with its better trained marksmen) in such instances, assigning exclusive powers to the police force of the relative Land. Questioned on television the day after the disaster, Defense Secretary Georg Leber noted how the situation had touched on an impasse in the constitution.[170] Chastened by events, Leber was later prepared to ignore such intricacies. Faced with (false) reports of a bomb-laden plane heading for the Olympic Stadium during the closing ceremony, he gave permission for it to be shot down if necessary by the Luftwaffe.[171] But a few days earlier, observing proceedings from the control tower of Fürstenfeldbruck, the federal representatives and Israeli specialists (who had arrived too late to make their presence felt)[172] could do little more than watch as "downright amateurism" unfolded around them.[173]

THE POLITICAL AFTERMATH

The attack left debris that would take months of diplomacy to clear. A hall of mirrors cast up multiple victims and multiple perpetrators. The Palestinians pointed to despair after decades of injustice and international abandonment.[174]

The Egyptians—whose athletes (along with those from Syria and Kuwait) left the Olympic village and, like other Arab nations and the GDR, absented themselves from the memorial service in the Olympic stadium on 6 September—reacted indignantly to being drawn into a crisis of someone else's making. The Israelis had suffered the most shocking psychological attack in their nation's short history. And the Germans had watched Munich shade into Dachau as Jewish blood trickled over the ruins of their Games. By the same token, the Palestinians had disrupted the Olympic peace, murdered Israelis, and committed crimes on German soil. The German authorities' incompetence had turned a delicate situation into a bloodbath. The Egyptians had looked away when asked for help. And the Israelis had underestimated their own security needs and remained intransigent over the negotiations. All four had complicated relations with each other and, vitally, could quote the others' mistakes to cover their own.

On 6 September, foreign minister Walter Scheel remarked to senior officials that "Life goes on," but his optimism was misplaced.[175] From the very beginning, every German statement came under intense scrutiny. By condemning Black September as a "criminal organization" and, crucially, placing responsibility on "those countries that [had] not prevented [it] in [its] actions," Gustav Heinemann's speech at the memorial service resonated strongly with the Israelis.[176] It matched almost verbatim deputy prime minister Yigal Allon's call for wider accountability when the athletes' remains returned to Israel,[177] and was warmly received by the government and public alike.[178] Ambassador Ben Horin reckoned he had "fundamentally contributed to the Israeli government's positive reaction to the events and conduct of the German authorities."[179] By the same token, however, Daume's words at the service had found favor with the Arabs. Expressing himself more vaguely than Heinemann, the OC president had commiserated "with the families and countries, while we put this day and its crude frenzies behind us," and adding, "the only consolation is that we do not determine our own fate, but that our present and future lies in the hands of a higher power."[180] His circumspection brought immediate thanks from the Deutsch-Arabische Gesellschaft, which believed his "measured thoughts, fittingly chosen for the general situation, causes and effects, had had a soothing effect."[181]

From the outset, therefore, it was clear that each side would be combing through the others' pronouncements. The West German authorities were caught up in a regional conflict but needed to display more bilateral cunning than in 1965. From nowhere, Black September had plunged German-Arab relations into serious doubt again.

FIGURE 21. Foreign Secretary Walter Scheel, Federal President Heinemann, and Willi Daume (left to right) at the memorial ceremony in the Olympic Stadium, 6 September 1972 (photo: Ludwig Wegmann, B 145 Bild-F037753-0007, courtesy of Bundesarchiv)

ARAB REACTIONS

While the Egyptian and West German governments were keen to maintain relations, regret and frustration quickly developed over allegations and expectations.[182] By 7 September an impasse had already been reached. On the one hand, the Egyptians' unwillingness to condemn the attack aroused the suspicion of the West German public. On the other, official spokesman Conrad Ahlers's blame of Egypt caused consternation[183] and forced his counterpart there to attack Bonn's failure to "respect its word" to the "Arab commandoes."[184] With the Arab League due to meet in the Egyptian capital from 9 September to 13 September and come under pressure from Palestinian resistance fighters to break ties with the Federal Republic, Ambassador Steltzer advised the Foreign Office to clarify its position. The resulting communication—which redoubled its commitment to good relations, absolved the Egyptians of culpability, but continued to hold out for a condemnation—did little to calm Cairo's nerves.[185] By the time it was handed to the new foreign minister on 9 September, Israel had attempted to intervene with the European foreign ministers[186] and the letter smacked of U.S.-Israeli influence.[187] Two days later, almost certainly under pressure from the Arab League, the PLO, and internal circles opposed to the Egypt's rapprochement with Western Europe,

FIGURE 22. Members of the Israeli team during the memorial ceremony (photo: Rue des Archives/AGIP, courtesy of Süddeutsche Zeitung Photo)

the Egyptian government was put onto the front foot again, replying to the missive with a statement "teeming with accusations against the federal government."[188] As the French Foreign Office advised the Germans, the issue had taken a definite turn for the worse, the Arab governments having "renewed their solidarity with the most radical faction of the Fedayin" for fear of their own populations and the terrorist leaders themselves.[189]

The Arabs' silence played badly with the West German public. Indeed, as an urgent paper prepared in the Ministry of Economic Cooperation on 11 September clearly shows, domestic pressure had led Bonn to make the wrong move. Amid calls from parliamentarians—most vociferously opposition leader Rainer Barzel—to cut development aid to countries unwilling to condemn the atrocity, the minister had tried to extract suitable statements from Yemen, Sudan, and Lebanon.[190] Brandt, however, had appealed for greater differentiation, and as the paper outlined, he was wise, if a little late, in doing so. Quite apart from the undesirability of destabilizing the region, the advanced state or completion of most of the Federal Republic's development projects gave it virtually no financial leverage. More importantly, in a tour d'horizon of the whole Middle East, the ministry outlined how volatile internal politics, awkward economic dependencies, and external military threat made it unthinkable for any Arab country—with the exception of Morocco, Jordan, and Lebanon[191]—to speak out against the attack.[192] Each had sent representatives to the terrorists' funeral in Libya;[193] and, as the paper concluded, despite the renowned "bad blood between them" on many issues, nothing—save Islam and the Arabic language—united the Arab states more than their repulsion of the common enemy Israel.

A cooler head impervious to the clamoring of public opinion would have saved Bonn from making demands that could never be met.

ISRAEL I

Initial calm, moreover, would have prevented a chain reaction. Incensed by West Germany's (unsuccessful) attempt to assuage the Arabs, Tel Aviv turned on Bonn. Until that point, the general rage in Israel had contrasted with the more moderate position of its government.[194] While the Germans' incompetence might have disappointed some politicians, they had not wished to erode worldwide goodwill.[195] The government might have tried to have the Games cancelled but, receiving little response from Washington or Bonn, it had kept its council and designated the funeral of the Israeli victims a "time of national mourning" (rather than "state funeral") to relieve foreign heads of state of the obligation to attend.[196] Against heavy criticism from the opposition, Meir's message of thanks on 7 September for the efforts to free the hostages was a clear attempt to temper the anti-German mood that had seized the country.[197] Despite its errors, West Germany, after all, had been the first country to intervene militarily on Israel's behalf. Meir's gratitude was doubtless motivated by other factors too. Aside from her warm relationship with Brandt, the Federal Republic was the country's third-largest trade partner and major aid benefactor.[198] At the same time, Israel had been forced to work harder to maintain special ties, West Germany's increasing standing in the international community reducing the value of this relationship with Israel as a litmus test of its democratic credentials. Despite Fürstenfeldbruck, then, Israel had a serious interest in preserving fruitful contact.

On 11 September, however, there was a sea change in Israel's tone. The Foreign Office's ill-fated missive to Egypt (9 September) and an ambiguous radio interview by Scheel (8 September) caused furor.[199] Like the Egyptians the same day, the Israeli press accused Bonn of "speaking two languages," and carried an explosive interview with Meir's deputy Yigal Allon.[200] In contradiction of the facts, Allon claimed the Israelis had alerted the Germans to a possible attack, had never been asked to consider a deal, and would naturally have understood had free passage been offered. Although Meir commented cautiously, the German embassy predicted further aggravation.[201] The next day, the cabinet had heavily criticized shortcomings in Israel's Olympic security plan, when Ambassador Ben Horin and an agent (believed to be General Zamir) came to report. As the embassy—correctly—predicted, "internal political reasons would mean that the initial, rather guarded recognition of partial Israeli responsibility would lead to louder criticism of the German failings."[202]

Two days after the closing ceremony, on 13 September, Ben Horin handed Brandt a damning report on Munich security and evoked President Heinemann's words at the memorial service to coax the Federal Republic into unequivocal allegiance against Arab terrorism. Genscher promptly rejected the indictments, but Heinemann's speech and its strong implication of Arab culpability proved a moot point.[203] Scheel had told Ben Horin that the government had approved it in advance, but either he was misinformed or had been soothing the Israelis at a difficult point: as a note from the Bundespräsidialamt clearly shows, the president composed his text without consultation.[204] Now Brandt had to negotiate his sentiments in the context of complex diplomacy, and—convinced that "the events in Munich had weakened the moderates in Arab capitals and increased the pressure applied by radical circles on governments and public media"—he did so by reinterpreting them in extraordinary fashion. Heinemann, Brandt told Ben Horin, had "deliberately dropped any restriction to the 'Arab' states" in order to "extend responsibility to other European governments, his own included" and France "because of [its] large number of Arab immigrant workers." It had clearly been a long week. Rapidly decaying relations with the Arab world had forced the chancellor to take back the only shred of diplomatic comfort that the Federal Republic had been able to offer Israel in its moment of deepest trauma.

Although it was agreed that "close contact [should] be maintained between German and Israeli agencies at all times," Ben Horin's meeting with Brandt signaled an unmistakable distance between the two countries' priorities.[205] As with the Arabs' stance toward Israel, Israel's position on the Arab world was rapidly hardening and complicating Bonn's intention to nurture good relations with both.[206] The Israeli and German governments were now set to react against rather than empathize with each other. In mid-October, the federal Innenausschuß's investigation, which exonerated the German authorities for the loss of life in Munich, was interpreted by the Israelis as apportioning blame to them.[207] Reports that Meir intended to criticize the Federal Republic sharply before the Knesset in return led to a demarche from Bonn and a plea from Brandt to avoid the topic of

Fürstenfeldbruck before the forthcoming general election. While Meir gave assurances she would not "put wind in the sails of the opposition," she reserved the right to justify herself domestically. In the event and to the German government's relief,[208] her speech was balanced.[209] Yet it was clear the situation was merely contained and unlikely to survive a further blow.

THE ARAB WORLD

If relations with Israel became heated in the second half of September and October, they boiled over elsewhere in the Middle East. In the wake of the attack, the government had declared it would pursue three distinct courses of action: talks with the United Nations on combating terror worldwide; political coordination in the EEC; and bilateral negotiations with the Arab states. The first two were well advanced by the end of the Games, Scheel voicing support for UN General Secretary Waldheim's proposal for an international convention on terrorism at a meeting of EEC foreign ministers in Rome on 12 September.[210] The third strategy—cooperating with the Arabs—however, was rendered almost impossible when Bonn heightened security to prevent the terrorists forcing the release of their three colleagues from German captivity.[211] PFLP terrorist Leila Khaled, whose good looks, cold blood, and political radicalism had shot her to celebrity status,[212] was suspected for some time of being on German soil, readying herself to strike.[213] A combination of German heavy handedness and a low tolerance threshold on the part of the Arabs precipitated a politically dangerous and pragmatically disadvantageous standoff. Relations plummeted several rungs, and a potential opening for joint surveillance of Black September by the West German and Egyptian secret services failed to materialize.[214]

The German authorities had moved swiftly on 5 September to increase security.[215] Across the country, Arab and Israeli diplomatic missions, airline offices, and shipping companies were put under protection, with similar precautions taken for German interests abroad. Immigration controls were radically increased for *all* Arabs, individuals being turned back at the slightest suspicion and tourist groups invariably banned. Lax controls on airlines—which had allowed terrorists to risk transporting weapons in the hold of charter flights[216]—were dramatically tightened.[217] The Länder were instructed to expel Arabs "in all legally justifiable cases," and proceeded to deport *all* foreigners living illegally in Germany, considering them particularly vulnerable to blackmail by terrorists.[218] On the premise that Palestinian terror groups also recruited from across the Arab world, visa requirements were extended to three previously exempt countries (Libya, Tunisia, and Morocco). Brandt had warned Ben Horin that a failure to distinguish between Arab groups would increase support for Black September.[219] But Germany's new measures fell into the same trap.[220] Morocco greeted the visa regulations "in part with alarm, in part with bitterness, but generally with incredulity,"[221] and President Bourguiba of Tunisia, having previously pledged to plead Germany's case with his neighbors,[222] felt "disavowed."[223] Soon, too, almost everyone in the Arab world seemed to have a friend or relative who had been affected.[224]

Although as few as one hundred official residents were asked to leave in the first five weeks, the number of illegal immigrants expelled is unknown.[225] At any rate, up to a quarter of the ten thousand Arabs seeking entry to the Federal Republic were rejected,[226] and complaints abounded.[227] The Deutsch-Arabische Gesellschaft argued that the Germans had legalized "discrimination against Arabs partout,"[228] and the Arab League raised the stakes by asking if it should withdraw its citizens altogether.[229] A hunger strike began on its premises in Bonn.[230] The German embassy in Cairo confirmed reports of the zealously uncouth handling of foreign students, workers, businessmen, tourists, and housewives at the Munich Airport, and feared reprisals against the German community in Egypt.[231] It urgently advised the Foreign Office to "bring security needs into line with foreign policy interests," while colleagues in Algeria reported open threats to vital oil and gas supplies.[232]

Not for the last time, however, the authorities were to complicate, rather than simplify, the lives of their ambassadors.[233] In early October, they increased the waiting time for visas[234] and outlawed the Palestinian workers union (General-Union Palästinensischer Arbeiter, GUPA) and student association (GUPS), whose president Al Frangi fled the Republic in anticipation of deportation on 28 September.[235] Under surveillance since 20 September,[236] GUPS had its assets seized and personnel rounded up in a series of lightening raids in fifteen cities on 4 October.[237] As the students were welcomed with open arms by the GDR,[238] savings books containing incongruous sums of money and recent transfers to the Middle East seemed to confirm suspicions.[239] Minor demonstrations in several university cities culminated in a ten-thousand-strong but peaceful rally in Dortmund organized by a range of German New Left groups and Maoist foreign organizations.

The response in the Middle East, by comparison, was inflammatory. Fuelled by a "distorted and emotional" media publishing anti-German articles on a daily basis, the public reacted "irascibly at times."[240] As the Foreign Office later realized, flames had been fanned by Israeli reports of information exchange and cooperation over border controls. Angry hordes stormed the German missions in Algiers and Damascus, one hundred students carried out a sit-in at the consulate in Karachi, and up to eight thousand protesters gathered in Lebanon. Across the region, the Federal Republic was equated with the Third Reich, the Kuwaiti newspaper *Al-Kabas,* to name but one example, depicting a "'new Nazism' . . . swooping down in West Germany in its ugliest form"[241] and printing a series of cartoons that culminated in the "Führer" Willy Brandt praying to Hitler and ignoring an Arab pleading for his life from a fire behind him.

With the situation in Cairo no better, the Egyptian government found itself in a quandary.[242] While bilateral discussions suggested that keeping the peace with Bonn remained a high priority,[243] it came under mounting pressure on regional and domestic fronts.[244] Unable to stray from his allies, Sadat joined Syria and Libya in announcing tit-for-tat immigration controls for West German citizens on 9 October.[245] From beyond the region too, the GDR—despite the near completion of Ostpolitik—mounted a major offensive to exploit its rival's "awkward position."[246] The East Germans flooded the Egyptian Foreign Office "not only on a daily basis," as its undersecretary reported, "but every hour and, he could almost say, nearly minute by minute."[247] On 15 October, Sadat commented publicly for the first time, referring to German security at the opening of parliament as "Nazi terrorism."[248] Reminded of the halcyon days of Hallstein, Steltzer, who initially urged caution, pleaded with Bonn to send the assurances that would offer an "almost desperate" Egyptian government much-needed relief from internal power struggles.[249] Despite his appointment as ambassador in August, the Egyptian government had still not completed the vital ceremonial formalities—a delay he interpreted as a clear "rebuke" that would cause considerable loss of face if not responded to in suitable manner.[250] The Foreign Office informed him it was playing a waiting game[251] and instructed him to remain in the field.[252] With the Federal Republic unwilling to modify its security, the situation looked set to deteriorate. Within days, however, a dramatic intervention had changed everything.

On 29 October, the terrorists struck again. The West German services had been on high alert about an attack for the previous two weeks, although they were unsure where it might occur. Intelligence sources had presented them with a range of possibilities: the kidnapping of a diplomat or an attack on German ships in Beirut harbor; an operation in the Federal Republic itself (possibly aided by the IRA, which had been observed liaising with two leading Fatah members in London); or the abduction of Manfred Schreiber, Hans Dietrich Genscher, and others.[253] On 20 October, the same signal that had been put out before Munich was transmitted from Baghdad and Cairo again,[254] and a list of the terrorists' possible goals, targets, and motives was assembled for a meeting of a standing committee scheduled for 30 October.[255] Before the committee met, however, the threat had already been realized. In the early hours of the morning, a Lufthansa jet en route from Damascus and Beirut to Frankfurt was hijacked by PFLP specialists who demanded the release of the three survivors of Fürstenfeldbruck and forced it to land for refueling in Cyprus before heading for Munich. At 11:00 A.M. the plane flew over the city's commercial airport at Riem, but turned eastward again when the hijackers were informed that the authorities would require a further ninety minutes to bring their comrades to the airfield. The new destination was Zagreb, and the terrorists demanded the three be flown there before they put down. The West Germans complied. In the early evening, the Lufthansa jet landed in Yugoslavia, the Black September terrorists (flown over on a Condor aircraft) joined their "liberators," and, against prior agreement, took off for Libya with the hostages still on board.[256] In Tripoli, they released the passengers within an hour of landing and held an international press conference amid a rapturous welcome from the locals.

The circumstances of the flight—not least its small number of male-only passengers—soon prompted conspiracy theories. The Israeli public was convinced that "the incident had been fixed between the terrorists and Lufthansa or the German authorities;"[257] the Zentralrat der Juden in Deutschland speculated that a previous German ransom of US$5 million had been invested directly in Munich and Zagreb;[258] and yet others claimed the PFLP had received the same sum to simulate the hijack.[259] Interviews in *One Day in September* indicate that German officials—including the normally circumspect Vogel—still harbor suspicions. Yet there is no proof, and there is good reason to doubt the alternative scenarios.[260] For one, as Matthias Dahlke has shown, relations with the Middle East had sunk so low that none of the usual Arab channels were prepared to help on the day, while the institutional incompetence that marred Munich was still much in evidence on the German side.[261] For another, the late arrival of the three survivors in Zagreb left the hijacked Lufthansa jet perilously low on fuel, landing with just thirty seconds to spare.[262] And finally, any German plot is unlikely to have involved Yugoslavia. In a bid to curry favor with the Arab states and bolster his country's nonaligned status, General Tito had claimed the massacre had been staged by "Israeli-Zionist groups" to legitimize heavy reprisals on Arab territories.[263] On 29 October, much to the cynicism of foreign observers, the Yugoslav leader walked a tightrope, doing just enough to appease the Arabs without alienating the Germans excessively.[264]

Whether fixed or not, the timing and side effects of the hijack certainly proved welcome, as the Ministry of the Interior noted, for the security of the country.[265] The accuracy of this assessment was soon confirmed by Arab partners. Libya, arguing it had allowed the plane to land to help the federal government out of a crisis, recorded its appreciation for the release,[266] and Morocco expressed relief.[267] And on 31 October, just two days after the incident, the Egyptian authorities contacted Ambassador Steltzer to arrange his ceremonial welcome in Cairo and seal the renewal of diplomatic relations.[268] In the immediacy of the event, Bonn might have taken Libya to task, demanding the extradition of the terrorists—a request met with open derision—and warning of consequences more dire than those in 1965 should any further incidents occur on German soil.[269] But it soon became apparent that Zagreb served the greater goal of righting the imbalance in Middle Eastern affairs since Munich. The cabinet duly treated the state of Bavaria's plans to demand the terrorists' return with as much distain as the Libyans had shown its own.[270]

ISRAEL II

If for the Arabs Zagreb had "brought satisfaction and led to a tendency to forgive the 'betrayal' and shootings at Fürstenfeldbruck magnanimously," it caused "huge ill-feeling" in Israel.[271] Not altogether inaccurately, the Israeli press suggested the German authorities were relieved to be rid of the terrorists,[272] and personal attacks on Brandt, with comparisons to the Nazi era, ensued.[273] Israeli schools were awash with protests, demonstrators flocked to the embassy, the ambassador's protection was increased, and concert tours, union visits, and bilateral governmental committee meetings cancelled.[274] As the embassy reported, the Federal Republic was facing "a new wave of anti-German sentiment . . . , which now engulf[ed] groups that had continued to give the Germans credit after Munich." Foreign minister Abba Eban declared Zagreb a "blow to the memory and dignity of the Munich victims;"[275] the Knesset saw "the heftiest and most critical anti-German [debate] since the disagreements over reparations in 1952";[276] the cabinet released a statement expressing its "confusion, consternation, anger, and indignation";[277] and Ben Horin was recalled from Bonn.[278] Zagreb had led "to a serious crisis" in bilateral relations that went far beyond the immediate post-Munich period, and with the Israeli ambassador withdrawn from the German capital, Bonn had to make the next move.[279] It came at the highest level—Brandt writing a personal letter that was read to Meir on 8 November. Its balance between justification for the saving of human life and renewed commitment to combating international terrorism, between regret at the tone of the Israeli press reaction and his conviction that nothing should disrupt the course of German-Israeli relations had the desired effect. Meir immediately distanced herself from the local press, calming its polemics with a governmental "guidance," and returning Ben Horin to Bonn the next day.[280]

But it was an uneasy truce. The immediate diplomatic crisis resolved, the Israeli ambassador went on the offensive again, evoking Heinemann's speech and demanding a hard line from Germany, during a candid and at times heated exchange with Secretary of State Frank at the Foreign Office on 15 November.[281] To the Germans' displeasure, Ben Horin announced to the evening news programs that Israel and the Federal Republic would be continuing their talks on Arab terrorism. The intention was unmistakable, and once again considering its bilateral discussions with the Arab world endangered, Bonn immediately instructed him to moderate his statements. Despite Tel Aviv's obvious disapproval, the Federal Republic was not prepared to waste the opportunity to right its relations with the Arab world, and the Foreign Office and its embassies moved quickly to correct any false impression.[282] Not surprisingly, Brandt's declaration of government after his election victory four days later took care to mention the country's relations with all parties in the Middle East.[283]

However this statement was received, Brandt's reelection marked a definite caesura in German-Israeli antagonism. Within days, Ben Horin visited the Foreign Office again, as well as President Heinemann, announcing "business as usual."[284] Despite the unseemly haste of Zagreb, relations seemed to settle quickly after Brandt's olive branch at the beginning of November. Tel Aviv University opened the first German institute in Israel, and after a brief hiatus caused by the criminal investigation of pro-Arab statements made by its student union, the Deutsche Sporthochschule established even closer links with the Wingate Institute.[285] In 1973, the young German athlete Heide Schüller, who had sworn the Olympic oath at the opening ceremony in Munich, was invited as guest of honor to the Makkabia dedicated to the memory of the murdered sportsmen. Although eliciting the Federal Republic's help in the fight against terrorism remained high on the agenda, toward the end of 1972 a new priority was emerging: persuading the newly mandated Brandt to set a date for his state visit to Israel.[286] Surveys conducted for the German embassy in the course of November showed encouraging signs.[287] And notwithstanding a slight rise in the number of Israelis opposed to the visit (up from 9.3 percent in May 1972 to 14.7 percent), this was more than balanced by the increase in those supporting the trip (up to 75 percent from 65.6 percent).[288] Despite a lingering reluctance to accept the Federal Republic's actions at Zagreb (60 percent of Israelis refusing to see the parallels with their own government's release of terrorists to save the lives of passengers on an El Al plane hijacked to Algeria and a kidnapped professor), the chancellor's arrival in Israel was eagerly awaited.[289]

. . .

By December 1972, therefore, the dust had begun to settle after Munich. The Federal Republic expressed disquiet to Arab representatives about intelligence of threats to Genscher, Merk and Schreiber despite the release of the terrorists.[290] But it received assurances (from Libya and Tunisia) that it had nothing to fear, the Munich attack having been a "folly" which had led to "in-depth discussions" in Arab circles,[291] and nothing would prevent the continued increase in trade between West Germany and the Arab world (doubling from 1970 to DM 11 billion by the end of 1973).[292] Meir would still rail against Zagreb as a "dreadful mistake" to receptive audiences at home.[293] But attention would soon shift to Brandt's historic visit in June 1973 and his resolution of debates with the SPD's governmental partner (FDP) over the definitional status of German-Israeli relations ("normal relations with special character"). Soon, with Mossad's revenge mission against Black September gathering pace, Israel and its Arab neighbors would have cause to take their eyes off Germany and look more intently at each other.

Diplomatically, therefore, the Munich massacre was a blip. By late autumn, the Olympics might have been associated across the Middle East with duplicity, incompetence, and Nazi brutality. Yet for the sovereign states, there was too much at stake. The Arabs needed to loosen the grip of the Soviets, settle divisions in their own ranks, and increase Western trade. And the Israelis, aware the rapprochement between their enemies and "special friends" could not be halted, moved to shore up as much of their relationship as possible. Even if the crisis evoked after Zagreb was "a calculated [one]," as the German ambassador later noted, it was born of high emotion and directed to a specific end.[294] Brandt's new mandate and the completion of Ostpolitik bolstered his position and he finally resolved important relations that had teased him in the earlier part of the year. Before 1972 was out, a line was drawn in the sand.

But diplomatic closure is not emotional closure. For the victims' families there could be no such forgetting—and legal proceedings ran until 2003. Contrary to common assumption—see *One Day in September*—the relatives received prompt compensation from Germany. The OC's general insurance policy provided DM 10,000 for each of the deceased, and the federal government made a one-off payment of US$1 million (DM 400,000 per widow, DM 100,000 per orphan or parent of the unmarried)—a considerable sum in the 1970s.[295] But at the heart of these gestures was the desire to deny all guilt—the government explicitly designating its contribution an act of generosity, with Daume cautious to keep the OC's sum at a level that denied complicity.[296] Yet the families' questions and quest for justice went unanswered. After the Landgericht München I dismissed negligence charges against Schreiber and Wolf in 1973, it took the relatives over twenty years to gain access to sufficient evidence to bring their own case to the same court in 1994. In all that time, the German authorities denied the existence of any such documentation. It wasn't until 1992 when an archivist saw Ankie Spitzer, the wife of murdered fencing coach Andre, on television and smuggled out data to her that the authorities were forced to release around four thousand files.[297] When they came to court, the relatives were undone by a cruel—and under the circumstances inexplicably exercised—technicality, the judge citing the German statute of limitations that requires negligence claims to be brought within three years of the relevant information becoming available. Despite the dubious nature of this outcome, the case was dismissed again on the same grounds in 2000 on the next rung of the judicial ladder, the Oberlandesgericht München. In 2003, before the Federal Court (Bundesgerichtshof, the highest court in the land) could make its findings, the parties settled out of court, the twenty-five surviving relatives receiving €3 million in total (as opposed to the DM 40 million they had originally demanded).[298] The terms of this settlement seem to have closed the book on further discussion. Tellingly, however, over thirty years on, costs were split between the original three partners—the city, Land, and state—and the authorities continued to deny liability *(Staatshaftung).*

The massacre, obviously, was the dominant event at the 1972 Olympics, but its relation to the Games and their legacy is complicated. In recent years, the memory of the Games has become increasingly tied to the tragic incident that interrupted them, but the immediate effects of the attack were as negligible as they were overwhelming. After a pause for a day, competitions resumed, medals were won, and reputations sealed and lost. In the years that followed, the stadium hosted other events and the excitement of the revolutionary opening lived on in those who had experienced it. The final chapter of this book will seek to draw conclusions about the Germans, their Games, and their changing relationship to triumph and tragedy.

8

Conclusion

Olympic Legacies

On the penultimate day of the Games, twelve hundred guests—including the International Olympic Committee (IOC), its outgoing and incoming presidents (Brundage and Killanin), and German politicians Heinemann, Brandt, and Goppel—had been expected at the Lenbachhaus gallery for an evening of champagne and sparkling conversation. But the terrorist attack several days before leadened the mood, and civic hospitality was cancelled as a mark of respect. Now extended by one day, the Games offered little joy or levity, as delegates, dignitaries, and athletes waited for a scaled-down closing ceremony before leaving Munich to its troubled Olympic legacy. When press officer Camillo Noel had delivered his text for the event on the eve of the Games to Vogel's successor, Mayor Georg Kronawitter, he could scarcely have imagined the irony of his words. Despite the excitement of the opening week, no one could have returned home with an overwhelming sense that "the examples of our ability to understand one another, to make friends and maintain peace" had proved "stronger than the risk of conflict and contestation."[1]

Kronawitter's aborted speech, which took in the international context of the Games and their potential hard and soft legacies for Germany, Munich, and the Olympic movement, nonetheless serves as a convenient frame to conclude our discussion of the Games, their making and significance. Certainly, as this book has shown, the Munich Olympics were "caught up in the currents of power and conflict in human society." They were caught, like the Federal Republic generally in the 1960s, between past and future. Indebted to, but emerging from the pathos of a nineteenth-century tradition, they were enabled by technocratic optimism and shaped by the futuristic rationality of the early computer age. Buffeted by student protest, they struggled to respond to radical youth demands while remaining faithful to the nonpolitical nature of the Games and the easygoing mood of its mainstream visitors. In the German Democratic Republic (GDR), they had a rival that exploited the Olympic movement to make quasipolitical gains that were inaccessible through normal diplomacy, but who approached the Munich event with thinly veiled enmity. That rival, however, had Brandt's rapprochement with the East to contend with, and ultimately the Soviet Union's strategic decisions within a complicated process of international relations. The West German authorities came up against forces beyond their own control too, when Palestinian terrorists interrupted the Games and threw their Middle Eastern initiatives out of kilter. Each of these currents moved at different speeds, at different times, and impacted on different aspects of the Games.

But these were only the external forces. As Johannes Paulmann—who has done much to advance the study of international representation—recently noted, "the *inner* dimensions of West German cultural diplomacy have so far not been studied adequately," and these must be considered here too.[2] Without wishing to reduce the often complex currents and influences presented in this book, it is worth noting the most significant factors in the inner evolution of the Munich event. First, there is the relation between individuals and collectives. On the one hand, despite the turmoil of 1967 through 1969, the Games would have been impossible without the deideologization that characterized the main political parties of the 1960s and allowed them to proceed invariably with unity of purpose. In the combined support of city, Land, and nation, they profited moreover from the centrist orientation of the Republic and its "cooperative federalism."[3] Yet, individuals held the upper hand. Without Daume's initiative, Vogel's determination, and both men's ambition, West Germany would not have contemplated hosting the Olympics at all. And without their steely resolve to produce the Games they wanted—variously for German sport, the Olympic movement, Munich, and the Federal Republic—the contours of the event would doubtless have developed differently. Echoing earlier complaints by Prince Georg von Opel, a West German IOC member who felt excluded by the closed and "cliquey" nature of the Organizing Committee (OC),[4] an internal Foreign Office report expressed irritation at the degree of autonomy enjoyed by the organizers—namely, "foreign partners could hardly believe that the federal government had practically zero influence on the OC."[5] Despite the factual inaccuracy of this statement—Bonn, like Bavaria and Munich, had significant representation on the executive board of the OC—it captures the essence of the enterprise. For, with Daume's vision and Vogel's blessing, selected representatives of the architectural, design, and PR elites that had constructed and projected the Federal Republic's image in the 1950s and 1960s formed a tight-knit group in Munich. Daume, as the OC's minute taker aptly concluded, was "a nutter, but an ingenious nutter."[6] It was his team's look, and the freedom to produce it without interference, that allowed the Games to speak to their times.

Second, there is the relation between the hosts and their chief guests, the IOC. Kronawitter might have cited the "Olympic Law" of ultimate sacrifice in easy conjunction with the endeavors of the city, but the Germans' engagement with a high-profile, outmoded, powerful, and self-deluded international body was far from easy. As Noel noted when sending Kronawitter his draft: "I have used my close knowledge of how things work in the Olympics to balance the content of the speech carefully and avoid any sort of pathos," warning nonetheless that "the subject matter [was] difficult."[7] Involvement with the strongly traditional IOC inevitably reopened a previous event that the organizers wished at once to forget and transcend. It was not simply that a veneration of the 1936 Games encouraged fringe members of the West German sports fraternity to vocalize their "Olympic imagination" at inappropriate moments, but that it contributed to Munich's selection in the first place and lurked unspoken in expectations (good and bad) around the world. Brundage, the biggest fan of a Germany that no longer existed, became an increasingly loose cannon, and Daume's expert knowledge and cunning was needed to negotiate the committees and corridors of the IOC. Yet at the same time, as governments of every political persuasion quickly appreciate—from Berlin to Moscow, Los Angeles to Beijing—Olympism is an open creed that permits the hosts to appropriate and radiate positive messages about themselves to unprecedented audiences across the globe. The fallacy of sport's assumed neutrality was its most powerful tool—one that generally worked well for the organizers except when turned upon them by Black September or the GDR.

And third, there was the relation between sport and political discourses in general. The (semi-)autonomous dynamic of sport could generate counterintuitive, even contradictory alignments. Jesse Owens's and the Israeli NOC's agreement with Brundage over respective boycott movements in the late 1960s and 1972 are prominent cases in point. But in Munich, despite the New Left's critique, sport harmonized well with pressing themes of the time in a series of ideological serendipities. While Daume opposed "gigantism" and kept Munich modest because of the IOC's aversion to the scale of Rome, Tokyo, and Mexico City, his attitude chimed with the rejection of the concept in postwar German architecture and helped ease the Games away from their infamous Berlin predecessor. An IOC keen to expand and trumpet its magnitude would have caused the organizers considerable problems. By the same token, Daume's long-held desire to democratize sport and his fixation with Huizinga's notions of play fitted neatly with the progressive mood of the era. Aicher, Behnisch, Grzimek, and Ruhnau found ready points of contact with the OC president, and translated the broader reform discourse of democracy, freedom, and participation that marked the Federal

Republic—even before its radicalization in 1968—into the Olympic landscape. And finally, in terms of aesthetic disposition, Daume's visual imagination met its perfect match in Aicher, who believed that trust and understanding developed from perception. Throughout the Olympic project, images, graphics, pictures, and material forms proved more effective than words.

Showing rather than telling had been the Federal Republic's modus operandi since the 1950s. Despite a strong belief in West German achievement, the exhibit at the Brussels World Fair of 1958 was marked by an "attitude of restraint" *(Haltung der Zurückhaltung)* and, "avoiding open propaganda and politics," used "architecture and things, rather than many words to make its point."[8] Bonn's conscious moderation continued through the 1960s—and, as Paulmann argues, still holds almost twenty years into the Berlin Republic.[9] In 1963, unsettling events such as the Nazi trials and the erection of the Berlin Wall caused the government to delay ten months before considering an invitation to participate at the next expo in Montreal, and the social tensions that gathered pace from the middle of the decade hardly encouraged them to let loose when 1967 arrived.[10] In the Canadian metropolis, Gutbrod and Otto's stunning architecture diminished the significance of the pavilion's content, but most importantly gave a sense of increased German confidence. Despite the desire to produce "an unconventional Germany" rather than a "German drama," national and international audiences perceived a clear development from the "sympathetic but all-too-obvious attempt to reestablish [the country] internationally" in Brussels to the "Swinging Germany" of Montreal.[11] The effect—initially unintended, as Sigel notes, but later seized upon as cultural capital—was magnified in Munich.[12] That is not to say that all caution was thrown to the wind in 1972. The Munich City Council fretted about the international custom for track-and-field judges to march into the stadium;[13] at the opening ceremony, Kurt Edelhagen scrupulously vetted tunes that were featured in 1936;[14] and the national anthem was played, not sung, while a simple "Welcome to Munich" replaced the words "Einigkeit und Recht und Freiheit" (unity, justice, freedom) on the scoreboard.[15] But the transformation of Otto's temporary and flexible solution to a specific architectural conundrum in Canada into—as he later sardonically noted—an "artificial form" and "Olympic rhapsody"[16] of permanent symbolism marks the high point of "modest" self-imaging in the history of the Bonn Republic.

Certainly, the FIFA soccer World Cup of 1974, which West Germany hosted and eventually won against Holland in Munich's Olympic Stadium, had a very different look. World Cups have never shared the Olympics' enthusiasm for symbols, and the soccer event appeared as primitive as the Mexico 1970 tournament did compared to its own Olympic predecessor of 1968.[17] But by the mid-1970s, it was the Munich Games, not their poor soccer relations, that formed the exception. After the late summer of 1972, Brandt won the Social Democratic Party's

(SPD) biggest mandate in the Bundestag but was later forced to resign; the consequences of Black September's attack for the security of megaevents were being realized for the first time against a backdrop of increased activity from the second generation of Red Army Faction commandoes; and in 1973, the OPEC (oil) crisis sent a dramatic shock through the world system. As Ulrich Pfeil recently observed: "There was nothing left of the 'dynamic times' of the long 1960s. . . . [There was] a sense of modernity and a striving for technocratic feasibility, but a 'change of direction' had already occurred and was questioning the euphoria of modernization. International terrorism, as well as an increasing awareness of the 'limits of growth' had demonstrated the vulnerability of Western industrial society."[18]

Thirty years earlier, Vogel reached a similar verdict in his closing remarks to the final meeting of OC members (Mitgliederversammlung) in 1977: "I'm not so certain . . . whether [the whole preparation of the Games] would work the same way under the conditions we face today, whether we would be able to bring everyone together under one roof with the same purpose."[19]

Thus, the Munich Games capture a moment.[20] They were the culmination of "the long 1960s": faith in planning, belief in modernity, and the desire to reform and democratize all levels of human activity. But, as this book has demonstrated, while they expressed social changes and political discourse, they far from simply reflected them. Taking 2,247 days to prepare and 1,758 to tidy up, they contested and constructed the spirit of the age as much as they accepted it.[21] Lasting sixteen days—or eleven until the terrorist attack—they were there one moment and gone the next, becoming unwittingly the farewell party of the "short summer of concrete utopia" (Ruck). Olympic Games, however, exist in three temporal dimensions. In addition to their long gestation and the epiphany of the event itself, they generate concrete and emotional legacies, and in time become subject to memorialization of another age's making. These effects are vital for an understanding of any Games, and in the case of Munich are best explained in relation to the three agencies that sponsored them: city, Land, and federal state.

"Much is left for the city when it's over." On 9 September in the Lenbachhaus, Kronawitter would have whisked his audience from the obvious infrastructural advantages the Games had brought toward the nobler but less tangible notions of "greater self-confidence and a little pride." Yet, the material legacy of the Olympics should never be underplayed, and particularly not in Munich. Several years earlier, in 1969, it was precisely this aspect that Vogel chose to highlight in his laudatio when Brundage was bestowed the honor of signing the city's Golden Book: "[Mr. President,] you mentioned that Pierre de Coubertin had two aims: namely that the Games should make healthier and stronger boys and girls and citizens. I think the Olympic idea has turned out to promote a third aim as well: to make better cities, to give cities subways and finer installations."[22]

Munich's long-term gains were many and various. Nearly three-quarters of the total DM 1.967 billion expenditure were invested in infrastructure (DM 1.35 billion to Munich, DM 94 million to Kiel) and, offset by the organizers' income of DM 359 million from ticket sales, television revenue, and private donations, the ephemeral sixteen days cost only DM 165 million.[23] Daume might have been exaggerating when he claimed the city's contribution of DM 154 million had soared in value to two or three billion, but the gains were certainly considerable: fabulous new sports facilities and parkland, six thousand apartments, 1,800 student flats, three schools with 7,650 places, and a large exhibition hall.[24] When it came to covering the future upkeep of the stadium, gymnastics hall, swimming pool, and cycle arena, the city brokered a further financial coup. According to the precedent of 1936, the federal government should have assumed responsibility for the various venues, but doubts about the durability of the roof made for protracted negotiations[25] and the city eventually agreed in June 1972 to accept a single payment of DM 130 million from Bonn, based on estimates that two-thirds of the sum would be consumed by 2000.[26] In reality, however, B+P's masterpiece required only minor repair until 1988, and regular income from the site (including DM 15 million per year from the Bayern Munich soccer club) covered maintenance and allowed the city to invest its windfall, which grew to DM 220 million by the millennium.[27]

To support the sites, the city's traffic infrastructure was dramatically improved between 1965 and 1972. Based on the German Federal Railway's existing grid, a star-shaped suburban rail system (S-Bahn) was completed with twelve separate lines and 134 stops, stretching thirty-five kilometers from the historic center into the region.[28] Tunneling through from Ostbahnhof and Hauptbahnhof to connect lines east and west of the river Isar and moving 4.2 kilometers of track underground paved the way for a pedestrian zone in the old part of the city between the hub at Marienplatz and Karlsplatz. The city's first two subway lines (U-Bahn) were also added, the first complementing the S-Bahn with a twelve-kilometer north-south axis, the second providing a speedy link between Marienplatz and the Olympic venues four kilometers away. And the building of two ring roads (Altstadtring and the Mittlerer Ring) was accelerated to ease the burden on the radial road grid and cope with the sharp rise in car ownership, which more than doubled to 377,000 in the decade leading up to 1970.[29] The Karlsplatz, in particular, believed to be the most congested square in Europe at the time, was greatly relieved.[30]

Much of this would have come about in due course, but the imminent arrival of the Games brought financial support and a sense of urgency.[31] The schedule of urban planner Herbert Jensen was cut in half, and the city gained what Frankfurt and Stuttgart took decades and much greater sums to achieve. Individual car use was reduced by 40 percent, and the banning of traffic from the city center—deemed to be one of the main achievements of Vogel's time in office—restored the city's historic luster.[32] However, there were serious drawbacks too. The construction of the Altstadtring ring road caused much aesthetic damage—disfiguring the Prinz-Carl-Palais, a gem of German neoclassical architecture and seat of the Bavarian minister president, crowding the façade of the Haus der Kunst, and bisecting two nineteenth-century boulevards (the Maximilianstrasse and Prinzregentenstrasse). More importantly, the time constraints under which the "great leap forward" was taken meant that politicians and planners had little opportunity to learn from their mistakes. The monocentric orientation of the S-Bahn became largely irreversible, as it increased commuter traffic between the center and the surrounding region and reinforced precisely the functionalist division between work and living spaces that Vogel had feared after reading Jacobs' critique of U.S. cities. Jensen's attempt to halt the "shapeless accidental development" and "dissolution of the city" was also quickly undone as the commercial center continued to expand and swallow large sections of residential neighborhoods (e.g., Lehel and Maxvorstadt) for business use. By 1974, Jensen's long-term vision, originally intended to last from the 1960s to 1990, was superseded by a new town development plan that replaced quantitative with qualitative growth, and encouraged polycentrism in the suburbs and region over the privileging of the center.[33]

Nonetheless, Munich became a more attractive city in which to live. Although its postwar population peaked in 1972, it was increasingly associated with the surrounding holiday region and regularly topped the popularity rankings.[34] Despite immediate fears that the subdued ending to the Games had cost the country dearly—the director of the German Tourism Agency (Deutsche Zentrale für Tourismus) predicting that millions would be required to compensate for lost advertising after the curtailment of Bavarian dancing in the closing ceremony—tourist numbers increased.[35] Notwithstanding a lack of detailed sources, it is clear the Games alerted domestic and overseas visitors to the city's charms. By 1985, for example, 5.8 million overnight stays placed it far ahead of its national rivals; some 44 percent of all visitors came from abroad; and the average stay (2.6 days) suggested that it no longer served as a transit point, as before the Games, but established itself as a destination in its own right.[36] For Munich citizens and tourists alike, the Olympic park proved a lasting attraction and could plausibly claim to have been Europe's most popular leisure facility in the late twentieth century. Statistics vary, but taking a conservative estimate: by 1977, it had drawn in over twenty-one million paying customers, between nine thousand and thirteen thousand active sports participants per week, and untold numbers of casual visitors—a total estimated in 1982 to have reached one hundred and twenty million.[37]

As Daume proudly noted in 1979, "In Munich there are no 'Olympic ruins,'" and despite the city's two soccer teams (Bayern and 1860 Munich) moving to a purpose-built stadium in 2005, this is still the case today.[38] But while statistics are easy to gather, the ideological legacy of the site is virtually impossible to ascertain.

At the turn of the century, when Bayern Munich had almost succeeded in convincing Behnisch to convert the stadium into a dedicated, closed-in soccer arena, a wide range of views were articulated. The liberal press championed the democratic, symbolic moment of 1972 (so desired by the organizers and feared by Frei Otto), while the fans themselves showed little respect for the site as a "lieu de memoire." Franz Beckenbauer, club president and chief organizer of the 2006 World Cup finals in Germany, spoke incautiously but doubtless for many when he described it as a "communist bowl" awaiting only "a few terrorists to come and blow it up."[39]

While the state of Bavaria stood to profit less directly from the Olympics than its capital or the Federal Republic in general, it could be satisfied with its investment. The Land benefited from infrastructural development (not least the conversion of the hockey, volleyball, and media sites into a still much used Hochschulsportanlage for Munich's two universities), commercial boosterism (Adidas, Siemens, etc.) and a tourist influx that extended well beyond the city's boundaries. And if the PR campaign capitalized on Munich's image, transferring it to the Land and the country at large, much of what the world perceived as typical of Munich applied equally to the Land. "Earthy," folkloristic *(Lederhosen* and *Dirndl),* and "life-embracing" (yodeling, beer, Oktoberfest)—Munich stood mutatis mutandis for Bavaria.[40] Most importantly, however, the Games marked an important stage in the Land's postwar development from a backward, agricultural economy to one of the richest states in the country by the 1980s. Despite the general fatigue in the region after the major push toward the Games and growing skepticism about modernization across the Federal Republic in the wake of the OPEC crisis, the Olympics, as Ferdinand Kramer noted, "created a new balance in the development of the metropolis of Munich and the State of Bavaria with a noteworthy acknowledgement of Munich's specific role in Bavaria as the state's gateway to the world."[41]

While the 1960s and 1970s model continues to resonate positively in reform discussions in the region and the city, there might even be evidence to support Kronawitter's hoped for "pride" and "greater self-confidence." Consolidating its stronghold as "the party that invented beautiful Bavaria," the Christian Social Union (CSU) appropriated the Games' strategy of presenting the Land as a bridge between modernity and tradition.[42] In its 1974 regional election campaign, a television slot spliced aerial shots of the tent roof with cows grazing happily in Alpine pastures; showed Franz Josef Strauß, the future minister-president, in Bavarian dress alongside the atomic research reactor at Garching; and played a swing version of the popular "Bayerischer Defiliermarsch" to remind viewers of the opening ceremony two years earlier.[43]

Tellingly, although Munich was heavily subsidized by and hosted the Games for "the whole country"—as Kronawitter planned to mention—they were never subsequently exploited for federal publicity. An unspoken cross-party agreement prevented their use in the November elections of 1972, and the embarrassment of Fürstenfeldbruck and the related diplomatic fallout in the Middle East placed them largely off-limits. Paradoxically, the Munich and Bavarian authorities contributed least financially and caused the most damage with their security failures, but came away with the greater tangible benefits. As we have seen, Kronawitter's hope "that the image of our city [would] retain a little luster," was certainly fulfilled. The fate of Brandt's wish to show the world a modern, democratic, and successful Germany, however, is altogether more difficult to determine. Despite the ecstatic reviews for the opening ceremony and the Olympic venues, the overall story is naturally entwined with the one event that Kronawitter's draft inevitably omitted to mention: the terrorist attack.

Initially, Brandt experienced intense disappointment that the Games would "not go down in history as a happy occasion" (chapter 1), and he couldn't have been cheered by the national press's speculation about the loss of image abroad.[44] Yet before the month was out, he seems to have changed his mind, telling the *Spiegel* at the height of the crisis with Egypt and Israel that the Federal Republic was "more highly regarded in the world than in 1969."[45] The impending federal election might have encouraged the chancellor's bullish mood, but his vacillation mirrored the bifurcation of viewpoints around the world. Olympic insiders, of course, rallied around the hosts. Daume received letters from foreign dignitaries and sports functionaries thanking the OC for its hospitality and praising it for its organizational endeavors. Philip Noel-Baker, the British Nobel Peace laureate who had been closely involved in London 1948 sent his "warmest congratulations on all that [he] achieved in the greatest Olympic Games which [had] ever taken place," claiming that British "television viewers all [said] . . . the Games were a magnificent experience."[46] But press coverage was more ambivalent. On the one hand, a *New York Times* editorial exculpated the authorities: "Since the attack on the Olympic Village was unprecedented, the West German government was unprepared and had to improvise as events unfolded. The terrorists had the advantage of surprise, and of the near-chaos that surprise produced."[47] But on the other, the massacre dominated the U.S. media for more than a week, with reports dissecting the Israeli refusal to negotiate, the West Germans' bungled rescue attempt, and the controversial decision to continue the Games.

Crucially, as Melani McAlister observed, "many accounts pointed out the terrible irony that these deaths had happened at Munich, where the West Germans had been self-consciously trying to counter the memories of the Nazi Games of 1936."[48] This is hardly surprising. Brandt's foreign minister Walter Scheel, after all, had told his ambassadors in 1970 the Games would show a different Germany from 1936 (see chapter 1); Aicher, Behnisch, and others had worked on the same principle; and the federal and Bavarian governments' investigation into the attack made exactly that point in mitigation of its light security at the village.[49] But while 1936 was intended as the inevitable foil against which the present and future Germany could be judged, the terrorist attack had inverted foreground and background. West Germany might well have been another country than the one that hosted the "Nazi Games," but Black September and the failed liberation attempt had locked the two together and turned Munich into a backward- rather than forward-looking event. This much is clear from another speech that was never given—one prepared for Daume by an unidentified writer for the final meeting of OC members in 1977. On that occasion, Daume ignored the draft he had been sent, opening instead with, "The Munich Olympics are old hat," (literally: "yesterday's snow") and closing the session, to applause and the sound of Almglocken, with a cheery "the Munich Olympics have left a warm after-glow—that is how it is, and that is how it will stay."[50] The text he decided to leave unread in the archive offered a grittier take on the Games, however, and came with a despondent note from its author: "None of the modern Olympics has made it into history. Only the first ones, because they were the beginning, and Berlin, because that's when the Nazis started to deceive the world . . . and from Munich the whole world will remember the terrorist attack. . . . There is no hope of any lasting glory."[51]

The unheard voice of 1977 had called it right. The terrorist attack hooks Munich uncomfortably to the 1936 Games, a phenomenon confirmed by the final pages of David Clay Large's recent academic account of the "Nazi Games," which repeat the trope of Munich's *intention*.[52] Popular Olympic history too is reductive—and the circumstances of adjacent Games proved less than conducive. The student massacre and black-power protests at Mexico City 1968, an African walkout and the financial disaster at Montreal 1976, and the tit-for-tat boycotts of Moscow 1980 and Los Angeles 1984 combined to place Munich at the heart of a crisis narrative.[53] Around the world, Munich is remembered for Mark Spitz, Olga Korbut, the terrorist attack, and the fact the West German "organizers were determined that everything about their Games should be different from those of 1936."[54] It is indicative of the shadow cast by 5 September that the organizers' *determination to show* a new Germany rather than the world's *realization that one existed* has become the historiographical default.

But for West Germany, as for other nations, cultural diplomacy had two dimensions. On the one hand, as Johannes Paulmann has stressed, "it served to establish and cultivate relations with foreign partners with the aim of rebuilding trust, furthering mutual understanding, and supporting national interests." On the other, it "also affected self-images at home," debates about how the country should present itself abroad contributing "markedly to the formation of identities in public institutions and societal groups."[55] If certain individuals—and in Paulmann's analysis these tend to belong to various elites—"observed themselves in the mirror of their own representations abroad," then the Olympics brought this process to more members and levels of society than any other event in the history of the Republic.[56] Unlike state visits, trade fairs, and expos in foreign countries, the Games became an unavoidable part of almost every citizen's daily existence. Bonn realized, in fact, that it needed their help to make the Games a success. In November 1970, an internal discussion paper in the Federal Press Office made the obvious point that the image visitors would "take home with them [would] essentially depend on the impressions [they] receive[d] in contact with Germans." While many were "used to living with foreigners (occupation troops, allied armies, guest workers, visits abroad, foreign tourists in Germany)," the 1972 Olympics needed to be "understood as a task to which all Germans felt obliged."[57] The chancellor reiterated this point in a speech to mark the ceremonial handover of the venues to the OC in June 1972: "The way the hosts comport themselves and the openness of our citizens to our guests are even more important [than the venues]. Let's disprove the notion . . . that 'friendly Germans' are the exception to the rule!"[58]

To this end, "taxi drivers, hotel employees, tourist guides, hostesses, and the man on the street" were all deemed "crucial,"[59] kept well informed (not least by a general PR campaign "Olympics of Hospitality"), and—although not to the same extent as in Mexico four years earlier—targeted by specific schemes.[60] Thousands of OC employees and hostesses were admonished to "show themselves particularly hospitable to foreigners,"[61] over two hundred thousand of whom were distinguished by special badges distributed during an "Olympic Guest" project *(Aktion Olympia-Gast)*.[62] Taxi drivers were supplied with an Olympic car badge to make them feel "somewhat official."[63] A poster campaign (*Die Welt zu Gast bei uns zuhause,* "The World a Guest in Our Home") and a mail-shot to 1.3 million homes around Munich offering various ticket incentives generated twenty thousand private beds to boost the meager ten thousand available in the city's hotels.[64] And the Glücksspirale lottery invited foreign celebrities—British *Avengers* star Patrick Macnee and émigré Croatian singer and actress Dunja Reiter—to appear on its television slots.

Despite such efforts, however, the mood preceding the Games was poor. Olympic sociologist Miquel de Moragas and others have posited that the host population's stance toward a megaevent changes through distinct phases: expectation (six to four years before), mistrust and criticism in the local press (four to two years before), agreement (one year before), and finally euphoria, local solidarity, and limited criticism (year of the Games).[65] In the Federal Republic, however, the picture was bleaker, with opinion polls showing a gradual slide until the eve of the event itself. In May 1966, a year after the IOC's decision in Rome, an EMNID survey had found 80 percent of West Germans in favor of the Games, with nine against and eleven undecided.[66] In the summer of 1971, when the mood should have reached a similar level again after a mid-cycle slump, the institute recorded only two-thirds supporting the Games, while some 29 percent expressed no opinion.[67] In September of that year, only twenty thousand people came out to hear high-profile speakers and watch the film *Munich—A City Invites* in sixty-two cities across the country on the evening of *Aktion Paukenschlag* (Drumbeat), the OC's major push to drum up grassroots support.[68] Liselott Diem, sent to Mainz, took pleasure in criticizing the poor organization and dreary speech outline sent by Klein's PR department.[69] And in February and March 1972, despite increased efforts by the OC, which lamented that the "personal identification . . . and joy about 'our Games' [was] still missing,"[70] the vital results had slipped again to 63 and 30 percent respectively.[71] Most worryingly for the organizers, only 56 percent of those from a higher education background (i.e., those most likely to hold opinion-forming positions) supported the Games, with some 15 percent, twice the national average (7 percent), against.[72] Just months before the starting pistol, Bonn was anticipating a poor return on its investment domestically.

Many factors contributed to the inauspicious standing. Advertising had initially concentrated on foreign audiences and was not launched in the Federal Republic until thirty months before the Games, when financial cuts had become the order of the day (see chapter 2). By 1972 the position had deteriorated further, a negligible subsidy of DM 100,000 to allow Paukenschlag volunteers to continue their work having to be rejected.[73] The 1971 version of the lottery show was poorly presented and badly received after technical problems diminished the chance of winning a major prize.[74] Even though two-thirds of the 3.5 million Olympic tickets were reserved for domestic use, only one in twenty-five Germans could buy one, and discontent spread further at the news that members of the Bavarian and federal parliaments could claim up to twenty each.[75] The press—in retrospect, incorrectly—heavily criticized the cost of the whole enterprise, such that neither federal government nor the Land or communes around the country were prepared to finance Olympic flags to decorate their towns and border crossings.[76] And in Munich itself, prominent cultural and architectural critics attacked the disfigurement of the historic center,[77] while residents complained about pollution, inflation, and the cost to local taxpayers.[78] The best the organizers could hope for was "grumbling consent."[79]

In the event, however, their fragile hopes were far exceeded. Asked a few days after the Games whether—"all things told, i.e., the serene atmosphere until the terrorist attack and then the terrorist attack itself"—they could be considered a success, 80 percent of West Germans replied in the affirmative, taking the polls back to their highpoint of 1966. 78 percent supported the IOC's decision to let the Games continue.[80] Despite the much praised performance of the West German team (particularly over the last few days), these are strikingly counterintuitive figures—not least because of those who supported the Games in the previous poll, the highest proportion did so in the belief they would contribute to peace and understanding.[81] And although anger was initially expressed at the police's mistakes—most prominently by Brandt himself[82]—and the press expected the "shots fired at Fürstenfeldbruck" to "reverberate around national politics for some time to come," the public spared the major politicians in the November elections.[83] Brandt secured the SPD's largest share of the vote, while his Free Democratic Party (FDP) colleagues Genscher and Scheel rose to record heights in the twelve months following the Games.[84] In his official report, Manfred Schreiber, too, felt comfortable defending his policing policy, weighing up the "once-in-a-century event of a militarily executed attack" against the "sum total of all the pleasures and meetings between the nations," and declared the security "a success."[85]

Taken together, these reactions require some explanation. For while it is impossible to judge how well the Games would have been received without the attack, it is clear that it did not hinder greater acceptance domestically. Certainly a paradox was at work. On the one hand—as a West German diplomat stationed in the Middle East observed one year on—the population had still not recovered from the "ruination" of their Games, the Olympic ideal, and the event's peaceful symbolism. Psychologically, "the way they brought matters to a conclusion [had been] rather inelegant and problematic" and continued to hamper the forgiving process and prevent Bonn from making necessary progress with the Palestinians.[86] Yet on the other, this ruination seemed to make the Germans value their Games all the more and close ranks emotionally with the victims. The two aspects were linked. At a memorial ceremony in Washington, Senator Edward Kennedy noted that "the terrorist attack had been a tragedy not only for the Israeli but also the German people," and his words caught the mood in the Federal Republic.[87] Axel Springer, the pro-Israeli media tycoon, sent his condolences to Golda Meir in a telegram that was reprinted in all his newspapers on 7 September. More significantly, journalists and politicians saw the massacre as a moment to transcend the past. As an editorial in the popular Munich *Abendzeitung* put it: "Historians will note that here in Munich, only a few kilometers from Dachau, at the location of a horrible crime, Germans have cried next to Israelis. From the perspective of history, the image of the Germans who mourn the dead of Israel will be a marker—a marker at the beginning of a road which one day leads two nations away from bitterness."[88] President Heinemann received over four hundred letters congratulating him on his speech at the memorial ceremony, some from companies with hundreds of signatories,[89] and a business in Reutlingen sponsored ten employees to work for up to four weeks in Israel on full salary.[90]

In the 1950s and 1960s, the West German public tended to sympathize with Israel in its hour of need—most prominently during the Six Day War and after an arson attack on an old people's home in Munich (1970).[91] But the reaction to the massacre eclipsed habitual empathies. The "common loathing of the crime" did not just "bring [the two nations] close together"—as Georg Kronawitter hoped at Munich City Council's memorial ceremony on 7 September[92]—but led to a conflation of real and symbolic victims.[93] The fact that a German police officer had died at Fürstenfeldbruck eased the public's conscience and contributed to a heightened identification with Israel. On 8 September, Fliegerbauer was given a well-attended civic funeral, at which Kronawitter and Goppel represented the city and Land and wreaths were laid on behalf of Heinemann and Brandt. The policeman was celebrated as a hero who had paid the ultimate price in his attempt to liberate innocent hostages from the hands of "fanatics blind with rage." At the end of the ceremony, a representative of the Israeli government expressed the condolences and gratitude of the Israeli people,[94] and in the *Münchner Jüdische Nachrichten,* Ernest Landau stressed: "Wracked with pain and grief, we stand, with the whole Jewish people, before the coffins of these eleven young Israelis and the police officer Anton Fliegerbauer."[95]

On a level distinct from Bonn's diplomatic fire-fighting across the Middle East in the last third of 1972, public discourse and practice shunned the Arab world as much as it embraced its Jewish rivals. On the day of the attack, the OC, the Olympic Press Center DOZ, Deutsche Bundesbahn, and several private companies were sent anonymous bomb threats demanding the release of the hostages and the sacking of Arab workers.[96] Soon afterward, Arab hostesses—despite some being daughters or wives of German citizens—and other employees in the Olympic village were removed to avoid confrontations.[97] The OC considered a similar move at the Vier Jahreszeiten Hotel, where the IOC was staying but desisted for fear of repercussions.[98] Twenty Tunisian participants at the Youth Camp departed for Austria "in fear of reprisals."[99] And many of the letters that Heinemann received demanded retaliatory measures against the Palestinians and their supporters. The reluctance of Egypt and its allies to condemn the attack did little to diffuse the situation, but the furor in the Federal Republic soon bled into another issue. Just as in the United States, where—as Melani McAlister noted—outrage at the senseless violence soon spilled over into well-worn debates about the futility or otherwise of the Vietnam War, the West German press and public linked the attack with its growing unease over foreign workers and immigration.[100] In fact, press coverage of the security theme—both in Munich and Zagreb—remained surprisingly thin, international terrorism disappearing off the radar as quickly as the three surviving perpetrators made good their escape to Libya.[101] What remained, however, was a fomenting anger toward foreigners in general—the *Spiegel* leading on 18 September, for instance, with stories such as "Imported Terror?" and "Arabs—not to be trusted."[102] Munich became a watershed for the 3.4 million guest workers in the Federal Republic. An election topic in October 1972, the country's *Ausländerpolitik* was revised in the recruitment stop of 1973 and grew significantly restrictive.[103]

The terrorist attack undoubtedly influenced the West Germans' view of their Olympics. In the immediate aftermath, surrogate victimhood in sympathy with Israel played into a much enhanced appreciation of the Games but mutated quickly into reprisals and policy change against foreign workers. Into the following year, it was this and a dislike of Palestinians that continued. For one small but significant group, however, the attack had precisely the opposite effect: the organizers. Daume, as his secretary later recalled, crumpled on hearing the news from Fürstenfeldbruck: "He looked not so much in pain as—dead. His face was lifeless and had the events of that terrible night written all over it."[104] Even at the end of the fortnight, he was uncertain about the IOC's majority decision to let the Games go on.[105] And at the memorial service in the Olympic Stadium, he appeared visibly shaken when proclaiming that "a celebration that . . . so clearly expressed the yearning of mankind for understanding, joy and peace, ha[d] been called into question."[106] Vogel, although convinced from the beginning the Games should continue, was equally devastated, noting that "the contrast to the bright colors of the days of peace [had] alerted the world to the horror of such atrocities and sharpened its conscience," before accompanying the bodies back to Israel.[107] For the others involved in the organization—as discussions and interviews with many of them at their thirty-year reunion in 2002 confirm—the Games came to an abrupt end after the massacre.[108] Some left the Olympic village (and were refused money owed to them), while those who stayed completed their tasks out of a heavy sense of duty.[109] We mention these reactions not merely as a footnote to the main narrative, or as a reminder of the need to differentiate, but because as the popular memory of Munich faded—the natural course, as Moragas maintains—those most closely involved in its organization carried it with them in interesting ways.

• • •

Although disappointing, it is hardly surprising that the IOC did nothing to remember the victims. With members from the Middle East but none from Israel, it was easiest to play its nonpolitical card and simply ignore the tragedy. Even before the Games finished, it had returned to business as usual—Brundage collecting signatories (including those of the marquis of Exeter, Jesse Owens, and Emil Zatopek) on a statement against commercialization and professionalization to take to an executive board meeting early in 1973.[110] And at its session in Varna later that year, members stood in silence, but only to mark the passing of one of their own number, Comte Paolo Thaon di Revel.[111] Yet in Munich—even at the height of popular support for Israel—the OC proved oddly reticent too. The day after the Games, Vogel rejected a suggestion from the German embassy in Washington (echoing one already received from the West German public) that the stadium be renamed after Moshe Weinberg, the Israeli wrestling coach killed in the

FIGURE 23. Memorial plaque in front of 31 Connollystraße (photo: Carsten Schiller)

initial struggle.[112] He remarked, "It would be inappropriately excessive and perpetuate the memory of the tragedy in the Olympic village."[113] In fact, the OC struggled to find any appropriate memorial. In 1973, realizing it would be impossible to sell the Connollystraße apartment on the open market, the OC donated it to the Max Planck Society, which still uses it today as a guest house for international fellows, a subtle tablet by the entrance commemorating the hostages. Even this minor gesture was ill-fated, though. When first unveiled in November 1972, it caused understandable offense in Israel for listing incorrect names and displaying a cross for the Star of David, and was duly replaced by the Munich Jewish community and the Central Council of Jews in Germany.[114] In the course of 1973, when Daume, Bieringer, and Hohenemser considered an idea from the publisher Günther Neske to commission a more substantial memorial for the Olympic village from a young Jewish artist, they came to the same conclusion as Vogel: namely "that any monumentalization of the tragic event should be avoided on German soil."[115]

Although Vogel had encouraged nearly seven hundred Jewish émigrés to return to Munich for the Games, invited Israeli mayors to attend at the city's expense, and in 1993, in keeping with his long-held views, would cofound the Verein "Gegen Vergessen—für Demokratie" (Association "Against Oblivion—For Democracy")—both he and Daume maintained their public silence as the years went on.[116] At the

OC's final meeting in 1977, no one mentioned the Israelis, Vogel introducing the only somber note to a mood of self-congratulation, when remembering three deceased colleagues: Ludwig Erhard (who had given his vital consent), Konrad Pöhner (the Bavarian finance minister), and Georg Brauchle (the deputy mayor who had worked tirelessly during the bid).[117] Neither of the two main organizers attended the low-key commemorative ceremonies on the first and tenth anniversaries of the massacre, journalists recalled a whole range of different aspects to the Games ten years on,[118] and by 1988 Daume was telling *GEO* magazine that the attack was "inconsequential in Germany" (literally, "only worth a footnote").[119] It was not until the 1990s that matters changed. Daume attended the twentieth anniversary service in 1992 organized by the German NOC, addressing some of the Israelis' families on the theme of continued Jewish suffering.[120] Three years later, the Wailing Beam *(Klagebalken)*, a DM 500,000 memorial by sculptor Fritz König, containing the names of the eleven hostages and Anton Fliegerbauer, was erected at the entrance to the stadium concourse. And in 1999, a further memorial was unveiled at Fürstenfeldbruck, where in his speech Vogel treated Jewish affliction in the twentieth century, from the Holocaust to the Munich Olympics and the desecration of forty-seven Jewish gravestones in German cemeteries in 1998.[121]

Over the 1980s and 1990s, much, of course, had changed in the culture of public memory. But to the nation's general transition from "Geschichtsvergessenheit" (historical amnesia) to "Geschichtsversessenheit" (an obsession with history) or even "ritualized confession of guilt" must be added the particular circumstances of the Munich event and its aftermath.[122] For one, the fragile but important truce between West German diplomats, Israel, and the Arab states toward the end of 1972 and the withholding of evidence from the victims' families until it was leaked in 1992 would have discouraged enthusiasm for commemorative events. For another, as Moragas and others note, if the Olympic Games return to prominence again, they do so invariably at some considerable distance. Given the general shape of German memorial culture, the opening of the court cases, and the scale of the tragedy itself, it is no surprise Munich's place in the popular memory has been determined by the attack. Kevin MacDonald's *One Day in September* (1999) and Steven Spielberg's September 11–influenced *Munich* (2005) contributed to that trend.[123] Windsurfer Gal Friedman's dedication of Israel's first Olympic gold medal (Athens 2004) to the murdered athletes and New York mayor Rudy Giuliani's incorporation of the massacre in his thoughts on global terrorism in 2001 confirm it.

This book has sought not to undermine that memorialization—which is, after all, a natural and much-studied historical process—but, whatever the Games might have bequeathed, to uncover the myriad processes of their making and significance at the time. Hosting or achieving success in megaevents can enhance many ordinary citizens' sense of pride and identity. Such moments are complex

FIGURE 24. View of the Olympic park and stadium from the Olympic mountain (photo: Carsten Schiller)

nodes of experience: intense then fleeting, they might nonetheless serve as important pulses in an incremental but uneven curve of national feeling. Along with 1972, the surprise World Cup victory in 1954 (itself recently memorialized) had positive identificatory effects, while victory in the same tournament hosted on home soil in 1974 struggled to compete. But one important footnote remains. For if Munich 1972 is now remembered by the majority for the terrorist attack and enjoyed perhaps—in a physical but emotionally intangible way—by those who use its park and sports facilities, then it retains a special importance for one particular group. Leaving aside the senior organizers—Daume and his general secretary Herbert Kunze from the reconstruction generation and Vogel, Aicher, Behnisch, Grzimek, and Ruhnau of the skeptical "1945ers"—the Games were carried by thousands of young adults in their twenties and thirties. Hostesses, administrative staff, reporters at the time—many went on to occupy influential positions in public life.

In his thought-provoking essay on the West German exhibit at the 1958 World Fair in Brussels, Johannes Paulmann observed that "the memories of contemporaries . . . point toward the essential role played by apparently minor things for the development of a collective memory in individuals," noting it is "promising to do further research on [the] individual imprinting of self-consciousness in everyday practice. Merely searching for the renewal and formation of a West German identity in the national debate of intellectuals and politicians," he comments, "appears to miss many of the essential mechanisms of cultural appropriation."[124] While researching this book, we had the opportunity to hear the memories of many younger people involved in the Games, and as Paulmann suspected, their "imprinting" is worthy of note.

For Werner Rabe—a young regional reporter, and now head of sport at Bayerischer Rundfunk—the Games proved a formative experience: a first encounter with the international scene on home territory and a feeling—not of "wir sind wieder wer" (we are someone again) as often claimed for 1954—but "endlich sind wir dabei" (at last we're there with everyone else).[125] For Klaus von Lindeiner, the OC's minute taker, general factotum for the official film, and later leading corporate lawyer—they brought the opportunity to interact at the highest administrative and cultural levels in national and international settings.[126] And for the hundreds of hostesses—some of whom trained their successors at Olympic Games through Los Angeles 1984 and went on to senior positions in event management—they offered the chance to participate in a once-in-a-lifetime event.[127] As their extensive questionnaire returns confirm, their primary motivation was West Germany's becoming part of the Olympics and being involved themselves ("dabei sein").[128] They were extensively trained (and as the 1972 returns suggest, bored) by the latest computer-generated learning methods—but remember few of the details now. Instead, what remains is the deep fulfillment of putting on a world event with members of their own generation. These emotions and experiences are more difficult to measure than the facts, figures, and decisions contained in countless meters of archive files. But they are no less real, and present in the tear that comes to the eye of Gertrude Krombholz—chief hostess at Spitz's swimming pool, later academic sports director at Munich's Technische Universität and leading functionary in the international Paralympics movement—as she digs out a letter sent by Daume in February 1972. Addressing the German hostesses, the OC president reminded them of their vital contribution to the Olympic Games and the Federal Republic with the words:

> A hostess is something you *are*. Fundamentally, it is not something you can learn. This skill comes from the heart and very essence of a woman. You have to bring it with you. We hope that you will do this, that you will bring this gift to the task at hand, and in so doing will derive pleasure from it. . . . You will be working for very little money, but you will have the honor of actively contributing to what is in its own way a unique event in the world. Without doubt, it will enrich your lives and personalities.[129]

Munich 1972 proved, indeed, to be an encouragement and an experience that propelled many young people into their professional lives. The common denominator to their memories is "participation." This was not a group that set off on a long march through the institutions or rode a wave of radical intent—but one that profited from the reform discussion of the "long 1960s" and took part in its single greatest practical experiment. In terms of human capital, this is Munich's major legacy.

NOTES

1. INTRODUCTION

1. U.S. National Archives College Park: Kissinger telcons, Boxes 15, 16, Nixon Presidential Materials. Our sincere thanks to Barbara Keys for passing this material on to us.

2. See David Edmonds and John Eidinow, *Bobby Fischer Goes to War: How the Soviets Lost the Most Extraordinary Chess Match of All Time* (New York, 2004).

3. See U.S. National Archives College Park: Kissinger telcons, Boxes 15, 16, Nixon Presidential Materials: telcons, 6 September 1972.

4. British journalist Gerald Seymour, quoted in Simon Reeve, *One Day in September: The Story of the 1972 Munich Olympics Massacre, a Government Cover-up and a Covert Revenge Mission* (London, 2000), p. 57.

5. Willy Brandt, *People and Politics: The Years 1960–1975* (New York, 1976), pp. 439–41.

6. A television journalist's commentary, cited in the *Daily Mail*, 24 July 2004.

7. See David Scott Diffrient, "Spectator Sports and Terrorist Reports: Filming the Munich Olympics, (Re)Imagining the Munich Massacre," *Sport in Society* 11, nos. 2–3, 2008, pp. 311–29.

8. David Miller, *Athens to Athens: The Official History of the Olympic Games and the IOC, 1894–2004* (Edinburgh, 2003), p. 195.

9. While Richard Mandell's *Munich Diary* provides useful information on the atmosphere of the 1972 Games, it is an eyewitness account published almost twenty years after the event without access to archival materials (*The Olympics of 1972: A Munich Diary* [Chapel Hill, 1991]).

10. See Uta Andrea Balbier, "'Der Welt das moderne Deutschland vorstellen': Die Eröffnungsfeier der Olympischen Spiele in München," in Johannes Paulmann, ed., *Auswärtige Repräsentationen: Deutsche Kulturdiplomatie nach 1945* (Cologne, 2005), pp. 105–19; Robert Geipel, Ilse Helbrecht, and Jürgen Pohl, "Die Münchner Olympischen

Spiele von 1972 als Instrument der Stadtentwicklungspolitik," in Hartmut Häußermann and Walter Siebel, eds., *Festivalisierung der Stadtpolitik: Stadtentwicklung durch große Projekte* (*Leviathan. Zeitschrift für Sozialwissenschaft*, Sonderheft 13, 1993), pp. 278–304; Ferdinand Kramer, "München und die Olympischen Spiele von 1972," in Christian Koller, ed., *Sport als städtisches Ereignis* (Ostfildern, 2008), pp. 239–52; Eva Maria Modrey, "Architecture as a Mode of Self-representation at the Olympic Games in Rome (1960) and Munich (1972)," *European Review of History: Revue européenne d'histoire* 15, no. 6, 2008, pp. 691–706; Ulrich Pfeil, "Die Olympischen Spiele 1972 und die Fußballweltmeisterschaft 1974: Fallbeispiele für die Verquickung von Sport, Politik und Gesellschaft," *Deutschland Archiv* 39, no. 3, 2006, pp. 415–23; Swantje Scharenberg, "Nachdenken über die Wechselwirkung von Architektur und Wohlbefinden: Das Olympiastadion in München, ein politischer Veranstaltungsort," in Matthias Marschik, Rudolf Müllner, Georg Spitaler, and Michael Zinganel, eds., *Das Stadion: Geschichte, Architektur, Politik, Ökonomie* (Vienna, 2005), pp. 153–74; Kay Schiller, "Death at the Munich Olympics," in Alon Confino, Paul Betts, and Dirk Schumann, eds., *Between Mass Death and Individual Loss: The Place of the Dead in Twentieth-Century Germany* (New York, 2008), pp. 129–50; Christopher Young, "Munich 1972: Re-presenting the Nation," in Alan Tomlinson and Christopher Young, eds., *National Identity and Global Sports Events: Culture, Politics, and Spectacle in the Olympics and the Football World Cup* (New York, 2006), pp. 117–32.

11. See Simone Derix, "Gruppenbild mit Industrielandschaft: Wie Krupp die Bundesrepublik Deutschland bei Staatsbesuchen bebilderte" and Frieder Günther, "Gespiegelte Selbstdarstellung: Der Staatsbesuch von Theodor Heuss in Großbritannien im Oktober 1958," in Paulmann, *Auswärtige Repräsentationen*, pp. 165–84 and 185–203; Christoph Oesterreich, "Umstrittene Selbstdarstellung: Der deutsche Beitrag zur Weltausstellung in Brüssel 1958," *Vierteljahrshefte für Zeitgeschichte* 48, 2000, pp. 127–53; Peter Alter, ed., *Der DAAD in der Zeit: Geschichte, Gegenwart und zukünftige Aufgaben—vierzehn Essays* (Bonn, 2000); Eckard Michels, *Von der Deutschen Akademie zum Goethe-Institut: Sprach- und auswärtige Kulturpolitik 1923–1960* (Munich, 2005).

12. Reeve, *One Day in September*, p. 51.

13. PAAA Berlin/Av. Neues Amt 2.233: Der Bundesminister des Auswärtigen, 16 April 1970.

14. Brundage, Speech at the IOC Session, 19 August 1972, in Organizing Committee for the Games of the XXth Olympiad Munich 1972, ed., *Die Spiele: The Official Report*, vol. 1: *The Organization* (Munich, 1972), p. 95. On Rome 1960, see David Maraniss, *Rome 1960: The Olympics That Changed the World* (New York, 2008); on Tokyo, Christian Tagsold, *Die Inszenierung der kulturellen Identität in Japan* (Munich, 2002); on Mexico City, Joseph L. Arbena, "Hosting the Summer Olympic Games: Mexico City, 1968," in Joseph Arbena and David G. LaFrance, eds., *Sport in Latin America and the Caribbean* (Wilmington, 2002), pp. 133–43; Michael Barke, "Mexico City 1968," in John R. Gold and Margaret M. Gold, eds., *Olympic Cities: City Agendas, Planning, and the World's Games, 1896 to 2012* (London, 2006), pp. 183–96; Claire and Keith Brewster, "Mexico City 1968: Sombreros and Skyscrapers," in Tomlinson and Young, *National Identity and Global Sports Events*, pp. 99–116; Kevin B. Witherspoon, *Before the Eyes of the World: Mexico and the 1968*

Olympic Games (De Kalb, IL, 2008); Eric Zolov, "Showcasing the 'Land of Tomorrow': Mexico and the 1968 Olympics," *Americas* 61, no. 2, 2004, pp. 159–88.

15. CULDA/Koebsel/III.1: Niederschrift über die 2. Sitzung der Mitgliederversammlung des Organisationskomitees für die Spiele der XX. Olympiade München 1972 e.V. am 18. März 1967 [hereafter abbreviated to 2. Mitgliederversammlung, likewise for other OC bodies].

16. Alan Tomlinson and Christopher Young, "Culture, Politics, and Spectacle in the Global Sports Event—An Introduction," in Tomlinson and Young, *National Identity and Global Sports Events,* pp. 1–14, 5.

17. Tony Judt, *Postwar: A History of Europe Since 1945* (New York, 2005), p. 820.

18. See Friedrich Kießling, "Täter repräsentieren: Willy Brandts Kniefall in Warschau. Überlegungen zum Zusammenhang von bundesdeutscher Außenrepräsentation und der Erinnerung an den Nationalsozialismus," in Paulmann, *Auswärtige Repräsentationen,* p. 206; see also Christoph Schneider, *Der Warschauer Kniefall: Ritual, Ereignis und Erzählung* (Konstanz, 2006); Adam Krzemiński, "Der Kniefall," in Étienne François and Hagen Schulze, eds., *Deutsche Erinnerungsorte: Eine Auswahl* (Munich, 2005), pp. 431–46.

19. When Daume apologized, Brandt allegedly responded: "Ah, Mr. Daume, don't worry. If the worst that can happen is that someone gives me a punch in the face." (IFS Archiv Hannover: Andreas H. Trebels, Lorenz Peiffer et al., Interview mit Prof. Dr. Willi Daume am 10./11. März 1994, transcript [hereafter Interview Daume, March 1994], p. 109)

20. Detlef Siegfried, "Zwischen Aufarbeitung und Schlußstrich: Der Umgang mit der NS-Vergangenheit in den beiden deutschen Staaten, 1958–1969," in Axel Schildt, Siegfried, and Karl Christian Lammers, eds., *Dynamische Zeiten: Die 60er Jahre in den beiden deutschen Gesellschaften* (Hamburg, 2000), p. 112.

21. Ibid., p. 99.

22. Helmut Dubiel, *Niemand ist frei von der Geschichte: Die nationalsozialistische Herrschaft in den Debatten des Deutschen Bundestages* (Munich, 1999), p. 92.

23. Edgar Wolfrum, *Geschichtspolitik in der Bundesrepublik Deutschland: Der Weg zur bundesrepublikanischen Erinnerung, 1948–1990* (Darmstadt, 1999), p. 247.

24. Ibid., p. 250.

25. Dubiel, *Niemand ist frei von der Geschichte,* p. 114.

26. Ibid., p. 133.

27. Gabriele Metzler, "Am Ende aller Krisen? Politisches Denken und Handeln in der Bundesrepublik der sechziger Jahre," *Historische Zeitschrift* 275, 2002, p. 63.

28. Michael Ruck, "Westdeutsche Planungsdiskurse und Planungspraxis der 1960er Jahre im internationalen Vergleich," in Heinz Gerhard Haupt and Jörg Requate, eds., *Aufbruch in die Zukunft: Die 1960er Jahre zwischen Plannungseuphorie und kulturellem Wandel: DDR, CSSR und Bundesrepublik Deutschland im Vergleich* (Weilerswist, 2004), p. 302.

29. See Anselm Doering-Manteuffel, "Westernisierung: Politisch-ideeller und gesellschaftlicher Wandel in der Bundesrepublik bis zum Ende der 60er Jahre," in Schildt, Siegfried, and Lammers, *Dynamische Zeiten,* especially pp. 321–27.

30. Klaus Schönhoven, "Aufbruch in die sozialliberale Ära: Zur Bedeutung der 60er Jahre in der Geschichte der Bundesrepublik," *Geschichte und Gesellschaft* 25, 1999, pp. 137–38.

31. Metzler, "Am Ende aller Krisen?," p. 92.

32. Daume remained in charge of the DSB until 1970 and the NOC until 1992.

33. IOC membership: 1956–1991; vice president of the IOC: 1972–1976; president of the admission committee: 1978–1992.

34. "'Willi Daume konnte Geige spielen . . .': Zeitzeugen erinnern sich," in *Willi Daume: Olympische Dimensionen. Ein Symposion* (Bonn, 2004), p. 104.

35. By a jury of *sport-intern* in January 2001.

36. Hans-Jochen Vogel, *Nachsichten: Meine Bonner und Berliner Jahre* (Munich, 2nd ed. 1996), p. 520.

37. Brazilian João Havelange became president of the world soccer body FIFA in 1974; Spaniard Juan Antonio Samaranch was elected IOC president in 1980.

38. Hubert Dwertmann and Lorenz Peiffer, eds., *Willi Daume: Eine Bibliographie seiner Schriften, Reden und Interviews* (Cologne, 2001), p. 16.

39. Andreas Höfer, "Willi Daume: Von der Machbarkeit der Utopie," in Manfred Lämmer, ed., *Deutschland in der Olympischen Bewegung: Eine Zwischenbilanz* (Frankfurt am Main, 1999), p. 322.

40. Attributed to the *Weltwoche* by Jürgen Leinemann, *Höhenrausch: Die wirklichkeitsleere Welt der Politiker* (Munich, 2006), p. 168.

41. Ulrich Herbert, "Liberalisierung als Lernprozeß: Die Bundesrepublik in der deutschen Geschichte—eine Skizze," in Herbert, ed. *Wandlungsprozesse in Westdeutschland: Belastung, Integration, Liberalisierung* (Göttingen, 2002), p. 44.

42. See Dirk Moses, "The Forty-Fivers: A Generation between Fascism and Democracy," *German Politics & Society* 17, no. 1, 1999, pp. 94–126.

43. Leinemann, *Höhenrausch,* p. 167.

44. Vogel, *Demokratie lebt auch vom Widerspruch* (Zurich, Munich, 2001), pp. 306–7; Schiller, "Death at the Munich Olympics," p. 133.

45. PAAA Berlin/B41/48: Vogel, Leningrad-Reise, June 1966.

46. Vogel, *Nachsichten,* p. 508; on "guilt," see also Vogel, *Demokratie lebt auch vom Widerspruch,* p. 312.

47. DOA/Nachlaß Daume/513: Draft of *GEO* magazine article (1988).

48. Ibid.

49. Hubert Dwertmann and Lorenz Peiffer, "Zwischen Kontinuität, systematischem Neuaufbau und Transformation: Willi Daume—das 'neue' Gesicht im bundesrepublikanischen Sport," in Michael Krüger, ed., *Transformation des deutschen Sports seit 1939* (Hamburg, 2001), pp. 135–51, 145.

50. IFS Archiv Hannover: Andreas H. Trebels, Lorenz Peiffer et al., Interview mit Prof. Dr. Willi Daume, Protokollierte und überarbeitete Fassung der 2. und 3. Interviewphase im Jahr 1994, transcript [hereafter Interview Daume, 2. und 3. Interviewphase 1994], p. 78.

51. Dwertmann and Peiffer, "Zwischen Kontinuität, systematischem Neuaufbau und Transformation," p. 145.

52. Ibid., p. 142.

53. Ibid., p. 145 and Giselher Spitzer, "Das Scheitern der internationalen Diskreditierung Willi Daumes durch die DDR," in *Olympisch bewegt: Festschrift zum 60. Geburtstag von Prof. Dr. Manfred Lämmer* (Cologne, 2003), pp. 375–84.

54. He became managing partner of an engineering firm, an ore trading company, and was on the supervisory board of a brewery and a bank.

55. *Willi Daume: Deutscher Sport 1952–1972* (Munich, 1973), p. 20.

56. Vogel, *Nachsichten,* p. 510 and *Die Amtskette: Meine 12 Münchner Jahre. Ein Erlebnisbericht* (Munich, 1972), p. 13.

57. Christian Ude, "Der Stadtpolitiker," in Herta Däubler-Gmelin, Helmut Schmidt, and Jürgen Schmude, eds., *Gestalten und Dienen. Fortschritt mit Vernunft* (Wiesbaden, 1996), p. 370.

58. Vogel, *Nachsichten,* p. 520.

59. See, for instance, Helmut Schmidt, "Hans Jochen Vogel zum Siebzigsten Geburtstag," in Däubler-Gmelin, Schmidt, and Schmude, *Gestalten und Dienen,* p. 16.

60. Vogel, "Grußwort," in *Willi Daume: Olympische Dimensionen,* p. 10.

61. "Willi Daumes Charisma und Körpersprache: Thomas Bach im Gespräch mit Andreas Höfer" and Ommo Grupe, "Willi Daume: Olympische Überzeugungen—der Sport, die Spiele," in *Willi Daume: Olympische Dimensionen,* p. 25 and p. 108.

62. See, for example, Schmidt, "Hans Jochen Vogel zum Siebzigsten Geburtstag," p. 17, and Leinemann, *Höhenrausch,* pp. 144–45.

63. Georg Kronawitter, "Zum Siebzigsten Geburtstag von Hans-Jochen Vogel," in Däubler-Gmelin, Schmidt, and Schmude, *Gestalten und Dienen.*

64. Vogel, "Grußwort," p. 10.

65. Vogel, *Nachsichten,* pp. 510, 518; Leinemann, *Höhenrausch,* p. 148; "Willi Daume konnte Geige spielen," pp. 85–86.

66. See Grupe, "Willi Daume."

67. *Willi Daume. Deutscher Sport,* p. 243.

68. Vogel, *Nachsichten,* pp. 507–8.

69. Vogel, *Demokratie lebt auch vom Widerspruch,* pp. 327–28.

70. See Michael Ruck, "Ein kurzer Sommer der konkreten Utopie—Zur westdeutschen Planungsgeschichte der langen 60er Jahre," in Schildt, Siegfried, and Lammers, *Dynamische Zeiten,* pp. 362–401.

71. David C. Young, *The Olympic Myth of Greek Amateur Athletics* (Chicago, 1984), p. ix.

72. PAAA Berlin/B41/86: Aufzeichnung, IOC-Tagung in Amsterdam, May 1970.

73. In particular, see John J. MacAloon, *This Great Symbol: Pierre De Coubertin and the Origins of the Modern Olympic Games* (Chicago, 1981); Richard Mandell, *The First Modern Olympics* (Berkeley, 1976); C.R. Hall, *Olympic Politics* (Manchester, 1992); Eugen Weber, "Pierre de Coubertin and the Introduction of Organized Sport in France," *Journal of Contemporary History* 5, no. 2, 1970, pp. 3–26; David C. Young, "Origins of the Modern Olympics," *International Journal of the History of Sport* 4, 1987, pp. 271–300 and *The Modern Olympics: A Struggle for Revival* (Baltimore, 1996).

74. Weber, "Pierre de Coubertin and the Introduction of Organized Sport in France," p. 15.

75. John M. Hoberman, "Toward a Theory of Olympic Internationalism," *Journal of Sport History* 22, 1995, pp. 1–37, 10.

76. See Pierre de Coubertin, "Die philosophischen Grundlagen des modernen Olympismus" (Berlin, August 1935), in *Pierre de Coubertin: Der Olympische Gedanke, Reden und Aufsätze* (Schondorf, 1967), pp. 150–54.

77. John R. Hoberman, *The Olympic Crisis: Sport, Politics, and the Moral Order* (New Rochelle, 1986), p. 29.

78. Ibid., p. 33.

79. Cited in Arnd Krüger, "What's the Difference between Propaganda for Tourism or for a Political Regime? Was the 1936 Olympics the First Postmodern Spectacle?" in John Bale and Mette Krogh Kristensen, eds., *Post-Olympism?: Questioning Sport in the Twenty-First Century* (Oxford, 2004), p. 37.

80. Brundage, Speech at the IOC Session in Munich, 19 August 1972.

81. See Allen Guttmann, *The Olympics: A History of the Modern Games* (Urbana, 2nd ed. 2002), pp. 125–40.

82. See in general *Willi Daume, Deutscher Sport 1952–1972;* the all-year ice remarks appear on p. 253.

83. Brundage, "The Fumbled Ball" (15 April 1967), cited in Hoberman, *The Olympic Crisis,* p. 53.

84. IOC Lausanne/Executive Board Minutes: Confidential letter from Brundage, 4 March 1969.

85. Hoberman, *The Olympic Crisis,* p. 51.

86. Barbara Keys, "Spreading Peace, Democracy, and Coca-Cola®: Sport and American Cultural Expansion in the 1930s," *Diplomatic History* 28, no. 2, 2004, p. 195.

87. Arnd Krüger, "United States of America: The Crucial Battle," in William J. Murray and Krüger, eds., *The Nazi Olympics: Sport, Politics, and Appeasement in the 1930s* (Urbana, rev. ed. 2003), pp. 50–58.

88. Allen Guttmann, *The Games Must Go On: Avery Brundage and the Olympic Movement* (New York, 1984), p. 81.

89. Ibid., p. 73.

90. Ibid., p. 90.

91. Interview Daume, March 1994, pp. 19–20.

92. See the case of Edgar Joubert (chapter 3).

93. Guttmann, *The Games Must Go On,* pp. 257–59.

94. Hoberman, *The Olympic Crisis,* pp. 54–56. By the Cold War, Brundage's ambivalent attitude to both sides brought severe criticism, particularly from the United States. During that time, he wrote a note to himself: "AB / Clever fellow / Imperialist / Fascist / Capitalist / Nazi / and now Communist." (Guttmann, *The Games Must Go On,* p. 150)

95. CULDA/Koebsel/III.1: 2. Mitgliederversammlung, 18 March 1967; 4. Mitgliederversammlung, 30 April 1969.

96. CULDA/Koebsel/III.1: 6. Mitgliederversammlung, 15 May 1971.

97. Johannes Paulmann, "Auswärtige Repräsentationen nach 1945: Zur Geschichte der deutschen Selbstdarstellung im Ausland," in Paulmann, *Auswärtige Repräsentationen,* pp. 1–32, especially 4–6.

98. Interview Daume, March 1994, p. 19.

99. Interview with Klaus von Lindeiner, November 2003.

100. CULDA/Koebsel/IV.1: 6. Vorstandssitzung, 25 May 1967.

101. IOC Lausanne/Brundage/Correspondences 1962–63: Otto Mayer to Brundage, 14 September 1963. The budget ran to $75,000 (DM 300,000) for between 200 to 250

participants. The flags around the city alone cost DM 30,000. Mayer concluded simply: "Can you imagine."

102. CULDA/Koebsel/IV.2: 21. Vorstandssitzung, 8–9 January 1971.

103. See Christiane Eisenberg, *"English Sports" und deutsche Bürger: Eine Gesellschaftsgeschichte, 1800–1939* (Paderborn, 1999), pp. 215–81.

104. Andreas Höfer, "Carl Diem: Ein Leben für den Sport," in Lämmer, *Deutschland in der Olympischen Bewegung*, p. 262.

105. The cases for and against Diem are well known. On the one hand, he was married to a Jew and helped Jews during the war. Despite the fact he was not a party member, his appeal to Olympic ideals to persuade German youths to fight to the death on the Reichssportfeld in the last days before Berlin's collapse to the Allies; his plans for a Großdeutsches Olympia (Greater German Olympics) (1939); inflammatory documents such as "Sturmlauf durch Frankreich" (Rampage through France) (1940); and his unsuccessful trip to Lausanne during the war to transfer the IOC's vital documentation to Berlin—are all evidence of a certain (self-)alignment (*Gleichschaltung*) with the regime. On the other hand, while his notion that sports offered the country nationalistic, militaristic, and biological benefits harmonized easily with Nazi viewpoints, his views stem from an older tradition of the volkish ideologies of Wilhelmine Germany. Moreover, such beliefs and rhetoric must also be seen in the context of the sport having to fight its corner against vociferous gymnastics rivals, such as Edmund Neuendorff (head of the German Turner and later party member) who vehemently opposed Olympic participation as an antipatriotic act. Despite the success of the Games, Diem's political opponents managed to curtail his career under National Socialism: he was relieved of his posts as general secretary of the Reichsausschuß für Leibesübungen and pro-rector of the Hochschule für Leibesübungen, and overlooked—in favor of General Walther von Reichenau—for party-sponsored membership of the IOC; see DSB-Präsidium, "Stellungnahme der Expertenkommission zu Werk und Person von Carl Diem (1882 bis 1962)," *Sozial- und Zeitgeschichte des Sports* 10, 1996, pp. 75–9; Hans Joachim Teichler, "Die Rolle Carl Diems in der Zeit und im zeitlichen Umfeld des NS-Regimes," *Sozial- und Zeitgeschichte des Sports* 10, 1996, pp. 56–74; Hubert Dwertmann, "Die Rolle Carl Diems im nationalsozialistischen Regime: Zum Gutachten H. J. Teichlers und zur Stellungnahme der Expertenkommission," *Sozial- und Zeitgeschichte des Sports* 10, 1996, pp. 7–47; Andreas Jungbauer, "Die Auseinandersetzung um 'Sportvater' Carl Diem—am Beispiel seiner Geburtsstadt Würzburg, die nun ihre größte Veranstaltungshalle umbenennt," *SportZeiten: Sport in Geschichte, Kultur und Gesellschaft* 4, 2004, pp. 93–101.

106. BAK/B322/433: Testament Carl Diem, 19 August 1961; Liselott Diem to Daume, December 1962.

107. Hoberman, *The Olympic Crisis*, pp. 45–50.

108. BAK/B322/433: Carl Diem to Daume, 1 December 1960.

109. BAK/B185/1920: Women's Association Fukuoka to Liselott Diem, October 1964.

110. DOA/Nachlaß Daume/560: Ansprache Th. Papathanassiadis.

111. Hoberman, *The Olympic Crisis*, p. 32.

112. Suzanne L. Marchand, *Down from Olympus: Archaeology and Philhellenism in Germany, 1750–1970* (Princeton, 1996), p. 351.

113. StAMü/Olympiade 1972/554: Auszug aus *sport intern* Nr. 3 (March 1970).

114. Marchand, *Down from Olympus*, pp. 368–9, 342.

115. Carl Diem, *Weltgeschichte des Sports*, vol. 1: *Von den Anfängen bis zur französischen Revolution;* vol. 2: *Der moderne Sport* (Stuttgart, 1960).

116. DOA/Nachlaß Daume/514: Laudatio Carl Diem, 1957.

117. BAK/B322/433: Daume to Schwarz, 7 June 1962; Schwarz to Daume, 19 June 1962; also Interview Daume, 2. und 3. Interviewphase 1994, p. 33.

118. Daume, "Die Olympiastadt und ihre Entstehung," *Münchner Stadtanzeiger*, 17 August 1972.

2. URBAN, STATE, AND NATIONAL CAPITAL

1. Allen Guttmann, *The Olympics: A History of the Modern Games* (Urbana, 2nd ed. 2002) p. 107.

2. Christopher Brasher, *Mexico 1968: A Diary of the XIXth Olympiad* (London, 1968), p. 1.

3. Martin H. Geyer, "Der Kampf um nationale Repräsentation: Deutsch-deutsche Sportbeziehungen und die 'Hallstein-Doktrin,'" *Vierteljahrshefte für Zeitgeschichte* 44, 1996, pp. 83–84; Tobias Blasius, *Olympische Bewegung, Kalter Krieg und Deutschlandpolitik 1949–1972* (Frankfurt am Main, 2001), pp. 292–93; Andreas Höfer, "Querelle d'allemand: Die gesamtdeutschen Olympiamannschaften (1956–1964)," in Manfred Lämmer, *Deutschland in der Olympischen Bewegung: Eine Zwischenbilanz* (Frankfurt am Main, 1999), p. 252.

4. BAK/B137/16432: Foreign Office to Interior Ministry, 11 April 1963.

5. Blasius, *Olympische Bewegung, Kalter Krieg und Deutschlandpolitik*, p. 293.

6. IOC Lausanne/JO ÉTÉ 1968/Correspondance Générale, Berlin 1963/Buenos Aires 1962–1963/Le Caire 1960–1962/Detroit: Brandt to Otto Mayer, 27 March 1963.

7. BAK/B137/16432: Aktennotiz, betr. Olympische Spiele 1968.

8. Interview mit Prof. Dr. Willi Daume am 10./11. März 1994, transcript (hereafter Interview Daume, March 1994), p. 8.

9. Ibid., p. 7.

10. These thoughts were percolating two years *before* Mexico City staged a yearlong arts festival in 1968.

11. Hans-Jochen Vogel, *Die Amtskette: Meine 12 Münchner Jahre. Ein Erlebnisbericht* (Munich, 1972), pp. 42, 96.

12. Robert Geipel, Ilse Helbrecht, and Jürgen Pohl, "Die Münchner Olympischen Spiele von 1972 als Instrument der Stadtentwicklungspolitik," in Hartmut Häußermann and Walter Siebel, eds., *Festivalisierung der Stadtpolitik: Stadtentwicklung durch große Projekte* (*Leviathan. Zeitschrift für Sozialwissenschaft*, Sonderheft 13, 1993), p. 280.

13. StAMü/Olympiade 1972/128.

14. Vogel, *Die Amtskette*, p. 98.

15. IFS Archiv Hannover: Lorenz Peiffer, Interview mit Dr. Hans-Jochen Vogel—ehemaliger Oberbürgermeister von München—am 13.2.1996, transcript [hereafter Interview Vogel, February 1996], p. 1.

16. Vogel, *Die Amtskette,* p. 95; StAMü/Olympiade 1972/69: Stadtratsvollversammlung, 20 December 1965; FES/Dep. HJV/Reden 1968: Rede Trauerfeier Georg Brauchle, 26 April 1968.

17. FES/1/HJVA 400235: Stadtplanungsausschuß, 4–5 July 1963; Vogel, *Die Amtskette,* p. 34.

18. FES/1/HJVA 400116: "München von morgen;" Rolf-Richard Grauhan, *Politik der Verstädterung* (Frankfurt am Main, 1974), p. 88.

19. FES/Dep. HJV/Reden 1968: "Gemeinden und Länder in der Bundesrepublik," Nuremberg, March 1968.

20. BayHStA/MWi/28400: Regierung von Oberbayern to Landeshauptstadt München, 18 December 1964 and 12 January 1965.

21. Vogel, *Die Amtskette,* pp. 131–32.

22. Detlev Klingbeil, "Münchens Wirtschafts- und Bevölkerungsentwicklung nach dem II. Weltkrieg," in Robert Geipel and Günter Heinritz, eds., *München: Ein sozialgeographischer Exkursionsführer,* Münchener geographische Hefte 55–56 (Kallmünz, 1987), pp. 56–57.

23. Nina Krieg, "Die 'Weltstadt mit Herz': Ein Überblick 1957 bis 1990," in Richard Bauer, ed., *Geschichte der Stadt München* (Munich, 1992), p. 413.

24. Egon Dheus, *Die Olympiastadt München* (Stuttgart, Cologne, Berlin, 1972), pp. 4–5.

25. Klingbeil, "Münchens Wirtschafts- und Bevölkerungsentwicklung," pp. 55, 65.

26. Detlev Klingbeil, "Grundzüge der stadtstrukturellen Entwicklung nach dem II. Weltkrieg," in Geipel and Heinritz, *München: Ein sozialgeographischer Exkursionsführer,* p. 126.

27. Robert Geipel, "Münchens Image und Probleme," in Geipel and Heinritz, *München: Ein sozialgeographischer Exkursionsführer,* p. 30; Klingbeil, "Münchens Wirtschafts- und Bevölkerungsentwicklung," p. 65.

28. StAMü/Olympiade 1972/73: Vogel, Speech at the IOC session, Rome, 26 *[sic]* April 1966.

29. Vogel, *Die Amtskette,* p. 106.

30. Ibid., pp. 133–34 and among a plethora of relevant speeches by Vogel, FES/Dep. HJV/Reden 1968: "Die Stadt im Wandel" (March 1968); FES/Dep. HJV/Reden 1970, Sept.-Dez.: "Die Stadt von morgen" (September 1970).

31. FES/Dep. HJV/Reden 1963–1964: Vortrag im Stadtmuseum, 9 April 1964.

32. Arbeitsgemeinschaft Stadtentwicklungsplan München, *München: Stadtentwicklungsplan. Gesamtverkehrsplan* (Munich, 1962), p. 8; Vogel, *Die Amtskette,* p. 38.

33. Dheus, *Die Olympiastadt München,* pp. 19–21.

34. Vogel, *Die Amtskette,* pp. 79–80.

35. See NOK-Archiv Frankfurt/4A8/12: Daume to Werner Peterssen, 7 December 1965; BayHStA/MWi/28400: Vogel to Goppel, 26 November 1965.

36. Thomas Schlemmer, Stefan Grüner, and Jaromír Balkar, "'Entwicklungshilfe im eigenen Lande'—Landesplanung in Bayern nach 1945," in Matthias Frese, Julia Paulus, and Karl Teppe, eds., *Demokratisierung und gesellschaftlicher Aufbruch: Die sechziger Jahre als Wendezeit der Bundesrepublik* (Paderborn, 2003), p. 403.

37. "München. Nur eine arme Stadt," *Der Spiegel,* 29 December 1965.

38. "Olympia in München kostet zuviel Geld," *Handelsblatt,* 6 December 1965.

39. See Alfons Frey, *Die industrielle Entwicklung Bayerns von 1925 bis 1975: Eine vergleichende Untersuchung über die Rolle der städtischen Agglomerationen im Industrialisierungsprozeß* (Berlin, 2003); Karl-Ulrich Gehlberg, "Dynamischer Wandel und Kontinuität: Die Ära Goppel (1962–1978)," in Max Spindler and Alois Schmid, eds., *Handbuch der bayerischen Geschichte* (Munich, 2nd ed. 2003), vol. IV/1, pp. 857–956.

40. BayHStA/MWi/28399: Betr.: Ausschließlichkeitsvereinbarungen, 29 July 1971.

41. Not only was Herbert Kunze, the general secretary of the OC, married to the daughter of Ernst Henne, the firm's most famous racing driver of the 1930s and owner of the largest Mercedes dealership in Munich, but Daume was closely tied to its press chief, Artur Keser, who ran the Games' publicity in the early stages.

42. CULDA/Koebsel/IV.2: 16. Vorstandssitzung, 27 June 1969; see the documentation on Daimler-Benz in StAMü/Olympia-Förderverein/569.

43. Organizing Committee for the Games of the XXth Olympiad Munich 1972, ed., *Die Spiele: The Official Report,* vol. 1: *The Organization* (Munich, 1972), p. 308; DOA/Nachlaß Daume/530: Daume to Vogel, 23 June 1969 and *Die Spiele: The Official Report,* vol. 1, pp. 333–34. Opel, Ford, Audi, and even the Italian manufacturer Fiat entered the car pool, too, when the OC's increasing demands exceeded the ability of the companies originally chosen to supply the vehicles.

44. For instance, spectators and athletes had to wait for half an hour to find out the official result of the 100-meter men's athletics competition (Rainer Nistl, "Mexiko als Maßstab für München," *Süddeutsche Zeitung,* 23 October 1968).

45. *Die Spiele: The Official Report,* vol. 1, p. 165; see also BAK/B185/2601: 20. Vorstandssitzung, 1 July 1970; Franz-Joachim Verspohl, *Stadionbauten von der Antike bis zur Gegenwart* (Gießen, 1976), p. 263.

46. CULDA/Koebsel/IV.2: 17. Vorstandssitzung, 21–22 November 1969, p. 49; see also the minutes of the Vorstand at their 18th, 19th, and 21st meetings and of the second meeting of the OC Beirat (CULDA/Koebsel/III.1) and *Die Spiele: The Official Report,* vol. 1, p. 157. In the end Junghans charged DM 290,000 and Longines only DM 10,000 less.

47. On the success of Adidas generally, see Barbara Smit, *Pitch Invasion: Three Stripes, Two Brothers, One Feud. Adidas, Puma and the Making of Modern Sport* (London, 2006). In 1972, West German sportswear manufacturers recorded an increase of 12 to 15 percent in their profits. (Verspohl, *Stadionbauten,* p. 263)

48. CULDA/Koebsel/IV.2: 19. Vorstandssitzung, 17 April 1970.

49. CULDA/OS72/4: Vermerk on 69th IOC Session Amsterdam, 19 May 1970.

50. *Die Spiele: The Official Report,* vol. 1, p. 109.

51. Richard Mandell, *The Olympics of 1972: A Munich Diary* (Chapel Hill, 1991), p. 6.

52. The IOC, however, voted sixty-seven to three in favor of the location (IOC Lausanne: 69th IOC Session Amsterdam, 12–16 May 1970).

53. Stenographischer Bericht über die 87. Sitzung des Bayerischen Landtags am 14.12.1965, pp. 3205–6 and Beilage 2368.

54. BAK/B106/30598: Cornelius von Hovora to Seibt, 19 November 1965.

55. Interview Daume, March 1994, p. 9.

56. Vogel, *Die Amtskette,* p. 99.

57. BAK/B106/30598: handwritten note, signed Althammer.

58. Erhard supposedly said "Wir können nicht immer Trübsal blasen." ("München. Nur eine arme Stadt," *Der Spiegel,* 29 December 1965)

59. Heinrich August Winkler, *Der lange Weg nach Westen,* vol. 2: *Deutsche Geschichte vom "Dritten Reich" bis zur Wiedervereinigung* (Munich, 2000), p. 233.

60. Manfred Görtemaker, *Geschichte der Bundesrepublik Deutschland von der Gründung bis zur Gegenwart* (Munich, 1999), p. 418.

61. See Alfred C. Mierzejewski, *Ludwig Erhard: A Biography* (Chapel Hill, 2004), p. 196.

62. See Ludwig Erhard, "Formierte Gesellschaft," in Karl Hohmann, ed., *Ludwig Erhard: Gedanken aus fünf Jahrzehnten. Reden und Schriften* (Düsseldorf, 1988), pp. 915–19.

63. Volker Hentschel, *Ludwig Erhard: Ein Politikerleben* (Munich, 1996), p. 601.

64. PAAA Berlin/94/1605: Auszug aus dem Kurzprotokoll über die 6. Kabinettssitzung am 2. Dezember 1965.

65. StAMü/Olympiade 1972/73: Daume to Vogel, 30 April 1966, Konstantin von Bayern to Vogel, 5 May 1966; ACSP/LG 5, WP 33: Konstantin von Bayern to Leo Wagner and Josef Rösing, 26 May 1966; ACSP/LG 5, WP 218: Mitteilung der CSU-Landesgruppe, *CSU-Correspondenz,* 27.4.1966; BayHStA/StK/14030: Strauß to Goppel, 24 February 1966; BayHStA/MF/80667: Goppel to Strauß, 9 March 1966. StAMü/Olympiade 1972/73 and BayHStA/StK/14030: Vogel to Barzel et al., 4 May 1966.

66. DOA/Nachlaß Daume/530: Daume to Konstantin von Bayern, 28 February 1968; DOA/Nachlaß Daume/534: Reichart to Vogel, 12 September 1968; correspondence in StAMü/BuR/3223; CULDA/Koebsel/IV.1/2: 11th, 13th, and 19th Vorstandssitzung.

67. The appointment arose after the provisional post-holder, Artur Keser (head of press for Daimler-Benz) fell ill. Klein was suggested to Daume by Karl-Günther von Haase, who was soon to become ambassador to London. Despite pleas from Daume, Vogel refused to withdraw his candidate who lost hands down after a grueling interview process with the OBG and the OC (DOA/Nachlaß Daume/528: Daume to Strauß, 11 July 1968; ACSP/Nachlaß Klein/122: Klein to Daume, 9 October 1968; DOA/Nachlaß Daume/534: Daume to Vogel, 4 September 1968, Vogel to Daume, 9 September 1968; BAK/B185/2367: 6. Vorstandssitzung der OBG, 30 August 1968; DOA/Nachlaß Daume/534: Daume to Berthold Beitz, 4 September 1968).

68. See Charlie Jeffrey, "German Federalism from Cooperation to Competition," in Maiken Umbach, ed., *German Federalism: Past, Present, Future* (Basingstoke, 2002), pp. 172–88.

69. *Die Spiele: The Official Report,* vol. 1, p. 41; Interview Daume, March 1994, p. 51.

70. See, for example, DOA/Nachlaß Daume/534: Daume to Paul Lücke, 18 February 1967, where he explains this issue with regards to the Beirat of the OC.

71. StAMü/Olympiade 1972/72 1–2: Ernst Knoesel, betr.: Bewerbung, 4 January 1966.

72. Ibid. and see BayHStA/StK/14030: Kurzfassung der Bewerbung.

73. See, for example, FES/Dep. HJV/Reden 1965–1966: "München, eine Stadt in der Zeit großer Veränderungen" (December 1966); FES/Dep. HJV/Reden 1967: "München als Olympia-Stadt" (October 1967).

74. Volker Kluge, *Olympische Sommerspiele: Die Chronik*, vol. 3: *Mexiko-Stadt 1968—Los Angeles 1984* (Berlin, 2000), p. 215.

75. See Cesar R. Torres, "Stymied Expectations: Buenos Aires' Persistent Efforts to Host Olympic Games," *Olympika: The International Journal of Olympic Studies* 16, 2007, pp. 54–57.

76. "Starker Beifall für München," *Sportinformationsdienst* [hereafter *sid*], 26 April 1966.

77. Interview Daume, March 1994, p. 33.

78. StAMü/BuR/3156: Daume and Vogel, Speeches at IOC session in Rome, 25 and 26 *[sic]* April 1966; see also NOK-Archiv Frankfurt/4A8/11: 2. Sitzung der AG Vorbereitung, 25 January 1966.

79. Figures taken from Kluge, *Olympische Sommerspiele: Die Chronik*, vol. 3, p. 214.

80. *Die Spiele: The Official Report*, vol. 1, p. 25.

81. Annex 8 to 62nd Session of the IOC, October 7 and 8, 1964, Nissei Kaikan, Tokyo, in: *Bulletin du Comité International Olympique* 89, February 1965, p. 80.

82. IFS Archiv Hannover/Archiv Fritz Hattig: Daume to F.C. Matthaei, 19 October 1966.

83. Ibid.

84. Otto Fischer, "Die Koffer für Rom sind gepackt," *Süddeutsche Zeitung*, 21 April 1966.

85. This despite the Munich working party's initial aim of staying within the "boundaries of what was permitted." (NOK-Archiv Frankfurt/4A8/11: 1. Sitzung der AG Vorbereitung, 11 January 1966)

86. StAMü/Olympiade 1972/509–1: Vogel to Brundage, 20 December 1965.

87. StAMü/Olympiade 1972/72 1–2: Vogel, Letter to IOC members, 27 January 1966. The offer was taken up by at least two IOC members, Reginald Stanley Alexander who represented Kenya and Alfredo Inciarte from Uruguay. (PAAA Berlin/94/1605: Diplogerma Montevideo to Foreign Office, 12 April 1966)

88. StAMü/Olympiade 1972/509–1: Vogel to Brundage, 20 December 1965. See Hart Cantelon, "Amateurism, High-Performance Sport, and the Olympics," in Kevin Young and Kevin B. Wamsley, eds., *Global Olympics: Historical and Sociological Studies of the Modern Games* (Amsterdam, 2005), pp. 83–101.

89. Interview Daume, March 1994, pp. 36–37. On Brundage and amateurism see Guttmann, *The Games Must Go On*, pp. 213–22.

90. The medals were given back again twenty-two years later by President Juan Antonio Samaranch.

91. NOK-Archiv Frankfurt/4A8/11: 1. Sitzung der AG Vorbereitung, 11 January 1966.

92. See, for example, StAMü/Olympiade 1972/72 1–2: Schmidt-Hildebrandt to Doug A. Gardner, 1 February 1966.

93. StAMü/Olympiade 1972/72 1–2: Schmidt-Hildebrandt to Alex Natan, 27 January 1966.

94. Interview Daume, March 1994, p. 113.

95. Ibid., p. 99.

96. BAK/B106/30600: Daume to von Hovora, 23 February 1966.

97. StAMü/BuR/3156: Correspondence between Vogel and Halford MacLeod, 7 January to 5 May 1966; StAMü/Olympiade 1972/73: Daume to Vogel, 12 April 1966.

98. PAAA Berlin/94/1605: Foreign Office to all embassies and consulates, 23 February 1966.

99. PAAA Berlin/94/1605: Embassy Rio de Janeiro to Foreign Office, 15 March 1966 and 28 April 1966.

100. PAAA Berlin/94/1605: Embassy Buenos Aires to Foreign Office, 19 April 1966.

101. Heide-Irene Schmidt, "Pushed to the Front: The Foreign Assistance Policy of the Federal Republic of Germany, 1958–1971," *Contemporary European History* 12, no. 4, 2003, pp. 474–75.

102. William Glenn Gray, *Germany's Cold War: The Global Campaign to Isolate East Germany, 1949–1969* (Chapel Hill, 2003), p. 188.

103. PAAA Berlin/B92/858: Zwischenbericht Sport, 10 May 1971.

104. Gray, *Germany's Cold War,* pp. 185–86.

105. BAK/B106/30600: Embassy Rabat to Foreign Office, 22 March 1966.

106. PAAA Berlin/94/1605: Embassy Rabat to Foreign Office, 30 March 1966.

107. NOK-Archiv Frankfurt/1.7/12: Foreign Office to Daume, 15 July and 30 September 1966; PAAA Berlin/94/1605: Foreign Office, Olympic support from African states, 5 July 1966 and Daume to Foreign Office, 2 November 1966.

108. StAMü/BuR/3176: Daume to Vogel, 11 December 1969.

109. PAAA Berlin/B92/849: Foreign Office to Interior Ministry, 19 August 1970.

110. Gray, *Germany's Cold War,* p. 186.

111. BAK/B122/5333 Embassy Rabat to Foreign Office, 18 March 1966.

112. BAK/B122/5333: Embassy Rabat to Foreign Office, 22 March 1966.

113. BAK/B122/5333: Development Aid for Morocco, 12 January 1966.

114. Schmidt, "Pushed to the Front," pp. 487–8.

115. BAK/B106/30600: Embassy Rabat to Foreign Office, 22 March 1966.

116. StAMü/BuR/3156: Daume, Speech at IOC session in Rome, 25 April 1966.

117. Interview Daume, March 1994, p. 99.

118. IFS Archiv Hannover/Archiv Fritz Hattig: Daume to Brundage, 25 January 1966.

119. BAK/B185/3038: Otto Haas, Werbung und Öffentlichkeitsarbeit in Afrika, 13 July 1970.

120. Ibid.

121. Ibid.

122. See CULDA/OS72/loose materials: Koch to Klein, 10 February 1971.

123. In Lagos, for instance, Daume claimed that while Africa was a "young continent," it owned the future in sporting terms. The Africans were more than welcome in Munich, he added, because of their "ability to join in festive celebrations." There was certainly sincerity in the somewhat condescending remark that the Africans, with their "talents for rhythm, music, and dance," would provide the ideal antidote to the pathos and political abuse of the Games, which he so abhorred. (CULDA/OS72/1.1: Daume, Afrika-Rede 1970 [Lagos])

124. Ibid. Such generous assistance was not offered to poorer Asian countries.

125. "Ganz Afrika wirbt für unser Olympia," *tz München,* 23 November 1970; BAK/B106/30657: Foreign Office to Interior Ministry, 6 January 1972.

126. "Olympia 1972 in München," *Die Welt,* 27 April 1966.

127. DOA/Nachlaß Daume/559.

128. DOA/Nachlaß Daume/528: Daume to Siegfried Balke, 3 May 1967.

129. DOA/Nachlaß Daume/559.

130. "Olympia in München kostet zuviel Geld," *Handelsblatt,* 6 December 1965.

131. BayHStA/StK/14030: Gleißner et al. to Vogel, 24 March 1966.

132. BAK/B106/30598: Vorläufige Kostenschätzung, 3 December 1965.

133. *Die Spiele: The Official Report,* vol. 1, p. 52.

134. StAMü/Olympiade 1972/128: Übersicht über die eingegangenen Antworten; StAMü/Olympiade 1972/69: Stadtratsvollversammlung, 20 December 1965.

135. See Holger Preuss, *The Economics of Staging the Olympics: A Comparison of the Games, 1972–2008* (Cheltenham, 2004), p. 259. The Games, no doubt, played an important role in the local price increases, although their exact impact is impossible to quantify.

136. Ibid., p. 32.

137. *The Games of the XVIII Olympiad Tokyo 1964: The Official Report of the Organizing Committee* (Tokyo, 1966), vol. 1/1, p. 66.

138. Preuss, *The Economics of Staging the Olympics,* p. 15; see also Daniel Latouche, "Montreal 1976," in John R. Gold and Margaret M. Gold, eds., *Olympic Cities: City Agendas, Planning, and the World's Games, 1896–2012* (London, 2007), pp. 197–217.

139. Mandell, *A Munich Diary,* p. 38.

140. See Preuss, *The Economics of Staging the Olympics,* pp. 66–8 and Hanwen Liao and Adrian Pitts, "A Brief Historical Review of Olympic Urbanization," *The International Journal of the History of Sport* 23, no. 7, 2006, p. 1240.

141. Deutscher Bundestag, 7. Wahlperiode, Drucksache VII/3066: Abschlußbericht über die Gesamtfinanzierung der Olympischen Spiele in München, 9 January 1975.

142. Monika Meyer-Künzel, *Städtebau der Weltausstellungen und Olympischen Spiele: Stadtentwicklung der Veranstaltungsorte* (Hamburg, 2001), p. 431.

143. See *Die Spiele: The Official Report,* vol. 1, pp. 69–70; see also BAB/SAPMO/DY 30/IVA2/10.02/-14: Information zu den Olympischen Sommerspielen 1972, 14 September 1971; IOC Lausanne/Schöbel/Correspondence 1966–1980: 69th session of the IOC, Amsterdam, May 1970. Agenda item 12: Statement by Heinz Schöbel; IOC Lausanne/Minutes of the 69th session of the IOC in Amsterdam, 12–16 May 1970.

144. *Die Spiele: The Official Report,* p. 66.

145. Roone Arledge, *Roone: A Memoir* (New York, 2003), p. 121.

146. CULDA/Vorhammer/OS72: Bericht des Olympiafördervereins 1966–1973.

147. *Die Spiele: The Official Report,* vol. 1, pp. 59–60.

148. See, for example, a range of press headlines from 1969: "Zehnstellige Ziffer," *Der Spiegel,* 28 July 1969; "Olympisches Preisrätsel," *Süddeutsche Zeitung,* 25–26 October 1969; "Zu kostspielige Spiele?" *Frankfurter Allgemeine Zeitung,* 18 November 1969.

149. Deutscher Bundestag, 5. Wahlperiode, Haushaltsausschuß, Drucksache 35 and Kurzprotokoll 3. Sitzung des Haushaltsausschusses am 8. Dezember 1965, pp. 15–20; see also Interview Vogel, February 1996, p. 5; Vogel, *Die Amtskette,* p. 100.

150. BayHStA/StK/14034: Correspondence between Goppel and Erhard, 14 June to 14 October 1966.

151. BayHStA/MWi/28395: Konsortialvertrag, 10 July 1967, Article 2.

152. The cost of development was as follows: by early 1968 the cost had risen by DM 300 million, in 1969, when the Federal Parliament was fully informed of expenditure increases for the first time, the total cost was estimated to run to DM 992 million. A year later the price tag had increased to 1.582 billion; see Deutscher Bundestag, 5. and 6. Wahlperiode, Drucksachen V/2796, V/3789 and VI/382.

153. Bayerischer Landtagsdienst, 21/130, 27 March 1968.

154. Discussion of the eastern wing of the roof, which was never built, can be found in StAMü/Olympiade 1972/405.

155. See StAMü/Olympiade 1972/672: 9. Aufsichtsratssitzung der OBG, 24 February 1969; 11. Aufsichtsratssitzung der OBG, 15 July 1969; BAK/B185/2371: 12. Aufsichtsratssitzung der OBG, 18 August 1969.

156. See DOA/Nachlaß Daume/530: Daume to Pöhner, 7 March 1968.

157. See StAMü/Olympiade 1972/771.

158. DOA/Nachlaß Daume/528: Daume to Goppel, 18 March 1968; see also DOA/Nachlaß Daume/528: Daume to Goppel, 8 March 1968; BayHStA/StK/14035: Vogel to Goppel, 12 February 1968 and Vogel to Strauß, 16 February 1968.

159. BayHStA/StK/14035: Jaumann to Strauß, 17 and 30 May 1968; BayHStA/StK/14035: Goppel to Benda, Strauß and Kiesinger, 12 July 1968.

160. StAMü/Olympiade 1972/128.

161. Deutscher Bundestag, 6. Wahlperiode, Haushaltsausschuß, Kurzprotokoll der 123. Sitzung vom 25.9.1968.

162. BayHStA/StK/14035: Goppel to Strauß, 18 June 1968.

163. BayHStA/MF/80645: Bund der Steuerzahler in Bayern to Strauß, 19 July 1969.

164. StAMü/Olympiade 1972/672: 11. Aufsichtsratssitzung der OBG, 15 July 1969.

165. Wolfgang Renzsch, *Finanzverfassung und Finanzausgleich: Die Auseinandersetzungen um ihre politische Gestaltung in der Bundesrepublik Deutschland zwischen Währungsreform und deutscher Vereinigung (1948–1990)* (Bonn, 1991), especially p. 292.

166. See Klaus Schönhoven, *Wendejahre: Die Sozialdemokratie in der Zeit der Großen Koalition, 1966–1969* (Bonn, 2004), pp. 332–39.

167. As reported in Deutscher Bundestag, 6. Wahlperiode, 1. Sonderausschuß für Sport und Olympische Spiele, Protokoll der 4. Sitzung vom 11.12.1969.

168. See, for example, FES/Dep. HJV/Reden 1971, Juli-Dez.: Address to the XXth World Congress of the International Union of Local Authorities on 19 July 1971 in Toronto.

169. See the relevant documentation in ACSP/Nachlaß Richard Jaeger/C: 38.

170. Much of the lobbying work on behalf of Munich and Bavaria was done by Erich Riedl (CSU), who was parliamentary aide to Richard Stücklen (one of the Bavarian members in Erhard's cabinet in favor of the Games) before becoming an MP, as well as Günther Müller (SPD), and Manfred Schmidt (SPD), the latter representing the constituencies of Munich-South and Munich-Center in the Bundestag; see, for example, Deutscher Bundestag, 6. Wahlperiode, 1. Sonderausschuß für Sport und Olympische Spiele, Protokoll der 3. Sitzung vom 4.12.1969.

171. BayHStA/StK/14036: Strauß to Goppel, 15 and 17 October 1969.

172. BayHStA/MF/80642: Schedl to Huber and Riedl, 23 January 1971.

173. BAK/B185/3035: Haas, Werbung und Öffentlichkeitsarbeit 1968–1972, p. 73.

174. StAMü/BuR/3174: Haas, Werbung und Öffentlichkeitsarbeit. Gesamtkonzeption und Etat, 15 January 1969; see also CULDA/OS72/13.1: 2. Öffentlichkeitsausschußsitzung, 10 November 1967.

175. Ibid.

176. The most important materials were as follows: four different series of advertising posters, eight different information brochures and magazines in up to nineteen languages, and a scale model of the Olympic venues for exhibitions. Two more short films were commissioned, which took their cue from *Munich—A City Applies* and brought it up to date—*Munich—A City Prepares* (1969) and *Munich—A City Invites* (1971).

177. CULDA/OS72/13.6: Munich Tourist Office to Haas, 5 August 1968. An Infratest poll was conducted in August and September 1969 and involved 1,100 participants (BAK/B185/1737: Infratest, Zusammenfassung 1969); see also *Die Spiele: The Official Report,* vol. 1, p. 197; CULDA/OS72/13.6: Infratest to Haas, 9 June 1969 and Haas to Daume, 15 July 1969; CULDA/OS72/13.1: 8. Öffentlichkeitsausschußsitzung, 22 June 1970.

178. Ibid.

179. CULDA/OS72/13.1: Hans Klein, Der Werbeaspekt der Informationsarbeit, 23 April 1971.

180. StAMü/BuR/3174: Haas, Werbung und Öffentlichkeitsarbeit, 15 January 1969.

181. Ibid.

182. BAK/B185/1737: Infratest, Zusammenfassung 1969.

183. StAMü/BuR/3174: Haas, Werbung und Öffentlichkeitsarbeit, 15 January 1969.

184. Cited in Mandell, *A Munich Diary,* p. 7.

185. StAMü/BuR/3174: Haas, Werbung und Öffentlichkeitsarbeit, 15 January 1969.

186. Ferdinand Kramer, "München und die Olympischen Spiele von 1972," in Christian Koller, ed., *Sport als städtisches Ereignis* (Ostfildern, 2008), pp. 248–49.

187. BAK/B185/902: Lecture held by Frau Dr. Rube.

188. BAK/B185/3035: Haas, Werbung und Öffentlichkeitsarbeit 1968–1972.

189. See CULDA/OS72/13.2: Konzeptionsvorschläge zur Insertionswerbung, 1 July 1971.

190. See BAK/B185/3038: Walter Schätz to Reichart, 3 April 1971; *Die Spiele: The Official Report,* vol. 1, p. 206.

191. *Die Spiele: The Official Report,* vol. 1, p. 197.

192. CULDA/OS72/13.4: Coca-Cola to Kunze, 20 September 1968.

193. BAK/B185/3035: Haas, Werbung und Öffentlichkeitsarbeit 1968–1972.

194. Ibid.

195. See CULDA/OS72/13.5: Norddeutscher Lloyd Bremen to Kunze, 22 August 1969.

196. CULDA/OS72/13.5: Haas, Olympiawerbung auf deutschen Passagierschiffen.

197. *Die Spiele: The Official Report,* vol. 1, pp. 236, 307.

198. Arledge, *Roone,* p. 139.

199. *Die Spiele: The Official Report,* vol. 1, p. 214.

200. Verspohl, *Stadionbauten,* p. 263. In 1972, 1.2 million color television sets were sold in West Germany.

201. "Olympia. Das totale Fernsehen," *Der Spiegel,* 28 August 1972, p. 24.

202. See CULDA/OS72/12.1: Protocol, 22 December 1966.

203. IFS Archiv Hannover/Archiv Fritz Hattig: Daume to Brundage, 26 January 1966.

204. CULDA/OS72/12.1: Joubert, Die Presseorganisation in Grenoble (May 1968).

205. CULDA/OS72/12.1: Joubert, Bemerkungen zur Presseorganisation von Mexiko (December 1968).

206. Ibid.

207. CULDA/OS72/13.1: 4. Öffentlichkeitsausschußsitzung, 25 September 1968.

208. *Die Spiele: The Official Report,* vol. 1, pp. 215, 217.

209. See Richard Mandell, *The Nazi Olympics* (New York, 1971).

210. Mandell, *A Munich Diary,* p. 14.

211. CULDA/OS72/13.1: Klein, Der Werbeaspekt der Informationsarbeit.

212. Mandell, *A Munich Diary,* p. 47.

213. Herbert Schneider, "Durst wird durch Bier erst schön," *Olympia Press* 3, August 1969.

214. *Olympia Press* 16, October 1970.

215. Klein, "Die Welt schaut auf München," in *Olympia in München: Offizielles Sonderheft der Olympiastadt München,* Sommer 1972, p. 72.

216. Arledge, *Roone,* p. 121.

217. CULDA/OS72/12.1: Report by Edgar Joubert, 14 April 1968.

3. THE LEGACY OF BERLIN 1936 AND THE GERMAN PAST

1. Allen Guttmann, "Berlin 1936: The Most Controversial Olympics," in Alan Tomlinson and Christopher Young, eds., *National Identity and Global Sports Events: Culture, Politics, and Spectacle in the Olympics and the Football World Cup* (New York, 2006), pp. 65–81.

2. *Der Spiegel,* 20 August 1972.

3. Hajo Bernett, "Das Bild der Olympischen Spiele von 1936 im Spiegel neuerer Publikationen," *Leibeserziehung: Monatsschrift für Wissenschaft und Unterricht* 21, no. 8, 1972, p. 276.

4. Ibid., pp. 276–77.

5. Hans Joachim Teichler, "Der Stellenwert der Olympischen Spiele 1936 in Berlin," in *Olympisch bewegt: Festschrift zum 60. Geburtstag von Prof. Dr. Manfred Lämmer* (Cologne, 2003), p. 210.

6. Friedrich Kießling, "Täter repräsentieren: Willy Brandts Kniefall in Warschau," in Johannes Paulmann, ed., *Auswärtige Repräsentationen: Deutsche Kulturdiplomatie nach 1945* (Cologne, 2005), p. 206.

7. See www.olympic.org/uk/games/index_uk.asp, retrieved 24 September 2008 and, most recently, Guy Walters, *Berlin Games: How Hitler Stole the Olympic Dream* (London, 2006) and David Clay Large, *Nazi Games: The Olympics of 1936* (New York, London, 2007).

8. See Maurice Roche, *Mega-events and Modernity: Olympics and Expos in the Growth of Global Culture* (London, 2000), p. 120.

9. Hans Joachim Teichler, "Coubertin und das Dritte Reich: Zur Vorgeschichte eines unveröffentlichten Coubertin-Briefs an Hitler aus dem Jahre 1937," *Sportwissenschaft* 12, no. 1, 1982, pp. 18–55.

10. Arnd Krüger, "United States of America: The Crucial Battle," in William J. Murray and Krüger, eds., *The Nazi Olympics: Sport, Politics, and Appeasement in the 1930s* (Urbana, rev. ed. 2003), p. 50.

11. Christopher Young, "'A Victory for the Olympic Idea': Berlin 1936 in Its Sporting and Socio-cultural Contexts," *Stadion: Internationale Zeitschrift für die Geschichte des Sports* 32, 2006, pp. 147–72.

12. Of the many books on Schmeling and Louis, see on this fight in particular David Margolick, *Beyond Glory: Max Schmeling vs. Joe Louis* (London, 2005).

13. See James Riordan, "The Workers' Olympics," in Alan Tomlinson and Garry Whannel, eds., *Five Ring Circus: Money, Power and Politics at the Olympic Games* (London, 1984), pp. 98–112.

14. Organisationskomitee für die XI. Olympiade Berlin 1936, ed. *The XIth Olympic Games Berlin, 1936, Official Report* (Berlin, 1937), vol. 1, p. 43.

15. Michael Bauer, *Die Olympischen Spiele 1932 in Los Angeles aus der Sicht des Kommandanten der deutschen Mannschaft Carl Diem* (Marburg, 1998), pp. 82–83.

16. Thomas Alkemeyer, *Körper, Kult und Politik: Von der "Muskelreligion" Pierre de Coubertins zur Inszenierung von Macht in den Olympischen Spielen von 1936* (Frankfurt am Main, 1996), pp. 12, 237, 260–61.

17. *The XIth Olympic Games Berlin, 1936, Official Report,* vol. 1, pp. 43, 67.

18. Roche, *Mega-events and Modernity,* p. 115.

19. *The XIth Olympic Games Berlin, 1936, Official Report,* vol. 1, p. 76; see also Christopher Young, "'In Praise of Jesse Owens': Technical Beauty at the Berlin Olympics 1936," *Sport in History* 28, no. 1, 2008, pp. 83–103.

20. William Edward Dodd Jr. and Martha Dodd, eds., *Ambassador Dodd's Diary, 1933–1938* (New York, 1941), p. 346.

21. See Wolfgang Gilleßen, *Das Olympische Dorf 1936* (Potsdam, 1996) and Susanne Dost, *Das Olympische Dorf 1936 im Wandel der Zeit* (Berlin, 2003).

22. Dodd and Dodd, *Ambassador Dodd's Diary,* p. 348.

23. Peter Gay, *My German Question: Growing up in Nazi Berlin* (New Haven, 1998), pp. 78–79.

24. BAK/B106/30603: *sid*-report, 28 January 1969. Brundage said "I am sure the 1972 Games will be a big success, both in terms of sport and art, because I know and respect the interest Germans have in the Olympic movement. I was in Munich for the first time in 1912 and saw the 1936 Games in Garmisch-Partenkirchen and Berlin. That's why I've got a good idea already."

25. Tobias Blasius, *Olympische Bewegung, Kalter Krieg und Deutschlandpolitik 1949–1972* (Frankfurt am Main, 2001), p. 47.

26. The correspondence in UIUC Archives/Brundage Collection/Box 118 tells a tale of friendship.

27. Cited in BAB/SAPMO/DY 30/IVB2/18/-37: Rudi Hellmann to Honecker, 27 January 1971.

28. IOC Lausanne/Stoytchev/Correspondence 1948–1984: Curriculum Vitae.

29. StAMü/Olympiade 1972/72 1–2: Bruno Schmidt-Hildebrandt to Alex Natan, 27 January 1966; Daume to Otto Haas, 21 February 1966. On Lübke's role in the exploita-

tion of concentration camp labor as site manager during the building of the Peenemünde V2 rocket plant in 1943, see Norbert Frei, "Hitlers Eliten nach 1945—eine Bilanz," in Frei, ed., *Karrieren im Zwielicht. Hitlers Eliten nach 1945* (Frankfurt am Main, 2001), p. 334.

30. IFS Archiv Hannover: Andreas H. Trebels, Lorenz Peiffer et al., Interview mit Prof. Dr. Willi Daume am 10./11. März 1994, transcript [hereafter Interview Daume, March 1994], p. 11.

31. StAMü/Olympiade 1972/562: Sylvio de Magalhaes Padilha to Vogel, 6 February 1966. Similar sentiments were expressed by Italian IOC member Giorgio de Stefani (StAMü/Olympiade 1972/562: de Stefani to Vogel, 31 December 1965).

32. CULDA/OS72/12.1: Report by Edgar Joubert, 14 April 1968; as just one example of many, CULDA/Koebsel/III.1: 5. Mitgliederversammlung des OK, 18 April 1970: "The president pointed out that the Germans were expected to organize everything perfectly."

33. See StAMü/Stadtratsprotokoll, 20 December 1965.

34. CULDA/Koebsel/IV.1: 8. Vorstandsssitzung, 22 November 1967. Daume was reporting to the OC on the pre-Olympic trial run in Mexico 1967.

35. Interview with Hans-Jochen Vogel, 10 November 2003.

36. StAMü/Olympiade 1972/71: Brundage to Daume, 25 November 1965.

37. StAMü/Olympiade 1972/73: Gespräch mit Brundage am 26. März 1966.

38. UIUC Archives/Brundage Collection/Box 53: Handwritten note of meeting with Vogel and Brauchle in 1966.

39. "Olympia-Trip in Rekordzeit," *Münchner Merkur,* 29 March 1966.

40. A rare example of the archaeology argument is found in CULDA/OS72/1.1: Transcript of interview given by Daume to *Prado,* February 1971.

41. StAMü/BuR/3156: Rede von Daume vor dem IOK in Rom am 25. April 1966, 1. Fassung.

42. Organizing Committee for the Games of the XXth Olympiad Munich 1972, ed., *Die Spiele: The Official Report,* vol. 1: *The Organization* (Munich, 1972), p. 25.

43. See Peter Heimerzheim, *Karl Ritter von Halt—Leben zwischen Sport und Politik* (St. Augustin, 1999).

44. Von Halt competed in the decathlon in the Stockholm Olympics, was decorated in the First World War, and became a banker with a private Jewish bank in 1922. In the realm of sport: he took responsibility for track-and-field events at the 1928 Olympics, was head of the German track-and-field team in Los Angeles 1932, and chief organizer of the 1936 Winter Olympics at Garmisch-Partenkirchen.

45. BStU/MfS HA IX/11 AS53/68b: Hauptabteilung IX/11, Materialien zu Angehörigen des "Freundeskreises Himmler," 3 October 1968.

46. Interview Daume, March 1994, p. 23; see also IFS Archiv Hannover: Andreas H. Trebels, Lorenz Peiffer et al., Interview mit Prof. Dr. Willi Daume, Protokollierte und überarbeitete Fassung der 2. und 3. Interviewphase im Jahr 1994, transcript [hereafter Interview Daume, 2. und 3. Interviewphase 1994], p. 81.

47. StAMü/BuR/3156: Rede von Daume vor dem IOK in Rom am 25. April 1966, 1. Fassung.

48. StAMü/BuR/3156: Stadt München to Frau von Halt, 31 March 1966.

49. DOA/Nachlaß Daume/561: Trauerrede Dr. von Halt, 11 August 1964.

50. DOA/Nachlaß Daume/561: Interview with *Bayernkurier,* 18 August 1964.

51. Allen Guttmann, *The Olympics: A History of the Modern Games* (Urbana, 2nd ed. 2002), pp. 113–23.

52. IOC Lausanne/Executive Board Minutes, Tehran, 2–8 May 1967.

53. Interview Daume, March 1994, p. 23.

54. StAMü/Olympiade 1972/72 1–2: Werner Solms to Schmidt-Hildebrandt, 8 February 1966.

55. NOK-Archiv Frankfurt/4A8/11: 2. Sitzung der AG Vorbereitung, 25 January 1966.

56. NOK-Archiv Frankfurt/6A8/10: Vorbereitung der Präsentation, Informationsreise Rom 8.-10.2.1966, 10 February 1966.

57. For instance, the working group decided to drop the plan to hold a reception for IOC members in the German Embassy in Rome before the decision; see StAMü/Olympiade 1972/73: Daume to Hans Heinrich Herwarth von Bittenfeld, 8 March 1966.

58. DOA/Nachlaß Daume/561: Trauerrede Dr. von Halt, 11 August 1964.

59. Willi Daume, "Eine Milliarde für die Olympischen Spiele?" *Olympisches Feuer* 6, 1966, p. 4.

60. DOA/Nachlaß Daume/534: Daume to Ludwig Huber, 4 May 1967; Daume to Vogel, 19 April 1967.

61. DOA/Nachlaß Daume/610: Rudolf Hagelstange to Dietz, 21 July 1971.

62. DOA/Nachlaß Daume/534: Daume to Huber, 4 May 1967; Daume to Vogel, 19 April 1967.

63. BStU/MfS ZA 3395/92: Hauptabteilung XX/3, Kunze, Herbert, 30 November 1966.

64. BStU/MfS ZA 26237/92: Baier, Bernhard, 6.4.1972.

65. BAK/B106/36101: Lebenslauf, Herbert Kunze, 20 August 1966.

66. "Ein Lagerleiter," *Deutsches Sport-Echo,* 9 August 1972.

67. March withdrew from the building committee on grounds of age and energy to pursue his own goals. (DOA/Nachlaß Daume/532: March to Heinz Noris, 11 January 1967)

68. DOA/Nachlaß Daume/530: Daume to Cornelius von Hovora, 5 September 1969; Daume to Vogel, 6 September 1969.

69. CULDA/Koebsel/IV.1: 6. Vorstandssitzung, 25 May 1967; and again, StAMü/BuR/3177: Daume to Vogel, 12 September 1966.

70. Interview Daume, March 1994, p. 67.

71. Hajo Bernett, *Guido von Mengden, 'Generalstabschef' des deutschen Sports* (Berlin, 1976); Horst Ueberhorst, "Guido von Mengden (1896–1982)," in *Die Gründerjahre des Deutschen Sportbundes: Wege aus der Not zur Einheit* (Schorndorf, 1991), vol. 2, pp. 143–45.

72. IOC Lausanne/Daume/Correspondence 1957–1972: Daume to Otto Mayer, 6 July 1964.

73. Interview Daume, March 1994, p. 67; Interview Daume, 2. und 3. Interviewphase 1994, p. 83.

74. The Stasi had a full file on von Mengden (BStU/MfS/AP/29974/92).

75. See Interview Daume, March 1994, pp. 67–68.

76. DOA/Nachlaß Daume/604: von Mengden to Daume, 16 February 1971.

77. Interview Daume, March 1994, p. 67.

78. For instance, regarding the application of Anton Keser for press chief. (DOA/Nachlaß Daume/534: Daume to Vogel, 1 September 1966)

79. Elizabeth Audrey Leckie Schlüssel, *Zur Rolle der Musik bei den Eröffnungs- und Schlußfeiern der Olympischen Spiele von 1896 bis 1972*, PhD diss. (Deutsche Sporthochschule Köln, 2001), pp. 589–90.

80. Interview Daume, March 1994, p. 67.

81. Walter Umminger, ed., *Olympisches Lesebuch* (Hannover, 1971), p. 88.

82. Ibid., p. 93.

83. PAAA Berlin/B41/353: Vermerk, Die Olympischen Spiele der Neuzeit (Umminger), 6 April 1971.

84. For a good overview of this development, see Mary Fulbrook, *German National Identity after the Holocaust* (Cambridge, 1999), pp. 103–41.

85. Umminger, *Olympisches Lesebuch*, p. 142.

86. BAK/B106/30629: Internationale Pressekonferenz der Gesellschaft zur Förderung des olympischen Gedankens in der DDR, 13 April 1971.

87. StAMü/Olympiade 1972/554 contains a long article from the Soviet press and, for instance, *Süddeutsche Zeitung*, 26 February 1971.

88. *Telegraf* Berlin, 25 February 1971.

89. See Liselott Diem, *Leben als Herausforderung*, 3 vols. (St. Augustin, 1986); Gerhard Hecker, August Kirsch, and Clemens Menze, eds., *Der Mensch im Sport: Festschrift zum 70. Geburtstag von Prof. Liselott Diem* (Schorndorf, 1976).

90. BAK/B106/30603: Dringender Anruf von Herrn Daume, 28 September 1976.

91. For example, Diem to Daume, 20 December 1961, where she recounts the ravishing reception laid on for her by Brundage in his hotel in Chicago (BAK/B322/433).

92. For instance, she found the idea of splitting the Olympic village into a men's and women's village "no longer up to date." (CULDA/OS72/loose materials: Diem to Walther Tröger, 28 March 1972)

93. See documentation in CULDA/OS72/6.4, 7.1 and 7.2 and the exhibition catalogue *100 Jahre deutsche Ausgrabung in Olympia* (Munich, 1972).

94. Aicher kept a tight control on the overall design concept (see chapter 4) but could not prevent Daume, an avid soft-toy collector, from pushing Waldi the Dachshund through as the Games' mascot. In triumph, Diem wrote to Aicher: "Dear Mr. Aicher, another announcement for your collection. We're knocking together Olympia-Waldi. It doesn't appear that the design office has pre-programmed this Waldi. Yours, Prof. L. Diem." (CULDA/OS72/loose materials: Diem to Aicher, 30 August 1971)

95. CULDA/OS72/loose materials: Diem to Klein, 26 March 1971.

96. CULDA/OS72/loose materials: Daume to Diem, 22 October 1969; Protokoll einer Besprechung mit Frau Diem am 22. September 1970.

97. CULDA/OS72/loose materials: Diem to Daume, 16 October 1969.

98. See documentation in CULDA/OS72/loose materials.

99. Interview with Friedhelm Brebeck, 7 February 2005.

100. BAK/B106/30603: Herbert Kunze to Hans-Dietrich Genscher, 3 October 1973; Vorlage für 27. Vorstandssitzung am 14.9.1973.

101. BAK/B106/30603: Betr. Offizieller Bericht, Herausgebervertrag.

102. BAK/B106/30603: 27. Vorstandssitzung, 14 September 1973.

103. BAK/B106/30603: Diem to Daume, 21 September 1973.

104. BAK/B106/30603: Kurt Bartenbach to Kunze, 1 October 1972.

105. There is a broad literature on Riefenstahl and *Olympia,* see, for example, the recent monograph by Steven Bach, *Leni: The Life and Work of Leni Riefenstahl* (London, 2007).

106. IOC Lausanne/Brundage/Correspondence, July to August 1972: Monique Berlioux to Brundage, 11 July 1972.

107. Clay Large, *Nazi Games,* p. 333.

108. Bach, *Leni,* pp. 172–73; UIUC Archives/Brundage Collection/Box 22: Carl Diem to Brundage, 22 March 1948; Brundage to Carl Diem, 1 June 1948.

109. IOC Lausanne/Brundage/Correspondence 1964–1965: Berlioux to Brundage, 19 November 1965.

110. BAK/B122/15032: Vermerk vom 10.8.1972 zur Einladungsliste zum Empfang des Bundespräsidenten am 26.8.1972.

111. Jürgen Trimborn, *Riefenstahl: Eine deutsche Karriere* (Berlin, 2002), pp. 485–87.

112. Ibid., p. 479

113. *Sunday Times,* 10 September 1972.

114. Trimborn, *Riefenstahl,* p. 485.

115. *Sunday Times,* 10 September 1972.

116. *Sunday Times,* 17 September 1972.

117. DOA/Nachlaß Daume/530: Daume to Otto Haas, 8 April 1969.

118. DOA/Nachlaß Daume/530: Daume to Schmeling, 18 March 1969.

119. Siegfried Gehrmann, "Symbol of National Resurrection: Max Schmeling, German Sports Idol," in Richard Holt, J. A. Mangan, and Pierre Lanfranchi, eds., *European Heroes: Myth, Identity, Sport* (London, 1996), pp. 112–13.

120. Volker Kluge, *Max Schmeling: Eine Biographie in 15 Runden* (Berlin, 2004), pp. 409–10.

121. Ibid., p. 411.

122. Max Schmeling, *8–9-aus* (Munich, 1956), p. 136; Max Schmeling, *Erinnerungen* (Frankfurt am Main, Berlin, 1977), pp. 322–24.

123. Schmeling, *8–9-aus,* p. 136.

124. Schmeling, *Erinnerungen,* p. 324.

125. Amy Bass, *Not the Triumph But the Struggle: The 1968 Olympics and the Making of the Black Athlete* (Minneapolis, London, 2002), p. 93; Clay Large, *Nazi Games,* pp. 88–90.

126. Ulrich Huhn in *Neues Deutschland,* 5 June 1970.

127. The various sources that have provided this explanation are given in Bass, *Not the Struggle but the Triumph,* p. 375, note 33.

128. Ibid., p. 93.

129. Clay Large, *Nazi Games,* p. 233; Douglas Hartmann, *Race, Culture, and the Revolt of the Black Athlete: The 1968 Olympic Protests and Their Aftermath* (Chicago, 2003), p. 64.

130. Bass, *Not the Struggle but the Triumph,* pp. 135–36.

131. Ibid., p. 64.

132. Ibid., p. 160.

133. Ibid., pp. 237, 79 (quotations in this order).

134. Ibid., pp. 237–38, 254.

135. IOC Lausanne/Executive Board Minutes, 8 September 1972; an excellent account is given in Vincent Matthew's well-regarded autobiography *My Race Be Won* (New York, 1974), pp. 335–76.

136. Jesse Owens, *I Have Changed* (New York, 1972), pp. 18–19.

137. Christopher Brasher, *Munich 1972* (London, 1972), p. 85.

138. Clay Large, *Nazi Olympics*, p. 155.

139. Etched on the shaft were the words "Fackelstaffel-Lauf Olympia-Berlin 1936" as well as a map of the route; on top of the protective disk, "Organisationskomitee für die XI. Olympiade Berlin 1936" and "Als Dank dem Träger"; and under it, "Krupp Nirosta V2A Stahl" and "Stiftung der Fried. Krupp A.G. Essen" (Walter Borgers, *Olympic Torch Relays 1936–1994* [Kassel, 1996], p. 49).

140. CULDA/OS72/3.1: 1. Sitzung des Fackellauf-Ausschusses, 2 March 1970. Aicher had begun his discussions with the aluminum company Südalumin in July 1969.

141. CULDA/OS72/3.2: von der Planitz, Entwicklung und augenblicklicher Stand des Fackelgriffs und Brennsatzes, 10 June 1970.

142. BAK/B185/1921: von der Planitz, Schriftwechsel Krupp-OK wegen Stiftung des Fackelgriffs, 23 September 1971. At a previous meeting in the general secretariat, Krupp was told that advertising would have to be "as subtle as possible." A letter from Krupp on 2 December 1970 had confirmed that the firm's symbol would appear on the base of the capsule. However, the official letter of offer on 5 March 1971 (CULDA/OS72/3.1) stated that the words Krupp-Stahl would appear on full display around the edge of the flame protector. Daume wrote a letter of acceptance without pointing out the discrepancy or showing it to Kunze at the general secretariat. To Kunze's annoyance, further meetings had to be called to settle the issue.

143. CULDA/OS72/3.2: von der Planitz, Herstellung des Fackelgriffes.

144. CULDA/OS72/3.2: von der Planitz, Entwicklung und augenblicklicher Stand des Fackelgriffs und Brennsatzes, 10 June 1970.

145. CULDA/OS72/3.2: von der Planitz, Fackellauf, 6 August 1970.

146. Previous weights were: Mexico 0.78kg, Tokyo 0.826kg, Rome 0.58kg, Melbourne 0.96kg, Helsinki 0.6kg, London 0.96kg (Borgers, *Olympic Torch Relays*, pp. 62, 70, 74, 83, 91, 101).

147. StAMü/Olympia-Förderverein/419: Olympia-Förderverein to Krupp AG, 28 November 1972.

148. Interview Daume, 2. und 3. Interviewphase 1994, p. 67.

149. William Manchester, *The Arms of Krupp, 1587–1968* (London, 1969), pp. 854–85.

150. Ibid., p. 902.

151. S. Jonathan Wiesen, *West German Industry and the Challenge of the Nazi Past, 1945–1955* (Chapel Hill, 2001), p. 137.

152. Interview Daume, 2. und 3. Interviewphase 1994, p. 65.

153. Manchester, *The Arms of Krupp*, p. 812.

154. Quotations from Simone Derix, "Gruppenbild mit Industrielandschaft: Wie Krupp die Bundesrepublik Deutschland bei Staatsbesuchen bebilderte," in Johannes Paulmann, ed.,

Auswärtige Repräsentationen: Deutsche Kulturdiplomatie nach 1945 (Cologne, 2005), pp. 175, 171.

155. Wiesen, *West German Industry,* pp. 97, 206.

156. Interview Daume, 2. und 3. Interviewphase 1994, p. 79.

157. Wiesen, *West German Industry,* pp. 201–2.

158. For example, in 1938, von Tschammer und Osten and Ritter von Halt helped Brundage win the contract to build a new German Embassy in Washington, which was postponed on the outbreak of World War II (Clay Large, *Nazi Games,* p. 99); on 1932 in particular, see Barbara Keys, "Spreading Peace, Democracy, and Coca-Cola®: Sport and American Cultural Expansion in the 1930s," *Diplomatic History* 28, no. 2, 2004, pp. 165–96.

159. Interview Daume, 2. und 3. Interviewphase 1994, p. 65.

160. Wiesen, *West German Industry,* p. 244.

161. StAMü/Olympia-Förderverein/419.

162. BAK/B185/1921: Betr. Olympia Fackeln, 21 March 1972.

163. StAMü/Olympia-Förderverein/419: *Kicker,* 29 November 1971, p. 3. There were very few complaints about Krupp's contribution. One notable exception came from Chlodwig Graf von Königsdorff, a distant relative of Alfried (DOA/Nachlaß Daume/532: von Königsdorff to Daume, 8 August 1966).

164. CULDA/OS72/3.2: Schilgen, Wie ich Schlußmann der Olympia-Fackelstaffel wurde (1956).

165. CULDA/OS72/3.1: 2. Sitzung des Fackellauf-Ausschusses, 15 July 1970.

166. CULDA/OS72/3.2: Diem, Der Grosstaffellauf *[sic]* Olympia-Muenchen startet am 28. Juli.

167. CULDA/OS72/loose materials: Ilse Robaschik-Kroeger to Diem (with her annotations), 23 August 1972.

168. CULDA/OS72/3.2: Ansprache anläßlich der Entzündung der olympischen Flamme in Olympia am 28. Juli 1972.

169. BAK/B136/5574: Vogel to Horst Ehmke, 13 July 1972.

170. CULDA/OS72/3.2: Bericht über den Olympischen Fackellauf 1972.

171. CULDA/OS72/3.1: 4. Sitzung des Fackellauf-Ausschusses, 15. March 1971.

172. CULDA/OS72/3.1: 5. Sitzung des Fackellauf-Ausschusses, 15. November 1971.

173. Peter Reichel, *Politik mit der Erinnerung: Gedächtnisorte im Streit um die nationalsozialistische Vergangenheit* (Frankfurt am Main, 1999), p. 182.

174. Wolfgang Schäche and Norbert Szymanski, *Das Reichssportfeld: Architektur im Spannungsfeld von Sport und Macht* (Berlin, 2001), pp. 139–45.

175. Clay Large, *Nazi Games,* p. 329. Additional information gratefully received from Andrei S. Markovits and his forthcoming book, *Global Players, Local Cultures* (Princeton University Press).

176. See documentation and correspondence in BAK/B106/36160, especially Klaus Schütz to Ernst Benda, 9 April 1968.

177. CULDA/Koebsel/IV.1: 6. Vorstandssitzung, 25 May 1967.

178. CULDA/Koebsel/IV.1: 10. Vorstandssitzung, 6 May 1968.

179. Reichel, *Politik mit der Erinnerung,* p. 184.

180. StAMü/Olympiade 1972/601: Klein to Peter Kuhn, 11 July 1969. The Munich team had a prominent role in Warsaw as the host of the next Games. On preparations and reports of this occasion, see BAK/B106/30616: Vorlage zur 15. Vorstandssitzung am 29.4.1969; Aufzeichnung über den 68. IOC-Kongreß in Warschau vom 4.-10.6.1969, 14 July 1969.

181. Wolfgang Schäche, "Von der Rennbahn zum Sportpark des 21. Jahrhunderts: Etappen einer komplexen Baugeschichte," in Senatsverwaltung für Stadtentwicklung Berlin, ed., *Panorama eines Bauwerks: Olympiastadion Berlin* (Berlin, 2001), pp. 41–5.

182. Reichel, *Politik mit der Erinnerung*, p. 184.

183. DOA/Nachlaß Daume/610: Daume to Board of Olympia-Förderverein, 6 April 1972.

184. Ibid. The Indian NOC had erroneously stated that Singh was dead, a precondition for street-naming in Munich. When the mistake was discovered, it was decided to leave the name as it stood: "Well, there are so many Singhs who were successful at the Olympics . . . that it's best just to leave it for the time being."

185. Clay Large, *Nazi Games*, pp. 265–77.

186. CULDA/OS72/loose materials: Liselott Diem to Klein, 19 August 1971.

187. "Carl Diem als 'persona non grata,'" *Aschaffenburger Volksblatt*, 3 August 1971.

188. CULDA/Koebsel/IV.3: 2. außerordentliche Vorstandssitzung, 23 August 1972. On the Dachau exhibition, see also Schiller, "Death at the Munich Olympics," p. 135.

189. CULDA/Koebsel/IV.3: 26. Sitzung des Vorstands des OK, 22 January 1973.

190. DOA/Nachlaß Daume/610: Daume to Board of Olympia-Förderverein, 6 April 1972.

191. CULDA/Koebsel/IV.1: 4. Vorstandssitzung, 2 December 1966.

192. CULDA/Koebsel/IV.1: 5. Vorstandssitzung, 17 March 1967.

193. By fifteen votes to six at the 2. Mitgliederversammlung, 18 March 1967 (CULDA/Koebsel/III.1).

194. See correspondence in BAK/B106/36142.

195. Gavriel D. Rosenfeld, *Munich and Memory: Architecture, Monuments, and the Legacy of the Third Reich* (Berkeley, Los Angeles, 2000), p. 86.

196. CULDA/Koebsel/III.1: 2. Beiratssitzung, 23 March 1970.

197. Rosenfeld, *Munich and Memory*, p. 94.

198. CULDA/OS72/3.1: 1. Sitzung des Fackellauf-Ausschusses, 2 March 1970.

199. CULDA/OS72/6.4: Konrad Pöhner to Herbert Hohenemser, 21 December 1967.

200. Sabine Brantl, *Haus der Kunst 1937–1997: Eine historische Dokumentation* (Munich, no date); for instance, Picasso, Frank Lloyd Wright, Cezanne (ninety-eight thousand visitors), van Gogh (one hundred and thirty thousand), Chagall (one hundred and four thousand), Gauguin (one hundred and twenty-six thousand).

201. Rosenfeld, *Munich and Memory*, p. 200.

202. Ibid., pp. 203–4.

203. Ibid., pp. 206–7.

204. CULDA/Koebsel/IV.2: 16. Vorstandssitzung, 27 June 1969; further details in *Die Spiele: The Official Report*, vol. 1, p. 237.

205. Rosenfeld, *Munich and Memory*, p. 208.

206. CULDA/OS72/6.4: Siegfried Wichmann to Hermann Reichart, 21 May 1969.

207. CULDA/OS72/3.1: Gestaltung der Feierlichkeiten beim Empfang des Olympischen Feuers, 19 January 1972.

208. *Die Spiele: The Official Report,* vol. 1, p. 235.

209. Further information about the exhibition itself can be found in *Die Spiele: The Official Report,* vol. 1, pp. 235–41 and the catalogue, *Weltkulturen und moderne Kunst: Die Begegnung der europäischen Kunst und Musik im 19. und 20. Jahrhundert mit Asien, Afrika, Ozeanien, Afro- und Indo-Amerika* (Munich, 1972).

210. "Die unerwiderte Liebe zur Kunst," *sid*-Olympia-Ausgabe, 9 September 1972.

211. IOC Lausanne/Brundage/Correspondence, September to December 1972: Brundage to Yvon d'Argencé, 16 September 1972.

212. *Die Spiele: The Official Report,* vol. 1, p. 237.

213. Ibid. In fact, the "Entartete Kunst" display took place in 1937, in Munich's Hofgartenarkaden, parallel to the "Große Deutsche Kunstaustellung," which was hosted in the Haus der deutschen Kunst.

214. Ibid.

215. See CULDA/OS72/6.4: Typescript Weltkulturen und moderne Kunst.

216. CULDA/OS72/6.4: Daume to Heinemann, 20 June 1970.

217. CULDA/OS72/6.3: Transcript of Daume interview with *Stern* magazine, 26 January 1971.

218. BAK/B122/10401: Ansprache des Bundespräsidenten auf der Tagung des IOK am 19. August 1972, 15 August 1972.

219. BAK/B122/15028: Empfang des Bundespräsidenten für den OK-Vorstand, 26 November 1969.

220. Daume was still expecting him to attend in June 1972 (CULDA/Koebsel/IV.3: 25. Vorstandssitzung, 25 June 1972).

221. BAK/B122/15030: Vermerk, 7 August 1972.

222. BAK/B122/15030: Vermerk, 23 March 1972.

223. CULDA/Koebsel/III.1: 2. Beiratssitzung, 23 March 1970.

224. CULDA/OS72/4: Konstituierende Sitzung des Protokoll-Ausschusses, 4 July 1970.

225. BAK/B106/36117: 3. Beiratssitzung, 24 September 1971.

226. CULDA/Koebsel/IV.3: 25. Vorstandssitzung, 25 June 1972. A full account of the various strands of negotiation can be read in StaMü/Olympiade/55.

227. Ibid.

228. *Münchner Merkur,* 5 September 1972.

229. See *Süddeutsche Zeitung,* 26–27 August 1972; *Frankfurter Rundschau,* 26 August 1972; *Münchener Jüdische Nachrichten,* 1 September 1972.

230. *Münchner Merkur,* 4 September 1972.

4. GERMANY ON THE DRAWING BOARD

1. Christoph Oesterreich, Umstrittene Selbstdarstellung: Der deutsche Beitrag zur Weltausstellung in Brüssel 1958," *Vierteljahrshefte für Zeitgeschichte* 48, 2000, p. 152; see also Winfried Nerdinger, "Aufbrüche und Kontinuitäten—Positionen der Nachkriegsar-

chitektur in der Bundesrepublik," in Nerdinger, ed., *Architektur der Wunderkinder: Aufbruch und Verdrängung in Bayern 1945–1960* (Salzburg, Munich, 2005), pp. 9–22.

2. Paul Betts, *The Authority of Everyday Objects: A Cultural History of West German Industrial Design* (Berkeley 2004), p. 9.

3. Johannes Paulmann, "Representation without Emulation: German Cultural Diplomacy in Search of Integration and Self-Assurance during the Adenauer Era," *German Politics and Society* 25, no. 2, 2007, pp. 168–200.

4. Nerdinger, "Aufbrüche und Kontinuitäten," pp. 15–16.

5. Betts, *The Authority of Everyday Objects,* pp. 190–91.

6. Paul Sigel, *Exponiert: Deutsche Pavillons auf Weltausstellungen* (Berlin, 2000), pp. 207–44.

7. PAAA Berlin/B90/763: Rolf Gutbrod, Der Deutsche Pavillon.

8. PAAA Berlin/B90/763: Arnold Bode, Der Deutsche Pavillon, 24 March 1965.

9. Cited in Oesterreich, "Umstrittene Selbstdarstellung," p. 147.

10. PAAA Berlin/B90/763: Memorandum from Ted Kaghan et al., 30 June 1966.

11. Sigel, *Exponiert,* pp. 237–38.

12. DOA/Nachlaß Daume/530: Daume to Hermann Jannsen, 29 February 1968.

13. BAK/B106/33054: Deutsches Mosaik (undated).

14. BAK/B122/10383: Daume to Heinemann, 19 March 1972.

15. DOA/Nachlaß Daume/530: Daume to Heinrich Köppler, 22 September 1969.

16. DOA/Nachlaß Daume/534: Vogel to Daume, 16 August 1967.

17. DOA/Nachlaß Daume/530 and 532: Daume to Unseld, 18 January 1968 and 10 July 1967.

18. "Willi Daume konnte Geige spielen", p. 100.

19. DOA/Nachlaß Daume/514: Vortrag Peking, Spring 1973; Deutscher Sportbund, ed., *Willi Daume: Deutscher Sport 1952–1972* (Munich, 1973), pp. 147–49.

20. BAK/B106/36163: Schmitz, 22 August 1969.

21. CULDA/Koebsel/IV.1: 7. und 10. Vorstandssitzung, 15 July 1967 and 6 May 1968. The committee was unimpressed at first and Vogel dragged his heels.

22. This was followed by a less successful series with young German artists.

23. Klaus Bieringer, "Kulturprogramm—ein olympischer Auftrag," in Volker Rattemeyer, ed., *Kunst + Design, Kultur Olympia. Willi Daume, Preisträger der Stankowski-Stiftung 1986* (Kassel, 1986), p. 27.

24. CULDA/OS72/13.7: Daume to Hohenemser, 27 June 1967; Daume to Pablo Picasso, 27 June 1967; Akten-Notiz, 19 May 1969; CULDA/Koebsel/IV.1: 7. Vorstandssitzung, 15 July 1967.

25. Interview with Klaus von Lindeiner, 5 November 2003; CULDA/Koebsel/IV.1: 10. Vorstandssitzung, 6 May 1968; CULDA/OS72/13.7: F. Andreas, Reisebericht, February 1969; CULDA/OS72/6.2: 6. Kunstausschußsitzung, 18–19 April 1969; Arbeitskreis Intendantenkonferenz, 16 June 1969; DOA/Nachlaß Daume/546: Daume to Hohenemser, 13 May 1969.

26. Herbert Hohenemser, "Edition Olympia München 72: Offenheit und Freiheit," in Rattemeyer, *Kunst + Design, Kultur Olympia,* p. 35.

27. See StAMü/BuR/3174.

28. "Hurra für Kokoschka," *Die Zeit,* 28 March 1969.

29. Ulrich Pabst, "Olympia und die Kunst," in Rattemeyer, *Kunst + Design, Kultur Olympia,* p. 22.

30. Hubert Dwertmann and Lorenz Peiffer, eds., *Willi Daume: Eine Bibliographie seiner Schriften, Reden und Interviews* (Cologne, 2001), p. 15; Ommo Grupe, "Willi Daume: Olympische Überzeugungen—der Sport, die Spiele," in Bundesinstitut für Sportwissenschaft and Deutsches Olympisches Institut, eds., *Willi Daume: Olympische Dimensionen. Ein Symposion* (Bonn, 2004), p. 25.

31. Allen Guttmann, *The Games Must Go On: Avery Brundage and the Olympic Movement* (New York, 1984), pp. 201–8.

32. Ibid., p. 205.

33. StAMü/Olympiade 1972/509–1: Vogel to Brundage, 20 December 1965.

34. IFS Archiv Hannover/Archiv Hattig: Daume to Brundage, 15 November 1965.

35. *Süddeutsche Zeitung,* 5 April 1966.

36. Address by Brundage in *Bulletin du Comité International Olympique* 95, August 1966, p. 70.

37. StAMü/Olympiade 1972/67: Antworten zum Fragebogen, 14 December 1965; BAK/B185/1815: Das 12-Punkte-Programm.

38. CULDA/OS72/6.2: Kunstausschußsitzung, 6–7 December 1968.

39. Bieringer, "Kulturprogramm—ein olympischer Auftrag," p. 26.

40. Others included *Bayern—Kunst und Kultur, 100 Jahre deutsche Ausgrabung in Olympia,* and *Olympia und Technik.*

41. Bieringer, "Kulturprogramm—ein olympischer Auftrag," p. 29.

42. See CULDA/OS72/6.2: 8. Intendantenkonferenzsitzung, 27 April 1971.

43. DOA/Nachlaß Daume/546: Kunstprogramm.

44. IOC Lausanne/Daume/Correspondence 1957–1972: Monique Berlioux to Daume, 15 December 1969; Executive Board Minutes, Dubrovnik, 23–27 October 1969; CULDA/Koebsel/IV.2: 16. Vorstandssitzung, 27 June 1969.

45. IOC Lausanne/69th IOC Session, Amsterdam, 12–16 May 1970; 70th IOC Session, Luxembourg, 15–17 September 1971; CULDA/OS72/4: Vermerk on 69th IOC Session Amsterdam, 19 May 1970.

46. IOC Lausanne/Executive Board Minutes, Sapporo, 29 January 1972; 72nd IOC Session, Sapporo, 31 January–1 February 1972.

47. Bieringer, "Kulturprogramm—ein olympischer Auftrag," p. 30.

48. Ibid., p. 26.

49. De Coubertin (1911) quoted in Arnd Krüger, "What's the Difference between Propaganda for Tourism or for a Political Regime? Was the 1936 Olympics the First Postmodern Spectacle?" in John Bale and Mette Krogh Kristensen, eds., *Post-Olympism?: Questioning Sport in the Twenty-First Century* (Oxford, 2004), p. 48. On Wagner see Thomas Alkemeyer, *Körper, Kult und Politik: Von der "Muskelreligion" Pierre de Coubertins zur Inszenierung von Macht in den Olympischen Spielen von 1936* (Frankfurt am Main, 1996), pp. 148–49, 151, 306, 409–12.

50. *The XIth Olympic Games Berlin, 1936, Official Report,* vol. 1, p. 42.

51. Ibid., p. 454.

52. Gunter Gebauer and Christoph Wulf, "Die Berliner Olympiade 1936: Spiele der Gewalt," in Gebauer, ed., *Olympische Spiele—die andere Utopie der Moderne. Olympia zwischen Kult und Droge* (Frankfurt am Main, 1996), p. 253.

53. CULDA/Koebsel/III.1: 2. Beiratssitzung, 23 March 1970.

54. Betts, *The Authority of Everyday Objects*, pp. 196–97.

55. See DOA/Nachlaß Daume/549: Aicher to Daume, 26 September 1966.

56. Interview with Rolf Müller, 10 April 2005.

57. See CULDA/Koebsel/IV.2: 12. Vorstandssitzung, 9 September 1969.

58. See StAMü/Olympiade 1972/117 and 118: Hubert Abreß, Vormerkungen, 20 March 1968 and 14 January 1969; see also DOA/Nachlaß Daume/549: Roth to Daume, 29 April 1968.

59. See StAMü/Olympiade 1972/117: Wirsing to Vogel, 9 December 1965 and 12 May 1966.

60. Peter M. Bode and Manfred Sack wrote regularly in support of Aicher's work.

61. DOA/Nachlaß Daume/549: Daume, Das visuelle Bild der Olympischen Spiele von München (September 1966).

62. Betts, *The Authority of Everyday Objects*, pp. 145, 151, 154, 158.

63. Ibid., p. 166.

64. DOA/Nachlaß Daume/549: Daume, Das visuelle Bild.

65. TU Mü-Weihst/ArchGrz: Otl Aicher, "zum 22. februar 1963," p. 2.

66. Otl Aicher, *die welt als entwurf* (Berlin, 1991), pp. 87–95.

67. See Otl Aicher, "Planung in Mißkredit. Zur Entwicklung von Stadt und Land," in Hans-Werner Richter, ed., *Bestandsaufnahme. Eine deutsche Bilanz, Sechsunddreißig Beiträge deutscher Wissenschaftler, Schriftsteller und Publizisten* (Munich, 1962), pp. 398–420, and Markus Rathgeb, *Otl Aicher* (London, 2006), p. 78.

68. HFG-Archiv Ulm/Ai.Az.80: Aicher, die olympischen spiele in münchen 1972, July 1975, p. 5.

69. Barbara Schüler, *"Im Geiste der Gemordeten . . .": Die "Weiße Rose" und ihre Wirkung in der Nachkriegszeit* (Paderborn, 2000), p. 406; see also HFG-Archiv Ulm/Ai.Az.1216: Aktennotiz, ferngespräch mit dr. hohenemser, 7 October 1966 (during which Aicher was informed of his appointment).

70. Interview with Friedhelm Brebeck, 7 February 2005.

71. Rathgeb, *Otl Aicher*, p. 22.

72. Otl Aicher, "über management: willi daume," in Rattemeyer, *Kunst + Design, Kultur Olympia*, pp. 14–15.

73. Otl Aicher, "Olympia und Kunst," in Norbert Müller and Manfred Messing, eds., *Auf der Suche nach der Olympischen Idee: Facetten der Forschung von Athen bis Atlanta* (Kassel, 1996), p. 18.

74. HFG-Archiv Ulm/Ai.Az.80: Aicher, die olympischen spiele in münchen 1972, juli 1975, p. 9.

75. BAK/B185/2155: Aicher, Das Erscheinungsbild der Olympischen Spiele, München 1972 (Vorstandsvorlage, 22 November 1967), p. 4.

76. StAMü/Olympiade 1972/117: Aicher, Olympische Spiele München 1972—ohne politischen Charakter, 3 July 1967.

77. HFG-Archiv Ulm/Ai.Az.80: Aicher, die olympischen spiele in münchen 1972, juli 1975, p. 1.

78. BAK/B185/2155: Aicher, Das Erscheinungsbild der Olympischen Spiele, München 1972, p. 4, our emphasis.

79. StAMü/Olympiade 1972/117: Aicher, Olympische Spiele München 1972, 3 July 1967.

80. BAK/B185/2155: Aicher, Das Erscheinungsbild der Olympischen Spiele, München 1972, p. 5.

81. See BAK/B185/3197: Richtlinien und Normen für die visuelle Gestaltung, June 1969.

82. BAK/B185/2155: Aicher, Das Erscheinungsbild der Olympischen Spiele, München 1972, p. 7.

83. Aicher, *typographie* (Berlin, 1988), pp. 172–73.

84. BAK/B185/2155: Aicher, Das Erscheinungsbild der Olympischen Spiele, München 1972, p. 7.

85. Rathgeb, *Otl Aicher,* pp. 81–82.

86. HFG-Archiv Ulm/Ai.Az.80: Aicher, die olympischen spiele in münchen 1972, juli 1975, p. 12.

87. Rathgeb, *Otl Aicher,* pp. 94–95.

88. Elizabeth Audrey Leckie Schlüssel, "Zur Rolle der Musik bei den Eröffnungs- und Schlußfeiern der Olympischen Spiele von 1896 bis 1972," PhD diss. (Deutsche Sporthochschule Köln, 2001), p. 677.

89. Ibid., p. 6.

90. Ibid., p. 4.

91. Richard Mandell, *The Olympics of 1972: A Munich Diary* (Chapel Hill, NC, 1991), p. 3.

92. HFG-Archiv Ulm/Ai.Az.80: Aicher, die olympischen spiele in münchen 1972, juli 1975, pp. 2–3.

93. See Rathgeb, *Otl Aicher,* pp. 77–112.

94. StAMü/Olympiade 1972/117: Aicher, Olympische Spiele München 1972—ohne politischen Charakter.

95. Ibid.; see also BAK/B185/3188: Aicher to Vogel.

96. BAK/B185/2155: Aicher, Das Erscheinungsbild der Olympischen Spiele, München 1972, p. 1.

97. On the mixed reaction to the final emblem, see *Süddeutsche Zeitung* and *Münchner Merkur,* 15–17 June 1968. The board discussed the issue at its 7th, 8th, and 10th meetings (see CULDA/Koebsel/IV.1).

98. See Moritz Scheibe, "Auf der Suche nach der demokratischen Gesellschaft," in Ulrich Herbert, ed., *Wandlungsprozesse in Westdeutschland: Belastung, Integration, Liberalisierung* (Göttingen, 2002), pp. 245–53.

99. Hans-Jochen Vogel, *Die Amtskette: Meine 12 Münchner Jahre. Ein Erlebnisbericht* (Munich, 1972), pp. 133–34.

100. Cited in Scheibe, "Auf der Suche nach der demokratischen Gesellschaft," p. 254.

101. Edgar Wolfrum, *Die geglückte Demokratie: Geschichte der Bundesrepublik Deutschland von ihren Anfängen bis zur Gegenwart* (Stuttgart, 2006), pp. 243, 275.

102. BAK/B185/2155: Aicher, Das Erscheinungsbild der Olympischen Spiele, München 1972, p. 6.

103. Heinrich Klotz, *Architektur in der Bundesrepublik* (Frankfurt am Main, 1977), pp. 57–60.

104. Fritz Auer, "Zur Entstehung des Olympiaprojektes vom Wettbewerb bis zur Auftragserteilung aus meiner Erinnerung" (January 1999), unpublished manuscript, p. 1.

105. Hans-Jochen Vogel, *Demokratie lebt auch vom Widerspruch* (Munich, 2001), p. 336.

106. DOA/Nachlaß Daume/542: Architektenwettbewerb, Sitzung des Preisgerichts, pp. 1–2.

107. Auer, "Zur Entstehung des Olympiaprojektes," p. 1.

108. "Aufgabe, Programm," in *Bauten der Olympischen Spiele 1972: Architekturwettbewerbe, Sonderband 1: 1969* (Stuttgart, 1969), p. I/4.

109. Clay Large, *Nazi Games*, pp. 153–54.

110. See also Swantje Scharenberg, "Nachdenken über die Wechselwirkung von Architektur und Wohlbefinden: Das Olympiastadion in München, ein politischer Veranstaltungsort," in Matthias Marschik, Rudolf Müllner, Georg Spitaler, and Michael Zinganel, eds., *Das Stadion: Geschichte, Architektur, Politik, Ökonomie* (Vienna, 2005), p. 156 and Organisationskomitee für die XI. Olympiade Berlin 1936, ed., *The XIth Olympic Games Berlin, 1936, Official Report* (Berlin, 1937), vol. 1, p. 149.

111. Auer, "Zur Entstehung des Olympiaprojektes," p. 1; see also Thomas Schmidt, *Olympische Stadien von 1896 bis 1988* (Berlin, 1994), pp. 124, 126.

112. Auer, "Zur Entstehung des Olympiaprojektes," pp. 3–4.

113. BAK/B185/2155: Aicher, Das Erscheinungsbild der Olympischen Spiele, München 1972, p. 6.

114. Architekten Behnisch & Partner, "Architekturtheoretische Anmerkungen zum Entwurf," in *Bauten der Olympischen Spiele 1972: Architekturwettbewerbe, Sonderband 1: 1969* (Stuttgart, 1969), p. IV/15.

115. Quoted in David Butwin, "It Isn't Whether You Win or Lose But How You Stage the Games," *The Arts Saturday Review*, 25 March 1972.

116. Interview with Carlo Weber, 29 September 2005.

117. Gavriel D. Rosenfeld, *Munich and Memory: Architecture, Monuments, and the Legacy of the Third Reich* (Berkeley, 2000), pp. 157–59.

118. Interview with Carlo Weber, 29 September 2005.

119. Interview Daume, March 1994, p. 49.

120. Karin Wilhelm, *Portrait Frei Otto* (Berlin, 1985), p. 71.

121. Auer, "Zur Entstehung des Olympiaprojektes," p. 7; see also Klotz, *Architektur in der Bundesrepublik*, p. 33.

122. DOA/Nachlaß Daume/542: Architektenwettbewerb, Niederschrift über die Sitzung des Preisgerichts, Tarnnummer 4350, p. 3.

123. Auer, "Zur Entstehung des Olympiaprojektes," p. 9.

124. StAMü/Olympiade 1972/723: Otto-Hermann Grüneberg, Dach-Entscheidungen (December 1974), p. 19.

125. Interview with Carlo Weber, 29 September 2005.

126. Interview with Rolf Müller, 10 April 2005.

127. See StAMü/Olympiade 1972/515: Tonbandprotokoll Eiermann-Rede, 19 October 1967 and Vogel, *Demokratie lebt auch vom Widerspruch*, p. 336.

128. See Peter M. Bode, "Plädoyer für Olympias hängende Dächer," *Süddeutsche Zeitung*, 27 October 1967, "Olympischer Stellungskrieg," *Süddeutsche Zeitung*, 26 January 1968 and "Heißumkämpftes Olympiadach: Stellungnahmen von Preisträgern, Gutachtern und Journalisten," *Süddeutsche Zeitung*, 13 February 1968.

129. *Süddeutsche Zeitung*, 18 October 1967.

130. See StAMü/Olympiade 1972/723: Grüneberg, Dach-Entscheidungen, p. 22.

131. Quoted in Franz-Joachim Verspohl, *Stadionbauten von der Antike bis zur Gegenwart* (Gießen, 1976), p. 269.

132. See, for example, "Ein Schuttberg wird 'Olympiahügel:' Prof. Frei Otto verteidigt die Zeltdachkonstruktion," in: *Hannoversche Allgemeine*, 17 October 1967; "Ein Konstrukteur über Münchens olympische Architektur: Frei Otto, der Erbauer des deutschen Pavillons in Montreal, nimmt zum preisgekrönten Olympiaentwurf Stellung," *Süddeutsche Zeitung*, 26 January 1968; "Kampf um Münchens Olympiazelt: Professor Frei Otto verteidigt den preisgekrönten Entwurf," *Rheinischer Merkur, Christ und Welt*, 23 February 1968.

133. See, for example, Winfried Nerdinger, ed., *Frei Otto—Das Gesamtwerk: Leicht bauen, natürlich gestalten* (Basel, Boston, and Berlin, 2005), p. 167.

134. These were Heinz Isler, later known for the thin concrete roofs of his Isler bowls (Isler Schalen), and, as project leader, Jörg Schlaich from the engineering firm Leonhardt and Andrä; see Peter Blundell-Jones, *Günter Behnisch* (Basel, 2000), p. 65; Frei Otto, "Das Zeltdach: Subjektive Anmerkungen zum Olympiadach (1973)," in Berthold Burckhardt, ed., *Frei Otto: Schriften und Reden, 1951–1983* (Wiesbaden, 1984), p. 101.

135. Otto, "Das Zeltdach," p. 103, note 14; Klotz, *Architektur in der Bundesrepublik*, p. 224.

136. Winfried Nerdinger, "Frei Otto: Arbeit für eine bessere 'Menschenerde,'" in Nerdinger, *Frei Otto—Das Gesamtwerk. Leicht bauen, natürlich gestalten*, p. 12.

137. Scharenberg, "Nachdenken über die Wechselwirkung," p. 160.

138. Organizing Committee for the Games of the XXth Olympiad Munich 1972, ed., *Die Spiele: The Official Report*, vol. 2: The Constructions (Munich, 1972), p. 180; StAMü/Olympiade 1972/723: Die Dach-Geschichte (press release), 4 November 1971.

139. Otto, "Das Zeltdach," p. 99.

140. Quoted in Scharenberg, "Nachdenken über die Wechselwirkung," p. 160.

141. Vogel, *Demokratie lebt auch vom Widerspruch*, pp. 336–38.

142. Andreas König, *Günther Grzimek: Ein Landschaftsarchitekt der Nachkriegszeit. Berufliche Entwicklung, Konzepte und Arbeiten* (Diplomarbeit, TU München-Weihenstephan, 1996), p. 6.

143. Günter Behnisch und Partner, "Zur Gesamtkonzeption 'Oberwiesenfeld,'" in *Sportbauten für die XX. Olympiade*, special issue of *der mensch und die technik: Technisch-wissenschaftliche Blätter der Süddeutschen Zeitung*, 29 December 1971, p. 1.

144. See König, *Günther Grzimek*, pp. 25–52.

145. René Spitz, *hfg ulm: the view behind the foreground. the political history of the ulm school of design, 1953–1968* (Stuttgart, London, 2002), p. 100.

146. Interview with Carlo Weber, 29 September 2005; König, *Günther Grzimek*, p. 80.

147. König, *Günther Grzimek*, p. 105, see also Aicher, *die welt als entwurf*, pp. 87–88.

148. Günther Grzimek, "Spiel und Sport im Olympiapark München," in Gerda Gollwitzer, ed., *Spiel und Sport in der Stadtlandschaft: Erfahrungen und Beispiele für morgen* (Munich, 1972), p. 12.

149. TU Mü-Weihst/ArchGrz: Grzimek, Olympialandschaft München, Oberwiesenfeld (early 1990s), p. 1; Grzimek, "Spiel und Sport im Olympiapark München," pp. 12–13.

150. *Die Spiele: The Official Report*, vol. 2, p. 179.

151. Grzimek, "Spiel und Sport im Olympiapark München," p. 12; see also Grzimek, "Bau der Landschaft, Construction of the Landscape," in *Bauten der Olympischen Spiele 1972: Architekturwettbewerbe, Sonderband 2: Bestandsaufnahme Herbst 1970* (Stuttgart, 1970), p. 38.

152. TU Mü-Weihst/ArchGrz: Grzimek, Olympialandschaft München, p. 1.

153. Günther Grzimek, *Gedanken zur Stadt- und Landschaftsarchitektur seit Friedrich Ludwig v. Sckell* (Munich, 1973), pp. 14–16.

154. Architects Behnisch & Partners, "Olympic Athletic Facilities Munich 1972," in *Bauten der Olympischen Spiele 1972: Architekturwettbewerbe, Sonderband 1: 1969* (Stuttgart, 1969), p. 2.

155. Auer, "Zur Entstehung des Olympiaprojektes," p. 3.

156. Grzimek, "Spiel und Sport im Olympiapark München," p. 12.

157. HFG-Archiv Ulm/Ai.Az.1223: Aicher, Projekt Regenbogenspiele, p. 1.

158. See Günther Grzimek, *Die Besitzergreifung des Rasens: Folgerungen aus dem Modell Süd-Isar. Grünplanung heute* (Munich, 1983).

159. König, *Günther Grzimek*, p. 13.

160. Frank Uekötter, *The Green and the Brown: A History of Conservation in Nazi Germany* (Cambridge, 2006), pp. 80, 157–160; David Blackbourn, *The Conquest of Nature: Water, Landscape and the Making of Modern Germany* (London, 2006), p. 277.

161. König, *Günther Grzimek*, p. 21.

162. *The XIth Olympic Games Berlin, 1936, Official Report*, vol. 1, p. 138.

163. Ibid., pp. 172–75; see also Alkemeyer, *Körper, Kult und Politik*, p. 324.

164. Quoted in Blackbourn, *The Conquest of Nature*, p. 262.

165. Günther Grzimek, "Landschaftsarchitektur," in *Bauten für Olympia 1972: München, Kiel, Augsburg. Building and Facilities for the Olympic Games* (Munich, 1972), p. 36.

166. Grzimek, "Bau der Landschaft, Construction of the Landscape," p. 38; TU Mü-Weihst/ArchGrz: Grzimek, Olympialandschaft München, p. 4; Interview with Carlo Weber, 29 September 2005.

167. TU Mü-Weihst/ArchGrz: Grzimek, Olympialandschaft München, pp. 4–5.

168. Herbert Schneider, "Durst wird durch Bier erst schön," *Olympia Press* 3, August 1969, pp. 38–40.

169. BAK/B185/2609 fol 1: 3. Gestaltungsausschußsitzung, 7 July 1967.

170. HFG-Archiv Ulm/Ai.Az.1228: Aicher, erscheinungsbild der olympischen spiele in münchen 1972, 13 January 1971, p. 1.

171. StAMü/BuR/3181: Olympia-Pressestelle, "München—Olympiastadt 1972," 17 April 1968.

172. CULDA/Koebsel/IV.2: 19. Vorstandssitzung, 17 April 1970; HFG-Archiv Ulm/Ai.Az.1208: Aicher to Hermann Reichart, 19 March, 6 May and 6 June 1971; Aicher to Daume, 12 May 1971; undated unpublished press release.

173. See DOA/Nachlaß Daume/610: Carl Mertz to Daume, 12 May 1971; interview with Friedhelm Brebeck, 7 February 2005.

174. CULDA/Koebsel/III.2: Olympia Großgaststätten to Wirtschaftsvereinigung Münchner Brauereien, 31 July 1973; Ansprüche der Wirtschaftsvereinigung Münchner Brauereien.

175. StAMü/Olympiade 1972/226: 15. Aufsichtsratssitzung der OBG, 18 December 1970, p. 17; Vogel to Ludwig Rosenberg (DGB), 2 May 1967.

176. Rosenfeld, *Munich and Memory,* p. 220.

177. StAMü/Olympiade 1972/226: 15. Aufsichtsratssitzung der OBG, 18 December 1970, p. 19; see also interview with Carlo Weber, 29 September 2005.

178. CULDA/OS72/6.6: Behnisch, Erläuterung der Entwurfsprinzipien für ein Friedensdenkmal auf dem Schuttberg, 12 November 1970.

179. HFG-Archiv Ulm/Ai.Az.1223: Aicher, Projekt Regenbogenspiele, p. 1.

180. StAMü/Olympiade 1972/681: Gemeinsame 14. Sitzung des Finanz- und Verwaltungsausschusses und 16. Aufsichtsratssitzung der OBG, 10 March 1971.

181. StAMü/Olympiade 1972/655: Eisgruber, Vormerkung, Vorsprache von Behnisch bei Vogel, 12 November 1971.

182. CULDA/OS72/6.6: Behnisch, Vorschlag für eine große Erdskulptur, Kurzfassung Walter de Maria, August 1970, p. 6.

183. See ibid., Anlagen. These included positive references from New York's MOMA and museums of art in Stockholm and Basel.

184. BAK/B185/2632: 3. Beiratssitzung, 24 September 1971; StAMü/Olympiade 1972/681: 17. Aufsichtsratsitzung der OBG, 16 November 1971; Reinhard Müller-Mehlis, "Der Propagandatrupp Bohrloch ist wieder aktiv," *Münchner Merkur,* 8 November 1971.

185. StAMü/Olympiade 1972/395: 17. Bauausschußsitzung der OBG, 11 November 1971; Abreß, Marginalia on a press conference report, 8 November 1971; StAMü/Olympiade 1972/681: 17. Aufsichtsratssitzung der OBG, 16 November 1971.

186. Alkemeyer, *Körper, Kult und Politik,* pp. 46–48, 213.

187. *Die Spiele: The Official Report,* vol. 1, p. 80.

188. Alan Tomlinson, "Olympic Spectacle: Opening Ceremonies and Some Paradoxes of Globalization," *Media, Culture and Society* 18, no. 4, 1996, pp. 583–602, 590–93.

189. BAK/B322/433: Carl Diem to Daume, 28 July 1960; Diem to Wolf Heinrich Prinz von Hannover, 6 February 1961.

190. BAK/B322/433: Diem to Wolfgang Schadewaldt, 4 January 1961.

191. BAK/B322/433: Paul Winter to Diem, 7 December 1960.

192. CULDA/OS72/3.3: Guido von Mengden, Eröffnungs- und Schlußfeier der Olympischen Spiele 1972, 7 March 1968; Deutscher Sportbeirat, Stellungnahme, 10 July 1969.

193. Ibid.

194. StAMü/BuR/3182: OK-Studienbericht über die Olympischen Spiele 1968, from which the following quotations are taken.

195. BAK/B106/30673: OK-Studienbericht.

196. *Gazette de Lausanne,* 14 October 1968, quoted in Leckie Schlüssel, *Zur Rolle der Musik,* p. 578.

197. The first three meetings of the DSB working party are covered in Leckie Schlüssel, *Zur Rolle der Musik,* pp. 544–50, from which the quotations are taken.

198. CULDA/OS72/6.3: Stellungnahme des Deutschen Sportbeirates, 1 July 1969.

199. CULDA/OS72/3.2: Daume to the Greek NOC, 16 January 1971.

200. CULDA/OS72/3.2: General Programm, Erster Entwurf des Kapitels "Fackellauf" (Koebsel, no date).

201. An account of these discussions can be read in exhaustive detail in Leckie Schlüssel, *Zur Rolle der Musik,* pp. 519–714, from which the following draws its main facts.

202. CULDA/OS72/6.2: 3. Kunstausschußsitzung, 18–19 April 1968.

203. Leckie Schlüssel, *Zur Rolle der Musik,* pp. 587–625.

204. Ibid., pp. 589–90.

205. Thus the short vita circulated to the group before his appointment (ibid., p. 669).

206. BAK/B185/2146: Wilhelm Killmayer to Bieringer, 12 August 1970.

207. Willi Daume, "Eine Milliarde für die Olympischen Spiele?" *Olympisches Feuer* 6, 1966, p. 3.

208. See Leckie Schlüssel, *Zur Rolle der Musik,* pp. 565–77, quotation p. 571.

209. CULDA/Koebsel/IV.2: 17. Vorstandssitzung, 21–22 November 1969.

210. CULDA/Koebsel/IV.2: 19. Vorstandssitzung, 17 April 1970.

211. *Frankfurter Rundschau,* 26 April 1971; *Süddeutsche Zeitung,* 26 April 1971.

212. See in particular CULDA/OS72/6.2: 3. Kunstausschußsitzung, 18–19 April 1968, with von Mengden present.

213. See also Uta Andrea Balbier, "'Der Welt das moderne Deutschland vorstellen:' Die Eröffnungsfeier der Olympischen Spiele in München," in Johannes Paulmann, ed., *Auswärtige Repräsentationen: Deutsche Kulturdiplomatie nach 1945* (Cologne, 2005), pp. 105–19.

214. Kip Keino (Africa), Jim Ryan (USA), Keino Kimihara (Asia), Derek Clayton (Australia).

215. "Aufgabe, Programm," p. I/7.

216. *Die Spiele: The Official Report,* vol. 1, p. 8 states that the children handed over their bows and posies unplanned. But this has to be doubted, since the possibility appeared in the first draft of the working party for the opening and closing ceremonies in December 1969. (Leckie Schlüssel, *Zur Rolle der Musik,* p. 600)

217. Leckie Schlüssel, *Zur Rolle der Musik,* p. 609.

218. BAK/B106/30673: Vorbericht zu 6. Kunstausschußsitzung, 18.-19. April 1969—Gestaltung des Olympischen Zeremoniells.

219. Leckie Schlüssel, *Zur Rolle der Musik,* pp. 634–47.

220. Ibid., p. 638. The words come from Bieringer's notes on a meeting with Edelhagen himself.

221. Ibid., pp. 644, 642.

222. CULDA/OS72/6.2: 7. Kunstausschußsitzung, 24–25 October 1969.

223. CULDA/Koebsel/IV.1: 14. Vorstandssitzung, 11 March 1969.

224. Leckie Schlüssel, *Zur Rolle der Musik*, p. 640.

225. Ibid., pp. 660–66.

226. Interview with Hans-Jochen Vogel, 10 November 2003.

227. Oesterreich, "Umstrittene Selbstdarstellung," p. 146.

228. BAK/B106/30673: Eckstein to Schmitz on ceremonies, 9 September 1969.

229. Bavaria was persuaded to foot the bill of around DM 20,000, so that "authentic Bavarian folk culture could have worldwide resonance." (BayHStA/StK/14058: Ludwig Huber to Daume, 24 May 1972, and related correspondence)

230. U. Kaiser, "Heiterer können wir nicht . . . ," *sid*-Olympia-Ausgabe, 26 August 1972, p. 20.

231. Mandell, *A Munich Diary*, p. 54.

232. All quotations taken from "Stimmen zur Eröffnungsfeier," *sid*-Olympia-Ausgabe, 26 August 1972. The story of Brigitte Maibohm comes from the authors' interview (19 November 2003) with her.

233. Cited in H.-J. Noack, "Auch Falin sprach von einem eindrucksvollen Beginn," *Frankfurter Rundschau*, 28 August 1972.

234. Rosenfeld, *Munich and Memory*, p. 156.

235. See, for instance, Balbier, "Der Welt das moderne Deutschland vorstellen," p. 106.

236. Cited in Noack, "Auch Falin sprach von einem eindrucksvollen Beginn."

5. AFTER "1968"

1. Michael Barke, "Mexico City 1968," in John R. and Margaret M. Gold, eds., *Olympic Cities: City Agendas, Planning, and the World's Games, 1896 to 2012* (London, 2006), p. 193.

2. Arif Dirlik, "The Third World," in Carole Fink, Philipp Gassert, and Detlef Junker, eds., *1968: The World Transformed* (Cambridge, 1998), pp. 311–12.

3. Tony Judt, *Postwar: A History of Europe Since 1945* (New York, 2005), p. 394.

4. Ibid., pp. 390, 398.

5. Detlef Siegfried, "Understanding 1968: Youth Rebellion, Generational Change and Postindustrial Society," in Axel Schildt and Siegfried, eds., *Between Marx and Coca-Cola: Youth Cultures in Changing European Societies, 1960–1980* (New York, 2006), pp. 61–63; Eric Hobsbawm, *Age of Extremes: The Short Twentieth Century, 1914–1991* (London, 1994), p. 445.

6. Detlef Siegfried, *Time is on my side: Konsum und Politik in der westdeutschen Jugendkultur der 60er Jahre* (Göttingen, 2006), p. 747.

7. Wolfgang Kraushaar, *Frankfurter Schule und Studentenbewegung: Von der Flaschenpost zum Molotowcocktail 1946–1995*, vol. 1: *Chronik* (Hamburg, 1998), pp. 304–5.

8. Rob Burns and Wilfried van der Will, *Protest and Democracy in West Germany: Extra-Parliamentary Opposition and the Democratic Agenda* (Basingstoke, 1988), pp. 109–11; Nick Thomas, *Protest Movements in 1960s West Germany: A Social History of Dissent and Democracy* (Oxford, 2003), pp. 173–75; Manfred Schreiber, "Das Jahr 1968 in München," in Venanz Schubert, ed., *1968: 30 Jahre danach* (St. Ottilien, 1999), p. 39.

9. See Gerd Koenen, *Das rote Jahrzehnt: Unsere kleine deutsche Kulturrevolution 1967–1977* (Cologne, 2001) and Siegfried, *Time Is on My Side*, pp. 706–29.

10. FES/Dep. HJV/Reden 1968: Speech on the Königsplatz, 23 April 1968; see also Hans-Jochen Vogel, *Die Amtskette: Meine 12 Münchner Jahre. Ein Erlebnisbericht* (Munich, 1972), pp. 182–84; Hans-Jochen Vogel, *Demokratie lebt auch vom Widerspruch* (Munich, 2001), pp. 299–301.

11. Andrei S. Markovits and Philip S. Gorski, *The German Left: Red, Green and Beyond* (Cambridge, 1993), pp. 94–95.

12. For the details see Vogel, *Die Amtskette*, pp. 213–47.

13. CULDA/Koebsel/III.1: 4. Mitgliederversammlungssitzung, 30 April 1969.

14. CULDA/OS72/13.5: Brauer, Aktenvermerk, 14 March 1972.

15. BAK/B136/5561.

16. Interview with Werner Rabe, 21 November 2003.

17. DOA/Nachlaß Daume/534: Daume to Vogel, 19 December 1968.

18. CULDA/Koebsel/IV.1: 15. Vorstandssitzung, 29 April 1969.

19. DOA/Nachlaß Daume/546: Hohenemser (also on behalf of Hans Dürrmeier, Anton Stankowski, Werner Wirsing) to Daume, 28 May 1969. Dürrmeier was chair of the PR committee, Hohenemser chair of the arts committee; Stankowski chair of the design committee, and Werner Wirsing a leading member of the latter. While Nestler went through with retiring from his position in protest with immediate effect (to return later in an important function for the Games as designer of the annex to the Haus der Kunst for the World Cultures exhibit), Hohenemser, along with Dürrmeier and Stankowski, remained in post.

20. BAK/B185/2155: Aicher, Das Erscheinungsbild der Olympischen Spiele, München 1972, p. 13.

21. CULDA/Koebsel/III.1: 4. Mitgliederversammlungssitzung, 30 April 1969.

22. Ibid.

23. "Rasse veredeln," *Der Spiegel*, 13 December 1971.

24. BAK/B185/2976: Peter Hoffmann, Zum Kampf der Wagen und Gesänge, Bayerischer Rundfunk, 20 October 1968.

25. CULDA/Koebsel/IV.1: 15. Vorstandssitzung, 29 April 1969.

26. On Ruhnau see Winfried Nerdinger, "Aufbrüche und Kontinuitäten—Positionen der Nachkriegsarchitektur in der Bundesrepublik," in Nerdinger, ed., *Architektur der Wunderkinder: Aufbruch und Verdrängung in Bayern 1945–1960* (Salzburg, 2005), pp. 14, 18 and Michael Hesse, ed., *Baumeister im Ruhrgebiet*, vol. 1: *Werner Ruhnau* (Gelsenkirchen, 2002).

27. CULDA/Koebsel/IV.2: 17. Vorstandssitzung, 21–22 November 1969.

28. CULDA/Koebsel/IV.2: 18. Vorstandssitzung, 23 January 1970.

29. CULDA Koebsel/IV.2.

30. Interview with Werner and Anita Ruhnau, 23 February 2004.

31. See, for example, Dietmar N. Schmidt, "Ein Jahrmarkt der Künste," *Frankfurter Rundschau*, 2 September 1972.

32. See CULDA/Koebsel/IV.3: 23. Vorstandssitzung, 11 October 1971.

33. Diem, "Mit Carl Orff im Olympiapark: 'Spielstraße—eine Beleidigung Olympias,'" *sid*-Olympia-Ausgabe, 5 September 1972.

34. Interview with Werner and Anita Ruhnau, 23 February 2004.

35. CULDA/Koebsel/IV.2: 21. Vorstandssitzung, 8–9 January 1971.

36. CULDA/OS72/6.9: Behnisch, Konzept "Kunst auf dem Oberwiesenfeld," 25 July 1969.

37. Paul Ryder Ryan, "Thing of a Day," *The Drama Review: TDR* 16, no. 4, December 1972, p. 66.

38. BAK/B185/2972: Zusammenfassung "Spiel im Sinn des totalen Theaters," 17 November 1968.

39. Interview with Werner and Anita Ruhnau, 23 February 2004.

40. BAK/B185/3188: Daume, "Moderne Lebensformen für den Sport," 25 April 1970, quoting directly from Huizinga.

41. John M. Hoberman, *Sport and Political Ideology* (Austin, 1984), p. 44.

42. BAK/B185/2980: 1. Sitzung "Arbeitskreis Straßentheater," 27 February 1970.

43. Deutscher Sportbund, ed. *Willi Daume: Deutscher Sport 1952–1972* (Munich, 1973), pp. 316–17.

44. See BAK/B185/2610: 1. and 2. Sitzung "Arbeitskreis Straßentheater," 27 February and 4 May 1970.

45. BAK/B185/2978: Göhling to Honecker, 23 June 1971.

46. Werner Ruhnau, *Spielstrassen (Bildende Kunst, Theater . . .)* (Castrop-Rauxel, no date), p. 16.

47. This interpretation was given in a contemporary documentary on the *Spielstraße* produced by London Weekend Television and broadcast by the BBC a few weeks after the Games.

48. BAK/B185/2980: Erich Promoli to Göhling, Planungsauftrag für babbelplast-Objekte, 22 February 1972.

49. Klaus Bieringer, "Kulturprogramm—ein olympischer Auftrag," in Volker Rattemeyer, ed., *Kunst + Design, Kultur Olympia. Willi Daume, Preisträger der Stankowski-Stiftung 1986* (Kassel, 1986), p. 29.

50. There were 650,000 people who attended the other cultural events (Organizing Committee for the Games of the XXth Olympiad Munich 1972, ed., *Die Spiele: The Official Report,* vol. 1: *The Organization* [Munich, 1972], p. 236).

51. CULDA/Koebsel/IV.3: 26. Vorstandssitzung, 22 January 1973.

52. See, for example, BAK/B185/2979: Hans Maier to OC, 9 September 1972.

53. Interview with Werner and Anita Ruhnau, 23 February 2004.

54. BAK/B185/2979: Frank Burckner, Die Geschichte der Olympischen Spiele. Szenario, 15 March 1971.

55. See *Die Spiele: The Official Report,* vol. 1, p. 252.

56. BAK/B185/2979: Burckner, Szenario, 15 March 1971.

57. BAK/B185/2979: Ruhnau to Burckner, 25 August 1971.

58. CULDA/OS72/6.7: Anke Roeder, Workshop Spielstraße, 27.6.1972.

59. Ryder Ryan, "Thing of a Day," p. 81.

60. CULDA/OS72/6.7: Roeder, Workshop Spielstraße, 27.6.1972.

61. Ryder Ryan, "Thing of a Day," p. 84.

62. Interview with Werner and Anita Ruhnau, 23 February 2004.

63. See Thomas Meyer, "Die Schizophrenie der Olympischen Restspiele," *Frankfurter Allgemeine Zeitung,* 11 September 1972.

64. CULDA/Koebsel/IV.3: 3. außerordentliche Vorstandssitzung, 6 September 1972.

65. H. Mislewitz, "Spielstraßen-Künstler protestieren," *Neue Rhein Zeitung,* 11 September 1972.

66. For the city's response to this critique, see StAMü/Olympiade 1972/194: Hubert Abreß to Katholische Landjugend Bayerns, 12 June 1970.

67. Hoberman, *Sport and Political Ideology,* p. 235.

68. Judt, *Postwar,* p. 401.

69. John M. Hoberman, *The Olympic Crisis: Sport, Politics, and the Moral Order* (New Rochelle, 1986), pp. 109–10.

70. Ulrike Prokop, *Soziologie der Olympischen Spiele: Sport und Kapitalismus* (Munich, 1971), p. 124.

71. StAMü/Olympiade 1972/194: Bero Rigauer, Die Sportkritik der neuen Linken, Thesenpapier für "Olympische Spiele contra und pro." Evangelische Akademie Tutzing, 3.-5.11.1970 and Noel to Vogel, 6 November 1970.

72. Joachim Neu, "Studentenschaft zwischen 'Olympismus' und 'Anti-Olympia': Die ambivalente Haltung des Hochschulsports zur Olympischen Bewegung unter besonderer Berücksichtigung des olympischen Jugend- und Studentenlagers München 1972," in Hans-Jürgen Schulke, ed., *Die Zukunft der Olympischen Spiele: Die Olympische Bewegung zwischen Moskau und Montreal* (Cologne, 1976), p. 198.

73. Ibid., pp. 199–200.

74. See, for example, Hans Klingbeil, "Goldmedaille für Weitspucken," *Düsseldorfer Nachrichten,* 26 January 1971 and Adolf Metzner, "Sie werden uns lynchen. München: Protestaktionen eines anti-olympischen Komitees," *Die Zeit,* 13 February 1970.

75. DOA/Nachlaß Daume/Texte Daume 2: "Olympische Spiele und soziale Modernität," 17 April 1972; BAK/B185/3188: Daume, "Moderne Lebensformen für den Sport," 25 April 1970.

76. DOA/Nachlaß Daume/42: "Sport für alle. Die Demokratisierung des Sports." Mexico City, 8 October 1968.

77. CULDA/Koebsel/IV.2: 17. Vorstandssitzung , 21–22 November 1969; see the preparatory volume Ommo Grupe, Dietrich Kurz, and Johannes Marcus Teipel, eds., *The Scientific View of Sport: Perspectives—Aspects—Issues* (Berlin, Heidelberg, New York, 1972) and the congress report, Grupe, Kurz, and Teipel, eds., *Sport in the Modern World—Chances and Problems* (Berlin, Heidelberg, New York, 1973).

78. BAK/B106/36163: Flitner, Bemerkungen zum Kongreß-Thema (July 1968).

79. Hans Lenk, *Leistungssport, Ideologie oder Mythos? Zur Leistungskritik und Sportphilosophie,* (Stuttgart, 1972), pp. 37–38.

80. *Die Spiele: The Official Report,* vol. 1, pp. 265–66.

81. CULDA/Koebsel/IV.2: 14. Vorstandssitzung, 11 March 1969.

82. CULDA/OS72/8.2: Erich Heine, Joachim Neu, and Franz Nitsch, Bericht über das Jugend- und Studentenlager, 1 November 1972.

83. Neu, "Studentenschaft zwischen Olympismus und Anti-Olympia," p. 205.

84. CULDA/OS72/8.2: Heine, Neu, and Nitsch, Bericht über das Jugend- und Studentenlager.

85. Harald Pieper, ed., *Olympische Zaungäste: Das andere Olympiabuch* (Frankfurt am Main, 1972), pp. 112, 98, 31.

86. See, for example, BayHStA/MInn/88570: Einsatz im Englischen Garten, 26. August 1972, 1 September 1972.

87. *Die Spiele: The Official Report,* vol. 1, p. 383.

88. DOA/Nachlaß Daume/29: Daume, Rede anläßlich der Eröffnung des Jugendlagers, 26 August 1972.

89. CULDA/OS72/8.3: Entwurf einer Lagerordnung.

90. *Die Spiele: The Official Report,* vol. 1, p. 384.

91. CULDA/OS72/8.3: 7. Jugendlagerausschußsitzung, 28 September 1970.

92. Pieper, *Olympische Zaungäste,* pp. 67–68.

93. CULDA/OS72/8.2: Anlagen 7 and 8.

94. CULDA/OS72/8.2: Anzahl der Verpflegungsteilnehmer vom 12.8.-16.9.1972.

95. Pieper, *Olympische Zaungäste,* p. 76; CULDA/OS72/8.2: ADH, Dokumentation zum olympischen Jugendlager, Rudolf Großkopff, "Über Vietnam wollten auch die Russen nicht diskutieren."

96. Pieper, *Olympische Zaungäste,* pp. 50, 84–85.

97. CULDA/OS72/8.2: Heine, Neu, and Nitsch, Bericht über das Jugend- und Studentenlager.

98. CULDA/OS72/8.1: BRD-Studentendelegation, Das Recht auf freie Meinungsäußerung/Freedom of Speech, 25 August 1972, flyer.

99. See "Protestversuch," *Frankfurter Allgemeine Zeitung,* 28 August 1972 and Peter Pragal, "Rote Fähnchen im olympischen Flaggenwald," *Süddeutsche Zeitung,* 1 September 1972.

100. CULDA/OS72/8.2: *Olympix, Zeitung für das olympische Jugendlager* 1, 21 August 1972.

101. CULDA/OS72/8.2: *Olympix,* 3/4, 7 September 1972.

102. Ibid.

103. CULDA/OS72/8.2: Hans-Joachim Körner, Bericht über das olympische Jugendlager, draft.

104. CULDA/OS72/8.2: *Olympix* 3/4, 7 September 1972.

105. Christiane Eisenberg, *"English Sports" und deutsche Bürger: Eine Gesellschaftsgeschichte, 1800–1939* (Paderborn, 1999), p. 418.

106. On Schreiber's appointment see the documentation in BAK/B185/3129.

107. See, for example, Manfred Schreiber, "Das Geschehen am 5./6. September," *Münchner Polizei* 19, 1972, pp. 4–10.

108. See Schreiber, "Das Jahr 1968 in München," pp. 36–37 and 50–52.

109. See Michael Sturm, " 'Wildgewordene Obrigkeit?' Die Rolle der Münchner Polizei während der "Schwabinger Krawalle," in Gerhard Fürmetz, ed., *"Schwabinger Krawalle": Protest, Polizei und Öffentlichkeit zu Beginn der 60er Jahre* (Essen, 2006), pp. 100–101; Thomas Kleinknecht and Michael Sturm, " 'Demonstrationen sind punktuelle Plebiszite:' Polizeireform und gesellschaftliche Demokratisierung von den Sechziger- zu den Achtzigerjahren," *Archiv für Sozialgeschichte* 44, 2004, pp. 208–11; Klaus Weinhauer, " 'Staatsbürger mit Sehnsucht nach Harmonie'—Gesellschaftsbild und Staatsverständnis in der Polizei,"

in Axel Schildt, Detlef Siegfried, and Karl Christian Lammers, eds., *Dynamische Zeiten: Die 60er Jahre in den beiden deutschen Gesellschaften* (Hamburg, 2000), pp. 453–54, 467–68.

110. See Schreiber, "Das Jahr 1968 in München," p. 39; Thomas, *Protest Movements,* pp. 173–5.

111. CULDA/Koebsel/IV.2: 17. Vorstandssitzung, 21–22 November 1969.

112. Ibid.

113. See StAMü/Olympiade 1972/602: Schreiber, Begründung eines Gesetzes über den Olympischen Frieden, 11 November 1972; Gesetz zum Schutz des Olympischen Friedens (31.5.1972), *Bundesgesetzblatt* 48, 1972, p. 865.

114. CULDA/Koebsel/IV.2: 20. and 21. Vorstandssitzung, 1 July 1970 and 8–9 January 1971.

115. CULDA/Koebsel/IV.9: Vorlage "Gesetz für den Olympischen Frieden."

116. BayHStA/MInn/88570: Polizeiführungsstab München to Heinrich v. Martin, 14 September 1972.

117. CULDA/Koebsel/IV.3: 2. außerordentliche Vorstandssitzung, 23 August 1972.

118. See BAK/B185/2977: Reinhard Rupprecht to Margot Berthold, 18 June 1970.

119. CULDA/OS72/6.7: Konzept der Spielstraße, Die künstlerischen Vorschläge incl. Kostenschätzung.

120. BAK/B185/2979: Gutachten des Instituts für Schall- und Wärmeschutz, Essen, 2 February 1972.

121. BAK/B185/3246: Ruhnau, betr.: Popmusik, 28 June 1972.

122. CULDA/OS72/6.9: Ruhnau to Promoli, 23 April 1971.

123. Siegfried, *Time Is on My Side,* p. 409.

124. BayHStA/MInn/88570: Beatveranstaltung im Kongreßsaal des Deutschen Museums (30.8.1972), 1 September1972.

125. BAK/B185/2979: Daniel Spiegel, Vermerk über ein Gespräch mit Georg Wolf am 12.6.1972.

126. BAK/B185/3246: Ronny d'Ancona to Spiegel, 12 May 1972.

127. "Pop-Musik für Olympia. 'Spielstraße' mit 3 Millionen Etat," *Der Musikmarkt,* no. 19, 1971.

128. BAK/B185/3246: Vermerk: Besprechung über das Auftreten von Beat-Gruppen, 5 May 1972.

129. BayHStA/MInn/88585: Schreiber, betr.: Veranstaltungen von Beatkonzerten, 12 June 1972.

130. BAK/B185/3246: Bavarian Interior Ministry, betr.: Veranstaltungen von Beatkonzerten, 26 June 1972.

131. BAK/B185/3246: Correspondence between Spiegel and Schreiber, 18 to 24 May 1972; BAK/B185/2979: Spiegel, Gespräch mit Georg Wolf am 12.6.1972.

132. BayHStA/MInn/88594: Vorbereitung der Olympischen Spiele, Wildes Lagern im Freien, 19 June 1972.

133. See, for instance, Schreiber's warning to refugees and foreign "guest workers" before the Games: "Perpetrators of any incident can reckon with the full force of law as it pertains to foreigners and asylum legislation. Should the intentions of the Federal Republic be

seriously impaired, measures will follow immediately resulting in the termination of residence within federal territory." (ACSP/Nachlaß Klein/42: Entwurf für eine Rede Manfred Schreibers an die ausländischen Mitbürger, August 1972)

134. BayHStA/MInn/88620: Merkblatt: Aufgaben, Ausbildung, Organisation und Arbeitsweise des Ordnungsdienstes und seine Abgrenzung zur Polizei, November 1971.

135. BayHStA/MInn/88564: Referat für Polizeikräfte aus dem Bereich Angewandte Psychologie.

136. See CULDA/Vorhammer/XI: Schulungs- und Informationsmappe für Führungskräfte des Ordnungsdienstes, May 1972.

137. BayHStA/MInn/88571: Mögliche Störsituationen während der Olympischen Spiele, 18 October 1971.

138. BAK/B185/3230: Manfred Schreiber, Tätigkeitsbericht der Abteilung XIII.

139. Ibid.

140. CULDA/Koebsel/IV.2: 21. Vorstandssitzung, 8–9 January 1971.

141. BayHStA/MInn/88570: Einsatz anläßlich des Jesus-Festivals am 2.9.1972, 14 September 1972.

142. Richard Mandell, *The Olympics of 1972: A Munich Diary* (Chapel Hill, NC, 1991), pp. 60–61.

143. "Die Größten," *Sport Illustrierte,* 19 September 1972, p. 63.

144. Heide Rosendahl, *Die Fahrten der Deutschen Sportjugend zu den Olympischen Spielen (1952–1964)* (Diplomarbeit, Sporthochschule Köln, Wintersemester 1968–69), pp. 5–7.

145. DOA/Nachlaß Daume/587: W. Hollmann to Daume, 15 February 1971.

6. EAST VERSUS WEST

1. Mary Elise Sarotte, *Dealing with the Devil: East Germany, Détente, and Ostpolitik, 1969–1973* (Chapel Hill, 2001), p. 249, note 48.

2. BAK/B137/8474: Interview des Bundeskanzlers mit *sid,* 23 March 1971.

3. William Glenn Gray, *Germany's Cold War: The Global Campaign to Isolate East Germany, 1949–1969* (Chapel Hill, 2003), p. 105.

4. Christoph Kleßmann, *Zwei Staaten, eine Nation: Deutsche Geschichte 1955–1970* (Bonn, 2nd ed. 1997), p. 102.

5. Gray, *Germany's Cold War,* pp. 69, 106.

6. Werner Kilian, *Die Hallstein-Doktrin: Der diplomatische Krieg zwischen der BRD und der DDR 1955–1973. Aus den Akten der beiden deutschen Außenministerien* (Berlin, 2001), p. 260.

7. Martin H. Geyer, "Der Kampf um nationale Repräsentation: Deutsch-deutsche Sportbeziehungen und die 'Hallstein-Doktrin,'" *Vierteljahrshefte für Zeitgeschichte* 44, 1996, p. 67; see also Martin H. Geyer, "On the Road to a German 'Postnationalism': Athletic Competition between the Two German States in the Era of Konrad Adenauer," *German Politics & Society* 25, no. 2, 2007, pp. 140–67.

8. Tobias Blasius, *Olympische Bewegung, Kalter Krieg und Deutschlandpolitik 1949–1972* (Frankfurt am Main, 2001), p. 249.

9. Geyer, "Der Kampf um nationale Repräsentation," p. 79.

10. IOC Lausanne/Brundage/Correspondences 1962–1963: Brundage to Otto Mayer, 6 April and 13 May 1963.

11. UIUC Archives/Brundage Collection/Box 130: Brundage to the West and East German NOCs, 2 June 1965.

12. Robert Edelman, "Moscow 1980: Stalinism or Good, Clean Fun?" in Alan Tomlinson and Christopher Young, *National Identity and Global Sports Events: Culture, Politics, and Spectacle in the Olympics and the Football World Cup* (New York, 2006), p. 156.

13. UIUC Archives/Brundage Collection/Box 50: Andrianow to the IOC.

14. DOA/Nachlaß Daume/Texte—Daume 1: Rede zum IOC-Kongreß in Baden-Baden, October 1963.

15. Edelman, "Moscow 1980," pp. 156–57.

16. UIUC Archives/Avery Brundage Collection/Box 50: Brundage to Andrianow, 18 March 1967.

17. Heinz Schöbel, *Olympia and its Games* (Leipzig, 1966).

18. Heinz Schöbel, "Die Verwirklichung des humanistischen Gehalts der olympischen Idee in der sozialistischen Gesellschaft," *Wissenschaftliche Zeitschrift DHfK* 12, no. 3, 1970, p. 12. On humanism see exactly this argument in Helmut Behrendt to Brundage, 12 September 1964 (UIUC Archives/Brundage Collection/Box 130).

19. UIUC Archives/Brundage Collection/Box 130: Schöbel to Brundage, 31 July 1969, from which the quotation is taken, and Box 62: Brundage to Schöbel, 27 November 1964 and 2 March 1965.

20. UIUC Archives/Brundage Collection/Box 62: The Life of Avery Brundage.

21. The East Germans presented Brundage with a set of Meissen porcelain; the West Germans with a ceramic bowl, a Meissen vase, and his favorite vintage wine, with a note from Daume—before the potentially prickly IOC session on the German question in Tehran in 1967—which said: "a very famous wine, reserved for kings (Olympic kings included)."

22. In 1972, "Johnny" Klein was responsible for the translation of Brundage's memoirs into German (*Avery Brundage—bekannt und unbekannt* [Munich, 1972]). The West Germans also invited him frequently to write prefaces for their celebratory volumes, often ghostwriting his piece in advance, for example, *Olympic Games 1964—Innsbruck—Tokyo*, a volume to celebrate the seventy-fifth anniversary of the "German" NOC.

23. See, for instance, Kilian, *Die Hallstein-Doktrin*, p. 252 and, in general, Blasius, *Olympische Bewegung, Kalter Krieg und Deutschlandpolitik*.

24. Geyer, "Der Kampf um nationale Repräsentation," p. 58.

25. IOC Lausanne/Daume/Correspondence 1957–1972: Daume to Brundage, 7 January 1957.

26. IOC Lausanne/Brundage/Correspondence 1962–1963: Mayer to Brundage, 16 January 1963.

27. BAK/B322/433: Liselott Diem to Daume, 20 December 1961.

28. IOC Lausanne/Brundage/Correspondence 1962–1963: Brundage to Mayer, 26 January 1963.

29. BAK/B137/16432: Embassy Tokyo to Foreign Office, 19 November 1964.

30. BAK/B137/16432: Daume, Speech at the IOC session in Tokyo, 7 October 1964.

31. BAK/B137/16432: Foreign Office to Interior Ministry and other ministries, 4 February 1965.

32. BAK/B137/16432: Embassy Tokyo to Foreign Office, 19 November 1964.

33. BAK/B137/16432: Foreign Office to Interior Ministry, Gesamtdeutsche Olympia-Mannschaft, 16 March 1965.

34. Uta Andrea Balbier, *Kalter Krieg auf der Aschenbahn: Der deutsch-deutsche Sport 1950–1972. Eine politische Geschichte* (Paderborn, 2007), pp. 124–25.

35. Lorenz Peiffer, Manuscript on East-West German Sports Relations (2005), pp. 9–10, 21.

36. PAAA Berlin/MfAA, C100/72: Büro Stibi an alle Länderabteilungen, 10 October 1965.

37. Peiffer, Manuscript, pp. 14–15.

38. BAK/B137/16432: Vermerk, Gesamtdeutsche Olympia-Mannschaft, 1 April 1965.

39. The Foreign Office calculated that since a simple majority of the sixty to sixty-two (out of a total of sixty-nine) IOC members was needed, thirty-two votes would suffice. According to feedback from their embassies, they could reckon with a minimum of thirty-six and a maximum of forty-five votes. (PAAA Berlin/B94/1604: Aufzeichnungen, 23 September 1965 and 30 September 1965, which includes comments of members from noncommunist countries)

40. Peiffer, Manuscript, p. 14.

41. UIUC Archives/Brundage Collection/Box 129: Daume to IOC members, 30 September 1965; DOA/Nachlaß Daume/561: Speech at the IOC session in Madrid, October 1965.

42. There were only five votes against the motion (Kilian, *Die Hallstein-Doktrin,* p. 270; Balbier, *Kalter Krieg auf der Aschenbahn,* p. 126).

43. Robert Geipel, Ilse Helbrecht, and Jürgen Pohl. "Die Münchner Olympischen Spiele von 1972 als Instrument der Stadtentwicklungspolitik," in Hartmut Häußermann and Walter Siebel, eds., *Festivalisierung der Stadtpolitik: Stadtentwicklung durch große Projekte, Leviathan. Zeitschrift für Sozialwissenschaft* (Sonderheft 13, 1993), p. 280.

44. BAB/SAPMO/DY 30/IV A2/18–4: Rudi Hellmann to Honecker, 11 March 1966.

45. For instance, at an extraordinary meeting of the West German NOC, 18 December 1965 (see Blasius, *Olympische Bewegung, Kalter Krieg und Deutschlandpolitik,* p. 293).

46. UIUC Archives/Brundage Collection/Box 130: Brundage to the West and East German NOCs, 2 June 1965.

47. Peiffer, Manuscript, p. 20.

48. Interview Vogel, February 1996, p. 1.

49. Hans-Jochen Vogel, *Die Amtskette: Meine 12 Münchner Jahre. Ein Erlebnisbericht* (Munich, 1972), p. 98.

50. There are two versions of this meeting. According to Vogel's 1972 account, Erhard's second concern related to the German-German problem and the question of East German participation in the Games if Munich's bid were successful (*Die Amtskette,* pp. 98–99). However, in a 1996 interview Vogel claimed that the latter played no role in the discussion (Interview Vogel, February 1996, p. 2). This version is confirmed in a memo from the meeting,

written by a civil servant in the chancellery. After listening to Daume's explanation why Berlin did not stand a chance for political reasons, Erhard declared "that given his generally positive attitude toward sport and the Olympics he would naturally be pleased to see the Games being held in the Federal Republic. . . . He would be in favor of Munich, but he needed to ask what costs would arise from it." (BAK/B136/5566: Grundschöttel, Vermerk über die Besprechung am 29. November 1965)

51. PAAA Berlin/94/1605: Auszug aus Kurzprotokoll über die 6. Kabinettssitzung am 2. Dezember 1965.

52. StAMü/Olympiade 1972/1–2: Lücke to Vogel, 8 Dezember 1965.

53. Kleßmann, *Zwei Staaten, eine Nation,* pp. 96–97.

54. Torsten Oppelland, *Gerhard Schröder (1910–1989): Politik zwischen Staat, Partei und Konfession* (Düsseldorf, 2002), p. 626.

55. StAMü/Olympiade 1972/524: Interior Ministry to Ernst Knoesel, 23 March 1966 (our emphasis) and Lydie Zanchi to Knoesel, 24 January 1966, 18 March and 23 March 1966; see also BayHStA/MWi/28395: Vogel to Cornelius von Hovora, 7 February 1966.

56. StAMü/BuR/3156: Entwurf der Antworten zum Fragebogen des IOK.

57. StAMü/Olympiade 1972/524: Zanchi to Knoesel, 23 March 1966.

58. Blasius, *Olympische Bewegung, Kalter Krieg und Deutschlandpolitik,* pp. 268–69.

59. BAK/B136/5566: Daume to Lücke, 21 February 1966.

60. NOK-Archiv Frankfurt/6A414: Daume to Andrianow, 15 April 1966 and, more conciliatory, 9 March 1966.

61. NOK-Archiv Frankfurt/6A414: Daume to Brundage, 18 April 1966.

62. NOK-Archiv Frankfurt/6A414: Andrianow, "Römischer Kalender," translation from *Sovietski Sport,* 13 April 1966.

63. BAB/SAPMO/DY 12/9245/BÜ365: Günther Heinze to Präsidium des Ministerrats, 15 March 1966; Alfred Heil, Aktennotiz für Sekretariatsmitglieder, 9 March 1965.

64. BAK/B106/36167: Foreign Office to Interior Ministry, 23 March 1966.

65. Blasius, *Olympische Bewegung, Kalter Krieg und Deutschlandpolitik,* pp. 296–97.

66. BAK/B106/36167: Hans Schäfer to Daume, 18 April 1966; see also StAMü/Olympiade 1972/524: Noel to Vogel, Draft declaration for the IOC, 15 April 1966.

67. StAMü/Olympiade 1972/524: von Hovora to Andreas Kohl, 4 April 1966.

68. BAK/B136/5566: Daume to Erhard, 20 April 1966.

69. PAAA Berlin 94/1605: Auszug aus Kurzprotokoll über die 23. Kabinettssitzung am 20. April 1966.

70. BAK/B136/5566: Mercker, Vormerkung für Lücke, 21 April 1966 and Daume to Erhard mit Zusatz von v. Herwarth, 22 April 1966.

71. StAMü/BuR/3156: Declaration without place, date, and signature and Vogel, *Die Amtskette,* p. 103; see also StAMü/Olympiade 1972/1–2: Lücke to Vogel, 8 Dezember 1965.

72. BAK/B136/5566: Ludger Westrick, Memo for Erhard, 21 April 1966.

73. BAK/B136/5566: Mercker to Daume, 22 April 1966.

74. BAK/B136/5566: Mercker to Gesamtdeutsches Ministerium, 23 April 1966; Daume to Erhard mit Zusatz von v. Herwarth, 22 April 1966; see also Interview Vogel, February 1996, pp. 11–2.

75. Cited in Blasius, *Olympische Bewegung, Kalter Krieg und Deutschlandpolitik,* p. 264.

76. PAAA Berlin/MfAA C100/72: Konzeption für weitere Tätigkeit der DDR-Sportverbände in den internationalen Förderationen (November 1965).

77. Lorenz Peiffer, "Die Madrider Entscheidung des IOC im Oktober 1965. Ein Wendepunkt in der Geschichte der deutsch-deutchen Sportbeziehungen," in Arnd Krüger and Wolfgang Buss, eds., *Transformationen: Kontinuituäten und Veränderungen in der Sportgeschichte* (Hoya, 2002), pp. 118–24. The figures for contests in the GDR (which were very similar to those which took place in the Federal Republic) were 1961: 738; 1966: 52; 1967: 48; 1968: 32; 1969: 43; 1970: 13; 1971: 8; 1972: 7.

78. See Gray, *Germany's Cold War,* pp. 140–41, 144–45, 159, 163, 174.

79. Ibid., p. 191.

80. Ibid., p. 187.

81. StAMü/Olympiade 1972/524: Infas report, 20 February 1967.

82. BAK/B137/16432: Auszug aus Kurzprotokoll über die 41. Kabinettssitzung am 31. August 1966.

83. StAMü/Olympiade 1972/524: Vogel to Willy Brandt, 12 September 1966.

84. BAK/B137/16432: Kabinettsvorlage betreffend Behandlung der Flaggen-, Hymnen- und Emblemfrage, September 1966.

85. Gray, *Germany's Cold War,* p. 219.

86. Ibid., p. 190.

87. BAK/B106/36168: Daume, Memorandum zur Flaggen- und Hymnen-Frage, 28 June 1968 (written by K. H. Gieseler).

88. Peiffer, Manuscript, p. 22. The joint teams were in handball, four times until 1961; and rowing, once in 1962.

89. Kilian, *Die Hallstein-Doktrin,* p. 264.

90. PAAA Berlin/B33/478: Embassy Mexico City, Politischer Jahresbericht 1965, 17 January 1966.

91. PAAA Berlin/B33/478: Foreign Office to Embassy Mexico City, no date.

92. PAAA Berlin/B94/1600: Werner Klingeberg to Foreign Office, 12 November 1966.

93. PAAA Berlin/B94/1600: Embassy Mexico City to Foreign Office, 24 October 1966.

94. This observation is based on assessments of the event by both Daume and the GDR; see PAAA Berlin/B94/1602: Daume to Foreign Office, 22 June 1967; BAB/SAPMO/DY 30/IVA2/18/4: Stellungnahme des Präsidiums des DTSB, 20 October 1966.

95. PAAA Berlin/B94/1600: Foreign Office to Embassy Mexico City, 19 September 1966.

96. BAB/SAPMO/DY 30/IVA2/18/4: Stellungnahme des Präsidiums des DTSB, 20 October 1966.

97. BAK/B106/36168: Gutachten von Karl Doehning.

98. BAK/B106/36168: Vermerk, Sowjetzonale Symbole bei Sportveranstaltungen, December 1967.

99. BAK/B106/36168: Daume, Memorandum zur Flaggen- und Hymnen-Frage, 28 June 1968.

100. DOA/Nachlaß Daume/534: Daume to Vogel, 28 November 1966.

101. BAB/SAPMO/DY 30/IVA2/18: Manfred Ewald to Honecker, Maßnahmen zur Weiterführung des Kampfes der Sportorganisationen, 11 October 1966.

102. PAAA Berlin/B94/1605: Besprechung über die Behandlung sowjetischer Symbole, 3 October 1967.

103. Gray, *Germany's Cold War,* p. 199.

104. Ibid., p. 200.

105. Blasius, *Olympische Bewegung, Kalter Krieg und Deutschlandpolitik,* pp. 280–83. Several letters from this period display a frank exchange of views on the relationship between Daume and State Secretary Rolf Lahr (StAMü/Olympiade 1972/524: Daume to Vogel, 8 December 1966; Vogel to Klaus Schütz, 12 December 1966; Schütz to Vogel, 23 December 1966).

106. BAK/B137/16432: Auszug aus Kurzprotokoll über die 41. Kabinettssitzung am 31. August 1966; PAAA Berlin/B90/870: Nagel, Diplogerma Mexiko, September 1968.

107. PAAA Berlin/B94/1605: Foreign Office to Interior Ministry, 14 April 1967.

108. PAAA Berlin/B94/1605: Vermerk, Sitzung des IOC in Teheran, 28 April 1967.

109. Blasius, *Olympische Bewegung, Kalter Krieg und Deutschlandpolitik,* p. 302.

110. PAAA Berlin/B94/1605: Aufzeichnung, Mannschafts-, Flaggen- und Hymnenfrage.

111. StAMü/Olympiade 1972/524: Daume, Notiz, 28 September 1967.

112. BAK/B137/36167: Kabinettsvorlage, Auswirkungen des Beschlusses des IOK, December 1968.

113. BAK/B106/36167: Gesamtdeutsche Belange bei der Organisation und Durchführung der Olympischen Spiele 1972, 14 August 1968.

114. Balbier, *Kalter Krieg auf der Aschenbahn,* p. 163.

115. PAAA Berlin/B90/870: Nagel, Diplogerma Mexiko, September 1968.

116. UIUC Archives/Brundage Collection/Box 130: Schöbel to Brundage, 29 September 1968.

117. BAK/B106/36168: Gespräch mit dem Attaché des NOK der "DDR" Horst Hübner am 17 August 1968.

118. *sid*-Olympia-Ausgabe, 12 October 1968.

119. IOC Lausanne/Daume/Correspondence 1957–1972: Brundage to Daume, undated draft, summer 1968.

120. UIUC Archives/Brundage Collection/Box 130: Schöbel to Brundage, 18 June 1968.

121. UIUC Archives/Brundage Collection/Box 130: Schöbel to Brundage, 11 October 1968.

122. BAK/B106/36167: Embassy Mexico City to Foreign Office, 13 October 1968.

123. Gray, *Germany's Cold War,* p. 204.

124. PAAA Berlin/B90/870: Nagel, Diplogerma Mexiko, September 1968.

125. PAAA Berlin/B90/870: Aufzeichnung, IOC-Beschluß in der deutschen Frage.

126. Blasius, *Olympische Bewegung, Kalter Krieg und Deutschlandpolitik,* pp. 305–7.

127. Mayor Drapeau told Vogel this personally and offered Montreal at the IOC session in Mexico; see BAK/B137/36167: Kabinettsvorlage, Auswirkungen des Beschlusses des IOK, December 1968; StAMü/Olympiade 1972/524: Daume to Vogel, 24 April 1967; Vogel to Brandt and Herbert Wehner, 8 July 1968.

128. BAK/B137/16432: Auszug aus Kurzprotokoll über die 144. Kabinettssitzung am 29. Oktober 1968.

129. BAK/B137/16432: Auszug aus Kurzprotokoll über die 142. Kabinettssitzung am 16. Oktober 1968.

130. BAK/B137/36167: Kabinettsvorlage, Auswirkungen des Beschlusses des IOK, December 1968.

131. Balbier, *Kalter Krieg auf der Aschenbahn*, p. 165.

132. StAMü/Olympiade 1972/524: Noel to Vogel, Auswertung der DDR-Sportpresse, insbesondere *Deutsches Sportecho*, 20 November 1968.

133. PAAA Berlin/MfAA C111/72: Betr. IOC-Beschluß vom 12.10.1968, 16 October 1968.

134. Joachim Scholtyseck, *Die Außenpolitik der DDR* (Munich, 2003), p. 118.

135. BAK/B137/16432: Auszug aus Kurzprotokoll über die 151. Kabinettssitzung am 18. Dezember 1968. It maintained, of course, that its action had no "relevance for international law" (StAMü/Olympiade 1972/524: Ernst Benda to Daume, 19 December 1968).

136. BAK/B137/16432: Auszug aus Kurzprotokoll über die 150. Kabinettssitzung am 11. Dezember 1968.

137. PAAA Berlin/B90/870: Aufzeichnung, Bezeichnung der beiden deutschen Olympischen Mannschaften, 24 January 1969.

138. BAK/B106/36167: Neufassung des Entscheidungsvorschläge (8 July 1969).

139. Gray, *Germany's Cold War*, pp. 232–33.

140. IFS Archiv Hannover/Handakte Martius: Foreign Office to all embassies and consulates (in non-NATO states), 1 April 1970.

141. Largely, although not entirely, as suggested by Blasius *Olympische Bewegung, Kalter Krieg und Deutschlandpolitik*, pp. 307–8; see PAAA Berlin/B41/86: Gespräch des Staatssekretärs mit Daume am 19. Februar 1971, 17 February 1971 and Betr.: Olympische Spiele München 1972, 17 March 1971.

142. See, for instance, Daume's speech at the ceremony to mark Bundespräsident Heinemann's patronage of the Games in November 1969 (BAK/B122/15028: Vermerk, Empfang des Bundespräsidenten, 26 November 1969) and, two years later, Brandt's speech at the third session of the OC Beirat on 24 September 1971 (BAK/B106/36117).

143. An excellent bibliographical overview is offered by Lorenz Peiffer and Matthias Fink, *Zum Forschungsstand der Geschichte von Körperkultur und Sport in der DDR: Eine kommentierte Bibliografie* (Cologne, 2003). See also Roland Naul and Ken Hardman, "Sport and Physical Education in the two Germanies, 1945–90," in Naul and Hardman, eds., *Sport and Physical Education in Germany* (London, 2002), pp. 29–76; Gertrud Pfister, *Frauen und Sport in der DDR* (Cologne, 2002); Andreas Ritter, *Wandlungen in der Steuerung des DDR-Hochleistungssports in den 1960er und 1970er Jahren* (Potsdam, 2003).

144. StAMü/Olympiade 1972/524: Noel to Vogel, Auswertung der Sportpresse der DDR, insbesondere *Deutsches Sportecho*, 20 November 1968.

145. BAB/SAPMO/DY 30/IVA2/10.02/-16: Informationen über die Sitzung der Parteikommission "Olympische Spiele 1972 in München" am 28. Oktober 1971; Hinweise für die politisch-ideologische Arbeit, 30 April 1970.

146. BAK/B137/16432: Anlage zum Schreiben vom 16 Juli 1969, Beispiele östlicher Propaganda gegen München.

147. Gesellschaft zur Förderung des olympischen Gedankens in der DDR (Heinz Koch, Dieter Wales, Helmuth Westphal, and Bernhard Wilk), *München 1972 Schicksalsspiele? Eine Dokumentation über den Mißbrauch der olympischen Bewegung und ihrer Spiele durch den deutschen Imperialismus* (Berlin, 1969). The volume had been conceived centrally in January 1969 with the working title *Die Olympischen Spiele 1972 dürfen keine Wiederholung der Olympischen Spiele 1936 werden* (BAB/SAPMO/DY 30/JIV2/3/-1491: Anlage Nr. 3 zum Protokoll Nr. 6, 22 January 1969).

148. See M. Iu. Prozumenshchikov, *Bol'shoi Sport and Bol'shaia Politika* (Moscow, 2004), p. 186. Our warmest thanks to Mike Froggatt for a summary of the relevant pages.

149. Andrianow, for instance, brought the issue of the "Hetzsender" up again, even after it had been settled (IOC Lausanne/Minutes of the 72nd session, 31 January-1 February 1972).

150. The West German Foreign Office was soon to assure itself that neither the GDR nor the USSR would boycott the Games over the issue (LA Speyer/Nachlaß Dr. Adolf Müller-Emmert, Bestand V91/225: Vermerk für Hermann Schmitt-Vockenhausen, August 1971). On the general issue, see Balbier, *Kalter Krieg auf der Aschenbahn*, pp. 213–15.

151. BAB/SAPMO/DY 30/JIV2/3/-1491: Anlage Nr. 3 zum Protokoll Nr. 6 vom 22.1.1969.

152. See Monika Kaiser, *Machtwechsel von Ulbricht zu Honecker: Funktionsmechanismen der SED-Diktatur in Konfliktsituationen 1962 bis 1972* (Berlin, 1997) and Sarotte, *Dealing with the Devil.*

153. BAB/SAPMO/DY 30/JIV2/202/11: Sergei Pawlow to Piotr Abrassimow (translation), 28 July 1969.

154. See Ronald Huster, "Streitobjekt Friedensfahrt. Sportliche und sportpolitische Rivalitäten im Ostblock," *Deutschland Archiv* 37, no. 3, 2004, pp. 448–57; Thomas Fetzer "Die gesellschaftliche Akzeptanz des Leistungssportsystems," in Teichler, ed., *Sport in der DDR: Eigensinn, Konflikte, Trends* (Cologne, 2003) p. 291; Grit Hartmann, *Goldkinder: Die DDR im Spiegel ihres Spitzensports* (Leipzig, 1997), pp. 223–25, 263.

155. BAB/SAPMO/DY 30/IVA2/10.02/-16: Beratung der Parteikommission, 30 January 1970.

156. The commission took over ultimate responsibility for the work previously conducted by the AG 72 at the GDR Foreign Office (Balbier, *Kalter Krieg auf der Aschenbahn*, pp. 210–11).

157. BAB/SAPMO/DY 30/IVA2/10.02/-17: Aufgaben, Arbeitsmethoden und Zusammensetzung der Parteikommission.

158. BAB/SAPMO/DY 30/IVA2/10.02/-16: Beratung der Parteikommission, 30 January 1970.

159. PA AA Berlin/MfAA C147/73: Unterredung zwischen Wildberger und Jaeschke am 23.12.1970, 5 January 1971.

160. BAB/SAPMO/DY 30/JIV2/3/-1589: Aufgabenstellung der Parteikommission, 18 December 1969.

161. BAB/SAPMO/DY 30/12/9245/BÜ365: Langfristige Konzeption für die außenpolitische Vorbereitung, II. Halbjahr 1969 und 1970.

162. Kaiser, *Machtwechsel von Ulbricht zu Honecker,* p. 362.

163. PAAA Berlin/MfAA C147/73: Direktive für die Vorbereitung und Durchführung einer Konsultativtagung.

164. PAAA Berlin/MfAA C147/73: Diskussionsbeitrag Ernst Scholz; Beratung der stellvertretenden Außenminister der Staaten des Warschauer Vertrages am 20. und 21. Mai 1969 in Berlin.

165. The AG 72's energy is seen in its extensive information exchange with the Foreign Ministry in Mongolia in 1971 (BAB/SAPMO/DY 30/IVA2/10.02/-18: Bericht über die Konsultationen am 14.5.1971 in der Mongolischen Volksrepublik, 18 June 1971).

166. These countries were North Korea, Mongolia, United Arab Republic (of Egypt and Syria), Western Sahara, Cuba, Sudan, and Iraq; see documentation in BAB/SAPMO/DY 30/JIV2/3/-1528; BAB/SAPMO/DY 30/IVA2/2.028/-35 and PAAA Berlin/MfAA C147/73.

167. BAB/SAPMO/DY 30/IVA2/2.028/-35: Information zu einigen aktuellen politischen Fragen, summer 1970.

168. BAB/SAPMO/DY 30/IVA2/2.028/-35: Zwischenbericht über den Stand und die bisherigen Ergebnisse der bilateralen Konsultationen, 1 June 1970.

169. BAB/SAPMO/DY 30/IVA2/10.02/-17: AG 72, Aktuelle Probleme der Vorbereitung der Olympischen Spiele 1972, 21 September 1970.

170. BAB/SAPMO/DY 30/IVA2/2.028/-35: Oskar Fischer to Albert Norden, 14 July 1970.

171. BAB/SAPMO/DY 30/IVA2/10.02/-17: AG 72, Aktuelle Probleme der Vorbereitung der Olympischen Spiele 1972, 21 September 1970.

172. BAB/SAPMO/DY 30/IV12/10.02/-17: Scholz to Ewald and Hellmann, 22 September 1970.

173. BAB/SAPMO/DY 30/IVA2/2.028/-35: Zwischenbericht über den Stand und die bisherigen Ergebnisse der bilateralen Konsultationen, 1 June 1970.

174. BAB/SAPMO/DY 30/IVA2/10.02/-17: Westabteilung, Aktennotiz, 3 December 1970.

175. See documentation in PAAA, Berlin/MfAA C147/73 and BAB/SAPMO/DY 30/IVA2/10.02/-17.

176. Christopher Young, "Carrying a German Flame: The Olympic Torch Relay and its Instrumentalization in the Age of Ostpolitik," *Historical Social Research/Historische Sozialforschung* 32, no. 1, 2007, pp. 118–19.

177. BAK/B106/30623: Auswertung der Ostpresse, 4. Bericht (April 1970 to March 1971).

178. PAAA Berlin/MfAA C147/73: Information über den Verlauf und die Ergebnisse einer Beratung vom 14.-16.12.1970 in Moskau.

179. See documentation in BAB/SAPMO/DY 30/IV12/10.02/-17 and BAB/SAPMO/DY 30/IVA2/2.028/-38.

180. BAB/SAPMO/DY 30/IVA2/10.02/-17: Information zur Ostsee-Kreuzfahrt der "Hanseatic" im September 1970, 1 October 1970.

181. BAB/SAPMO/DY 30/IVA2/18/-11: Gespräch mit Pawlow am 16.10.1970 in Leningrad, 3 November 1970.

182. Young, "Carrying a German Flame," pp. 125–33.

183. BAB/SAPMO/DY 30/IVA2/10.02/-17: Konsultationsgespräch mit Vertretern des ZK der KPdSU in Moskau, 3 March 1970.

184. BAK/B106/30623: Auswertung der Ostpresse, 3. Bericht (September 1969 to April 1970).

185. PAAA Berlin/B41/86: Bewerbung von Los Angeles um die Olympischen Spiele 1976, 28 April 1970.

186. PAAA Berlin/B41/86: Olympische Spiele 1976; Kandidatur von Los Angeles, 4 May 1970.

187. LA Speyer/Nachlaß Dr. Adolf Müller-Emmert, Bestand V91/225: Daume to Müller-Emmert, 10 March 1970.

188. BAB/SAPMO/DY 30/IVA2/10.02/-17: Konsultationsgespräch mit Vertretern des ZK der KPdSU in Moskau, 3 March 1970. As an East German document shows, Daume reassured the Russians in Moscow that the three German delegates did indeed vote for the Soviet capital (BAB/SAPMO/DY 12/3181: Niederschrift über Gespräche, March 1971).

189. PAAA Berlin/B41/86: Olympische Spiele 1976; Kandidatur von Los Angeles, 4 May 1970.

190. PAAA Berlin/B41/86: Tagung des IOC in Amsterdam (7.-16. Mai 1970). The voting was as follows. Round one: Montreal twenty-five, Moscow twenty-three, Los Angeles seventeen. Round two: Montreal forty-one, Moscow twenty-eight.

191. BAB/SAPMO DY 30/IVA2/10.02/17: Heinze to Wildberger, 28 July 1970.

192. LA Speyer/Nachlaß Dr. Adolf Müller-Emmert, Bestand V91/225: Bericht über einen Besuch in der Sowjetunion, 21 December 1970.

193. PAAA Berlin/B41/86: Progress Report German Cultural Relations with Eastern Europe in 1968.

194. PAAA Berlin/B41/86: Hans Georg Steltzer to Vogel, 4 March 1971; Vogel to Steltzer, 22 January 1971; Reichel, Kulturarbeit in den osteuropäischen Ländern, 12 March 1971.

195. BAK/B106/30623: Auswertung der Ostpresse, 5. Bericht (March to July 1971).

196. Christopher Young, "'Nicht mehr die herrlichste Nebensache der Welt': Sport, West Berlin and the Four Powers Agreement 1971," in *German Politics and Society* 25, no. 1, 2007, pp. 28–45.

197. BAK/B137/8474: Berliner Senator für Familie, Jugend und Sport an Ausschuß für innerdeutsche Beziehungen am 1. Juli 1971; PAAA Berlin/B41/86: Leichtathletikländerkampf Bundesrepublik Deutschland-Sowjetunion in Leningrad, 13 August 1970.

198. LA Speyer/Nachlaß Dr. Adolf Müller-Emmert, Bestand V91/225: Vermerk für Hermann Schmitt-Vockenhausen, August 1971.

199. CULDA/OS72/6.2: 12. Kunstausschußsitzung, 1 October 1971; Margot Berthold, Absprache mit Haas und Bieringer, Ausstellung "Sport und Kunst in der Sowjetunion" im Kunstverein München, 21 December 1971.

200. PAAA Berlin/B41/123: BPA Ostinformation, Deutschland-UdSSR, Radio Moskau (deutsch), Interview mit Promyslow über seine Reise in die BRD.

201. DOA/Nachlaß Daume/560: Pawlow, Körperkultur und Sport in der UdSSR, Mai 1972.

202. DOA/Nachlaß Daume/608: Programm für den Besuch von Sergei Pawlowitsch Pawlow von 23.-28.5.1972 in München.

203. PAAA Berlin/B41/122: Besuch sowjetischer Parlamentarier in der Bundesrepublik Deutschland, Gespräch mit dem Herrn Bundeskanzler, 15 June 1972.

204. PAAA Berlin/B41/122: Gesprächsvorschlag, Empfang einer sowjetischen Parlamentarier-Delegation durch den Bundesaußenminister.

205. PAAA Berlin/B41/122: Besuch sowjetischer Parlamentarier in der Bundesrepublik Deutschland; Gespräch mit dem Bundesaußenminister, 15 June 1972.

206. BAB/SAPMO/DY 30/IVA2/10.02/-18: Vermerk über ein Gespräch mit S. Nowoshilow am 17.3.1971.

207. BAB/SAPMO/DY 30/IVA2/10.02/-18: Hellmann to Wildberger, 28 July 1971.

208. BAB/SAPMO/DY 30/IVA2/10.02/-18: Information über Auffassungen in den sozialistischen Bruderländern, 24 December 1971.

209. CULDA/OS72/3.2: Bericht über den Olympischen Fackellauf.

210. BAK/B106/30604: Geschenk des NOK der CSSR an OK, 3 October 1974.

211. Details of the care taken with the Soviet delegation are given in StAMü/Olympiade 1972/521.

212. Sarotte, *Dealing with the Devil*, pp. 131–34.

213. BAB/SAPMO/DY 30/IVB2/18/-37: Vorschläge der Sportleitung der UdSSR, 17 April 1972.

214. BAB/SAPMO/DY 30/IVB2/18/37: Hellmann to Honecker, 20 April 1972.

215. See BAB/SAPMO/DY 30/IVA2/10.02/-18.

216. BAK/B106/30685: Fernschreiben to von Hovora, no sender and date (summer 1971), Reise von Herrn Daume zur Spartakiade; see also UIUC Archives/Brundage Collection/Box 128: Ruegsegger to Brundage.

217. Balbier, *Kalter Krieg auf der Aschenbahn*, pp. 219–20.

218. See documentation in BAB/SAPMO/DY 30/IVA2/10.02/-18 and BAB/SAPMO/DY12/3181.

219. See PAAA Berlin/B41/86: Tagung des IOC in Amsterdam (7.-16. Mai 1970).

220. PAAA Berlin/B41/86: Gespräch des Staatssekretärs mit Daume am 19. Februar 1971, 17 February 1971. The GDR report on Daume's trip to Moscow makes clear how strictly the West German followed the Foreign Office's advice to avoid political topics (BAB/SAPMO/DY 12/3181: Niederschrift über Gespräche, March 1971).

221. Balbier, *Kalter Krieg auf der Aschenbahn*, pp. 216–17.

7. THE END OF THE GAMES

1. Susan L. Carruthers, *The Media at War: Communication and Conflict in the Twentieth Century* (Basingstoke, 1999), p. 170.

2. Original commentary taken from the ABC television documentary *Our Greatest Hopes, Our Worst Fears: The Tragedy of the Munich Games* (2002).

3. Ibid.

4. See Richard Mandell, *The Olympics of 1972: A Munich Diary* (Chapel Hill, 1991) pp. 52–54.

5. *Our Greatest Hopes.*

6. PAAA Berlin/B36/462: Foreign Office to Vogel, 14 December 1972.

7. PAAA Berlin/B36/296: Embassy Tel Aviv to Foreign Office, 30 August and 20 September 1967.

8. Carole Fink, "Turning Away from the Past: West Germany and Israel, 1965–1967," in Philipp Gassert and Alan E. Steinweis, eds., *Coping with the Nazi Past: West German Debates on Nazism and Generational Conflict, 1955–1975* (New York, 2006), p. 279.

9. See, for example, FES/Dep. HJV/Reden 1963–1964: Vogel, Bericht über die Israel-Reise (April 1964); Anthony Kauders, *Democratization and the Jews: Munich, 1945–1965* (Lincoln, 2004), pp. 212–14, 216.

10. Fink, "Turning Away from the Past," p. 285.

11. PAAA Berlin/B36/457 contains a series of reports on Abba Eban's visit.

12. PAAA Berlin/B36/462: Embassy Tel Aviv to Foreign Office, 1 December 1972.

13. PAAA Berlin, B36/547: Embassy Tel Aviv to Foreign Office, Kulturpolitischer Jahresbericht, 15 February 1972.

14. PAAA Berlin/Av. Neues Amt 2.233: Embassy Tel Aviv to Foreign Office, 23 July 1970.

15. BAK/B106/50117: Embassy Tel Aviv to Foreign Office, 12 August 1969.

16. PAAA Berlin/Av. Neues Amt 2.233: Embassy Tel Aviv to Foreign Office, 14 April 1969.

17. PAAA Berlin/Av. Neues Amt 2.233: Embassy Tel Aviv to Foreign Office; Inbar to Walther Tröger, 25 August 1970; PAAA Berlin/B36/547: Embassy Tel Aviv to Foreign Office, Kulturpolitischer Jahresbericht, 15 February 1972.

18. Manfred Lämmer, "Der Beitrag des Sports zur deutsch-israelischen Verständigung" (lecture manuscript).

19. PAAA Berlin/B36/465: Borussia Mönchengladbach in Israel, 3 April 1970.

20. PAAA Berlin/B36/547: Embassy Tel Aviv to Foreign Office, Kulturpolitischer Jahresbericht, 15 February 1972.

21. Lämmer, "Der Beitrag des Sports."

22. DOA/Nachlaß Daume/594: Herbert Liebmann, "Im Basketball ist Israel Weltklasse," draft corrected by Daume, 19 March 1969.

23. Lämmer, "Der Beitrag des Sports."

24. BAK/B322/433: Daume to Deutsche Sporthochschule Köln, 20 December 1962; Liselott Diem to Daume, 6 June 1963, includes a report of the trip written for the Interior Ministry.

25. DOA/Nachlaß Daume/594: Robert Atlasz and Michael Kevehazi to Daume, 20 June 1971.

26. See correspondence in StAMü/BuR/3555.

27. IOC Lausanne/Daume/Correspondence 1957–1972: Otto Mayer to Daume, 10 January 1964.

28. DOA/Nachlaß Daume/530: Daume to 20 IOC members, 19 March 1969; Daume to Inbar, 31 March 1969.

29. DOA/Nachlaß Daume/530: Daume to Inbar, 25 June 1969.

30. The expulsion of this African nation, it was feared, could create a "dangerous precedent for all states, including Israel" (PAAA Berlin/Av. Neues Amt 2.257: Embassy Tel Aviv to Foreign Office, 22 August 1972).

31. PAAA Berlin/Av. Neues Amt 2.257: Embassy Tel Aviv to Foreign Office, 9 December 1970.

32. PAAA Berlin/Av. Neues Amt 2.257: Embassy Tel Aviv to Foreign Office, 15 August 1972.

33. PAAA Berlin/Av. Neues Amt 2.257: Embassy Tel Aviv to Foreign Office, 8 September 1971.

34. PAAA Berlin/Av. Neues Amt 2.257: Embassy Tel Aviv to Foreign Office, 15 August 1972.

35. PAAA Berlin/Av. Neues Amt 2.257: Embassy Tel Aviv to Foreign Office, 29 August 1972.

36. *The Jerusalem Post,* 27 August 1972: "The friendship and warmth generated in Munich's futuristic Olympic stadium . . . Munich, the spawning ground of the Nazi movement between the two world wars, spared no pains to provide a fiesta atmosphere which contrasted with Hitler's 1936 Olympics in Berlin. . . . But here was not a political overtone to be seen."

37. The twenty-eight consisted of fifteen athletes (in seven sports) and thirteen coaches and officials.

38. PAAA Berlin/Av. Neues Amt 2.257: Embassy Tel Aviv to Foreign Office, 29 August and 1 September 1972.

39. PAAA Berlin/Av. Neues Amt 2.257: Embassy Tel Aviv to Foreign Office, 29 August 1972.

40. PAAA Berlin/Av. Neues Amt 2.257: Embassy Tel Aviv to Foreign Office, 15 August and 1 September 1972.

41. PAAA Berlin/Av. Neues Amt 2.257: Embassy Tel Aviv to Foreign Office, 1 September 1972.

42. Paul Noack, *Die Außenpolitik der Bundesrepublik Deutschland* (Stuttgart, 2nd ed. 1981), p. 106.

43. Werner Kilian, *Die Hallstein-Doktrin: Der diplomatische Krieg zwischen der BRD und der DDR 1955–1973. Aus den Akten der beiden deutschen Außenministerien* (Berlin, 2001), p. 156.

44. Markus A. Weingardt, *Deutsche Israel- und Nahostpolitik: Die Geschichte einer Gratwanderung seit 1949* (Frankfurt am Main, 2002), p. 200.

45. See William Glenn Gray, *Germany's Cold War: The Global Campaign to Isolate East Germany, 1949–1969* (Chapel Hill, 2003), pp. 174–95.

46. DOA/Nachlaß Daume/594: Embassy Algiers to Daume, 6 June 1972. Foreign ministries represented were: Hungary, Romania, USSR, GDR, Yugoslavia, Bulgaria, Morocco, Tunisia, Libya, Mauritania, Senegal.

47. PAAA Berlin/B36/296: Press conference Abba Eban, 24 February 1970.

48. PAAA Berlin/B36/546: Stand der deutsch-israelischen Beziehungen, 16 June 1971.

49. Helga Haftendorn, *Deutsche Außenpolitik zwischen Selbstbeschränkung und Selbstbehauptung 1945–2000* (Stuttgart, 2001), p. 233.

50. Weingardt, *Deutsche Israel- und Nahost-Politik*, pp. 200–12.

51. Ibid., p. 198.

52. Ibid., p. 219.

53. PAAA Berlin/B36/462:"Die Lage im Nahen Osten" (17. Januar 1972).

54. PAAA Berlin/B36/462: Foreign Office to Vogel, 14 December 1972.

55. PAAA Berlin/B36/462: Embassy Tel Aviv to Foreign Office, 22 November 1971.

56. PAAA Berlin/B36/544: Meir to Brandt, 29 November 1971.

57. PAAA Berlin/B36/544: Brandt to Meir, 26 January 1972.

58. PAAA Berlin/B36/545: Meir to Brandt, 6 February 1972.

59. PAAA Berlin/B36/545: Telex from Baghdad to Foreign Office, 1 February 1972.

60. PAAA Berlin/B36/545: von Mirow, Damascus, to Foreign Office, 3 February 1972; von Arndt, Khartoum, to Foreign Office, 9 February 1972; von Werner, Tripoli, to Foreign Office, 17 February 1972.

61. PAAA Berlin/B36/545: Zu Drahtbericht aus Kairo, 11 February 1972; von Werner, Tripoli, to Foreign Office, 17 February 1972.

62. PAAA Berlin/B36/545: Redies, 8 February 1972.

63. PAAA Berlin/ B36/545: Embassy Tel Aviv to Foreign Office, 9 February 1972.

64. PAAA Berlin/B36/545: von Nowak, Beirut, to Foreign Office, 9 February 1972.

65. PAAA Berlin/B36/545: von Jesser, Cairo, to Foreign Office, 9 February 1972.

66. PAAA Berlin/B36/545: Gespräch des Bundeskanzlers mit dem tunesischen Botschafter, 24 February 1972.

67. PA AA Berlin/B36/545: Aufzeichnung, 14 February 1972.

68. PAAA Berlin/B36/547: Beziehungen Israels zur EG, 22 June 1972.

69. PAAA Berlin/B36/544: Embassy Tel Aviv to Foreign Office, 22 June 1972.

70. PAAA Berlin/B36/544: Rumpf, 20. Jahrestag des Luxemburger Abkommens, 4 July 1972.

71. PAAA Berlin/B36/544: Entwurf einer Erklärung des Herrn Bundeskanzlers, 26 Juli 1972. Further drafts on 3 and 22 August.

72. PAAA Berlin/B36/544: Aufzeichnung, 20. Jahrestag des Luxemburger Abkommens, 9 August 1972.

73. PAAA Berlin/B36/544: Alex Wachsmuth, "Jahrestag. Israel wird den Jahrestag des Abkommens ignorieren," *Deutsche Presse Agentur,* undated.

74. BAK/B106/146540: Günther Nollau to von Brockdorff-Ahlefeldt (*Bild*), 13 September 1972; Alexander Wolff, "When the Terror Began," *Time,* 2 September 2002.

75. Aaron J. Klein, *Striking Back: The 1972 Munich Olympics Massacre and Israel's Deadly Response* (New York, 2005), p. 32.

76. This was recently confirmed in an interview with Bassam Abu Sharif, a former senior advisor to Arafat; see Sebastian Dehnhardt, Uli Weidenbach, and Manfred Oldenburg, *Der Olympia-Mord (München '72—Die wahre Geschichte)* (2006).

77. Christopher Andrew and Vasili Mitrokhin, *The World Was Going Our Way: The KGB and the Battle for the Third World* (New York, 2005), p. 251.

78. Simon Reeve, *One Day in September: The Story of the 1972 Munich Olympics Massacre, a Government Cover-up and a Covert Revenge Mission* (London, 2000), p. 33.

79. John K. Cooley, *Green March, Black September: The Story of the Palestinian Arabs* (London, 1973), p. 122.

80. Klein, *Striking Back*, p. 32.

81. See Thomas Skelton-Robinson, "Im Netz verheddert: Die Beziehungen des bundesdeutschen Linksterrorismus zur Volksfront für die Befreiung Palästinas," in Wolfgang Kraushaar, ed., *Die RAF und der linke Terrorismus* (Hamburg, 2006), vol. 2, p. 847.

82. Klein, *Striking Back*, pp. 14–15.

83. BAK/B106/146540: Nollau to von Brockdorff-Ahlefeldt, 13 September 1972.

84. Interview with Dan Alon, 29 January 2006.

85. BAK/B106/146541: Otto Heindl, Einstellungsverfügung zum Ermittlungsverfahren gegen Manfred Schreiber und Georg Wolf wegen des Vorwurfs der fahrlässigen Tötung, 5 February 1973, pp. 10, 14.

86. Ibid., p. 13.

87. "Mal der eine Falke, mal der andere Taube." Interview mit Manfred Schreiber, *Der Spiegel*, 11 September 1972.

88. Subsequently, the two Asian men could only leave their room at 4:00 P.M. after intense negotiation (BStU/Auszug aus Akte MfS/HA XX/3–505: Martin Kramer, Dieter Wales, and Wolfgang Gitter, Dokumentation über die Ereignisse des 5. Septembers im Olympischen Dorf, pp. 70, 76–77).

89. Reeve, *One Day in September*, p. 58.

90. For further details see Jim McKay, *The Real McKay: My Wide World of Sports* (New York, 1998), pp. 209–11, 217.

91. Reeve, *One Day in September*, p. 219, note 25.

92. Interview with Dan Shilon in Kevin MacDonald, *One Day in September* (1999).

93. Presse- und Informationsamt der Bundesregierung and Pressestelle der Bayerischen Staatskanzlei, *Dokumentation: Der Überfall auf die israelische Olympiamannschaft* (Bonn, Munich, 1972), p. 21.

94. Reeve, *One Day in September*, p. 67.

95. BAK/B106/146540: Deutscher Bundestag, Innenausschuß, Kurzprotokoll der 91. Sitzung am 18. September 1972, p. 8. The Sicherheitsausschuß of the Bavarian parliament reached similar conclusions.

96. Bundesregierung and Staatskanzlei, *Dokumentation*, pp. 21 and 36: While the West German authorities took Brundage's point into consideration, it is clear that it was not the basis for their decision to try the liberation by force.

97. Matthias Dahlke, *Der Anschlag auf Olympia '72: Die politischen Reaktionen auf den internationalen Terrorismus in Deutschland* (Munich, 2006), p. 27.

98. "Das Massaker von München," *Der Stern*, 17 September 1972.

99. Reeve, *One Day in September*, p. 54; BAK/B106/146541: Heindl, Einstellungsverfügung, p. 13.

100. BayHStA/MInn/88625: Vorschläge der Bevölkerung, 5 September 1972.

101. BAK/B106/146541: Heindl, Einstellungsverfügung, p. 15. As an alternative, the Palestinians offered for two of their number to stay in the Federal Republic as exchange hostages to guarantee that the Israelis would be released in Egypt and taken to Israel; see Reeve, *One Day in September*, p. 68.

102. Bundesregierung and Staatskanzlei, *Dokumentation,* pp. 22–23.

103. Ibid., p. 28.

104. Hans-Dietrich Genscher, *Erinnerungen* (Berlin, 2nd ed. 1995), pp. 153–54.

105. Interview with Bruno Merk in MacDonald, *One Day in September.*

106. Bundesregierung and Staatskanzlei, *Dokumentation,* p. 36.

107. BAK/B106/146541: Heindl, Einstellungsverfügung, pp. 12–13, 19.

108. BStU/Auszug aus Akte MfS/HA XX/3–505: Kramer, Wales, Gitter, Dokumentation, p. 77; see also Interview with Heinz Hohensinn in MacDonald, *One Day in September;* Interview with Manfred Ommer in Dehnhardt, Weidenbach, and Oldenburg, *Der Olympia-Mord.*

109. Policeman Walter Renner claims that Schreiber gave the game away by alerting the hidden marksmen that Issa was starting a practice run. By contrast, the Munich public prosecutor later concluded that without seeing the police, the terrorist had become increasingly distrustful and deemed it safer to demand transportation by bus; see Interview with Walter Renner in Dehnhardt, Weidenbach, and Oldenburg, *Der Olympia-Mord;* BAK/B106/146541: Heindl, Einstellungsverfügung, p. 29.

110. Klein, *Striking Back,* p. 72; BAK/B106/146541: Heindl, Einstellungsverfügung, p. 28; Interviews with Heinz Hohensinn in Dehnhardt, Weidenbach, and Oldenburg, *Der Olympia-Mord* and MacDonald, *One Day in September.*

111. BAK/B106/146541: Heindl, Einstellungsverfügung, pp. 28–29; Bundesregierung and Staatskanzlei, *Dokumentation,* p. 61; "Hätte man doch Mosche Dajan geschickt," *Der Spiegel,* 18 September 1972.

112. The marksmen were not issued with the appropriate weapons, night-vision equipment, body armor, or walkie-talkies (despite every member of the Ordnungsdienst in the Olympic village carrying one); see "Hätte man doch Mosche Dajan geschickt," *Der Spiegel,* 18 September 1972; BAK/B106/146541: Heindl, Einstellungsverfügung, p. 25.

113. See Reeve, *One Day in September,* p. 100; Klein, *Striking Back,* p. 75. According to the Munich public prosecutor the killing of the hostages happened earlier, "probably straight after the first exchange of fire" (BAK/B106/146541: Heindl, Einstellungsverfügung, p. 34).

114. Interviews with Schreiber and Heinz-Peter Gottelt in Dehnhardt, Weidenbach, and Oldenburg, *Der Olympia-Mord;* see also BAK/B106/146541: Heindl, Einstellungsverfügung, p. 30.

115. Schreiber, "Das Geschehen am 5./6. September," p. 8; BAK/B106/146541: Heindl, Einstellungsverfügung, p. 22.

116. Interview with anonymous marksman in Dehnhardt, Weidenbach, and Oldenburg, *Der Olympia-Mord.* A generally overlooked statement at the time by Schreiber suggests this was an important reason: "You can imagine that a marksman who has only shot at targets would have to overcome a psychological barrier the first time he has a person in his sights on whom he has to pull the trigger. He only has to be uncertain for a fraction of a second to miss. In human terms, I would not judge this uncertainty negatively; I find it, actually, understandable." ("Das Massaker von München," *Der Stern,* 17 September 1972, p. 225; see also "Hätte man doch Mosche Dajan geschickt," *Der Spiegel,* 18 September 1972).

117. Melani McAlister, *Epic Encounters: Culture, Media, and U.S. Interests in the Middle East, 1945–2000* (Berkeley, 2001), p. 182.

118. BAK/B106/146540: BfV, Ermittlungen nach Helfern und Hintermännern, 6 September 1972.

119. Dahlke, *Der Anschlag auf Olympia '72,* for example, p. 107.

120. Klein, *Striking Back,* pp. 92–93.

121. ACSP/Nachlaß Jaeger C50: Hans Langemann, Die Entwicklung außenpolitischer Störfelder, 25 June 1971.

122. BayHStA/MInn/88598: Bayerisches Landesamt für Verfassungsschutz, Informationen (1.4.1972–30.6.1972).

123. See BAK/B185/3230: Schreiber, Konzeption für den Ordnungsdienst, 12 June 1970.

124. "Hätte man doch Mosche Dajan geschickt," *Der Spiegel,* 18 September 1972.

125. Ibid.

126. Alan Hart, *Arafat* (London, 2nd ed. 1994), p. 310; Cooley, *Green March, Black September,* pp. 123–24.

127. Reeve, *One Day in September,* p. 216, note 31.

128. Klein, *Striking Back,* p. 40; Reeve, *One Day in September,* p. 1.

129. BAK/B106/146540: BfV, Ermittlungen nach Helfern und Hintermännern, 6 September 1972.

130. Jamal Al-Jishey (nineteen, using the *nom de guerre* Samer Mohamed Abdulah or Abdulah); his uncle, Adnan Al-Jishey (twenty-five, Ibrahim Masoud Badran or Badran); Mohammed Safady (nineteen, El Safadi, also called Abed A[/E]l Kade[/i]r Al D[a]'nawy); Khalid Jawad; Afif Ahmed Hamid; Ahmed Sheik Taa (Abu Hallah or Abu el Alah).

131. There is no evidence to suggest they had been involved in building the Olympic village or were part of the short-term personnel working there during the Games (Bundesregierung and Staatskanzlei, *Dokumentation,* p. 16). This rumor circulated on the day, IM "Händel" (the GDR super heavyweight weightlifting bronze medalist Gerd Bonk) reporting it had been started by members of the Ordnungsdienst and the stewards (BStU/Reg.-Nr. XIV/781/71/Karl-Marx-Stadt, Akte IM "Händel": Bericht zu Olympischen Spielen 1972, Teil I, 12 September 1972, p. 41).

132. Interview with the father of Muhammed Massalha in Dehnhardt, Weidenbach, and Oldenburg, *Der Olympia-Mord.*

133. See Ulrike Meinhof, "Die Aktion des Schwarzen September in München: Zur Strategie des antiimperialistischen Kampfes, November 1972," in *Rote Armee Fraktion: Texte und Materialien zur Geschichte der RAF* (Berlin, 1997), p. 151.

134. See, for example, Wolfgang Kraushaar, "Antizionismus als Trojanisches Pferd: Zur antisemitischen Dimension in der Kooperation von Tupamaros West-Berlin, RAF und RZ mit den Palästinensern," in Kraushaar, *Die RAF und der linke Terrorismus* (Hamburg, 2006), vol. 1, pp. 676–95, esp. 689–91.

135. Ibid., p. 690.

136. Wolfgang Kraushaar, *Die Bombe im Jüdischen Gemeindehaus* (Hamburg, 2005), p. 209.

137. See "Aus Kunzelmanns Akten: Attentatspläne für Olympia," *Süddeutsche Zeitung,* 29 July 1970.

138. Quoted in "Störenfriede bei Olympia," *Augsburger Allgemeine Zeitung,* 28 July 1971.

139. In Kevin MacDonald's *One Day in September,* the narrator Michael Douglas suggests that the Black September commando was aided by members of the East German team in getting access to the village and reconnoitering it. For a historian who accepted this as fact, see Mary Elise Sarotte, *Dealing with the Devil: East Germany, Détente, and Ostpolitik, 1969–1973* (Chapel Hill, 2001), pp. 141–42 and 249, note 48.

140. See BStU/Auszug aus Akte MfS/HA XX/3–505.

141. BStU/MfS-ZAIG 14716: "Flamme", Information A/1846/9/1972.

142. BAK/B106/146541: BfV to Interior Ministry, 13 October 1972.

143. Interview with Markus Wolf, 22 February 2006; see also Markus Wolf, *Man Without a Face: The Autobiography of Communism's Greatest Spymaster* (New York, 1997), p. 300.

144. BStU/AS 432/73, Bd.1a: AG Ausländische Festivalteilnehmer, Abschlußeinschätzung "Banner," 15 August 1973, p. 182.

145. BStU/MfS-BdL-Dok. 1802: Mielke, Befehl Nr. 13/73, 18 April 1973.

146. BStU/AS 432/73, Bd.1b: AG AF, Konzeption, 18 June 1973, esp. pp. 132, 145.

147. See, for example, BStU/AS 432/73, Bd.2: AG AF, Bericht, 25 July 1973, pp. 153–54.

148. BAK/B106/146540: Nollau to von Brockdorff-Ahlefeldt, 13 September 1972 and [Antworten auf] [w]eitere Fragen der *Bild*-Redakteure, no date; see also Klein, *Striking Back,* p. 39; Hart, *Arafat,* p. 313.

149. BAK/B106/146541: BfV to Interior Ministry, 2 October 1972.

150. BfV, *Sicherheitsgefährdende Bestrebungen von Ausländern 1972,* 1 February 1973, p. 24.

151. BAK/B106/146541: LKA Wiesbaden, Al Frangi, 30 September 1972. Tellingly, alarm clocks started ringing in East Berlin when intelligence indicated that Al Frangi along with other unidentified members of Black September intended to come to the 1973 World Youth Festival; see BStU/AS 432/73, Bd.5: AG AF, Einschätzung zur Information 527/73, 23 July 1973, pp. 115–16.

152. BAK/B185/3230: Schreiber, Konzeption für den Ordnungsdienst, 12 June 1970.

153. *Village News,* 5 September 1972.

154. Mandell, *A Munich Diary,* pp. 33, 86.

155. See interviews with Abu Daoud in *München 1972: "Ich bereue nichts!"* (Spiegel TV, 2006) and Dehnhardt, Weidenbach, and Oldenburg, *Der Olympia-Mord.*

156. Interviews with Olympic hostesses, 26 July 2002.

157. BAK/B106/146541: Heindl, Einstellungsverfügung, p. 9.

158. BAK/B185/3230: Schreiber, Tätigkeitsbericht der Abteilung XIII, pp. 83–84. This still left over thirty on patrol.

159. BayHStA/MInn/88599: Anordnung von Sicherheitsstufen für gefährdete Besucher, 26 July 1972.

160. BAK/B185/3230: Schreiber, Informationsbesuch [in Rio, Sao Paolo, Buenos Aires, Lima], 30 November 1971.

161. Ken Connor, *Ghost Force: The Secret History of the SAS* (London, 1998), p. 211.

162. Bundesregierung and Staatskanzlei, *Dokumentation,* p. 16.

163. See Klein, *Striking Back,* pp. 20–21, 27–28.

164. See Bundesregierung and Staatskanzlei, *Dokumentation,* pp. 12–13 and BAK/B106/146541: Heindl, Einstellungsverfügung, p. 8.

165. DOA/Nachlaß Daume/594: Liebmann, "Im Basketball ist Israel Weltklasse," 19 March 1969.

166. See Klein, *Striking Back,* p. 250.

167. Ibid., p. 17. On the British reaction to Munich, see Christopher Andrew, *The Defence of the Realm: The Authorized History of MI5* (London, 2009), pp. 612–14.

168. Connor, *Ghost Force,* pp. 205, 211.

169. Klein, *Striking Back,* p. 56.

170. Quoted in Dahlke, *Der Anschlag auf Olympia '72,* p. 30.

171. Interview with Georg Leber in Dehnhardt, Weidenbach, and Oldenburg, *Der Olympia-Mord.* On the incident see documentation in BayHStA/MInn/88624/2.

172. Bundesregierung and Staatskanzlei, *Dokumentation,* p. 23; Klein, *Striking Back,* p. 57; Interview with Victor Cohen in Dehnhardt, Weidenbach, and Oldenburg, *Der Olympia-Mord.*

173. "Die schlimmste Nacht der Bundesrepublik," *Der Spiegel,* 11 September 1972.

174. Hans-Peter Schwarz, ed., *Akten zur Auswärtigen Politik der Bundesrepublik Deutschland 1972,* vol. 2: *1. Juni bis 30. September 1972* (Munich, 2003), vol. 2, document 267, p. 1245, note 8.

175. Dahlke, *Der Anschlag auf Olympia '72,* p. 65.

176. Organizing Committee for the Games of the XXth Olympiad Munich 1972, ed., *Die Spiele: The Official Report,* vol. 1: *The Organization* (Munich, 1972), p. 38.

177. "Those Arab states that help terrorists are no less guilty of the crime in Munich than the murderers themselves—and for that reason, these states will have to bear the responsibility for this act of terrorism" (cited in *Münchner Jüdische Nachrichten,* 17 September 1972). Allon had to hold the speech in place of Golda Meir who was attending her sister's funeral.

178. BAK/B122/15033: Shazar to Heinemann, 6 September 1972.

179. BAK/B122/15033: Vermerk, Rede des Bundespräsidenten am 6.9.1972; on another occasion Schwarz, *Akten zur Auswärtigen Politik 1972,* vol. 2, document 267, pp. 1243–47.

180. *Die Spiele: The Official Report,* vol. 1, p. 38.

181. DOA/Nachlaß Daume/566: Alfred H. Jacob to Daume, 8 September 1972.

182. Schwarz, *Akten zur Auswärtigen Politik 1972,* vol. 2, document 259, pp. 1193–96.

183. Ibid., p. 1193, note 2.

184. Ibid., p. 1193, note 3.

185. BAK/B122/15033: Telex 2 from Cairo to Foreign Office, 11 September 1972.

186. BAK/B122/15033: Telex from Cairo to Foreign Office, 9 September 1972.

187. Ibid.

188. BAK, B122/15033: Telex 1 from Cairo to Foreign Office, 11 September 1972.

189. BAK/B122/15033: Telex from Paris to Foreign Office, 11 September 1972.

190. See documentation in BAK/B213/16508.

191. In fact, only Jordan condemned the attack.

192. BAK/B213/16508: Herzog, Abbruch der E-Hilfe, 11 September 1972; Krumpholz, Entwicklungshilfe für arabische Länder, 11 September 1972.

193. Schwarz, *Akten zur Auswärtigen Politik 1972,* vol. 2, p. 1232, note 7.

194. Ibid., document 289, pp. 1360–62.

195. *Münchner Jüdische Nachrichten,* 17 September 1972: At the Trauerfeier in Lod, for instance, Yigal Allon had regretted that security in the village had been "insufficient." This matched the Federal Republic's regret that the Israeli government had not been prepared to negotiate with the terrorists.

196. German representatives at the Trauerfeier were: Werner Wichmann (for the Zentralrat der Juden in Deutschland), Hans Lamm (President of the Israelitische Kultusgemeinde München), and Vogel.

197. Schwarz, *Akten zur Auswärtigen Politik 1972,* vol. 2, p. 1360, note 3.

198. PAAA Berlin/B36/546: Israel-Reise des Senatspräsidenten von Bremen, 22 December 1972.

199. BAK/B122/15033: Embassy Tel Aviv to Foreign Office, 11 September 1972.

200. BAK/B122/15033: "Bonn spricht zwei Sprachen," *Maariv,* 11 September 1972.

201. BAK/B122/15033: Embassy Tel Aviv to Foreign Office, 12 September 1972.

202. Schwarz, *Akten zur Auswärtigen Politik 1972,* vol. 2, document 289, pp. 1360–62.

203. Ibid., p. 1535, note 5.

204. BAK/B122/15033: Vermerk, 7 September 1972.

205. Schwarz, *Akten zur Auswärtigen Politik 1972,* vol. 2, document 267, pp. 1243–47.

206. Ibid., document 289, pp. 1360–62.

207. Ibid., document 332, pp. 1534–37.

208. Ibid., p. 1615, note 4.

209. Ibid., document 332, especially p. 1536, note 10.

210. Ibid., vol. 2, p. 1245, note 6.

211. BAK/B106/146540: Terroristische Aktivitäten arabischer Untergrundorganisationen, 8 September 1972.

212. See Skelton-Robinson, "Im Netz verheddert," pp. 841–42.

213. See BayHSta/MInn/88623/2: Einreise der vermutlichen Khaled, Layla am 24.8.1972, 7 September 1972.

214. Schwarz, *Akten zur Auswärtigen Politik 1972,* vol. 2, document 280, pp. 1311–12.

215. See documentation in BAK/B141/30899.

216. Events at Amsterdam's Schiphol Airport, even after the Munich attack, give an indication of the general lack of attention paid to airport security in Europe. On 23 October, a Jordanian traveling on an Algerian diplomatic passport was caught with an arsenal of weapons, ammunition, hand grenades, and letter-bombs (BAK/B106/146541: Sicherheitslage in der Bundesrepublik Deutschland, 2 November 1972).

217. BAK/B106/146540: Maßnahmen zur Verhinderung weiterer Anschläge.

218. BAK/B106/146540: Sofortige Abschiebung illegaler Ausländer.

219. Schwarz, *Akten zur Auswärtigen Politik 1972,* vol. 2, document 267, pp. 1243–47.

220. Ibid., document 318, pp. 1476–82.

221. Ibid., p. 1245, note 9.

222. Ibid., document 265, pp. 1231–34.

223. Ibid., p. 1234, note 13.

224. Ibid., document 318, pp. 1476–82.

225. To be precise: in keeping with the Ministry of Interior's assessment of the small core of Palestinians living in the country capable of providing logistical assistance for terrorist

attacks, only 121 had been forced to leave (with a further seventy-nine still on the wanted list) during the height of the expulsions. (BAK/B106/146540: Nollau to von Brockdorff-Ahlefeldt, 13 September 1972; BAK/B213/16508: Deutsch-arabische Beziehungen, Auswirkungen der verschärften Sicherheitsbestimmungen, 20 October 1972)

226. BAK/B106/146541: Einreisekontrollen und -beschränkungen gegenüber Personen aus arabischen Staaten. A different source puts the figure at around 10 to 15 percent (BAK/B106/146541: Ausländerrechtliche Maßnahmen gegen Araber, 4 October 1972).

227. See documentation in BAK/B106/146543.

228. BAK/B106/146541: Alfred H. Jacob to Scheel.

229. BAK/B106/146541: Telex from Cairo to Foreign Office, 2 October 1972.

230. Ibid.

231. BAK/B106/146543 Telex from Cairo to Foreign Office, 25 September 1972.

232. BAK/B106/146543: Telex from Algiers to Foreign Office, 2 October 1972.

233. BAK/B213/16508: Deutsch-arabische Beziehungen, Auswirkungen der verschärften Sicherheitsbestimmungen, 20 October 1972.

234. BAK/B106/146541: Einreisekontrollen und -Beschränkungen gegenüber Personen aus arabischen Staaten.

235. As a result of the Black September commando's attempt to contact him, Al Frangi was arrested. His home was searched but no incriminating evidence was found, and he was released. Anticipating his imminent deportation, he left the Federal Republic on his own accord on 28 September and flew to Cairo where he complained about his treatment to the local correspondent of the ZDF. He rightly claimed that the Algerian embassy had not been allowed to contact him despite his diplomatic immunity. During what Arab governments with some justification called the "pogrom mood," his supposed role as a contact person for the Black September Commando was used as one of a number of reasons by the federal Interior Ministry when forbidding the GUPS on 3 October (Dahlke, *Der Anschlag auf Olympia '72*, pp. 47–48).

236. BAK/B106/146540: Observationsmaßnahmen gegen Funktionäre der GUPS und der GUPA, 20 September 1972.

237. BAK/B106/146541: GUPS, Verbotsverfügung, 3 October 1972.

238. PAAA Berlin/B36/544: Embassy Cairo to Foreign Office, 10 October 1972.

239. BAK/B106/146541: Vollzug der Vereinsverbote Gups/Gupa.

240. BAK/B213/16508: Deutsch-arabische Beziehungen, Auswirkungen der verschärften Sicherheitsbestimmungen, 20 October 1972; "Antideutsche Kampagne der Araber," *Süddeutsche Zeitung*, 12 October 1972.

241. BAK/B106/146543: "Brandt the Führer!!," *Al-Kabas*, 6 October 1972 [translation].

242. Schwarz, *Akten zur Auswärtigen Politik 1972*, vol. 2, p. 1476, note 2.

243. Ibid., document 318, pp. 1476–82 (and 1477, note 6).

244. Ibid., document 348, pp. 1600–1602.

245. Ibid.

246. Ibid.

247. Ibid., p. 1479, note 16.

248. BAK/B106/146543: Embassy Cairo to Foreign Office, 16 October 1972.

249. Schwarz, *Akten zur Auswärtigen Politik 1972,* vol. 2, document 348, pp. 1600–1602.

250. Ibid., p. 1381, note 8.

251. Ibid., p. 1602, note 8.

252. Ibid., p. 1600, note 2.

253. See documentation in BAK/B106/146541.

254. BAK/B106/146541: Mögliche wichtige Operationen der Fedayeen, 23 October 1972; Terroristentätigkeit, 22 October 1972.

255. BAK/B106/146541: Unterrichtung des Ständigen Ausschusses am 30.10.1972.

256. For details of complications over instructions to the Condor crew, see Dahlke, *Der Anschlag auf Olympia '72,* pp. 22–23.

257. Schwarz, *Akten zur Auswärtigen Politik 1972,* vol. 3, p. 1686, note 3.

258. PAAA Berlin/B36/544: Redies an das Büro Staatssekretär, 13 November 1972.

259. Klein, *Striking Back,* p. 128.

260. Klaus Kinkel, then state secretary at the Ministry of the Interior, categorically denied any conspiracy (see Dehnhardt, Weidenbach, and Oldenburg, *Der Olympia-Mord*).

261. Dahlke, *Der Anschlag auf Olympia '72,* pp. 21, 24.

262. Klein, *Striking Back,* p. 127.

263. BAK/B122/15033: Telex from Belgrade to Foreign Office, 13 September 1972.

264. Schwarz, *Akten zur Auswärtigen Politik 1972,* vol. 3, document 356, pp. 1635–38.

265. BAK/B106/146541: Sicherheitslage in der Bundesrepublik Deutschland, 2 November 1972.

266. Schwarz, *Akten zur Auswärtigen Politik 1972,* vol. 3, p. 1700, note 4.

267. PAAA Berlin/B36/547: Telex from Rabat to Foreign Office, 3 November 1972.

268. Schwarz, *Akten zur Auswärtigen Politik 1972,* vol. 2, p. 1381, note 8.

269. PAAA Berlin/B36/544: Gespräch Staatssekretär Frank mit Ben Horin, 15 November 1972.

270. Schwarz, *Akten zur Auswärtigen Politik 1972,* vol. 3, document 372, pp. 1699–1700; PAAA Berlin/B36/544: Jüngste Entwicklung der deutsch-israelischen Beziehungen.

271. BAK/B213/16508: Deutsch-arabische Beziehungen, 1 December 1972.

272. Schwarz, *Akten zur Auswärtigen Politik 1972,* vol. 3, document 352, pp. 1615–17.

273. PAAA Berlin/B36/544: Jüngste Entwicklung der deutsch-israelischen Beziehungen.

274. PAAA Berlin/B36/544: Ott to Foreign Office, 23 November 1972; BAK/B36/546: Israel-Reise des Senatspräsidenten von Bremen, Koschnick, 22 December 1972.

275. Weingardt, *Deutsche Israel- und Nahost-Politik,* p. 222.

276. Schwarz, *Akten zur Auswärtigen Politik 1972,* vol. 3, p. 1617, note 11.

277. PAAA Berlin/B36/544: Sprechzettel für das Gespräch mit Ben Horin am 15. November 1972.

278. Schwarz, *Akten zur Auswärtigen Politik 1972,* vol. 3, p. 1617, note 11.

279. PAAA Berlin/B36/544: Jüngste Entwicklung der deutsch-israelischen Beziehungen.

280. PAAA Berlin/B36/544: Sprechzettel für das Gespräch mit Botschafter Ben Horin am 15. November 1972; Telex from Tel Aviv to Foreign Office, 9 November 1972.

281. PAAA Berlin/B36/544: Gespräch Dr. Frank mit Ben Horin, 15 November 1972; see also Dahlke, *Der Anschlag auf Olympia '72,* pp. 70–71.

282. PAAA Berlin/B36/544: Telex from Tel Aviv to Foreign Office, 17 November 1972.

283. PAAA Berlin/B36/544: Telex from Tel Aviv to Foreign Office, 20 November 1972; Telex from Cairo to Foreign Office, 27 November 1972.

284. PAAA Berlin, B36/544: Telex from Tel Aviv to Foreign Office, 23 November 1972; Gespräch des israelischen Botschafters mit dem Bundespräsidenten (29. November 1972), 1 December 1972.

285. Lämmer, "Der Beitrag des Sports."

286. PAAA Berlin/B36/544: Telex from Tel Aviv to Foreign Office, 23 November 1972.

287. PAAA Berlin/B36/545: Umfrage in Israel zur Reise des Bundeskanzlers, 15 December 1972; Telex from Tel Aviv to Foreign Office, 18 December 1972.

288. PAAA Berlin/B36/545: Telex from Tel Aviv to Foreign Office, 12 and 14 December 1972.

289. PAAA Berlin/B36/545: Telex from Tel Aviv to Foreign Office, 5 December 1972.

290. Schwarz, *Akten zur Auswärtigen Politik 1972*, vol. 3, document 400, pp. 1794–95.

291. Ibid., document 422, pp. 1880–83.

292. Weingardt, *Deutsche Israel- und Nahost-Politik*, p. 223. By 1979, it had risen consistently to DM 39 billion.

293. PAAA Berlin/B36/544: Telex from Tel Aviv to Foreign Office, 18 December 1972.

294. Cited in Dahlke, *Der Anschlag auf Olympia '72*, p. 71.

295. See BAK/B185/2604: 27. Vorstandssitzung, 14 September 1973.

296. Daume wrote to Vogel, for instance: "As a result of the generous donation by the Federal Government a new situation has arisen. This makes the expenditure of budgetary means by the OC no longer necessary. Too much could naturally easily create the impression of a confession of responsibility" (FES/1/HJVA400100: Daume to Vogel, 27 September 1972).

297. Reeve, *One Day in September*, pp. 180–87.

298. Klein, *Striking Back*, p. 90.

8. CONCLUSION

1. StAMü/BuR/3247: Noel to Kronawitter, 25 August 1972; Ansprache von Oberbürgermeister Kronawitter beim Olympia-Empfang am 9. September 1972, 25 August 1972.

2. Johannes Paulmann, "Representation without Emulation: German Cultural Diplomacy in Search of Integration and Self-Assurance during the Adenauer Era," *German Politics and Society* 25, no. 2, 2007, p. 169, our emphasis.

3. Charlie Jeffrey, "German Federalism from Cooperation to Competition," in Maiken Umbach, ed., *German Federalism: Past, Present, Future* (Basingstoke, 2002), pp. 172–88.

4. Elizabeth Audrey Leckie Schlüssel, "Zur Rolle der Musik bei den Eröffnungs- und Schlußfeiern der Olympischen Spiele von 1896 bis 1972," PhD dissertation (Deutsche Sporthochschule Köln, 2001), p. 540.

5. Ulrich Pfeil, "Die Olympischen Spiele 1972 und die Fußballweltmeisterschaft 1974: Fallbeispiele für die Verquickung von Sport, Politik und Gesellschaft," *Deutschland Archiv* 39, no. 3, 2006, pp. 418–19.

6. Interview with Klaus von Lindeiner, 5 November 2003.

7. StAMü/BuR/3247: Noel to Kronawitter, 25 August 1972.

8. Paulmann, "Representation without Emulation," pp. 169, 189.

9. Ibid., p. 194.

10. Paul Sigel, *Exponiert: Deutsche Pavillons auf Weltausstellungen* (Berlin, 2000), p. 216.

11. Ibid., pp. 222, 237, 238.

12. Ibid., p. 244.

13. StAMü/Ratssitzungsprotokolle: Fragestunde in der Stadtratsvollversammlung, 25 July 1972.

14. PAAA Berlin/Av. Neues Amt 2.257: "Das Münchner Orchester studiert die Nationalhymnen ein," *Maariv,* 25 May 1972.

15. See Leckie Schlüssel, *Zur Rolle der Musik,* pp. 589–607.

16. Sigel, *Exponiert,* p 243.

17. Alan Tomlinson and Christopher Young, "Culture, Politics, and Spectacle in the Global Sports Event—An Introduction," in Tomlinson and Young, eds., *National Identity and Global Sports Events: Culture, Politics, and Spectacle in the Olympics and the Football World Cup* (New York, 2006), pp. 4–6.

18. Pfeil, "Die Olympischen Spiele 1972 und die Fußballweltmeisterschaft 1974," p. 423.

19. DOA/Nachlaß Daume/198: 12. Mitgliederversammlung, 25 June 1977.

20. Edgar Wolfrum, *Die geglückte Demokratie: Geschichte der Bundesrepublik Deutschland von ihren Anfängen bis zur Gegenwart* (Stuttgart, 2006), pp. 324–26.

21. CULDA/OS72/loose materials: Erfreulich positive Schlußbilanz (press release), 25 June 1972.

22. StAMü/Olympiade 1972/509–1: Ansprache beim Besuch von Brundage am 27. Januar 1969.

23. Deutscher Bundestag, 7. Wahlperiode, Drucksache VII/3066: Abschlußbericht über die Gesamtfinanzierung der Olympischen Spiele in München, 9 January 1975.

24. DOA/Nachlaß Daume/198: 12. Mitgliederversammlung, 25 June 1977.

25. See Deutscher Bundestag, 6. Wahlperiode, 1. Sonderausschuß für Sport und Olympische Spiele, Protokoll der 5. Sitzung vom 22.1.1970.

26. Deutscher Bundestag, 6. Wahlperiode, Drucksache VI/3665, Anlage 3.

27. Monika Meyer-Künzel, *Städtebau der Weltausstellungen und Olympischen Spiele: Stadtentwicklung der Veranstaltungsorte* (Hamburg, 2001), p. 425.

28. Egon Dheus, *Die Olympiastadt München* (Stuttgart, 1972), p. 269.

29. Detlev Klingbeil, "Grundzüge der stadtstrukturellen Entwicklung nach dem II. Weltkrieg," in Robert Geipel and Günter Heinritz, eds., *München: Ein sozialgeographischer Exkursionsführer,* Münchener geographische Hefte 55–56 (Kallmünz, 1987), p. 119.

30. Detlev Klingbeil, "Epochen der Stadtgeschichte und der Stadtstrukturenentwicklung," in Geipel and Heinritz, *München: Ein sozialgeographischer Exkursionsführer,* p. 98.

31. Dheus, *Die Olympiastadt München,* p. 270.

32. See e.g. FES/Dep. HJV/Reden 1972: Ludwig Koch, Abschiedsansprache für Vogel (Juli 1972) and Hans-Jochen Vogel, *Die Amtskette: Meine 12 Münchner Jahren. Ein Erlebnisbericht,* (Munich, 1972), p. 152.

33. Robert Geipel, Ilse Helbrecht, and Jürgen Pohl, "Die Münchner Olympischen Spiele von 1972 als Instrument der Stadtentwicklungspolitik," in Hartmut Häußermann

and Walter Siebel, eds., *Festivalisierung der Stadtpolitik: Stadtentwicklung durch große Projekte, Leviathan. Zeitschrift für Sozialwissenschaft* (Sonderheft 13, 1993), pp. 297–98.

34. See Robert Geipel, "Münchens Image und Probleme," in Geipel and Heinritz, *München: Ein sozialgeographischer Exkursionsführer*, p. 38.

35. *Frankfurter Rundschau*, 12 September 1972.

36. Detlev Klingbeil, "Münchens Wirtschafts- und Bevölkerungsentwicklung nach dem II. Weltkrieg," in Geipel and Heinritz, *München: Ein sozialgeographischer Exkursionsführer*, p. 50.

37. DOA/Nachlaß Daume/198: 12. Mitgliederversammlung, 25 June 1977; CULDA/OS72/loose materials: Werner Göhner, "Olympia hat sich gelohnt" (press release), 25 June 1977.

38. DOA/Nachlaß Daume/Texte Daume 2: "Munich's Olympic Park," 18 April 1979.

39. Christopher Young, "Kaiser Franz and the Communist Bowl: Memory in Munich's Olympic Stadium," *American Behavioural Scientist* 46, no. 11, 2003, p. 1479.

40. BayHStA/StK/14032: Sonderprogramm für prominente ausländische Gäste, 5 October 1971.

41. Ferdinand Kramer, "München und die Olympischen Spiele von 1972," in Christian Koller, ed., *Sport als städtisches Ereignis* (Ostfildern, 2008), pp. 246–47.

42. See Herbert Riehl-Heyse, *CSU: Die Partei, die das schöne Bayern erfunden hat* (Munich, 1979); see also Claire Sutherland, "Nation, Heimat, Vaterland: The Reinvention of Concepts by the Bavarian CSU," *German Politics* 10, no. 3, 2001, pp. 13–26.

43. We owe this information to Claus Brügmann of the ACSP of the Hanns-Seidel-Stiftung, Munich.

44. Matthias Dahlke, *Der Anschlag auf Olympia '72: Die politischen Reaktionen auf den internationalen Terrorismus in Deutschland* (Munich, 2006), p. 89.

45. Ibid., p. 72.

46. DOA/Nachlaß Daume/566: Noel-Baker to Daume, 20 September 1972.

47. "Frustrating Terrorists," reprinted in *International Herald Tribune*, 11 September 1972.

48. Melani McAlister, *Epic Encounters: Culture, Media, and U.S. Interests in the Middle East, 1945–2000* (Berkeley, 2001), p. 180.

49. Presse- und Informationsamt der Bundesregierung and Pressestelle der Bayerischen Staatskanzlei. *Dokumentation: Der Überfall auf die israelische Olympiamannschaft* (Munich, 1972), pp. 4–5.

50. DOA/Nachlaß Daume/198: 12. Mitgliederversammlung, 25 June 1977.

51. DOA/Nachlaß Daume/198: Aphorismen zur Auflösung des Organisationskomitees.

52. David Clay Large, *Nazi Games: The Olympics of 1936* (New York, 2007), pp. 332–36.

53. The relevant chapter in Guttmann's overview *The Olympics: A History of the Modern Games* (Urbana, 2nd ed. 2002) is entitled "A Time of Troubles" (pp. 125–40).

54. Clay Large, *Nazi Games*, p. 333.

55. Paulmann, "Representation without Emulation," p. 169; see also Johannes Paulmann, "Auswärtige Repräsentationen nach 1945: Zur Geschichte der deutschen Selbst-

darstellung im Ausland," in Paulmann, ed., *Auswärtige Repräsentationen: Deutsche Kulturdiplomatie nach 1945* (Cologne, 2005), p. 2.

56. Paulmann, "Representation without Emulation," p. 170.

57. BAK/B106/30639: Studie für die Sitzung der "Arbeitsgruppe Olympia" am 9. November 1970.

58. BAB/SAPMO/02/IVA2/10.02/-16: München '72. Interne Informationen 5.

59. BAK/B106/30639: Studie für die Sitzung der "Arbeitsgruppe Olympia" am 9. November 1970.

60. Claire Brewster and Keith Brewster, "Mexico City 1968: Sombreros and Skyscrapers," in Alan Tomlinson and Christopher Young, eds., *National Identity and Global Sports Events: Culture, Politics, and Spectacle in the Olympics and the Football World Cup* (New York, 2006), pp. 110–11.

61. CULDA/OS72/13.1: 11. Öffentlichkeitsausschußsitzung, 19 October 1971.

62. BAK/B185/3035: Haas, Werbung und Öffentlichkeitsarbeit 1968–1972.

63. CULDA/OS72/13.1: Arbeitskreis PR, 19 October 1971.

64. Organizing Committee for the Games of the XXth Olympiad Munich 1972, ed., *Die Spiele: The Official Report,* vol. 1: *The Organization* (Munich, 1972), p. 302.

65. Miquel de Moragas, Ana Belen Moreno, and Christopher Kennett, "The Legacy of the Symbols: Communication and the Olympic Games," in Moragas, Moreno, Kennett, and Nuria Puig, eds., *The Legacy of the Olympic Games 1984–2000: International Symposium, Lausanne, 14th, 15th, and 16th November 2002* (Lausanne, 2003), pp. 279–88.

66. BAK/B136/5561: BPA, Dem Herrn Bundeskanzler, 7 July 1966.

67. BAK/B106/30639: BPA, EMNID 6/1, Fazit, 11 August 1971.

68. *Die Spiele: The Official Report,* vol. 1, p. 212.

69. CULDA/OS72/Diem-Briefwechsel: Diem to Daume, 5 October 1971.

70. BAK/B185/2809: Vorlage zur 23. Vorstandssitzung am 11. Oktober 1971: Public Relations Programm für die Bundesrepublik.

71. Hartmut Becker, "Die Einstellung der Bevölkerung der Bundesrepublik zu den Olympischen Spielen in München," *Leibeserziehung: Monatsschrift für Wissenschaft und Unterricht* 21, no. 8, August 1972, p. 286.

72. Ibid.

73. CULDA/OS72/13.7: Brauer, Aktenvermerk, 20 April 1972.

74. CULDA/OS72/13.4: Lammers, Werbung und Öffentlichkeit zur Glücksspirale 1971, 7 October 1971. Paradoxically, as the public mood slipped, the lottery's success increased in 1972 (for figures see *Die Spiele: The Official Report,* vol. 1, pp. 64–6).

75. "20 Olympia-Karten je Abgeordneter," *Abendzeitung München,* 25 June 1971.

76. CULDA/OS72/13.1: Deutscher Städtetag to Haas, 24 February and 10 April 1972, correspondence between Bayerische Staatskanzlei and Bayerischer Städteverband, 21 December 1971 and 12 January 1972; Aktennotiz, Beflaggung der Grenzübergangsstellen, 29 March 1972.

77. See, for example, Joachim Kaiser, "München als (un)heimliche Lebensform" and Peter M. Bode, "München verliert sein Gesicht. Anmerkungen zur städtebaulichen Entwicklung einer Millionenstadt," *Süddeutsche Zeitung,* 20–22 May 1972.

78. BPA, *Emnid Informationen 1971*, p. 18.

79. CULDA/OS72/13.1: 11. Öffentlichkeitsausschußsitzung, 19 October 1971.

80. Hartmut Becker, "Die Beurteilung der Spiele der XX. Olympiade in München durch die Bevölkerung der Bundesrepublik," *Monatsschrift zur Wissenschaft und Praxis des Sports* 22, no. 6, June 1973, pp. 204–5.

81. Twenty-two percent, followed by nineteen because of the good they would do to the country's image abroad, and ten because the world would see Germany as it "really is today" (BAK/B106/30639: BPA, EMNID 2/2, Zusammenfassung, 12 April 1972).

82. Despite a dementi issued by Brandt claiming that whatever he had said in the direct aftermath had been misquoted, the press quoted him directly as describing Fürstenfeldbruck as a "dreadful display of German helplessness and incompetence" on 17 September (BAK/B106/146540: Deutscher Bundestag, Innenausschuß, Kurzprotokoll der 91. Sitzung am 18. September 1972; "Das Massaker von München," in *Der Stern*, 17 September 1972).

83. Dahlke, *Der Anschlag auf Olympia '72*, p. 89.

84. Ibid., p. 94.

85. BAK/B185/3230: Schreiber, Tätigkeitsbericht der Abt. XIII.

86. BAK/B122/15033: Embassy Rabat to Foreign Office, 18 September 1973.

87. According to a *dpa*-Meldung quoted in Bundespresseamt, Olympia-Sonderdienst, no. 2, 8 September 1972.

88. Horst Vetten, "Was bleibt von diesen Spielen?" *Abendzeitung München*, 11 September 1972.

89. See, for example, BAK/B122/15033: Bergbau AG Westfalen, Heesen, to Heinemann, with a list of signatures, 6 September 1972; for other examples see BAK/B122/15033 and 15034.

90. FES 1/HJVA 400099: W. O. to Ben-Horin, 7 September 1972.

91. Markus A. Weingardt, *Deutsche Israel- und Nahost-Politik: Die Geschichte einer Gratwanderung seit 1949* (Frankfurt am Main, 2002), p. 190, and also p. 234 (on the Yom-Kippur War of 1973); PAAA Berlin/B36/457: Deutschland-Berichte, 6. Jahrgang, Nr. 3, March 1970.

92. Quoted in Otto Fischer, "Gemeinsame Abscheu—gemeinsame Hoffnung," *Süddeutsche Zeitung*, 8 September 1972.

93. See Kay Schiller, "Death at the Munich Olympics," in Alon Confino, Paul Betts, and Dirk Schumann, eds., *Between Mass Death and Individual Loss: The Place of the Dead in Twentieth-Century Germany* (New York, 2008), p. 131.

94. Heiner Müller, "Ein Opfer im Kampf gegen Gewalt," *Süddeutsche Zeitung*, 9–10 September 1972.

95. Ernest Landau, "Der blutige Dienstag," *Münchner Jüdische Nachrichten*, 8 September 1972.

96. BayHStA/MInn/88627/1: KEZ/Staatsschutz, Morgenmeldung, 5 *[sic]* September 1972.

97. BAK/B185/911: Emmy Schwabe, Aktennotiz for Dr. Hegels, 9 September 1972; Reichart to Troeger, 9 September 1972.

98. Dahlke, *Der Anschlag auf Olympia '72*, pp. 90–91.

99. BayHStA/MInn/88623/2: Betr. Ausreise von Tunesiern, 6 September 1972.

100. McAlister, *Epic Encounters,* pp. 180–81.

101. Dahlke, *Der Anschlag auf Olympia '72,* pp. 88–101. Tellingly, many individuals had written to the federal Ministry of Justice asking that the three terrorists be given free passage (see BAK/B141/30902).

102. *Der Spiegel,* 18 September 1972.

103. See Karen Schönwälder, *Einwanderung und ethnische Pluralität: Politische Entscheidungen und öffentliche Debatten in Großbritannien und der Bundesrepublik von den 1950er bis zu den 1970er Jahren* (Essen, 2001), pp. 595–601.

104. "'Willi Daume konnte Geige spielen . . . :' Zeitzeugen erinnern sich," in Bundesinstitut für Sportwissenschaft and Deutsches Olympisches Institut, eds., *Willi Daume: Olympische Dimensionen. Ein Symposion* (Bonn, 2004), p. 96.

105. *sid*-Olympia-Ausgabe, 11 September 1972.

106. *Die Spiele: The Official Report,* vol. 1, p. 38.

107. Hans-Jochen Vogel, "Olympischer Terror," *sid*-Olympia-Ausgabe, 6 September 1972.

108. Our thanks to Brigitte Maibohm for allowing access to this event.

109. Karl-Otto Saur, "Krach nach Kündigung von Olympia-Hostessen," *Süddeutsche Zeitung,* 9–10 September 1972.

110. IOC Lausanne/Executive Board Meeting, 2–5 February 1973: Brundage, Statement at the Games of the XXth Olympiad.

111. IOC Lausanne/Minutes of the 74th IOC session, Varna, 5–7 October 1973.

112. FES/1/HJVA 400099: O. B. to Vogel, 8 September 1972.

113. StaMü/Olympiade 1972/521: Noel to Vogel, 12 September 1972, with handwritten comments by Vogel.

114. Dahlke, *Anschlag auf Olympia '72,* p. 70.

115. StAMü/Olympiade 1972/601: Bieringer, Vermerk vom 7. März 1973; ACSP/Nachlaß Klein/39: Günther Neske to Klein, 6 September 1972.

116. StAMü/Olympiade 1972/129: Einladung und Betreuung städtischer Gäste, 23 March 1970. The invitation came with a ticket for a sporting and cultural event and an offer of assistance with accommodation. It is unclear how many accepted (BayHStA/StK/1403: Steinkohl to Kessel, 27 June 1972).

117. DOA/Nachlaß Daume/198: 12. Mitgliederversammlung, 25 June 1977.

118. See, for example, the daily series "Olympische Spiele—heute vor 10 Jahren," *Süddeutsche Zeitung,* 26 August—11 September 1972.

119. DOA/Nachlaß Daume/513: Draft of *GEO* magazine article (1988).

120. DOA/Nachlaß Daume/5, 40: Daume, Commemorative Address.

121. Hans-Jochen Vogel, "Stichworte für eine Ansprache," in Angelika Fox, *Olympia-Attentat 1972: Begleitheft zur Errichtung der Gedenkstätte für die ermordeten israelischen Sportler und den deutschen Polizeibeamten am 5. September 1999 in Fürstenfeldbruck* (Fürstenfeldbruck, 1999), pp. 74–75.

122. Of the many treatments of this topic, see in particular Aleida Assmann and Ute Frevert, *Geschichtsvergessenheit/Geschichtsversessenheit: Vom Umgang mit deutschen Vergangenheiten nach 1945* (Stuttgart, 1999) and Mary Fulbrook, *German National Identity after the Holocaust* (Cambridge, 1999), p. 235, from which the quotation is taken.

123. On *Munich* see Nigel Morris, *The Cinema of Steven Spielberg: Empire of Light* (London, 2007), pp. 359–75.

124. Paulmann, "Representation Without Emulation," p. 193.

125. Interview with Werner Rabe, 21 November 2003.

126. Interview with Gertrude Krombholz, 12 November 2003.

127. Interviews at the thirty-year reunion of Olympic organizers, 26 July 2002.

128. See BAK/B185/886–893.

129. Privatarchiv Gertrude Krombholz: Daume to Olympic hostesses, February 1972.

BIBLIOGRAPHY

1. ARCHIVAL SOURCES

ACSP: Archiv für Christlich-Soziale Politik der Hanns-Seidel-Stiftung, München
- Nachlaß Jaeger, Richard
- Nachlaß Klein, Hans
- LG: CSU-Landesgruppe

BAB: Bundesarchiv Berlin
- SAPMO: Stiftung Archiv der Parteien und Massenorganisationen der DDR

BAK: Bundesarchiv Koblenz
- B106: Bundesministerium des Innern
- B122: Bundespräsidialamt
- B136: Bundeskanzleramt
- B137: Bundesministerium für innerdeutsche Beziehungen
- B141: Bundesministerium der Justiz
- B185: Organisationskomitee für die Spiele der XX. Olympiade München, e.V.
- B213: Bundesministerium für wirtschaftliche Zusammenarbeit
- B322: Deutscher Sportbund

BayHStA: Bayerisches Hauptstaatsarchiv, München
- MF: Bayerisches Staatsministerium der Finanzen
- MInn: Bayerisches Staatsministerium des Innern
- MWi: Bayerisches Staatsministerium der Wirtschaft
- StK: Bayerische Staatskanzlei

BStU: Bundesbehörde für die Stasi-Unterlagen, Berlin

CULDA: Carl und Liselott Diem Archiv, Sporthochschule Köln
- Koebsel
- Nachlaß Liselott Diem

OS72: Olympische Spiele 1972
Vorhammer
DOA: Deutsche Olympische Akademie, Frankfurt am Main
Nachlaß Daume, Willi
FES: Friedrich-Ebert-Stiftung Bonn
Dep. HJV: Depositum Hans-Jochen Vogel
HFG-Archiv Ulm: Archiv der Hochschule für Gestaltung
Ai.Az.: Otl Aicher Archiv
IFS Archiv Hannover: Archiv des Instituts für Sportwissenschaft der Universität Hannover
Archiv Fritz Hattig
Handakte Martius
IOC Lausanne: Archives of the International Olympic Committee, Lausanne
Correspondence Brundage, Avery, 1962–63, 1964–1965, 1972
Correspondence Daume, Willi, 1957–1972
Correspondence Schöbel, Heinz, 1966–1980
Correspondence Stoytchev, Vladimir, 1948–1984
Minutes of Executive Board Meetings
LA Speyer: Landesarchiv Speyer (des Landes Rheinland-Pfalz)
Nachlaß Dr. Adolf Müller-Emmert (Bestand V91/225)
NOK-Archiv Frankfurt: Archiv des Nationalen Olympischen Komittees für Deutschland, Frankfurt am Main
PAAA Berlin: Politisches Archiv des Auswärtigen Amts, Berlin
Privatarchiv Gertrude Krombholz
StAMü: Stadtarchiv München
BuR: Bürgermeister und Rat
Olympia-Förderverein
Olympiade 1972
Ratsprotokolle
TU Mü-Weihst/ArchGrz: Technische Universität München-Weihenstephan
Archiv Günther Grzimek
UIUC Archives: Archives of the University of Illinois Urbana-Champaign
Avery Brundage Collection
U.S. National Archives College Park
Nixon Presidential Materials

2. INTERVIEWS

Authors' interviews
with Dan Alon, 29 January 2006
with Friedhelm Brebeck, 7 February 2005
with Gertrude Krombholz, 12 November 2003
with Klaus von Lindeiner, 5 November 2003
with Rolf Müller, 10 April 2005

with Werner Rabe, 21 November 2003
with Werner and Anita Ruhnau, 23 February 2004
with Hans-Jochen Vogel, 10 November 2003
with Carlo Weber, 29 September 2005
with Markus Wolf, 22 February 2006
with several hostesses at the thirty-year reunion of Olympic organizers, 26 July 2002

Andreas H. Trebels, Lorenz Peiffer et al., Interview mit Prof. Dr. Willi Daume am 10./11. März 1994, transcript (IFS Archiv Hannover).

Andreas H. Trebels, Lorenz Peiffer et al., Interview mit Prof. Dr. Willi Daume, Protokollierte und überarbeitete Fassung der 2. und 3. Interviewphase im Jahr 1994, transcript (IFS Archiv Hannover).

Lorenz Peiffer, Interview mit Dr. Hans-Jochen Vogel—ehemaliger Oberbürgermeister von München—am 13.2.1996, transcript (IFS Archiv Hannover).

3. PUBLISHED SOURCES AND SECONDARY LITERATURE

100 Jahre deutsche Ausgrabung in Olympia, Munich, 1972.

Aicher, Otl. "Planung in Mißkredit. Zur Entwicklung von Stadt und Land," in Hans-Werner Richter, ed., *Bestandsaufnahme. Eine deutsche Bilanz, Sechsunddreißig Beiträge deutscher Wissenschaftler, Schriftsteller und Publizisten,* Munich, 1962, pp. 398–420.

———. "über management: willi daume," in Volker Rattemeyer, ed., *Kunst + Design, Kultur Olympia. Willi Daume, Preisträger der Stankowski-Stiftung 1986,* Kassel, 1986, pp. 12–17.

———. *die welt als entwurf,* Berlin, 1991.

———. "Olympia und Kunst," in Norbert Müller and Manfred Messing, eds., *Auf der Suche nach der Olympischen Idee: Facetten der Forschung von Athen bis Atlanta,* Kassel, 1996, pp. 16–22.

Alkemeyer, Thomas. *Körper, Kult und Politik: Von der "Muskelreligion" Pierre de Coubertins zur Inszenierung von Macht in den Olympischen Spielen von 1936,* Frankfurt am Main, 1996.

Alter, Peter, ed. *Der DAAD in der Zeit: Geschichte, Gegenwart und zukünftige Aufgaben—vierzehn Essays,* Bonn, 2000.

Andrew, Christopher. *The Defence of the Realm: The Authorized History of MI5,* London, 2009.

Andrew, Christopher, and Vasili Mitrokhin. *The World Was Going Our Way: The KGB and the Battle for the Third World,* New York, 2005.

Arbeitsgemeinschaft Stadtentwicklungsplan München, *München: Stadtentwicklungsplan. Gesamtverkehrsplan,* Munich, 1962.

Arbena, Joseph L. "Hosting the Summer Olympic Games: Mexico City, 1968," in Arbena and David G. LaFrance, eds., *Sport in Latin America and the Caribbean,* Wilmington, DE, 2002, pp. 133–43.

Arledge, Roone. *Roone: A Memoir,* New York, 2003.

Assmann, Aleida, and Ute Frevert. *Geschichtsvergessenheit/Geschichtsversessenheit: Vom Umgang mit deutschen Vergangenheiten nach 1945,* Stuttgart, 1999.

Bach, Steven. *Leni: The Life and Work of Leni Riefenstahl,* London, 2007.

Balbier, Uta Andrea. "'Der Welt das moderne Deutschland vorstellen:' Die Eröffnungsfeier der Olympischen Spiele in München," in Johannes Paulmann, ed., *Auswärtige Repräsentationen: Deutsche Kulturdiplomatie nach 1945*, Cologne, 2005, pp. 105–19.

———. *Kalter Krieg auf der Aschenbahn: Der deutsch-deutsche Sport 1950–1972. Eine politische Geschichte*, Paderborn, 2007.

Bar-Zohar, Michael, and Eitan Haber. *Massacre in Munich: The Manhunt for the Killers behind the 1972 Olympics Massacre*, Guilford, CT, 3rd ed. 2005.

Barke, Michael. "Mexico City 1968," in John R. and Margaret M. Gold, eds., *Olympic Cities: City Agendas, Planning, and the World's Games, 1896 to 2012*, London, 2006, pp. 183–96.

Bass, Amy. *Not the Triumph But the Struggle: The 1968 Olympics and the Making of the Black Athlete*, London, 2002.

Bauer, Michael. *Die Olympischen Spiele 1932 in Los Angeles aus der Sicht des Kommandanten der deutschen Mannschaft Carl Diem*, Marburg, 1998.

Bauten der Olympischen Spiele 1972: Architekturwettbewerbe, Sonderband 1: 1969, Stuttgart, 1969.

Bauten der Olympischen Spiele 1972: Architekturwettbewerbe, Sonderband 2: Bestandsaufnahme Herbst 1970, Stuttgart, 1970.

Bauten für Olympia 1972: München, Kiel, Augsburg. Building and Facilities for the Olympic Games, Munich, 1972.

Becker, Hartmut. "Die Einstellung der Bevölkerung der Bundesrepublik zu den Olympischen Spielen in München," *Leibeserziehung: Monatsschrift für Wissenschaft und Unterricht* 21, no. 8, August 1972, pp. 283–86.

———. "Die Beurteilung der Spiele der XX. Olympiade in München durch die Bevölkerung der Bundesrepublik," *Monatsschrift zur Wissenschaft und Praxis des Sports* 22, no. 6, June 1973, pp. 204–6.

Bender, Peter. *Die "Neue Ostpolitik" und ihre Folgen: Vom Mauerbau bis zur Vereinigung*, Munich, 3rd ed. 1995.

Bernett, Hajo. "Das Bild der Olympischen Spiele von 1936 im Spiegel neuerer Publikationen," *Leibeserziehung: Monatsschrift für Wissenschaft und Unterricht* 21, no. 8, 1972, pp. 275–78.

———. *Guido von Mengden, 'Generalstabschef' des deutschen Sports*, Berlin, 1976.

Betts, Paul. *The Authority of Everyday Objects: A Cultural History of West German Industrial Design*, Berkeley, 2004.

Bieringer, Klaus. "Kulturprogramm—ein olympischer Auftrag," in Volker Rattemeyer, ed., *Kunst + Design, Kultur Olympia. Willi Daume, Preisträger der Stankowski-Stiftung 1986*, Kassel, 1986, pp. 26–30.

Blackbourn, David. *The Conquest of Nature: Water, Landscape and the Making of Modern Germany*, London, 2006.

Blasius, Tobias. *Olympische Bewegung, Kalter Krieg und Deutschlandpolitik 1949–1972*, Frankfurt am Main, 2001.

Blundell-Jones, Peter. *Günter Behnisch*, Basel, 2000.

Borgers, Walter. *Olympic Torch Relays 1936–1994*, Kassel 1996.

Brandt, Willy. *People and Politics: The Years 1960–1975*, New York, 1976.

Brantl, Sabine. *Haus der Kunst 1937–1997: Eine historische Dokumentation*, Munich, no date.

Brasher, Christopher. *Mexico 1968: A Diary of the XIXth Olympiad,* London, 1968.

———. *Munich 1972,* London, 1972.

Brewster, Claire, and Keith Brewster. "Mexico City 1968: Sombreros and Skyscrapers," in Alan Tomlinson and Christopher Young, eds., *National Identity and Global Sports Events: Culture, Politics, and Spectacle in the Olympics and the Football World Cup,* New York, 2006, pp. 99–116.

Burckhardt, Berthold, ed. *Frei Otto: Schriften und Reden, 1951–1983,* Wiesbaden, 1984.

Burns, Rob, and Wilfried van der Will. *Protest and Democracy in West Germany: Extra-Parliamentary Opposition and the Democratic Agenda,* Basingstoke, 1988.

Cantelon, Hart. "Amateurism, High-Performance Sport, and the Olympics," in Kevin Young and Kevin B. Wamsley, eds., *Global Olympics: Historical and Sociological Studies of the Modern Games,* Amsterdam, 2005, pp. 83–101.

Carl-Diem Institut an der Deutschen Sporthochschule, ed., *Pierre de Coubertin: Der Olympische Gedanke, Reden und Aufsätze,* Schondorf, 1967.

Carruthers, Susan L. *The Media at War: Communication and Conflict in the Twentieth Century,* Basingstoke, 1999.

Clay Large, David. *Nazi Games: The Olympics of 1936,* New York, 2007.

Connor, Ken. *Ghost Force: The Secret History of the SAS,* London, 1998.

Cooley, John K. *Green March, Black September: The Story of the Palestinian Arabs,* London, 1973.

Dahlke, Matthias. *Der Anschlag auf Olympia '72: Die politischen Reaktionen auf den internationalen Terrorismus in Deutschland,* Munich, 2006.

Daume, Willi. "Eine Milliarde für die Olympischen Spiele?" *Olympisches Feuer* 6, 1966, pp. 1–5.

Däubler-Gmelin, Herta, Helmut Schmidt, and Jürgen Schmude, eds. *Gestalten und Dienen. Fortschritt mit Vernunft: Festschrift zum 70. Geburtstag von Hans-Jochen Vogel,* Wiesbaden, 1996.

de Moragas, Miquel, Ana Belen Moreno, and Christopher Kennett. "The Legacy of the Symbols: Communication and the Olympic Games," in Moragas, Moreno, Kennett, and Nuria Puig, eds., *The Legacy of the Olympic Games 1984–2000: International Symposium, Lausanne, 14th, 15th, and 16th November 2002,* Lausanne, 2003, pp. 279–88.

Dehnhardt, Sebastian, Uli Weidenbach, and Manfred Oldenburg. *Der Olympia-Mord. (München '72—Die wahre Geschichte),* television documentary, 2006.

Derix, Simone. "Gruppenbild mit Industrielandschaft: Wie Krupp die Bundesrepublik Deutschland bei Staatsbesuchen bebilderte," in Johannes Paulmann, ed., *Auswärtige Repräsentationen: Deutsche Kulturdiplomatie nach 1945,* Cologne, 2005, pp. 165–84.

Deutscher Sportbund, ed. *Willi Daume: Deutscher Sport 1952–1972,* Munich, 1973.

Dheus, Egon. *Die Olympiastadt München,* Stuttgart, 1972.

Diem, Carl. *Weltgeschichte des Sports,* vol. 1: *Von den Anfängen bis zur französischen Revolution;* vol. 2: *Der moderne Sport,* Stuttgart, 1960.

Diem, Liselott. *Leben als Herausforderung,* 3 vols., St. Augustin, 1986.

Diffrient, David Scott. "Spectator Sports and Terrorist Reports: Filming the Munich Olympics, (Re)Imagining the Munich Massacre," *Sport in Society* 11, nos. 2–3, 2008, pp. 311–29.

Dirlik, Arif. "The Third World," in Carole Fink, Philipp Gassert, and Detlef Junker, eds., *1968: The World Transformed,* Cambridge, 1998, pp. 295–317.

Dodd, Jr., William Edward, and Martha Dodd, eds. *Ambassador Dodd's Diary, 1933–1938,* New York, 1941.

Doering-Manteuffel, Anselm. "Westernisierung: Politisch-ideeller und gesellschaftlicher Wandel in der Bundesrepublik bis zum Ende der 60er Jahre," in Axel Schildt, Detlef Siegfried, and Karl Christian Lammers, eds., *Dynamische Zeiten: Die 60er Jahre in den beiden deutschen Gesellschaften,* Hamburg, 2000, pp. 311–41.

Dost, Susanne. *Das Olympische Dorf 1936 im Wandel der Zeit,* Berlin, 2003.

DSB-Präsidium. "Stellungnahme der Expertenkommission zu Werk und Person von Carl Diem (1882 bis 1962)," *Sozial- und Zeitgeschichte des Sports* 10, 1996, pp. 75–79.

Dubiel, Helmut. *Niemand ist frei von der Geschichte: Die nationalsozialistische Herrschaft in den Debatten des Deutschen Bundestages,* Munich, 1999.

Dwertmann, Hubert. "Die Rolle Carl Diems im nationalsozialistischen Regime: Zum Gutachten H. J. Teichlers und zur Stellungnahme der Expertenkommission," *Sozial- und Zeitgeschichte des Sports* 10, 1996, pp. 7–47.

Dwertmann, Hubert, and Lorenz Peiffer, eds. *Willi Daume: Eine Bibliographie seiner Schriften, Reden und Interviews,* Cologne, 2001.

———. "Zwischen Kontinuität, systematischem Neuaufbau und Transformation: Willi Daume—das 'neue' Gesicht im bundesrepublikanischen Sport," in Michael Krüger, ed., *Transformation des deutschen Sports seit 1939: Jahrestagung der dvs-Sektion Sportgeschichte vom 16.-18.6.2000 in Göttingen,* Hamburg, 2001, pp. 135–51.

Edelman, Robert. "Moscow 1980: Stalinism or Good, Clean Fun?" in Alan Tomlinson and Christopher Young, eds., *National Identity and Global Sports Events: Culture, Politics, and Spectacle in the Olympics and the Football World Cup,* New York, 2006, pp. 149–61.

Edmonds, David, and John Eidinow. *Bobby Fischer Goes to War: How the Soviets Lost the Most Extraordinary Chess Match of All Time,* New York, 2004.

Eisenberg, Christiane. *"English Sports" und deutsche Bürger: Eine Gesellschaftsgeschichte, 1800–1939,* Paderborn, 1999.

Fetzer, Thomas. "Die gesellschaftliche Akzeptanz des Leistungssportsystems," in Hans Joachim Teichler, ed., *Sport in der DDR: Eigensinn, Konflikte, Trends,* Cologne, 2003, pp. 273–357.

Fink, Carole. "Turning Away from the Past: West Germany and Israel, 1965–1967," in Philipp Gassert and Alan E. Steinweis, eds., *Coping with the Nazi Past: West German Debates on Nazism and Generational Conflict, 1955–1975,* New York, 2006, pp. 276–93.

Fox, Angelika. *Olympia-Attentat 1972: Begleitheft zur Errichtung der Gedenkstätte für die ermordeten israelischen Sportler und den deutschen Polizeibeamten am 5. September 1999 in Fürstenfeldbruck,* Fürstenfeldbruck, 1999.

Frey, Alfons. *Die industrielle Entwicklung Bayerns von 1925 bis 1975: Eine vergleichende Untersuchung über die Rolle der städtischen Agglomerationen im Industrialisierungsprozeß,* Berlin, 2003.

Fulbrook, Mary. *German National Identity after the Holocaust,* Cambridge, 1999.

Games of the XVIII Olympiad Tokyo 1964: The Official Report of the Organizing Committee, 2 vols., Tokyo, 1966.

Gay, Peter. *My German Question: Growing up in Nazi Berlin*, New Haven, CT, 1998.

Gebauer, Gunter, and Christoph Wulf. "Die Berliner Olympiade 1936: Spiele der Gewalt," in Gebauer, ed., *Olympische Spiele—die andere Utopie der Moderne. Olympia zwischen Kult und Droge*, Frankfurt am Main, 1996, pp. 247–55.

Gehlberg, Karl-Ulrich. "Dynamischer Wandel und Kontinuität: Die Ära Goppel (1962–1978)," in Max Spindler and Alois Schmid, eds., *Handbuch der bayerischen Geschichte*, Munich, 2nd ed. 2003, vol. IV/1, pp. 857–956.

Gehrmann, Siegfried. "Symbol of National Resurrection: Max Schmeling, German Sports Idol," in Richard Holt, J. A. Mangan, and Pierre Lanfranchi, eds., *European Heroes: Myth, Identity, Sport*, London, 1996, pp. 101–13.

Geipel, Robert. "Münchens Image und Probleme," in Geipel and Günter Heinritz, eds., *München: Ein sozialgeographischer Exkursionsführer*, Münchener geographische Hefte 55–56, Kallmünz, 1987, pp. 17–42.

Geipel, Robert, Ilse Helbrecht, and Jürgen Pohl. "Die Münchner Olympischen Spiele von 1972 als Instrument der Stadtentwicklungspolitik," in Hartmut Häußermann and Walter Siebel, eds., *Festivalisierung der Stadtpolitik: Stadtentwicklung durch große Projekte, Leviathan. Zeitschrift für Sozialwissenschaft*, Sonderheft 13, 1993, pp. 278–304.

Genscher, Hans-Dietrich. *Erinnerungen*, Berlin, 2nd ed. 1995.

Gesellschaft zur Förderung des olympischen Gedankens in der DDR [Heinz Koch, Dieter Wales, Helmuth Westphal, Bernhard Wilk], ed., *München 1972 Schicksalsspiele? Eine Dokumentation über den Mißbrauch der olympischen Bewegung und ihrer Spiele durch den deutschen Imperialismus*, Berlin, 1969.

Geyer, Martin H. "Der Kampf um nationale Repräsentation: Deutsch-deutsche Sportbeziehungen und die 'Hallstein-Doktrin,'" *Vierteljahrshefte für Zeitgeschichte* 44, 1996, pp. 55–86.

———. "On the Road to a German 'Postnationalism:' Athletic Competition between the Two German States in the Era of Konrad Adenauer," *German Politics & Society* 25, no. 2, 2007, pp. 140–67.

Gilleßen, Wolfgang. *Das Olympische Dorf 1936*, Potsdam, 1996.

Gollwitzer, Gerda, ed. *Spiel und Sport in der Stadtlandschaft: Erfahrungen und Beispiele für morgen*, Munich, 1972.

Gordon, Robert S. C., and John London. "Italy 1934: Football and Fascism," in Alan Tomlinson and Christopher Young, eds., *National Identity and Global Sports Events: Culture, Politics, and Spectacle in the Olympics and the Football World Cup*, New York, 2006, pp. 41–63.

Görtemaker, Manfred. *Geschichte der Bundesrepublik Deutschland von der Gründung bis zur Gegenwart*, Munich, 1999.

Grauhan, Rolf-Richard. *Politik der Verstädterung*, Frankfurt am Main, 1974.

Gray, William Glenn. *Germany's Cold War: The Global Campaign to Isolate East Germany, 1949–1969*, Chapel Hill, 2003.

Grupe, Ommo. "Willi Daume: Olympische Überzeugungen—der Sport, die Spiele," in Bundesinstitut für Sportwissenschaft and Deutsches Olympisches Institut, eds., *Willi Daume: Olympische Dimensionen. Ein Symposion*, Bonn, 2004, pp. 25–37.

Grupe, Ommo, Dietrich Kurz, and Johannes Marcus Teipel, eds. *The Scientific View of Sport: Perspectives—Aspects—Issues,* New York, 1972.

——, eds. *Sport in the Modern World—Chances and Problems,* New York, 1973.

Grzimek, Günther. *Gedanken zur Stadt- und Landschaftsarchitektur seit Friedrich Ludwig v. Sckell: Vortrag in der Bayrischen Akademie der Schönen Künste aus Anlaß der Verleihung des Friedrich Ludwig v. Sckell-Ehrenringes,* Munich, 1973.

——. *Die Besitzergreifung des Rasens: Folgerungen aus dem Modell Süd-Isar. Grünplanung heute,* Munich, 1983.

Günther, Frieder. "Gespiegelte Selbstdarstellung: Der Staatsbesuch von Theodor Heuss in Großbritannien im Oktober 1958," in Johannes Paulmann, ed., *Auswärtige Repräsentationen: Deutsche Kulturdiplomatie nach 1945,* Cologne, 2005, pp. 185–203.

Guttmann, Allen. *The Games Must Go On: Avery Brundage and the Olympic Movement,* New York, 1984.

——. *The Olympics: A History of the Modern Games,* Urbana, 2nd ed. 2002.

——. "Berlin 1936: The Most Controversial Olympics," in Alan Tomlinson and Christopher Young, eds., *National Identity and Global Sports Events: Culture, Politics, and Spectacle in the Olympics and the Football World Cup,* New York, 2006, pp. 65–81.

Haftendorn, Helga. *Deutsche Außenpolitik zwischen Selbstbeschränkung und Selbstbehauptung 1945–2000,* Stuttgart, 2001.

Hall, C. R. *Olympic Politics,* Manchester, 1992.

Hart, Alan. *Arafat,* London, 2nd ed. 1994.

Hartmann, Douglas. *Race, Culture, and the Revolt of the Black Athlete: The 1968 Olympic Protests and Their Aftermath,* Chicago, 2003.

Hartmann, Grit. *Goldkinder: Die DDR im Spiegel ihres Spitzensports,* Leipzig, 1997.

Hecker, Gerhard, August Kirsch, and Clemens Menze, eds. *Der Mensch im Sport: Festschrift zum 70. Geburtstag von Prof. Liselott Diem,* Schorndorf, 1976.

Heimerzheim, Peter. *Karl Ritter von Halt—Leben zwischen Sport und Politik,* St. Augustin, 1999.

Hentschel, Volker. *Ludwig Erhard: Ein Politikerleben,* Munich, 1996.

Herbert, Ulrich. "Liberalisierung als Lernprozeß: Die Bundesrepublik in der deutschen Geschichte—eine Skizze," in Herbert, ed., *Wandlungsprozesse in Westdeutschland: Belastung, Integration, Liberalisierung,* Göttingen, 2002, pp. 7–49.

Hesse, Michael, ed. *Baumeister im Ruhrgebiet,* vol. 1: *Werner Ruhnau,* Gelsenkirchen, 2002.

Hoberman, John M. *Sport and Political Ideology,* Austin, 1984.

——. *The Olympic Crisis: Sport, Politics, and the Moral Order,* New Rochelle, NY, 1986.

——. "Toward a Theory of Olympic Internationalism," *Journal of Sport History* 22, 1995, pp. 1–37.

Hobsbawm, Eric. *Age of Extremes: The Short Twentieth Century, 1914–1991,* London, 1994.

Höfer, Andreas. "Carl Diem: Ein Leben für den Sport," in Manfred Lämmer, ed., *Deutschland in der Olympischen Bewegung: Eine Zwischenbilanz,* Frankfurt am Main, 1999, pp. 261–65.

——. "Querelle d'allemand: Die gesamtdeutschen Olympiamannschaften, 1956–1964," in Manfred Lämmer, ed., *Deutschland in der Olympischen Bewegung: Eine Zwischenbilanz,* Frankfurt am Main, 1999, pp. 209–59.

———. "Willi Daume: Von der Machbarkeit der Utopie," in Manfred Lämmer, ed., *Deutschland in der Olympischen Bewegung: Eine Zwischenbilanz,* Frankfurt am Main, 1999, pp. 321–26.

Hohenemser, Herbert. "Edition Olympia München 72: Offenheit und Freiheit," in Volker Rattemeyer, ed., *Kunst + Design, Kultur Olympia. Willi Daume, Preisträger der Stankowski-Stiftung 1986,* Kassel, 1986, pp. 34–39.

Hohmann, Karl, ed. *Ludwig Erhard: Gedanken aus fünf Jahrzehnten. Reden und Schriften,* Düsseldorf, 1988.

Huster, Ronald. "Streitobjekt Friedensfahrt. Sportliche und sportpolitische Rivalitäten im Ostblock," *Deutschland Archiv* 37, no. 3, 2004, pp. 448–57.

Jeffrey, Charlie. "German Federalism from Cooperation to Competition," in Maiken Umbach, ed., *German Federalism: Past, Present, Future,* Basingstoke, 2002, pp. 172–88.

Judt, Tony. *Postwar: A History of Europe Since 1945,* New York, 2005.

Jungbauer, Andreas. "Die Auseinandersetzung um 'Sportvater' Carl Diem—am Beispiel seiner Geburtsstadt Würzburg, die nun ihre größte Veranstaltungshalle umbenennt," *SportZeiten: Sport in Geschichte, Kultur und Gesellschaft* 4, 2004, pp. 93–101.

Kaiser, Monika. *Machtwechsel von Ulbricht zu Honecker: Funktionsmechanismen der SED-Diktatur in Konfliktsituationen 1962 bis 1972,* Berlin, 1997.

Kauders, Anthony. *Democratization and the Jews: Munich, 1945–1965,* Lincoln, NE, 2004.

Keys, Barbara. "Spreading Peace, Democracy, and Coca-Cola®: Sport and American Cultural Expansion in the 1930s," *Diplomatic History* 28, no. 2, 2004, pp. 165–96.

Kießling, Friedrich. "Täter repräsentieren: Willy Brandts Kniefall in Warschau. Überlegungen zum Zusammenhang von bundesdeutscher Außenrepräsentation und der Erinnerung an den Nationalsozialismus," in Johannes Paulmann, ed., *Auswärtige Repräsentationen: Deutsche Kulturdiplomatie nach 1945,* Cologne, 2005, pp. 205–24.

Kilian, Werner. *Die Hallstein-Doktrin: Der diplomatische Krieg zwischen der BRD und der DDR 1955–1973. Aus den Akten der beiden deutschen Außenministerien,* Berlin, 2001.

Klein, Aaron J. *Striking Back: The 1972 Munich Olympics Massacre and Israel's Deadly Response,* New York, 2005.

Klein, Hans. *Avery Brundage—bekannt und unbekannt,* Munich, 1972.

Kleinknecht, Thomas, and Michael Sturm. " 'Demonstrationen sind punktuelle Plebiszite:' Polizeireform und gesellschaftliche Demokratisierung von den Sechziger- zu den Achtzigerjahren," *Archiv für Sozialgeschichte* 44, 2004, pp. 181–218.

Kleßmann, Christoph. *Zwei Staaten, eine Nation: Deutsche Geschichte 1955–1970,* Bonn, 2nd ed. 1997.

Klingbeil, Detlev. "Epochen der Stadtgeschichte und der Stadtstrukturenentwicklung," in Robert Geipel and Günter Heinritz, eds., *München: Ein sozialgeographischer Exkursionsführer,* Münchener geographische Hefte 55–56, Kallmünz, 1987, pp. 67–100.

———. "Grundzüge der stadtstrukturellen Entwicklung nach dem II. Weltkrieg," in Robert Geipel and Günter Heinritz, eds., *München: Ein sozialgeographischer Exkursionsführer,* Münchener geographische Hefte 55–56, Kallmünz, 1987, pp. 101–40.

———. "Münchens Wirtschafts- und Bevölkerungsentwicklung nach dem II. Weltkrieg," in Robert Geipel and Günter Heinritz, eds., *München: Ein sozialgeographischer Exkursionsführer,* Münchener geographische Hefte 55–56, Kallmünz, 1987, pp. 43–66.

Klotz, Heinrich. *Architektur in der Bundesrepublik*, Frankfurt am Main, 1977.

Kluge, Volker. *Olympische Sommerspiele: Die Chronik*, vol. 3: *Mexiko-Stadt 1968—Los Angeles 1984*, Berlin, 2000.

———. *Max Schmeling: Eine Biographie in 15 Runden*, Berlin, 2004.

Koenen, Gerd. *Das rote Jahrzehnt: Unsere kleine deutsche Kulturrevolution 1967–1977*, Cologne, 2001.

König, Andreas. *Günther Grzimek: Ein Landschaftsarchitekt der Nachkriegszeit. Berufliche Entwicklung, Konzepte und Arbeiten*, Diplomarbeit, TU München-Weihenstephan, 1996.

Kramer, Ferdinand. "München und die Olympischen Spiele von 1972," in Christian Koller, ed., *Sport als städtisches Ereignis*, Ostfildern, 2008, pp. 239–52.

Kraushaar, Wolfgang. *Frankfurter Schule und Studentenbewegung: Von der Flaschenpost zum Molotowcocktail 1946–1995*, vol. 1: *Chronik*, Hamburg, 1998.

———. *Die Bombe im Jüdischen Gemeindehaus*, Hamburg, 2005.

———. "Antizionismus als Trojanisches Pferd: Zur antisemitischen Dimension in der Kooperation von Tupamaros West-Berlin, RAF und RZ mit den Palästinensern," in Kraushaar, ed., *Die RAF und der linke Terrorismus*, Hamburg, 2006, vol. 1, pp. 676–95.

Krieg, Nina. "Die 'Weltstadt mit Herz:' Ein Überblick 1957 bis 1990," in Richard Bauer, ed., *Geschichte der Stadt München*, Munich, 1992, pp. 413–24.

Krüger, Arnd. "United States of America: The Crucial Battle," in William J. Murray and Krüger, eds., *The Nazi Olympics: Sport, Politics, and Appeasement in the 1930s*, Urbana, IL, rev. ed. 2003, pp. 44–69.

———. "What's the Difference between Propaganda for Tourism or for a Political Regime? Was the 1936 Olympics the First Postmodern Spectacle?" in John Bale and Mette Krogh Kristensen, eds., *Post-Olympism?: Questioning Sport in the Twenty-First Century*, Oxford, 2004, pp. 33–49.

Krzemiński, Adam. "Der Kniefall," in Étienne François and Hagen Schulze, eds., *Deutsche Erinnerungsorte: Eine Auswahl*, Munich, 2005, pp. 431–46.

Latouche, Daniel. "Montreal 1976," in John R. Gold and Margaret M. Gold, eds., *Olympic Cities: City Agendas, Planning, and the World's Games, 1896–2012*, London, 2007, pp. 197–217.

Leckie Schlüssel, Elizabeth Audrey. "Zur Rolle der Musik bei den Eröffnungs- und Schlußfeiern der Olympischen Spiele von 1896 bis 1972," PhD dissertation, Deutsche Sporthochschule Köln, 2001.

Leinemann, Jürgen. *Höhenrausch: Die wirklichkeitsleere Welt der Politiker*, Munich, 2006.

Lenk, Hans. *Leistungssport, Ideologie oder Mythos? Zur Leistungskritik und Sportphilosophie*, Stuttgart, 1972.

Liao, Hanwen, and Adrian Pitts. "A Brief Historical Review of Olympic Urbanization," *The International Journal of the History of Sport* 23, no. 7 (2006), pp. 1232–52.

MacAloon, John J. *This Great Symbol: Pierre De Coubertin and the Origins of the Modern Olympic Games*, Chicago, 1981.

MacDonald, Kevin. *One Day in September*, film documentary, 1999.

Manchester, William. *The Arms of Krupp, 1587–1968*, London, 1969.

Mandell, Richard. *The Nazi Olympics*, New York, 1971.
———. *The First Modern Olympics*, Berkeley, 1976.
———. *The Olympics of 1972: A Munich Diary*, Chapel Hill, NC, 1991.
Maraniss, David. *Rome 1960: The Olympics That Changed the World*, New York, 2008.
Marchand, Suzanne L. *Down from Olympus: Archaeology and Philhellenism in Germany, 1750–1970*, Princeton, 1996.
Margolick, David. *Beyond Glory: Max Schmeling vs. Joe Louis*, London, 2005.
Markovits, Andrei S., and Philip S. Gorski. *The German Left: Red, Green and Beyond*, Cambridge, 1993.
Marwick, Arthur. *The Sixties: Cultural Revolution in Britain, France, Italy, and the United States, c. 1958—c. 1974*, Oxford, 1998.
Matthew, Vincent. *My Race Be Won*, New York, 1974.
McAlister, Melani. *Epic Encounters: Culture, Media, and U.S. Interests in the Middle East, 1945–2000*, Berkeley, 2001.
McKay, Jim. *The Real McKay: My Wide World of Sports*, New York, 1998.
Meinhof, Ulrike. "Die Aktion des Schwarzen September in München: Zur Strategie des antiimperialistischen Kampfes, November 1972," in *Rote Armee Fraktion: Texte und Materialien zur Geschichte der RAF*, Berlin, 1997, pp. 151–77.
Metzler, Gabriele. "Am Ende aller Krisen? Politisches Denken und Handeln in der Bundesrepublik der sechziger Jahre," *Historische Zeitschrift* 275, 2002, pp. 57–103.
Meyer-Künzel, Monika. *Städtebau der Weltausstellungen und Olympischen Spiele: Stadtentwicklung der Veranstaltungsorte*, Hamburg, 2001.
Michels, Eckard. *Von der Deutschen Akademie zum Goethe-Institut: Sprach- und auswärtige Kulturpolitik 1923–1960*, Munich, 2005.
Mierzejewski, Alfred C. *Ludwig Erhard: A Biography*, Chapel Hill, NC, 2004.
Miller, David. *Athens to Athens: The Official History of the Olympic Games and the IOC, 1894–2004*, Edinburgh, 2003.
Modrey, Eva Maria. "Architecture as a Mode of Self-representation at the Olympic Games in Rome (1960) and Munich (1972)," *European Review of History: Revue européenne d'histoire* 15, no. 6, 2008, pp. 691–706.
Morris, Nigel. *The Cinema of Steven Spielberg: Empire of Light*, London, 2007.
Moses, Dirk. "The Forty-Fivers: A Generation between Fascism and Democracy," *German Politics & Society* 17, no. 1, 1999, pp. 94–126.
München 1972: "Ich bereue nichts!" Spiegel television documentary, 2006.
Naul, Roland, and Ken Hardman. "Sport and Physical Education in the two Germanies, 1945–90," in Naul and Hardman, eds., *Sport and Physical Education in Germany*, London, 2002, pp. 29–76.
Nerdinger, Winfried, ed. "Aufbrüche und Kontinuitäten—Positionen der Nachkriegsarchitektur in der Bundesrepublik," in Nerdinger, ed., *Architektur der Wunderkinder: Aufbruch und Verdrängung in Bayern 1945–1960*, Salzburg, 2005, pp. 9–22.
———. "Frei Otto: Arbeit für eine bessere 'Menschenerde,'" in Nerdinger, ed., *Frei Otto—Das Gesamtwerk: Leicht bauen, natürlich gestalten*, Basel, 2005, pp. 8–16.
Neu, Joachim. "Studentenschaft zwischen 'Olympismus' und 'Anti-Olympia:' Die ambivalente Haltung des Hochschulsports zur Olympischen Bewegung unter besonderer

Berücksichtigung des olympischen Jugend- und Studentenlagers München 1972," in Hans-Jürgen Schulke, ed., *Die Zukunft der Olympischen Spiele: Die Olympische Bewegung zwischen Moskau und Montreal,* Cologne, 1976, pp. 193–215.

Noack, Paul. *Die Außenpolitik der Bundesrepublik Deutschland,* Stuttgart, 2nd ed. 1981.

Ochs, Christoph. "Aktion 'Banner': Operativer Einsatz, Taktik und Strategie des MfS während der X. Weltfestpiele 1973," *Deutschland Archiv* 36, no. 6, 2003, pp. 981–90.

Oesterreich, Christoph. "Umstrittene Selbstdarstellung: Der deutsche Beitrag zur Weltausstellung in Brüssel 1958," *Vierteljahrshefte für Zeitgeschichte* 48, 2000, pp. 127–53.

Oppelland, Torsten. *Gerhard Schröder (1910–1989): Politik zwischen Staat, Partei und Konfession,* Düsseldorf, 2002.

Organisationskomitee für die XI. Olympiade Berlin 1936, ed. *The XIth Olympic Games Berlin, 1936, Official Report,* 2 vols., Berlin, 1937.

Organizing Committee for the Games of the XXth Olympiad Munich 1972, ed. *Die Spiele: The Official Report,* 3 vols., Munich, 1972.

Our Greatest Hopes. Our Worst Fears: The Tragedy of the Munich Games, ABC television documentary, 2002.

Owens, Jesse. *I Have Changed,* New York, 1972.

Pabst, Ulrich. "Olympia und die Kunst," in Volker Rattemeyer, ed., *Kunst + Design, Kultur Olympia. Willi Daume, Preisträger der Stankowski-Stiftung 1986,* Kassel, 1986, pp. 18–23.

Paulmann, Johannes. "Auswärtige Repräsentationen nach 1945: Zur Geschichte der deutschen Selbstdarstellung im Ausland," in Paulmann, ed., *Auswärtige Repräsentationen: Deutsche Kulturdiplomatie nach 1945,* Cologne, 2005, pp. 1–32.

———. "Representation without Emulation: German Cultural Diplomacy in Search of Integration and Self-Assurance during the Adenauer Era," *German Politics and Society* 25, no. 2, 2007, pp. 168–200.

Peiffer, Lorenz. "Die Madrider Entscheidung des IOC im Oktober 1965. Ein Wendepunkt in der Geschichte der deutsch-deutschen Sportbeziehungen," in Arnd Krüger and Wolfgang Buss, eds., *Transformationen: Kontinuituäten und Veränderungen in der Sportgeschichte,* Hoya, 2002, pp. 118–24.

Peiffer, Lorenz, and Matthias Fink. *Zum Forschungsstand der Geschichte von Körperkultur und Sport in der DDR: Eine kommentierte Bibliografie,* Cologne, 2003.

Pfeil, Ulrich. "Die Olympischen Spiele 1972 und die Fußballweltmeisterschaft 1974: Fallbeispiele für die Verquickung von Sport, Politik und Gesellschaft," *Deutschland Archiv* 39, no. 3, 2006, pp. 415–23.

Pfister, Gertrud. *Frauen und Sport in der DDR,* Cologne, 2002.

Pieper, Harald, ed. *Olympische Zaungäste: Das andere Olympiabuch,* Frankfurt am Main, 1972.

Presse- und Informationsamt der Bundesregierung and Pressestelle der Bayerischen Staatskanzlei. *Dokumentation: Der Überfall auf die israelische Olympiamannschaft,* Bonn, Munich, 1972.

Preuss, Holger. *The Economics of Staging the Olympics: A Comparison of the Games, 1972–2008,* Cheltenham, 2004.

Prokop, Ulrike. *Soziologie der Olympischen Spiele: Sport und Kapitalismus,* Munich, 1971.

Prozumenshchikov, M. Iu. *Bol'shoi Sport and Bol'shaia Politika,* Moscow, 2004.

Rathgeb, Markus. *Otl Aicher,* London, 2006.

Reeve, Simon. *One Day in September: The Story of the 1972 Munich Olympics Massacre, a Government Cover-up and a Covert Revenge Mission,* London, 2000.

Reichel, Peter. *Politik mit der Erinnerung: Gedächtnisorte im Streit um die nationalsozialistische Vergangenheit,* Frankfurt am Main, 1999.

Renzsch, Wolfgang. *Finanzverfassung und Finanzausgleich: Die Auseinandersetzungen um ihre politische Gestaltung in der Bundesrepublik Deutschland zwischen Währungsreform und deutscher Vereinigung (1948–1990),* Bonn, 1991.

Riehl-Heyse, Herbert. *CSU: Die Partei, die das schöne Bayern erfunden hat,* Munich, 1979.

Riordan, James. "The Workers' Olympics," in Alan Tomlinson and Garry Whannel, eds., *Five Ring Circus: Money, Power and Politics at the Olympic Games,* London, 1984, pp. 98–112.

Ritter, Andreas. *Wandlungen in der Steuerung des DDR-Hochleistungssports in den 1960er und 1970er Jahren,* Potsdam, 2003.

Roche, Maurice. *Mega-events and Modernity: Olympics and Expos in the Growth of Global Culture,* London, 2000.

Rosenfeld, Gavriel D. *Munich and Memory: Architecture, Monuments, and the Legacy of the Third Reich,* Berkeley, 2000.

Ruck, Michael. "Ein kurzer Sommer der konkreten Utopie—Zur westdeutschen Planungsgeschichte der langen 60er Jahre," in Axel Schildt, Detlef Siegfried, and Karl Christian Lammers, eds., *Dynamische Zeiten: Die 60er Jahre in den beiden deutschen Gesellschaften,* Hamburg, 2000, pp. 362–401.

———. "Westdeutsche Planungsdiskurse und Planungspraxis der 1960er Jahre im internationalen Vergleich," in Heinz Gerhard Haupt and Jörg Requate, eds., *Aufbruch in die Zukunft: Die 1960er Jahre zwischen Plannungseuphorie und kulturellem Wandel: DDR, CSSR und Bundesrepublik Deutschland im Vergleich,* Weilerswist, 2004, pp. 289–325.

Ruhnau, Werner. *Spielstrassen, Bildende Kunst, Theater . . . ,* Castrop-Rauxel, no date.

Ryder Ryan, Paul. "Thing of a Day," *The Drama Review: TDR* 16, no. 4, December 1972, pp. 62–91.

Sarotte, Mary Elise. *Dealing with the Devil: East Germany, Détente, and Ostpolitik, 1969–1973,* Chapel Hill, NC, 2001.

Schäche, Wolfgang. "Von der Rennbahn zum Sportpark des 21. Jahrhunderts: Etappen einer komplexen Baugeschichte," in Senatsverwaltung für Stadtentwicklung Berlin, ed., *Panorama eines Bauwerks: Olympiastadion Berlin,* Berlin, 2001, pp. 15–47.

Schäche, Wolfgang, and Norbert Szymanski. *Das Reichssportfeld: Architektur im Spannungsfeld von Sport und Macht,* Berlin, 2001.

Scharenberg, Swantje. "Nachdenken über die Wechselwirkung von Architektur und Wohlbefinden: Das Olympiastadion in München, ein politischer Veranstaltungsort," in Matthias Marschik, Rudolf Müllner, Georg Spitaler, and Michael Zinganel, eds., *Das Stadion: Geschichte, Architektur, Politik, Ökonomie,* Vienna, 2005, pp. 153–74.

Scheibe, Moritz. "Auf der Suche nach der demokratischen Gesellschaft," in Ulrich Herbert, ed., *Wandlungsprozesse in Westdeutschland: Belastung, Integration, Liberalisierung,* Göttingen, 2002, pp. 245–77.

Schiller, Kay. "Death at the Munich Olympics," in Alon Confino, Paul Betts, and Dirk Schumann, eds., *Between Mass Death and Individual Loss: The Place of the Dead in Twentieth-Century Germany,* New York, 2008, pp. 129–50.

Schlemmer, Thomas, Stefan Grüner, and Jaromír Balkar. "'Entwicklungshilfe im eigenen Lande'—Landesplanung in Bayern nach 1945," in Matthias Frese, Julia Paulus, and Karl Teppe, eds., *Demokratisierung und gesellschaftlicher Aufbruch: Die sechziger Jahre als Wendezeit der Bundesrepublik,* Paderborn, 2003, pp. 379–450.

Schmeling, Max. *8-9-aus,* Munich, 1956.

———. *Erinnerungen,* Frankfurt am Main, Berlin, 1977.

Schmidt, Heide-Irene. "Pushed to the Front: The Foreign Assistance Policy of the Federal Republic of Germany, 1958–1971," *Contemporary European History* 12, no. 4, 2003, pp. 473–507.

Schmidt, Thomas. *Olympische Stadien von 1896 bis 1988,* Berlin, 1994.

Schneider, Christoph. *Der Warschauer Kniefall: Ritual, Ereignis und Erzählung,* Konstanz, 2006.

Schöbel, Heinz. *Olympia and its Games,* Leipzig, 1966.

———. "Die Verwirklichung des humanistischen Gehalts der olympischen Idee in der sozialistischen Gesellschaft," *Wissenschaftliche Zeitschrift DHfK* 12, no. 3, 1970, pp. 9–16.

Scholtyseck, Joachim. *Die Außenpolitik der DDR,* Munich, 2003.

Schönhoven, Klaus. "Aufbruch in die sozialliberale Ära: Zur Bedeutung der 60er Jahre in der Geschichte der Bundesrepublik," *Geschichte und Gesellschaft* 25, 1999, pp. 123–45.

———. *Wendejahre: Die Sozialdemokratie in der Zeit der Großen Koalition, 1966–1969,* Bonn, 2004.

Schönwälder, Karen. *Einwanderung und ethnische Pluralität: Politische Entscheidungen und öffentliche Debatten in Großbritannien und der Bundesrepublik von den 1950er bis zu den 1970er Jahren,* Essen, 2001.

Schreiber, Manfred. "Das Geschehen am 5./6. September," *Münchner Polizei* 19, 1972, pp. 4–10.

———. "Das Jahr 1968 in München," in Venanz Schubert, ed., *1968: 30 Jahre danach,* St. Ottilien, 1999, pp. 35–52.

Schüler, Barbara. *"Im Geiste der Gemordeten . . . :" Die "Weiße Rose" und ihre Wirkung in der Nachkriegszeit,* Paderborn, 2000.

Schwarz, Hans-Peter, ed. *Akten zur Auswärtigen Politik der Bundesrepublik Deutschland 1972,* vol. 2: *1. Juni bis 30. September 1972,* Munich, 2003.

Siegfried, Detlef. "Zwischen Aufarbeitung und Schlußstrich: Der Umgang mit der NS-Vergangenheit in den beiden deutschen Staaten, 1958–1969," in Axel Schildt, Siegfried, and Karl Christian Lammers, eds., *Dynamische Zeiten: Die 60er Jahre in den beiden deutschen Gesellschaften,* Hamburg, 2000, pp. 114–47.

———. *Time is on my side: Konsum und Politik in der westdeutschen Jugendkultur der 60er Jahre,* Göttingen, 2006.

———. "Understanding 1968: Youth Rebellion, Generational Change and Postindustrial Society," in Axel Schildt and Siegfried, eds., *Between Marx and Coca-Cola: Youth Cultures in Changing European Societies, 1960–1980,* New York, 2006, pp. 59–81.

Sigel, Paul. *Exponiert: Deutsche Pavillons auf Weltausstellungen,* Berlin, 2000.

Skelton-Robinson, Thomas. "Im Netz verheddert: Die Beziehungen des bundesdeutschen Linksterrorismus zur Volksfront für die Befreiung Palästinas," in Wolfgang Kraushaar, ed., *Die RAF und der linke Terrorismus,* Hamburg, 2006, vol. 2, pp. 828–904.

Smit, Barbara. *Pitch Invasion: Three Stripes, Two Brothers, One Feud. Adidas, Puma and the Making of Modern Sport,* London, 2006.

Spitz, René. *hfg ulm: the view behind the foreground. the political history of the ulm school of design, 1953–1968 / hfg ulm: der blick hinter den vordergrund. die politische geschichte der hochschule für gestaltung 1953–1968,* Stuttgart, London, 2002.

Spitzer, Giselher. "Das Scheitern der internationalen Diskreditierung Willi Daumes durch die DDR," in Institut für Sportgeschichte and Carl und Liselott Diem-Archiv der Deutschen Sporthochschule Köln, eds., *Olympisch bewegt: Festschrift zum 60. Geburtstag von Prof. Dr. Manfred Lämmer,* Cologne, 2003, pp. 375–84.

Sturm, Michael. "'Wildgewordene Obrigkeit?' Die Rolle der Münchner Polizei während der 'Schwabinger Krawalle,'" in Gerhard Fürmetz, ed., *"Schwabinger Krawalle:" Protest, Polizei und Öffentlichkeit zu Beginn der 60er Jahre,* Essen, 2006, pp. 59–105.

Sutherland, Claire. "Nation, Heimat, Vaterland: The Reinvention of Concepts by the Bavarian CSU," *German Politics* 10, no. 3, 2001, pp. 13–26.

Tagsold, Christian. *Die Inszenierung der kulturellen Identität in Japan,* Munich, 2002.

Teichler, Hans Joachim. "Coubertin und das Dritte Reich: Zur Vorgeschichte eines unveröffentlichten Coubertin-Briefs an Hitler aus dem Jahre 1937," *Sportwissenschaft* 12, no. 1, 1982, pp. 18–55.

———. "Die Rolle Carl Diems in der Zeit und im zeitlichen Umfeld des NS-Regimes," *Sozial- und Zeitgeschichte des Sports* 10, 1996, pp. 56–74.

———. *Die Sportbeschlüsse des Politbüros: Eine Studie zum Verhältnis von SED und Sport mit einem Gesamtverzeichnis und einer Dokumentation ausgewählter Beschlüsse,* Cologne, 2002.

———. "Der Stellenwert der Olympischen Spiele 1936 in Berlin," in Institut für Sportgeschichte and Carl und Liselott Diem-Archiv der Deutschen Sporthochschule Köln, eds., *Olympisch bewegt: Festschrift zum 60. Geburtstag von Prof. Dr. Manfred Lämmer,* Cologne, 2003, pp. 209–22.

Thomas, Nick. *Protest Movements in 1960s West Germany: A Social History of Dissent and Democracy,* Oxford, 2003.

Tomlinson, Alan. "Olympic Spectacle: Opening Ceremonies and Some Paradoxes of Globalization," *Media, Culture and Society* 18, no. 4, 1996, pp. 583–602.

Tomlinson, Alan, and Christopher Young. "Culture, Politics, and Spectacle in the Global Sports Event—An Introduction," in Tomlinson and Young, eds., *National Identity and Global Sports Events: Culture, Politics, and Spectacle in the Olympics and the Football World Cup,* New York, 2006, pp. 1–14.

Torres, Cesar R. "Stymied Expectations: Buenos Aires' Persistent Efforts to Host Olympic Games," *Olympika: The International Journal of Olympic Studies* 16, 2007, pp. 43–75.

Trimborn, Jürgen. *Riefenstahl: Eine deutsche Karriere,* Berlin, 2002.

Ueberhorst, Horst. "Guido von Mengden (1896–1982)," in Deutscher Sportbund, ed., *Die Gründerjahre des Deutschen Sportbundes: Wege aus der Not zur Einheit,* Schorndorf, 1991, vol. 2, pp. 143–45.

Uekötter, Frank. *The Green and the Brown: A History of Conservation in Nazi Germany*, Cambridge, 2006.

Umminger, Walter, ed. *Olympisches Lesebuch*, Hannover, 1971.

Verspohl, Franz-Joachim. *Stadionbauten von der Antike bis zur Gegenwart*, Gießen, 1976.

Vogel, Hans-Jochen. *Die Amtskette: Meine 12 Münchner Jahre. Ein Erlebnisbericht*, Munich, 1972.

———. *Nachsichten: Meine Bonner und Berliner Jahre*, Munich, 2nd ed. 1996.

———. *Demokratie lebt auch vom Widerspruch*, Zurich, Munich, 2001.

Walters, Guy. *Berlin Games: How Hitler Stole the Olympic Dream*, London, 2006.

Weber, Eugen. "Pierre de Coubertin and the Introduction of Organized Sport in France," *Journal of Contemporary History* 5, no. 2, 1970, pp. 3–26.

Weingardt, Markus A. *Deutsche Israel- und Nahostpolitik: Die Geschichte einer Gratwanderung seit 1949*, Frankfurt am Main, 2002.

Weinhauer, Klaus. "'Staatsbürger mit Sehnsucht nach Harmonie'—Gesellschaftsbild und Staatsverständnis in der Polizei," in Axel Schildt, Detlef Siegfried, and Karl Christian Lammers, eds., *Dynamische Zeiten: Die 60er Jahre in den beiden deutschen Gesellschaften*, Hamburg, 2000, pp. 444–70.

Weltkulturen und moderne Kunst: Die Begegnung der europäischen Kunst und Musik im 19. und 20. Jahrhundert mit Asien, Afrika, Ozeanien, Afro- und Indo-Amerika, Munich, 1972.

Wenzel, H. "Der Mißbrauch der Olympischen Spiele des Jahres 1936 für die Kriegsinteressen der deutschen Faschisten," *Theorie und Praxis der Körperkultur* 16, 1967, pp. 678–85.

———. "Die Stellung der deutschen Großbourgeoisie zu den Olympischen Spielen 1936," *Theorie und Praxis der Körperkultur* 16, 1967, pp. 582–87.

Westphal, Helmut. "Die Mahnung der Olympischen Spiele des Jahres 1936," *Theorie und Praxis der Körperkultur* 15, 1966, pp. 780–6.

Wiesen, S. Jonathan. *West German Industry and the Challenge of the Nazi Past, 1945–1955*, Chapel Hill, NC, 2001.

Wilhelm, Karin. *Portrait Frei Otto*, Berlin, 1985.

"'Willi Daume konnte Geige spielen . . .:' Zeitzeugen erinnern sich," in Bundesinstitut für Sportwissenschaft and Deutsches Olympisches Institut, eds., *Willi Daume: Olympische Dimensionen. Ein Symposion*, Bonn, 2004, pp. 85–106.

"Willi Daumes Charisma und Körpersprache: Thomas Bach im Gespräch mit Andreas Höfer," in Bundesinstitut für Sportwissenschaft and Deutsches Olympisches Institut, eds., *Willi Daume: Olympische Dimensionen. Ein Symposion*, Bonn, 2004, pp. 107–14.

Winkler, Heinrich August. *Der lange Weg nach Westen*, vol. 2: *Deutsche Geschichte vom "Dritten Reich" bis zur Wiedervereinigung*, Munich, 2000.

Witherspoon, Kevin B. *Before the Eyes of the World: Mexico and the 1968 Olympic Games*, De Kalb, IL, 2008.

Wolf, Markus. *Man Without a Face: The Autobiography of Communism's Greatest Spymaster*, New York, 1997.

Wolfrum, Edgar. *Geschichtspolitik in der Bundesrepublik Deutschland: Der Weg zur bundesrepublikanischen Erinnerung, 1948–1990*, Darmstadt, 1999.

———. *Die geglückte Demokratie: Geschichte der Bundesrepublik Deutschland von ihren Anfängen bis zur Gegenwart,* Stuttgart, 2006.

Young, Christopher. "Kaiser Franz and the Communist Bowl: Memory in Munich's Olympic Stadium," *American Behavioural Scientist* 46, no. 11, 2003, pp. 1476–90.

———. "'A Victory for the Olympic Idea:' Berlin 1936 in its Sporting and Socio-cultural Contexts," *Stadion: Internationale Zeitschrift für die Geschichte des Sports* 32, 2006, pp. 147–72.

———. "Munich 1972: Re-presenting the Nation," in Alan Tomlinson and Young, eds., *National Identity and Global Sports Events: Culture, Politics, and Spectacle in the Olympics and the Football World Cup,* New York, 2006, pp. 117–32.

———. "Carrying a German Flame: The Olympic Torch Relay and its Instrumentalization in the Age of Ostpolitik," *Historical Social Research/Historische Sozialforschung* 32, no. 1, 2007, pp. 116–36.

———. "'Nicht mehr die herrlichste Nebensache der Welt:' Sport, West Berlin and the Four Powers Agreement 1971," *German Politics and Society* 25, no. 1, 2007, pp. 28–45.

———. "'In Praise of Jesse Owens:' Technical Beauty at the Berlin Olympics 1936," *Sport in History* 28, no. 1, 2008, pp. 83–103.

Young, David C. "Origins of the Modern Olympics," *International Journal of the History of Sport* 4, 1987, pp. 271–300.

———. *The Modern Olympics: A Struggle for Revival,* Baltimore, 1996.

Zolov, Eric. "Showcasing the 'Land of Tomorrow:' Mexico and the 1968 Olympics," *Americas* 61, no. 2, 2004, pp. 159–88.

INDEX

WEIMAR AND NOW: GERMAN CULTURAL CRITICISM

Edward Dimendberg, Martin Jay, and Anton Kaes, General Editors

1. *Heritage of Our Times,* by Ernst Bloch
2. *The Nietzsche Legacy in Germany, 1890–1990,* by Steven E. Aschheim
3. *The Weimar Republic Sourcebook,* edited by Anton Kaes, Martin Jay, and Edward Dimendberg
4. *Batteries of Life: On the History of Things and Their Perception in Modernity,* by Christoph Asendorf
5. *Profane Illumination: Walter Benjamin and the Paris of Surrealist Revolution,* by Margaret Cohen
6. *Hollywood in Berlin: American Cinema and Weimar Germany,* by Thomas J. Saunders
7. *Walter Benjamin: An Aesthetic of Redemption,* by Richard Wolin
8. *The New Typography,* by Jan Tschichold, translated by Ruari McLean
9. *The Rule of Law under Siege: Selected Essays of Franz L. Neumann and Otto Kirchheimer,* edited by William E. Scheuerman
10. *The Dialectical Imagination: A History of the Frankfurt School and the Institute of Social Research, 1923–1950,* by Martin Jay
11. *Women in the Metropolis: Gender and Modernity in Weimar Culture,* edited by Katharina von Ankum
12. *Letters of Heinrich and Thomas Mann, 1900–1949,* edited by Hans Wysling, translated by Don Reneau
13. *Empire of Ecstasy: Nudity and Movement in German Body Culture, 1910–1935,* by Karl Toepfer
14. *In the Shadow of Catastrophe: German Intellectuals between Apocalypse and Enlightenment,* by Anson Rabinbach
15. *Walter Benjamin's Other History: Of Stones, Animals, Human Beings, and Angels,* by Beatrice Hanssen
16. *Exiled in Paradise: German Refugee Artists and Intellectuals in America from the 1930s to the Present,* by Anthony Heilbut
17. *Cool Conduct: The Culture of Distance in Weimar Germany,* by Helmut Lethen, translated by Don Reneau
18. *In a Cold Crater: Cultural and Intellectual Life in Berlin, 1945–1948,* by Wolfgang Schivelbusch, translated by Kelly Barry
19. *A Dubious Past: Ernst Jünger and the Politics of Literature after Nazism,* by Elliot Y. Neaman
20. *Beyond the Conceivable: Studies on Germany, Nazism, and the Holocaust,* by Dan Diner
21. *Prague Territories: National Conflict and Cultural Innovation in Franz Kafka's Fin de Siècle,* by Scott Spector
22. *Munich and Memory: Architecture, Monuments, and the Legacy of the Third Reich,* by Gavriel D. Rosenfeld

23. *The Ufa Story: A History of Germany's Greatest Film Company, 1918–1945*, by Klaus Kreimeier, translated by Robert and Rita Kimber
24. *From Monuments to Traces: Artifacts of German Memory, 1870–1990*, by Rudy Koshar
25. *We Weren't Modern Enough: Women Artists and the Limits of German Modernism*, by Marsha Meskimmon
26. *Culture and Inflation in Weimar Germany*, by Bernd Widdig
27. *Weimar Surfaces: Urban Visual Culture in 1920s Germany*, by Janet Ward
28. *Graphic Design in Germany: 1890–1945*, by Jeremy Aynsley
29. *Expressionist Utopias: Paradise, Metropolis, Architectural Fantasy*, by Timothy O. Benson, with contributions by Edward Dimendberg, David Frisby, Reinhold Heller, Anton Kaes, and Iain Boyd Whyte
30. *The Red Count: The Life and Times of Harry Kessler*, by Laird M. Easton
32. *The Dark Mirror: German Cinema between Hitler and Hollywood*, by Lutz Koepnick
33. *Rosenzweig and Heidegger: Between Judaism and German Philosophy*, by Peter Eli Gordon
34. *The Authority of Everyday Objects: A Cultural History of West German Industrial Design*, by Paul Betts
35. *The Face of East European Jewry*, by Arnold Zweig, with fifty-two drawings by Hermann Struck. Edited, translated, and with an introduction by Noah Isenberg
36. *No Place Like Home: Locations of Heimat in German Cinema*, by Johannes von Moltke
37. *Berlin Alexanderplatz: Radio, Film, and the Death of Weimar Culture*, by Peter Jelavich
38. *Berlin Electropolis: Shock, Nerves, and German Modernity*, by Andreas Killen
39. *A Concise History of the Third Reich*, by Wolfgang Benz, translated by Thomas Dunlap
40. *Germany in Transit: Nation and Migration, 1955–2005*, edited by Deniz Göktürk, David Gramling, and Anton Kaes
41. *Weimar on the Pacific: German Exile Culture in Los Angeles and the Crisis of Modernism*, by Ehrhard Bahr
42. *The 1972 Munich Olympics and the Making of Modern Germany*, by Kay Schiller and Chris Young

Text: 10/12.5 Minion Pro
Display: Minion Pro
Indexer: Kevin Millham
Compositor: Westchester Book Group
Printer and binder: Maple-Vail Book Manufacturing Group